Theorising Surveillance

Theorizing Surveillance
The panopticon and beyond

edited by

David Lyon

Routledge
Taylor & Francis Group

LONDON AND NEW YORK

First published by Willan Publishing 2006
This edition published by Routledge 2011
2 Park Square, Milton Park, Abingdon, Oxon OX14 4RN
711 Third Avenue, New York, NY 10017

Routledge is an imprint of the Taylor & Francis Group

Hardback
ISBN-13: 978-1-84392-192-9

Paperback
ISBN-13: 978-1-84392-191-2

British Library Cataloguing-in-Publication Data

A catalogue record for this book is available from the British Library

Project managed by Deer Park Productions, Tavistock, Devon
Typeset by GCS, Leighton Buzzard, Beds.

Contents

Acknowledgements

The international research workshop out of which the chapters for this book grew was part of the 'Globalization of Personal Data' project, funded by the Social Sciences and Humanities Research Council of Canada. The Surveillance Project, which hosted the workshop, is a highly congenial and collegial environment in which to work, for which I am very grateful. Joan Sharpe, Project Manager, deserves thanks for her coordination of the workshop and Emily Smith, a Project Researcher, has been an unflappable and buoyant editorial assistant on this book.

David Lyon
Queen's University

Notes on the contributors

Kirstie Ball is Senior Lecturer in Organization Studies at the Open University Business School, Milton Keynes, UK. Her research interests include surveillance in organizations and society, subjectivity and the body, and discourse analytic organizational research. She is also a founding editor of the journal *Surveillance and Society* (www.surveillance-and-society.org).

Didier Bigo is Professor of International Relations at Sciences-Po Paris, France. He is also Visiting Professor in the Department of War Studies at King's College, London, UK. Since 1990, he has worked as an Associate Researcher at the Center for International Studies and Research/National Foundation of Political Science (CERI/FNSP), and is the Scientific Coordinator of the 6th PCRD of the European Commission on Security. The programme is called CHALLENGE (http://www.libertysecurity.org) and involves 23 universities for 5 years on the illiberal practices of the liberal regime after September 11, 2001. The main focus of his current research is the state of exception, surveillance, resistance and freedom and his main publication is: Didier Bigo and Elspeth Guild, *Controlling Frontiers* (Ashgate 2005).

William Bogard is a Professor of Sociology at Whitman College, Walla Walla, Washington, USA. He is the author of *The Simulation of Surveillance: Hypercontrol in Telematic Societies* (Cambridge University Press 1996) and is currently engaged in research on haptic surveillance and social control.

Mark Cole is an educationist by profession and currently works as the Head of Learning and Development at Queen Elizabeth Hospital, London, UK. He is registered on the Ed.D. (Taught Doctorate in Education) programme at the University of Greenwich, London, UK, where he is researching reflective practice in the context of health care delivery, but he also maintains an interest in issues of surveillance in general. Mark has published in a number of educational journals on the theory and practice of informal learning in general and his paper on the signage that accompanies closed-circuit television (CCTV) systems in the UK appeared in *Surveillance and Society* in 2004.

Lynsey Dubbeld is Post-doctoral Fellow at the Centre for Science, Technology, Health and Policy Studies in the Faculty of Business, Public Administration and Technology at Twente University, the Netherlands. Her publications include an empirical-conceptual exploration of the privacy aspects of public video surveillance systems, and a book on prison architecture and social control. She is currently working on a multidisciplinary project concerning issues of privacy and security in the context of telemonitoring systems in the health care sector.

Greg Elmer is the Bell Globemedia Research Chair and Director of the Infoscape Research Lab at Ryerson University, Toronto, Ontario, Canada. He is also author and editor of three books: *Profiling Machines: Mapping the Personal Information Economy* (MIT Press 2004), *Critical Perspectives on the Internet* (Rowman and Littlefield 2002), and with Mike Gasher (Concordia University) *Contracting Out Hollywood: Runaway Productions and Foreign Location Shooting* (Rowman and Littlefield 2005). He is currently working on two book projects, one on the architecture and politics of the Internet entitled *The Bundled Internet*, and the other with Andy Opel (Florida State University), tentatively entitled *Dissent During Wartime*.

Oscar H. Gandy, Jr. is the Herbert I. Schiller Term Professor at the Annenberg School for Communication at the University of Pennsylvania, Philadelphia, USA. *Beyond Agenda Setting* (Ablex 1982) and *The Panoptic Sort* (Westview 1993) are two books that explore public policy formation and privacy. An edited volume, *Framing Public Life* (Lawrence Erlbaum Associates 2001), explores the ways in which policy related discourse takes shape and does its work. *Communication and Race* (Oxford University Press 1998) explores the ways in which structures at the cognitive, discursive, and market level are implicated in the reproduction of race relations.

Gary Genosko is Canada Research Chair in Technoculture in the Department of Sociology at Lakehead University, Thunder Bay, Ontario, Canada. His current research is on informatic subjugation in Canada. He is author/editor of some 14 volumes on contemporary continental thought.

Stephen Graham is Professor of Human Geography at Durham University in the UK. He has a background in urbanism, planning and the sociology of technology. His research addresses the intersections of urban places, mobilities, technology, war, surveillance and geopolitics. His books include *Telecommunications and the City* (Routledge 1996), *Splintering Urbanism* (Routledge 2001) (both with Simon Marvin), the *Cybercities Reader* (Routledge 2003) and *Cities, War and Terrorism* (Blackwell 2004).

Josh Greenberg is Assistant Professor in the School of Journalism and Communication at Carleton University, Ottawa, Ontario, Canada. His research interests are in political communication, particularly the role of news media in social problems construction and the relations of cooperation and conflict between reporters and news sources. He has published on these topics in numerous journals and books. He is currently co-investigator (with Sean Hier) on a Social Science and Humanities Research Council of Canada (SSHRC) funded project examining surveillance practices and social problems in Canada, and is principal investigator of a SSHRC-funded study examining the growth of the Public Relations Industry in Canada.

Kevin D. Haggerty is the Director of the Criminology Program in the Department of Sociology at the University of Alberta, Edmonton, Alberta, Canada. He has written widely on issues of surveillance, policing, risk, governance and research ethics. In 2006 he co-edited the book *The New Politics of Surveillance and Visibility* (University of Toronto Press) with Richard V. Ericson.

Sean P. Hier is Assistant Professor of Sociology, University of Victoria, British Columbia, Canada. His current research, funded through the Social Science and Humanities Research Council of Canada (SSHRC), focuses on CCTV surveillance in Canada (with Josh Greenberg). He has recently published papers in *Social and Legal Studies* (2004), *Socialist Studies* (2005, with Kevin Walby), *Canadian Ethnic Studies* (2006, with Kevin Walby), and *Theoretical Criminology* (2006). (shier@uvic.ca)

Hille Koskela is a Senior Lecturer in the Department of Geography, University of Helsinki, Finland. Her research interests include women's fear of violence in urban space, video surveillance and the politics of control, public attitudes towards surveillance, urban security politics, and most recently, webcams as voluntary visual representations on the Internet. She has published several articles in journals such as *Surveillance and Society, Urban Geography, Progress in Human Geography, Geoforum*, and *Gender, Place and Culture*. (hille.koskela@helsinki.fi)

Maria Los is Professor of Criminology at the University of Ottawa and an Adjunct Professor at the Institute of European and Russian Studies and the Department of Legal Studies, Carleton University, Ottawa, Canada. Her publications include *Crime and Markets in Post-Communist Democracies* (Special Issue of *Law, Crime and Social Change* 2003), *Privatizing the Police-State: the Case of Poland* (with Andrzej Zybertowicz, St. Martin's Press 2000), *The Second Economy in Marxist States* (St. Martin's Press 1990), *Communist Ideology, Law and Crime* (St. Martin's Press 1988), *Multi-Dimensional Sociology* (with Adam Podgorecki, Routledge 1979) and numerous articles in several languages.

David Lyon is Queen's Research Chair in the Sociology Department and Director of the Surveillance Project at Queen's University, Kingston, Ontario, Canada. He is the author of *The Electronic Eye: The Rise of Surveillance Society* (Polity 1994); *Surveillance Society: Monitoring Everyday Life* (Open University Press 2001); *Surveillance after September 11* (Polity 2003); co-editor with Elia Zureik of *Computers, Surveillance and Privacy* (University of Minnesota Press 1996) and editor of *Surveillance as Social Sorting* (Routledge 2003). (david.lyon@queensu.ca)

Toshimaru Ogura is a Professor in the Department of Economics (Political Economy) at Toyama University, Toyama, Japan. He works as an activist in ICT, privacy and human rights with several human rights/ privacy/civil liberty groups in Japan, including the Networkers against Surveillance Taskforce (NaST, an online NGO) and the Anti Surveillance Network. He has written many articles about communication rights and anti-surveillance issues.

Andy Opel is an Assistant Professor and Area Head of the Media Production Program in the Department of Communication at Florida State University, Tallahassee, USA. His research interests include alternative media, social movements and environmental communication. Recent work includes an analysis of the *Media Activism and Reform Movement, Micro Radio and the FCC: Media Activism and the Struggle Over Broadcast Policy* (Praeger 2004) and a co-edited volume, *Representing Resistance: Media, Civil Disobedience and the Global Justice Movement* (Praeger 2003). Andy also works in digital video and his latest project, *Cargo Bike,* is an eco-horror short about a bicycle that eats SUV drivers. (aopel@fsu.edu)

Scott Thompson is currently a Research Assistant on the Social Science and Humanities Research Council of Canada (SSHRC) funded study of Alcohol Administration and Social Control in Northern Ontario at Lakehead University, Thunder Bay, Ontario, Canada. His current focus is on pre-electronic case studies of surveillance and social sorting in Canada.

Kevin Walby is a PhD candidate in the Department of Sociology and Anthropology at Carleton University, Ottawa, Ontario, Canada. His recent publications appear in the *Canadian Journal of Criminology and Criminal Justice* (2005), *Canadian Ethnic Studies* (2006, with Sean Hier), and *Culture and Organization* (2006). His research interests include critical criminology, surveillance and governance studies, institutional ethnography, and Canada's commercial sex trade industry. (kwalby@connect.carleton.ca)

Part I

Introduction

Chapter 1

The search for surveillance theories

David Lyon

The field of 'surveillance studies' has grown rapidly over the past two decades, spurred by both rapid developments in governance and new technologies on the one hand, and fresh initiatives in theoretical explanation on the other. While surveillance practices are as old as human history, they took some rather specific forms in the modern world, becoming routine and systematic, based especially on individuation and on bureaucratic organization (Dandeker 1990). From the last part of the twentieth century onwards, it became clear that new technologies would be implicated decisively in surveillance processes, as computer-based systems augmented older paper file and face-to-face modes (Marx 1988; Rule 1974). At the same time, the work of Michel Foucault stimulated new approaches to understanding surveillance. His book, *Discipline and Punish* (1979), was central to the new debates, even though surveillance appeared as a theme in several of Foucault's works.

The panopticon concept has caught the imagination of many researchers, for better or worse. The prison architecture invented by the Bentham brothers but elaborated by Jeremy Bentham became the crucial 'diagram' for Foucault's work on surveillance. Interestingly, it encapsulated both an emphasis on self-discipline as the archetypical modern mode, supplanting previous coercive and brutal methods, and a focus on the classificatory schemes by which sovereign power would locate and differentiate treatment of the variety of prisoners. Whether these two approaches are ever brought together in Foucault's work is

3

unclear; the more recent work of Agamben suggests not (Agamben 1998). However, while Foucault prompted a new 'panopticism' in theorizing surveillance, others quickly claimed that his work was flawed (e.g. Ignatieff 1977) or that one had to go beyond Foucault to understand contemporary electronic technology-dependent surveillance (Webster and Robins 1986; Zuboff 1988).

I commence with a conundrum: the more stringent and rigorous the panoptic regime, the more it generates active resistance, whereas the more soft and subtle the panoptic strategies, the more it produces the desired docile bodies. But that is only a starting point, still within the panoptic frame. My comments move, secondly, to the range of theories available, whether inside the panoptic frame or not, and the possibilities for dialogue and mutual learning presented if we bring together the classical and the cultural, the critical and the post-structuralist. The even larger frame behind these is the realm of metatheory. Surveillance theories are also situated within these debates and are inevitably informed by them. They relate to history, humanity and, yes, to life itself. All these comments serve as entry points into a lively debate about 'theorizing surveillance' represented by the authors of this book, to whose ideas I offer trailers or previews in the final part.

Moral panoptics and the panopticommodity

The panopticon refuses to go away. Despite the appearance of a number of critiques (e.g. Bauman 1992; Bogard 1996; Lyon 1993; Mathiesen 1997), the idea of the panopticon still appears routinely in surveillance discourses. The reasons for this are manifold but clearly one of them is that the panopticon is such a rich and multifaceted concept. It is capable of interpretation in a number of ways, and of course draws upon the major problematics of modernity. It helps in the exploration of knowledge and power, highlights the Enlightenment elevation of vision (partly expressing and partly parodying Christian notions of omniscience that it sought to dethrone; Lyon 1991) and is imbricated with a quest for social order and for progressive social change. We cannot evade some interaction with the panopticon, either historically or in today's analyses of surveillance. It may be best, as Roy Boyne (2000) suggested a few years ago, to accept the panoptic presence, even if only as the ghost lurking within the post-panoptic world. That is the strategy adopted here.

Rooted in Enlightenment privileging of vision as a means to order and control, today the complex dialectics of watching and being watched are still central to regulation and to governance even if – or just because – we acknowledge both in the shift to 'dataveillance' and the growth of many other forms of mediated watching by the few of the many as well as the many of the few. If not as an actual architecture expressed in stone and cement, the panopticon still functions as an ideal, a metaphor and a set of practices. The utopian vision machine (alluded to by Paul Virilio 1994) continues to drive initiatives such as the US Department of Homeland Security. The idea of omniscient visibility lies behind many schemes from urban planning to military intelligence. And the practices of unseen observation and categorical discrimination are encountered on a daily basis beneath the CCTV cameras and on the phone to the call centre. This is why surveillance studies is so intellectually engaging and politically relevant, and why the panopticon will continue to play the role of a marker.

At the sharp end of the panoptic spectrum lies the prison which, even if it was antedated by the workshop, still expresses panoptic power at its most extreme. It is here that one might expect the panopticon to evidence its effects most powerfully, producing if not Bentham's morally reformed individuals, at least Foucault's docile bodies. Of course, there is a sense in which the panopticon must ever be an uncompleted project and will tighten the focus whenever opacity threatens to undo it. Yet the maximum security prison, such as Kingston Penitentiary (KP), also turns out to be a place of uneven but not infrequent refusal, of revolt, and of ingenious escape attempts. KP has always been controversial, both for its treatment of prisoners and for their responses. Not only this, the 'supermax' prison evidences some seemingly curious reversals of panoptic principles in behaviours that, as Lorna Rhodes eloquently puts it, may actually 'diagnose us all' (1998: 308).

Lorna Rhodes has managed to undertake an unusual and very illuminating empirical study, exploring the lives of inmates in a Washington State supermax (2004). Among other things, she observes prisoners engaged in self-mutilation – one deliberately and repeatedly hits his hands on a stone wall in an exercise yard, causing laceration and bleeding – and in faeces-throwing and smearing within and beyond their cells. Such prisoners are diagnosed as 'behaviorally disturbed' but Rhodes examines their 'behaviours' as means of diagnosing the panopticon. The technology of power intended to produce a 'calculated manipulation' of the body (Foucault 1979: 202) actually produces more than this. As she says, the 'perfection' of the mechanism actually calls forth its opposite (1998: 286). This resistance may not be liberatory – indeed, it invites further control – but it calls in question both the panopticon and our representations of it.

5

Summarizing Rhodes in her own words, the prisoner '... discovers that his body, the very ground of the panoptical relation, is also its potential undoing; he has within himself the makings of a perverse opacity' (1998: 287). Beyond the bare life – mere existence – (Agamben 1998) to which the supermax inmate is reduced, suggests Rhodes, is the human who will always find ways of transcending that situation. The most panoptic circumstances do not necessarily produce the most docile bodies. Prisoners may experience their bodies as abandoned – but then they use them to assert themselves. The disciplinary spaces actually invite and magnify disorder, pollution and noise. As they throw faeces, self-mutilate and create disturbances, they produce selves for the observer, but they also treat their bodies as bodies for the observer, turning private and destructive bodily acts into spectacles.

This understanding of the panopticon, says Rhodes, diagnoses a view from nowhere; of a vision that undermines vision. Self-cutting prisoners, for example, react against the negative visibility that would produce 'compliant selves' by making themselves even more visible. These are strategic acts. They subvert not merely the immediate situation of the prisoner, but also, by extension, the basic seeing/being seen dissociation that the panopticon is intended to sustain. Ordinary citizens in Kingston or in Washington State today do not see inside the prisons as such citizens paid money to do when they were first built (and as Bentham intended); the prisons are hidden from sight. Yet these glimpses inside the supermax are very revealing, not just for what they show of prisoners' lives and their paradoxical resistance, but for what they reveal about the limits of Western Enlightenment rationalities based on the privileging of vision.

If the supermax represents the sharp end of the panoptical spectrum, however, it is also worth travelling the other way to look at the soft end. While the panopticon has been invoked in analyses of prisons, workplaces and government departments, it may also throw light on zones of consumption and entertainment. Oscar Gandy's ground-breaking work on the 'panoptic sort' (1993) demonstrates clearly the ways in which consumers are filtered through a *triage* that distinguishes and treats differently those of more and less worth to the corporation. More recently Mark Andrejevic (2004) has shown how *Big Brother* is now a television trope for late modern unrealities that serves to domesticate and justify surveillance to both watchers and the watched. The apparently least-panoptic forms of surveillance are ones in which a paradoxical docility is achieved in the name of freely chosen self-expression. Perhaps we should call it the 'panopticommodity'.

In *Reality TV: The Work of Being Watched*, Andrejevic shows how scientific management is applied to consumers rather than workers, to improve their 'productivity' for the corporation. Yet for him, the consumers of TV may also be thought of as 'workers' who view advertising for the 'payment' of programming content (2004: 98). To ensure that the consumers do their work, audiences are monitored and demographic profiling is done to check that the work of watching is not wasted. Traditionally, of course, this enterprise has been very limited. Surveillance is acceptable in the workplace, perhaps, but less so in the realm of consumer 'freedom'. In this realm, detailed monitoring depends on the consent of the subject, so for a long time TV companies relied on ratings as a rough guide to audiences. But first cable TV and now digital delivery promise to overcome such obstacles, such that the 'work of being watched' can now – in principle – be developed more fully.

The success of interactive online marketing may be traced, suggests Andrejevic, to the ways in which the labour of watching is integrated with the labour of being watched (2004: 102). While TV depended on a separate ratings industry to monitor viewers, e-commerce depends on the monitoring of consumers while they are surfing the Internet. Of course, you need consumers who are properly prepared for this process, who see the benefits of surveillance and who know that the new economy is good for them. This time, TV comes up with the answer – 'reality TV', that is. For Andrejevic, reality TV shows such as *Road Rules* provide precisely the right messages and encourage the appropriate attitudes for the online economy. Individuality can be rescued from mass society through customized production, and customization depends on surveillance. Equating pervasive monitoring with creativity and self-expression is a hallmark of reality TV.

Participants in reality TV shows appear to be untrained 'ordinary people' engaged in everyday life, whose activities are caught on camera because they managed to get on to the show. It seems 'real', unscripted, and 'controlled' by the participants themselves, who seem to make of the show what they will. Despite the *de facto* editing and the show producers' inducements to create interest, participants are willing to exchange access to the rhythms and intimacies of everyday life for minimal compensation (and a prize at the end of the show). They are encouraged to 'be themselves' and 'wear their hearts on their sleeves'. As one producer says, 'We try to cast people who have a natural openness' (Andrejevic 2004: 106). There is a reward for displaying your body and its activities. It is gratifying to be watched; close surveillance is de-stigmatized.

To make the connection between reality TV and online economy, Gandy's finding is quoted, that TV watchers are more inclined to think that businesses can better meet individual needs and that those bothered about privacy have something to hide (Gandy 1993: 165). The surveillance-

7

based economy persuades individuals that they count when all it wants is to count them. Gaze is no longer a threat of mass homogeneity but a promise of mass individuation; the person is no longer just one of the crowd, but the individuation is commodified. This is what Reg Whitaker (1999) calls the 'participatory panopticon' or what I dub the 'panopticommodity', in which people market themselves. Self-disclosure apparently equates with freedom and authenticity. But you individuate only by submitting to mass surveillance. So in this case too, in so far as we believe that our customized products express our individuality and our creativity, we are diagnosed by the panopticommodity.

Paradoxically, then, the sharp end of the panoptic spectrum may generate moments of refusal and resistance that militate against the production of docile bodies, whereas the soft end seems to seduce participants into a stunning conformity of which some seem scarcely conscious. Either way, so far from displacing the spectacle with self-discipline, the spectacle returns decisively, once more parading the body before audiences. But the audiences differ, as well. While in the supermax the display is catalysed by the presence of the audience; in reality TV the audience is retained by a careful manipulation of the display. At both ends of the spectrum, too, human creativity, spontaneity and autonomy – beyond bare life – are at stake. At the sharp end these are asserted through desperate acts, while at the soft end they are subverted through disingenuous art.

Now, my conundrum relies on a provocative polarization of the 'moral pan(opt)ics' and the 'panopticommodity'. One may wish to interrogate more closely each situation, exploring for instance the differences in display of the surveillance subjects in each case, or the similarities and differences between the prison walls and the domestic walls in which the surveillance is enacted. Again, one might inquire how the 'untrained' TV contestants differ from the 'spontaneous' protesters in the supermax, or whether there may be an exchange (implied in the panopticommodity) in the prison setting as well. Exploring these may well involve further empirical as well as theoretical investigation, but this is not my purpose here.

This conundrum, then, is one way of addressing broad issues of surveillance theory. As we can see, even within the panoptic frame, conclusions deduced from such theory are far from self-evident and may be colourfully counterintuitive. *En passant*, however, we may note that several central issues are thrown into sharp relief through even a cursory awareness of the conundrum. Questions of the body and of technologies, of productive power and active resistance, and of the hiddenness or mutuality of vision are but three such. But other puzzles, to do with political economy, of governance and of morality, for example, are never far from the surface. These questions are asked both within and beyond the panoptic frame of surveillance studies, and that tension is itself one that is maintained, sometimes tautly, throughout this book.

From the classics to the post-structural and back

Today, the panopticon is still in question. Is it the case that the panopticon perfects disciplinary power (as Jeremy Bentham clearly thought and as the earlier Foucault sometimes hints) or might there be some peculiar and paradoxical outcomes of panoptic power that Foucault overlooked? How far should the panopticon be permitted to guide the analysis of surveillance? Have other explanatory tools – even those also found in Foucault, such as treatment of the plague (Norris 2002) or the confession (Cole, this volume) – been neglected because of the panopticon's prominence? Or, more radically, is the panopticon a diversion, a distraction from much more important issues that we miss at our peril through an obsessive fixation with the prison diagram? Where else might one search for suitable theory?

Without intending to establish 'surveillance studies', some early social scientists mapped the field in a preliminary way, drawing attention to modern disciplines of capitalist supervision (Marx) or bureaucratic record-keeping (Weber), or the accenting of the eye in the urban metropolis (Simmel), or the disciplinary response to growing social inequality (Durkheim). Each of these may yield significant explanatory clues. It is also helpful to view these 'pre-panoptic' ideas more broadly within the 'scopic regimes of modernity' (Jay 1994), dating from Descartes. Narrowing this down to how some may 'watch over' others, it is already clear that the 'watching' may be metaphorical (the work-timing machines in the factory, the office files, and the city plan) as well as physical.

As I indicate, though, it took Foucault, writing in the later twentieth century, to pinpoint a precise shift to modern scopic regimes, in the panopticon, with its powerful explanatory proposals. Yet the panopticon is a prison, and for that as well as other reasons its generalizability is in question. The post-panoptics (see Boyne 2000), such as Deleuze, Hardt and Negri, and Agamben, see other factors at work, not only new technologies but new political regimes. Agamben's work, in particular, offers fresh insights on 'sovereign power' and 'bare life', ideas that relate closely to new surveillance regimes of categorizing and exclusion (see Bigo, this volume). But even these lack attention to crucial dimensions such and socio-economic class, gender and ethnicity which today must be applied in areas of literal (CCTV) as well as literary (data-mining) 'watching'; not to mention 'watch lists'.

9

I have argued elsewhere (Lyon 2001: 107–25) that rich veins of surveillance theory already exist, in several modes. But surveillance theories produced within what might be called a modernist frame are as incomplete as those that some would dub postmodern. Or so I submit. Modern ones relate to the nation-state, bureaucracy, techno-logic and political economy, whereas the postmodern ones tend to focus on the ways in which digital technologies 'make a difference'. The one set relies on Marx, Simmel, Weber, Durkheim, and the other on Lyotard, Baudrillard and Foucault. And of course, they do not appear, ultimately, in neat 'sets'. This is merely a handy heuristic.

I suggested in *Surveillance Society* that the work of Ericson and Haggerty in *Policing the Risk Society* (1997) and of Stephen Graham and Simon Marvin in *Telecommunications and the City* (1996) are exemplary for the ways that they bring together these different theoretical strands. In Ericson and Haggerty's work, Ulrich Beck meets Michel Foucault (and, later, Gilles Deleuze; see Haggerty and Ericson 2000) and in Graham and Marvin's, Jean Baudrillard encounters critical geographers. Moreover, I suggested that they do so in the context of empirical work of observation and analysis of institutions and systems. Ericson and Haggerty demonstrate how policing has become bound up with the priorities of insurance companies and Graham and Marvin expose the ways that banks and retail outlets are implicated in the reproduction of geospatial inequalities. Those kinds of studies, which seek strong theory but also draw theory into the explanation of empirical realities, are pursued here as well.

The challenge as I see it is to move beyond the fads and fashions of social and political theory that so easily dismiss previous work as boring, irrelevant or stuck in the wrong paradigm. Classical theories offer fascinating possibilities for exploring the production and uses of surveillance systems, or the beliefs and values that enliven and inhabit them, and the best will, as C. Wright Mills memorably said, connect history and biography, link 'personal troubles and public issues' (1959). At the same time, such theories are also critical, always raising questions about how much we can take, or how the surveillance situations we examine contain the seeds of their own destruction, or how surveillance power is dangerously concentrated in one agency or institution, or how repressive forms of surveillance may relate to broader circumstances such as polarized social and economic inequalities.

Cultural theories, on the other hand, focus on matters such as the constitution of the subject by discursive – including digital – means, on simulation and on speed. Theories of media and technology are vital to this enterprise, raising as they do how far new technologies assume powers of their own, how far they are fused with the human (or serve to propel us into the post-human) and how far they contribute to the structuring of social relations. Such debates are exciting ones, but they too have to remain as debates, not as fixed verities. For all their insight, for example, Hardt and Negri's 'information empire' (2000) has been taken to task by Mark Poster (2005) who berates their 'dystopian gestures' about information technology. And again, he does so not merely for a theory-for-theory's-sake position, but for their failure to offer empirical examples for the generalizations they make.

One of Poster's own neologisms in this context is the 'humachine' and as soon as we begin to address such items we are clearly also in the realm of metatheory. Yet in a world where technological dependence renders us radically reliant on machines – some workers are now required to have implanted chips (Libbenga 2006) – these issues are not 'merely theoretical' either. Are we dealing with subject theories of the human, or with something more post-human; with realms of production, or realms of culture? Is the body rendered superfluous in a post-human world or is it, as feminist analysts such as Katherine Hayles (1999) suggest, as material – and as spiritual – as ever? If we acknowledge the social significance of technology, are we doing so as an Ellul (1964), a Virilio, or Zizek (2002) might do, or are we claiming (as Scott Lash 2001) that the critique of information can only be immanent?

Certain distinguished theorists have always helped us to lift our eyes beyond the immediate and proximate to the truly significant aporias and conundrums of contemporary life. One thinks of Hannah Arendt (1963) and her subtle consideration of the ways that modernity produced the Holocaust, later picked up by Zygmunt Bauman (1991) and now by Giorgio Agamben (1998). Bauman has also been intrigued by the panopticon, writing about it illuminatingly in many of his books (e.g. 1988) and connecting it with the most profound issues of political freedom in the twentieth and twenty-first centuries. Today Agamben again argues for the 'inner solidarity between democracy and totalitarianism' (1998: 10) and suggests that the camp, not the city, is paradigmatic for politics today (see French, forthcoming, for a contemporary exploration of this in the context of Canadian anti-terrorist initiatives).

Agamben's work, like Bauman's and Arendt's, also speaks to surveillance theories. The panopticon was a distinct and bounded area; now, he says, zones of indistinction are crucial, and in fact, are the locus of power. Where (as he argues) Arendt or Foucault failed to connect their analyses of the world of power with those of everyday life, Agamben now proposes that sovereign power and bare life converge in the camp. As Didier Bigo argues, however, one way this happens is through mechanisms of surveillance power that create and perpetuate the 'ban'. And as some of these 'mechanisms' are technological, we also must examine the virtualizing of the 'ban'. Does carrying a national ID card or a Permanent Resident Card also express the 'zone of indistinction' and the 'ban' each time it is swiped or scanned?

The ongoing quest for surveillance theory

It seems clear that some constructive contributions to surveillance theory are needed. Surveillance theory cannot ignore the panopticon but it can surely move beyond it. Quite which directions will be taken 'beyond' is a matter of ongoing debate. First the ground has to be cleared. Kevin Haggerty makes no bones about his project: 'Tear down the walls'! He comments effectively on 'demolishing the panopticon', a project that has several significant rationales. His key point is that what might be called panopticism as an all-embracing model or paradigm should be abandoned. And rather than contribute any single such explanatory model in place of the panopticon, Haggerty hints that another Foucaldian theme, governmentality, should be seen as a source of useful insights that serve to frame a range of activities under the surveillance studies rubric.

Didier Bigo picks up this theme by proposing some quite specific forms of analysis that relate 'security' with surveillance studies in the context of early twenty-first century global developments. For this time, Bigo insists, the inclusive panopticon simply will not work as a heuristic. In its place, he explores the implications of his alternative exclusion-stressing formulation, deriving partly from Agamben, the 'ban-opticon'. The governmentality of uncertainty, fear and unease, argues Bigo, is characterized above all by 'exceptional' practices, extraordinary measures, that paradoxically are now routine. These involve profiling and containing foreigners at the same time as promoting the 'normative imperative of mobility'. Increasingly, he demonstrates, the idea is advanced of the formation of a 'world empire' to protect us all from 'fanatics'. But while this may be seen in various agreements, legal developments and new institutions, these should not deflect attention from the routine technologies of control that surveillance studies attempts to illuminate. Bigo pleads for further analysis of security and surveillance that is attuned to our times and prepared to confront current political trends driven by what might be called the 'security-informational complex'.

Sounds Orwellian? Curiously enough, the early surveillance studies literature, dating from the 1970s and 1980s, used not Foucault but

Orwell as its model. Work done in political and sociological analysis was frequently framed with the idea of a 'total surveillance' state or society derived from the *Nineteen-Eighty-Four* scenario (see e.g. Rule 1974; Flaherty 1989). The 'totalitarian' tendencies of bureaucratic, liberal states were explored particularly in relation to new technologies. The idea of totalitarian threats has reappeared recently, and is effectively and expansively discussed in the work of Maria Los. She takes the reader beyond twentieth-century engineered 'scientific totalitarianism' to the potentials for unintentional totalitarian effects flowing out of contemporary developments of risk management and social sorting. Where once the 'file' was crucial, Los posits the 'data double' as its current equivalent and proposes a 'surveillance-directed' character type to go with it (Hille Koskela pushes this further in her comments on the desire for surveillance). For Los, the real risks of contemporary global surveillance systems lie in their very local, social and personal outcomes. Surveillance makes itself indispensable, she says, by displacing morality, and undermines any notion of truth by preferring the data image to the lived reality of the personal narrative.

But what if the surveillance system itself is less than it is perceived to be? What if, despite the best efforts of Homeland Security and its ilk, those rhizomatic networks of pulsating data cannot finally be controlled and directed? This is the more emancipatory notion explored by William Bogard in his Deleuzean elaboration of 'lines of flight'. Post-panoptic surveillance is deterritorialized as well as rhizomic and as such resists exclusionary control strategies. In the panopticon, which is a 'machinic' assemblage, material flows are joined and separated. But in enunciative assemblages, words are attached to things by relations of power. The soul-training of the panopticon with its moulded subjects gives way to flexibly modulated hybrid subjects, suited to varying circumstances. But lines of flight within these latter systems include file-sharing, decryption, using proxies and sousveillance as well as conventional political anti-surveillance strategies. Does this mean, as Felix Guattari (1990) provocatively puts it, that there may be 'safety in the machine'? Bogard's reply brings Heidegger (1977) into the conversation but concludes with a carefully qualified yes.

If Bogard obliges us to rethink the spaces of surveillance, from territory to deterritorialization, then Gary Genosko and Scott Thompson make us think again about time, or at least temporality. In a welcome intervention, they observe that what in surveillance studies is all-too-quickly assumed to be an outcome of computerization – social sorting – may actually be observed in some patently 'pre-computer' contexts. But not only is history problematized, in the case of the racialized classification and targeting system of the Liquor Control Board of Ontario, but also the present and the *futur anterieur* are examined in relation to surveillance. In the present, ironically, presence is downplayed in the paradoxical unreality of 'real time'. While the camera that captures the image of the child murderer does so in the instant the event occurs, it is its role in the future, not the present, that counts. Yet that future is itself seen in simulated forms, say these authors (thus also connecting their work with Bogard's); like in the Ontario casinos where face-recognition systems compare players' images with those of 'known launderers and cheats'. It is the simulated assemblage that matters here; it creates the future as 'already over'.

For anyone who would write surveillance theory in the twenty-first century, the aftermath of September 11 hovers hauntingly overhead. In a timely piece on the 'survivor society', Greg Elmer and Andy Opel relate the future that is 'already over' to the War on Terror. Briskly sidestepping Bentham and Foucault, their focus is specifically on how the 'war effort' attempts to pre-empt certain outcomes and even to induce a sense of inevitability: when such-and-such happens, the new condition will be ... Simulation and forecasting models appear in conjunction with 'the privatization of self-preservation' through appropriate purchases and vigilance. In other words, they explore another logic behind extensive wiretaps, detentions without trial and the like, that operates alongside or (they hint) beyond conventional surveillance logics of automating and integrating new technological apparatuses. It is a 'survivor society' logic in which citizens are called upon to suspend disbelief, assume that the US Administration has things in hand, and remember that 'morality, critical thinking and dissent' inhibit the smooth functioning of society.

While territorialities and temporalities are given focused attention by Bogard, Genosko and Thompson, and Elmer and Opel, others who analyse the lived realities of surveillance also notice the significance of these dimensions. But they bring other aspects of surveillance into the picture, notably, in the next four cases, the cultures of surveillance, or the contexts in which surveillance occurs. These touch on specific ways in which subjects are involved in their surveillance, using the very different 'technologies' of the webcam, the cardiac monitor, 'Continuing Professional Development' and public Closed Circuit Television (CCTV). In each case, however, the focus is not only the artefacts themselves but on their interaction with the subjects. And each treatment also allows the mutating empirical situation to challenge theory.

Hille Koskela's examination of 'citycams' takes us to Finland, where some such systems are quite ambiguous. She details some Joensuu citycams that were installed originally for crime control purposes but now serve to 'promote' the city (but the process is also in some instances reversed, and, from some points of view, is one-and-the-same process anyway). And in relation to the much better known Times Square cameras and internet publicity, Koskela quotes Terranova's comment that 'the society of the spectacle, simulation and virtual reality' (2001: 130) collapse into one another. But this also seems true of 'home webcams' where surveillance becomes a desirable opportunity for self-display in front of the camera. The exposed participants become willing and active subjects of surveillance who simultaneously reclaim their bodies, or at least representations of them. Not self-repression but self-expression characterizes this surveillance, which, importantly, is on the terms of the watched, not the watcher. Theoretically, panoptic ideas are radically destabilized, and complexities of power relations are foregrounded. Moreover, suggests Koskela, webcams open a new liminal space, 'in between' material and virtual spaces, which awaits further analysis.

If there is something immediately plausible about webcams offering opportunities for active subjects to redefine aspects of surveillance experiences, the same is probably not true of cardiac telemonitoring. The medical gaze is often taken to be relentlessly one-way, objectifying and normalizing. The application of technology would seem simply to reinforce this. Yet Lynsey Dubbeld examines the telemonitoring of cardiac patients with a view to assessing how far the panopticon (and associated dystopic theoretical viewpoints) offers any illumination, given that at least some features of the panoptic circumstance are present. She finds little if any help in that quarter but suggests instead that the notion of the 'co-construction of users' within Science and Technology Studies (STS) does speak to the need for 'balanced and not inherently negative' forms of analysis. She argues that co-construction avoids pessimistic and deterministic theories of surveillance, and permits close investigation of the actual use of devices and systems in socio-technical practices, in ways that both acknowledge the embodiment and the choices of subjects and, interestingly, their involvement in processes that may produce forms of exclusion.

Dubbeld's comments about the role of the surveilled subject are well taken, and some aspects of the role of the subject in surveillance are also taken up in Mark Cole's revealing analysis of continuing professional development (CPD) as a 'technology of the self'. This is a programme directed at health care professionals in the UK, though readers from elsewhere will recognize analogues in their own professional and national settings, too. Health care professionals are, understandably, expected to 'keep up to date' in their fields, but many feel that the scrutable journalling and note-taking evidenced in CPD also threatens their autonomy. So, asks Cole, is the expected 'reflective practice' in fact a 'confession of competence' in the Foucaldian sense of 'confession', that turns the subject into a 'stock-taking administrator'? In a nuanced study that contributes in its own right to the debate over the confession, Cole shows how the CPD may be read as surveillance by the state through its proxies. At the same time, critical reflection may also be read as a means of caring for the self and thus as an emancipatory tool permitting professionals to 'speak truth to power'.

In a fourth exploration of actual surveillance circumstances involving specific technological systems and a variety of actors, Hier, Walby and Greenberg comment on the (slow) growth of CCTV in public sites in Canada. In this case, it is only indirectly that subjects are involved in their own surveillance (although as these are public systems there is a sense in which they may well be). Rather, and this is already a query about panoptic models, the 'top-down' theoretical assumption underpinning some accounts of CCTV is probed with a view to demonstrating a more complex reality. So far from representing neat asymmetries of power, reasons for deploying CCTV, at least in London, Ontario, seem to rest on 'grievances' (leading to efforts to eliminate harmful activities) as well as 'risks' (leading to individualized responsibility and the reduction of harm through ethical conduct). Local politicians, businesspersons and ordinary citizens may all be involved in forms of governance that put more cameras on the streets. How this actually affects the character of the surveillance that follows (does it become less 'top-down'?) is a further question raised by this analysis.

In a final series of chapters the issue of surveillance theory is confronted once again, but now seen through the lens of global military and capitalist power as well as in terms of specific strategies of resistance. Stephen Graham leads off with a call to attend to matters of military power that have in some ways – astonishingly – slipped through the academic cracks. He argues that surveillance studies must come to terms with the military origins and normalization of new surveillance techniques and illustrates the argument with reference to their uses in the urban battlespaces of the Middle East and other areas of the global south. The new 'network centric warfare' depends on 'situational awareness' provided by novel urban surveillance techniques. The older Revolution in Military Affairs (RMA), which assumed that open space such as deserts would be the cockpits of 'virtual war', is challenged by the realities of urban insurgency for which not only high-resolution satellite images but also algorithmic CCTV ('Combat Zones that See') are used to identify and eliminate targets remotely. Among several important conclusions Graham draws from this is that the programmes and discourses of the new RMA 'embed stark biopolitical judgments about the varying worth of human subjects, according to their location...' as revealed by surveillance.

If Graham's troubling critique of urban war-zone strategies reminds us sharply of the military drivers of contemporary surveillance, Toshimaru Ogura stresses that the growth of contemporary surveillance is also deeply rooted in the expanding global capitalist system. As such, he insists, it requires not only careful critique but also constructive proposals and exemplars for resistance. The problem here is that, unlike military surveillance that has some rather obviously destructive and fatal aspects to it, some features of the political economy of capitalist societies are geared to increasing efficiency and productivity. The promotion of 'electronic government', for instance, relies on just such 'unquestionable' benefits that seem simultaneously to provide for increased democratic participation through citizen access to documentary records. One of the outcomes proposed by Ogura is the potential emergence of a new identity politics structured around the critique of 'identity exploitation'.

Kirstie Ball, too, is very aware of the capitalist context, given her well-known interest in the flexible production evidenced in call centres, but she broadens her angle of vision here to speak of new biometric identifiers, and makes two further observations of note. One has to do with the ways that resistance to surveillance already occurs at an everyday and local level and is centred on the body, and the other with ways that feminist theory has insights to offer that are unavailable elsewhere. By retracing her theoretical steps through analyses of the body and of organization studies she discloses several important possibilities for resistance. She concludes that the 'core issue for any embodied sociology of surveillance' must be '... whose body information is appropriated, how it is encoded ... reapplied, how effectively this fixes and how it is resisted'. Like Maria Los, she shows how biometrics are treated as a source of truth, but also indicates how such assumptions may be destabilized. And because she sees how the macro-level tensions are focused in local organizational practices, Ball locates some specific sites and moments for active resistance.

Interestingly enough, Oscar Gandy also starts with the body – or at least with materials extracted from it – in his critique of 'rational discrimination' that may occur, for instance, courtesy of the human genome project. In his case, the question revolves around racial profiling that is facilitated by automated processes of discrimination. Especially since 9/11, notes Gandy, the *cumulative disadvantage* has increased to some specific population groups, resulting from surveillance. Building on the theoretical insights of Bowker and Star on 'sorting things out'

(1999), Gandy tightens the focus to look at its implications for rational discrimination and racial profiling. But he does so, not only in the notorious context of 'national security' but also in that of differential health care delivery – which may also engender a new eugenics. Gandy not only exposes the fallacies and consequent injustices of such processes, he also pleads for other approaches that are not tarred with the same brush.

Conclusion

I began with a conundrum within panoptic theory, namely that the most powerfully panoptic schemes seem to generate high levels of resistance while the softest and most benign-seeming produce sometimes startling levels of compliance. Leaving aside the question of what may be learned, theoretically, from this conundrum, I also observed that key theoretical problems, concerning the body and technologies, the articulation or the tension between watching and being watched, and questions of productive power and active resistance, are also raised in the contrasting cases of the supermax and reality TV. Other issues are not far behind, too – and these are picked up in later chapters – such as the role of major social, economic and political forces represented by global consumer capitalism, military power and the 'security-informational complex' in catalyzing, driving, reinforcing and on occasion diverting or constraining surveillance developments.

Without careful theorizing, the growth of contemporary surveillance will be seen only in relatively shallow and superficial ways in media accounts and policy reports that depend only on descriptive and statistical data. As the chapters of this book demonstrate, however, while surveillance is still thoroughly ambiguous and its origins and growth may be subtle and sophisticated, some aspects of surveillance are far too important to be left without explanatory guides and theoretical argument. And this is also why, as several chapters hint or illustrate, surveillance theory cannot ultimately be disengaged from the ethical and the political tasks. It is abundantly clear that the panopticon – itself caught in the opposing gravitational fields of Christianity and the Enlightenment – can never be looked to paradigmatically for all the theoretical clues, even though some of its features will continue to stimulate and direct some research endeavours. For much of its work, as this volume attests, surveillance theory for the twenty-first century is obliged to look beyond the panopticon.

References

Agamben, G. (1998) *Homo Sacer: Sovereign Power and Bare Life* (Stanford: Stanford University Press).

Andrejevic, M. (2004) *Reality TV: The Work of Being Watched* (New York: Rowman and Littlefield).

Arendt, H. (1963) *Eichmann in Jerusalem: A report on the banality of evil* (New York: Penguin).

Bauman, Z. (1988) *Freedom* (Buckingham: Open University Press).

Bauman, Z. (1991) *Modernity and the Holocaust* (Cambridge: Polity Press).

Bauman, Z. (1992) *Intimations of Postodernity* (London: Routledge).

Bogard, W. (1996) *The Simulation of Surveillance* (New York: Cambridge University Press).

Bowker, G.C. and Starr, S.L. (1999) *Sorting Things Out: Classification and its Consequences* (Cambridge, MA: MIT Press).

Boyne, R. (2000) 'Post-Panopticism', *Economy and Society*, 29 (2), 285–307.

Dandeker, C. (1990) *Surveillance, Power and Modernity* (Cambridge: Polity Press).

Ellul, J. (1964) *The Technological Society* (New York: Vintage).

Ericson, R.V. and Haggerty, K.D. (1997) *Policing the Risk Society* (Toronto: University of Toronto Press).

Flaherty, D. (1989) *Protecting Privacy in Surveillance Societies* (Chapel Hill: University of North Carolina Press).

Foucault, M. (1979) *Discipline and Punish: The Birth of the Prison* (New York: Vintage).

French, M. (forthcoming) 'In the Shadow of Canada's Camps', under submission to *Social and Legal Studies*.

Gandy, O.H. (1993) *The Panoptic Sort: A Political Economy of Personal Information* (Boulder, CO: Westview).

Graham, S. and Marvin, S. (1996) *Telecommunications and the City: Electronic Spaces, Urban Places* (London and New York: Routledge).

Guattari, F. (1990) 'On Machines', *Journal of Philosophy and the Visual Arts*, 6, 8–17.

Haggerty, K. and Ericson, R. (2000) 'The surveillant assemblage', *British Journal of Sociology*, 51 (4), 605–22.

Hardt, M. and Negri, A. (2000) *Empire* (Cambridge, MA: Harvard University Press).

Hayles, N. K. (1999) *How we became posthuman: virtual bodies in cybernetics, literature and informatics* (Chicago: University of Chicago Press).

Heidegger, M. (1977) *The Question concerning Technology* (New York: Harper and Row).

Ignatieff, M. (1977) *A Just Measure of Pain: the penitentiary in the industrial revolution, 1750–1850* (New York: Pantheon Books).

Jay, M. (1994) *Downcast Eyes: The Denigration of Vision in Twentieth Century French Thought* (Berkeley, CA: University of California Press).

Lash, S. (2001) *Critique of Information* (London: Sage).

Libbenga, J. (2006) 'Video surveillance outfit chips workers', *The Register*, Friday 10 February 2006. Available at: www.theregister.com/2006/02/10/employees_chipped/

Lyon, D. (1991) 'Bentham's Panopticon: From Moral Architecture to Electronic Surveillance', *Queen's Quarterly*, 98 (3), 596–617.

Lyon, D. (1993) 'An Electronic Panopticon? A Sociological Critique of Surveillance Theory', *The Sociological Review*, 41 (3).

Lyon, D. (2001) *Surveillance Society: Monitoring Everyday Life* (Buckingham: Open University Press).

Marx, G.T. (1988) *Under Cover: Police Surveillance in America* (Berkeley, CA: University of California Press).

Mathiesen, T. (1997) 'The viewer society: Michel Foucault's "Panopticon" revisited', *Theoretical Criminology*, 1 (2), 215–34.

Mills, C.W. (1959) *The Sociological Imagination* (New York: Oxford University Press).

Norris, C. (2002) 'From personal to digital: CCTV, the panopticon and the technological mediation of suspicion and social control', in D. Lyon (ed.) *Surveillance and Social Sorting: Privacy Risk and Automated Discrimination* (London: Routledge).

Poster, M. (2005) 'Hardt and Negri's Information Empire: A Critical Response', *Cultural Politics*, 1 (1), 101–17.

Rhodes, L. (1998) 'Panoptical Intimacies', *Public Culture*, 10 (2), 285–311.

Rhodes, L. (2004) *Total Confinement: Madness and Reason in the Maximum Security Prison* (Berkeley, CA: University of California Press).

Rule, J. (1974) *Private Lives: Public Surveillance* (London: Allen Lane).

Terranova, T. (2001) 'Demonstrating the Globe: Virtual Action in the Network Society', in D. Holmes (ed.) *Virtual Globalization. Virtual Spaces/Tourist Spaces* (London: Routledge), pp. 95–113.

Virilio, P. (1994) *The Vision Machine* (Bloomington, IN: Indiana University Press).

Webster, F. and Robins, K. (1986) *Information Technology: A Luddite Analysis* (Norwood, NJ: Ablex).

Whitaker, R. (1999) *The End of Privacy: How Total Surveillance is Becoming a Reality* (New York: New Press).

Zizek, S. (2002) *Welcome to the Desert of the Real* (London and New York: Verso).

Zuboff, S. (1988) *In the Age of the Smart Machine: The Future of Work and Power* (New York: Basic Books).

Part 2

Post-Panoptic Surveillance Theory

Chapter 2

Tear down the walls: on demolishing the panopticon[1]

Kevin D. Haggerty[2]

Introduction

The panopticon is oppressive. Since Foucault's famous reinterpretation of Bentham's utopian project of prison architecture, the panopticon has stood for sinister manifestations of power/knowledge. Today, however, the panopticon is oppressive in an entirely different sense. That is because the panopticon is now considerably more than a brick and mortar edifice, but is also easily the leading scholarly model or metaphor for analysing surveillance. In this latter role the panopticon has also become oppressive. The sheer number of works that invoke the panopticon is overwhelming. More problematically, the panoptic model has become reified, directing scholarly attention to a select subset of attributes of surveillance. In so doing, analysts have excluded or neglected a host of other key qualities and processes of surveillance that fall outside of the panoptic framework. The result has been that the panoptic model has been over-extended to domains where it seems ill-suited, and important attributes of surveillance that cannot be neatly subsumed under the 'panoptic' rubric have been neglected.

Analysts familiar with the work of Thomas Kuhn will detect some suggestive resonances between the current situation of surveillance studies and Kuhn's understanding of the operation of 'normal science'. Rivalling Foucault's *Discipline and Punish* as one of the most important books of its generation, Kuhn's *The Structure of Scientific Revolutions* (1970) advances a non-rationalist model for understanding scientific change. Central to his approach is the notion of paradigms, which are exemplars of research practice (Hoyingen-Huen 1993; Horwich 1993). In the day-to-day world of normal science, researchers uncritically employ and extend such models, using them as established examples of good practice. Indeed, for Kuhn, it is the acceptance of shared paradigms which makes normal science possible.

As normal science progresses, it inevitably produces a number of anomalous counter-instances. Such anomalies are not easily assimilated into the paradigm and are typically set aside as curiosities to be explained in the fullness of time within the existing paradigm. If the anomalies persist, increase in quantity, arrive with increasing frequency or are simply too weighty to ignore, then the field is primed for a paradigm shift. In such a context, research becomes more speculative and wide-ranging as researchers explore alternative models that might help explain the anomalies. When a new model is finally embraced, the field undergoes a paradigm shift. The old exemplar is abandoned as a new model for future inquiry comes to command the field. Such shifts are not exclusive to world-historical scientific revolutions, but can also characterize developments in a professional subspecialty (Kuhn 1970: 49). Scientific communities do not embrace new paradigms because they solve the pressing issues of their field, but because they offer a suggestive promissory model for future inquiry. Their major achievement is to serve as the foundation for future research practice.

The field of surveillance studies now mirrors the situation of a normal science on the cusp of a paradigm shift. For a quarter-century the panopticon has been the exemplar for inquiries into surveillance. In the process, however, a host of anomalous findings have emerged that do not match what is conventionally understood to be the panoptic model of surveillance. My analysis here details some, but by no means all, of the important anomalies that do not fit that orientation. It suggests that these are sufficiently numerous, weighty and significant to reveal the panopticon to be of limited relevance for appreciating the contemporary dynamics of surveillance. The concluding discussion articulates some reservations about the prospect or desirability for the emergence of a new model for understanding surveillance, proposing instead that surveillance studies conceptualize surveillance in relation to particular governmental projects.

Yet another tour of the panopticon

Eighteenth-century social reformer Jeremy Bentham (1995) proposed the panopticon penitentiary as a utopian project for curing a number of social ills. It had a unique architectural form which sought to maximize the visibility of inmates through the arrangement of space and the play of lighting. Inmates would be isolated in individual cells that circled a central observation tower. Guards in the tower could monitor the inmates while themselves remaining unseen. In this way a few watchers could scrutinize the behaviour of many inmates.

This system of visibility was to operate in conjunction with explicitly articulated behavioural norms in an effort to transform an inmate's behaviour. Hence, it was essential that prisoners be aware that at any given moment they were, or might be, under scrutiny. This constitutes the disciplinary component of the panopticon, which sought to instil a form of productive 'soul training' designed to encourage an inmate to reflect upon the minutia of their behaviour in a subtle and ongoing effort to transform their selves in prescribed directions.

Foucault's (1977) discussion of the panopticon is a brilliant analysis of the particularities of this unique architectural project. However, if that were the extent of his ambitions it is unlikely that his work would have circulated beyond a handful of historians and criminologists. It certainly would not have emerged as one of the most popular concepts in contemporary social thought if Foucault had not also proposed that the principles inherent in the panopticon themselves served as a model for understanding the operation of power in contemporary society. Consequently, he claims that the panoptic schema 'was destined to spread through the social body; its vocation was to become a generalized function' (Foucault 1977: 207). Panoptic schemes, following Foucault, become a principal means for managing a host of different populations through the dispersion of disciplinary power more generally.

My reservations are with how this claim to generalization has been embraced in the study of surveillance. It is a profound understatement to say that the panopticon dominates the study of surveillance. This influence takes various forms. Most common are those analyses which detected panoptic attributes in any number of surveillance arrangements, extending panoptic thinking to various new domains. Others have drawn attention to how computerization has augmented longstanding bureaucratic ambitions through processes of 'dataveillance', and advanced the notion of an 'electronic panopticon' to recognize the important role played by these new technologies in the routine operation of surveillance (Lyon 1994; Gordon 1990). Others have suggested that the sheer expansion in the volume of contemporary surveillance calls for a radicalization of Foucault's thesis, and proposed the notion of a 'superpanopticon' to recognize this escalation in the volume of social monitoring (Poster 1990: 93).

Recently there has been a distinct shift towards a more critical tone in the literature. More authors are self-consciously accentuating the limitations of the panopticon for understanding contemporary surveillance (Bauman 1992; Yar 2003). Roy Boyne (2000), for example, outlines a number of reasons why the panopticon model might not fit contemporary dynamics in surveillance and power more generally. He concludes by suggesting that analysts can best visually represent this problematic relationship by placing the terms 'panopticon', 'panoptical' and 'panopticism' under erasure – drawing a line through them as a way to simultaneously represent their presence while denying their continuing relevance. Nonetheless, by even his own account, Boyne believes that the panopticon can still serve as a model against which to compare contemporary developments in surveillance and power relations (2000: 303).

In addition to the superpanopticon, electronic panopticon and post-panopticon, there are references to the 'omnicon' (Goombridge 2003), 'ban-opticon' (Bigo this volume), 'global panopticon' (Gill 1995), 'panspectron' (De Landa 1991), 'myoptic panopticon' (Leman-Langois 2003), 'fractal panopticon' (De Angelis 2001), 'industrial panopticon' (Butchart 1996), 'urban panopticon' (Koskela 2003), 'pedagopticon' (Sweeny 2004), 'polyopticon' (Allen 1994), 'synopticon' (Mathiesen 1997), 'panoptic discourse' (Berdayes 2002), 'social panopticism' (Wacquant 2001), 'cybernetic panopticon' (Bousquet 1998), and the 'neo-panopticon' (Mann, Nolan and Wellman 2003). These proliferating opticons signal the point that I am accentuating. Each new 'opticon' points to a distinction, limitation, or way in which Foucault's model does not completely fit the contemporary global, technological or political dynamics of surveillance. At the same time, the inability to abandon the metaphor signals that the panopticon now stands for surveillance itself. At times it appears that characterizing surveillance as 'panoptic' is little more than a force of habit as opposed to a sober evaluation of whether the surveillance practices under description conform to Foucault's (or Bentham's) model. This is distinctive of this particular moment in the study of surveillance – a moment that might be short-lived, or might extend for many more years – characterized by a deeply ambivalent relation to the panopticon.

Ultimately, we arrive at a situation distinguished by a host of different stances towards the panopticon and panoptic processes, ranging from straightforward extensions of this model to more critical efforts to place the concept under erasure. Nonetheless, Bentham's famous design still retains pride of place in studies of surveillance. My position here is more extreme, as I believe that changes in surveillance processes and practices are progressively undermining the relevance of the panoptic model for understanding contemporary surveillance. Foucault continues to reign supreme in surveillance studies and it is perhaps time to cut off the head of the king. The panoptic model masks as much as it reveals, foregrounding processes which are of decreasing relevance, while ignoring or slighting dynamics that fall outside of its framework. The following analysis details this claim through an examination of several attributes of contemporary surveillance which exceed the express dynamics of panoptic surveillance.

Purposes of surveillance

For Foucault, panoptic surveillance serves both immediate and more general purposes. In the first instance its 'soul training' component seeks to transform individuals such that they shape their behaviour in prescribed directions. Hence, the panopticon's 'major effect' was 'to induce in the inmate a state of conscious and permanent visibility that assures the automatic functioning of power' (Foucault 1977: 201). The more general purpose of this transformation was related to a unique historical context; specifically to the requirements of industrial capitalism which sought to instil in the labouring classes a distinctive temporal and bodily discipline which meshed with the routines of the emergent factory system (Thompson 1991).

Since Bentham's initial formulation, one of the greatest changes in the operation of surveillance has been the proliferation of new purposes for surveillance, many of which transcend the functions initially envisioned for the panopticon. In some ways this connects with both Foucault's and Bentham's interest in the panopticon, as both saw it as an ideal form that could be enlisted in the service of various functions, including education, medical treatment and punishment. All such projects, however, share a common rationalizing thread in that they sought to foster gains in the efficiency and economy of power. Surveillance now serves a host of other purposes.

As Bauman (1992) has observed, a key transformation in the wider context of panopticism has been the development of an increasingly global transnational capitalism. Greater automation, computerization and the ability to rely upon unskilled and semi-skilled workers in other

27

countries has reduced the needs for unskilled domestic labour. This, in turn, reduces the impetus towards incorporating the 'dangerous classes' into the workforce. Even a cursory glimpse at the routine operation of contemporary penal regimes reveals that disciplinary strategies designed to reintegrate inmates into society and the labour market have largely been abandoned in favour of forms of surveillance in the service of social exclusion. Such visibility marks the boundaries between those who are seduced into mainstream society through market processes and the global capitalist system, versus those who are abandoned to their fates in the warehouses of the modern prison industrial complex (Garland 2001).

Outside of the prison, surveillance is used for a plethora of projects, including deterrence, consumption, entertainment, titillation, health promotion, education, governance, accountability, child-rearing and military conquest (Haggerty 2006; Dandeker 1990). While surveillance regimes are designed with particular purposes in mind, they often evolve in unanticipated ways. Uses are not necessarily established in advance, but are emergent, resulting from the creative insights of individuals who envision novel possibilities for systems developed for entirely different purposes. Hence, at the societal level, it is increasingly difficult to suggest that surveillance serves a single coherent purpose, such as 'social control', or even a limited set of purposes.

This proliferation of surveillance has also meant that more and more people at home, work or leisure are constituted as viewers. Such surveillance is not just a function of rationalizing regulatory projects, but can also be enjoyable. Both watching others and exposing oneself can, at times, be pleasant entertainment activities, and are themselves occasionally part of larger processes of identify formation. Web blogs, for example, allow for a leisurely scrutiny of the ruminations and images of otherwise unknown individuals through access to texts and images that were previously embedded in private settings such as diaries, or available only through interpersonal rituals of access and revelation, as with family photograph albums. The proliferation of 'reality' shows suggests the extent to which watching others subject themselves to a remarkable degree of public scrutiny can itself be a pleasurable activity (Doyle 1998). In her analysis of webcams, Koskela (2004) suggests that for women who are continually cautioned and badgered about the dangers of revealing too much in inappropriate contexts, acts of revelation can themselves be experienced as a form of empowerment. That surveillance can be experienced from both sides of the lens as 'fun' or liberating does not fit neatly within the preoccupations of the panoptic model.

Hierarchies of visibility

The types of surveillance accentuated in the panoptic model typically involve the monitoring of people who reside at a lower point in the social hierarchy; with physicians monitoring patients, guards watching inmates and supervisors keeping an eye on workers. In this, it is reminiscent of the functioning of a microscope, where specific marginalized or dangerous groups are situated under the unidirectional gaze of the powerful who can watch while remaining unseen by their charges.

While powerful institutions continue to use surveillance to scrutinize less powerful groups, an exclusive focus on that dynamic elides a vital development in contemporary surveillance. Traditional hierarchies of visibility are being undermined and reconfigured. Surveillance is not directed exclusively at the poor and dispossessed, but is now omnipresent, with people from all segments of the social hierarchy coming under scrutiny according to the their lifestyle habits, consumption patterns, occupations and the institutions with which they are aligned (Nock 1993). This increased visibility of the powerful is most apparent when individuals are transformed from respected citizen to social pariah. At those junctures the reams of data about the behaviours, actions, communications and movements of powerful individuals – much of which was arguably always available for media and official scrutiny – is capitalized on. Surveillance then undergoes a qualitative transformation from routine recording and analysis of aggregate trends to a motivated scrutiny of the documentary traces and data doubles that proliferate around powerful individuals (and most everyone else) as they go about their daily affairs. The multiplication of the sites of surveillance ruptures the unidirectional nature of the gaze, transforming surveillance from a dynamic of the microscope to one where knowledge and images of unexpected intensity and assorted distortions cascade from viewer to viewer and across institutions, emerging in unpredictable configurations and combinations, while undermining the neat distinction between watchers and watched through a proliferation of criss-crossing, overlapping and intersecting scrutiny.

Surveillance, nonetheless, continues to play an important role in establishing and reinforcing social inequalities. Groups are differentially positioned to be able to exploit these surveillance potentialities, and their abilities to do so are often structured according to traditional social cleavages. Nonetheless, today there is undeniably a greater visual and documentary scrutiny of the powerful than at any point in

29

the past. New technologies contribute to this transformation. The Web, for example, now provides opportunities for a virtual archaeology of the documentary traces of the powerful. The mass media have fostered a form 'synopticism', whereby the many are able to monitor the few (Mathiesen 1997). Citizens can scrutinize the demeanour, foibles and idiosyncrasies of powerful individuals to an entirely unprecedented extent. This is no minor development, and we are only on the cusp of appreciating the implications of this change. It raises questions about potential transformations to the politics of surveillance. If, as seems to be the case, powerful agents become increasingly attuned to the degree of scrutiny to which they are subjected and the reams of information they inadvertently surrender on a regular basis, they will likely develop a self-interest in the politics of surveillance. Previously this was something that they were free to ignore because they correctly assumed that such issues were predominately a concern of the poor and dispossessed. One scenario for the possible implications of this development would see privacy becoming yet another marker of class privilege as powerful groups secure spaces of comparative privacy for themselves, while leaving the poor ever more exposed to scrutiny. A countervailing tendency, however, would anticipate that the entrance of powerful individuals into the politics of surveillance in self-interested efforts to secure some modicum of personal privacy might inadvertently offer other groups a host of new legal, technological or discursive resources that they can exploit in their own struggles against surveillance.

Targets of surveillance

Panoptic surveillance is fundamentally concerned with monitoring people. However, in the contemporary context, an exclusive concentration on studying the processes whereby humans are observed neglects an enormous volume of surveillance. An electronic clipping service, for example, sends me a list of references to articles published on the topic of surveillance in the past week. This usually amounts to about 45 references, and only a fraction of them deal with monitoring human beings in any conventional sense. The majority of these articles document surveillance developments in the world of science and medicine, with titles such as 'Modeling Human Cancer Genotype-Phenotype Correlations in Mice', 'Low Grazing Angle Radar Imaging Experiments Over the South Falls Sandbank', and 'Epidemiologic Surveillance and Disease Control'.

Science studies have done an excellent job of accentuating the place of systems of visible scrutiny in the development of Western science (Rouse 1993; Lynch 1985). Much of this surveillance is not directed at humans; although this point must be qualified. Humans can be implicated in some of these processes in a more tangential fashion, as is the case with the massive global system for disease surveillance which records the presence of various classes of microbes. This documentation usually commences by some form of disassembling of their microbial hosts, which are often human, such that microbes can be detected, isolated and rendered into various forms of inscription. However, within surveillance studies little attention seems to be paid to the scrutiny of these human/technological hybrids (Haraway 1991), and much less attention has been directed to the scrutiny of entities which we might agree are entirely non-human.

Given the sheer volume of surveillance directed at non-human phenomena, the neglect of such practices represents a serious oversight. Advances in satellite imaging, for example, now allow for a remarkable scrutiny of the planet. While such systems can certainly be used to monitor human behaviour, they are more routinely used to detail the distinctive heat signature of specific crops or the natural devastation brought by tsunamis. The fact that these and other devices monitor non-human entities does not reduce their social significance, but raises a host of complicated normative issues. On the one hand, the proliferation of inexpensive sensors has spurred scientific efforts to tag any number of natural entities, from trees, to bears, to whales. Such tagging contributes to an expanding natural inventory, often motivated by efforts to transform unknown 'wild' phenomena into 'natural resources'. As such, these developments raise questions about how advances in the surveillance of nature might transform our conception of 'nature' or 'wildlife' and whether new abilities to visualize and document nature mark an important quantitative development in the centuries-old ambition by 'man' to secure dominion over the natural world. On the other hand, the surveillance of nature has occasionally brought profound social benefits. Consider the monitoring of animal-borne microbes that can infect humans. A case can be made that such surveillance has monumentally benefited the human species and secured the viability of particular human communities. The panoptic model does not seem to have inspired many analysts to explore the social and political implications of these and other forms of the surveillance of nature.

Agents of surveillance

Who or what conducts surveillance? Echoing his focus on the human targets of surveillance, Foucault directs our attention to the human guards sitting unseen in the central tower. While in an ideal panoptic setting humans need not be present for the system to function, entirely absent from Foucault's account is the use of new information technologies. Foucault's failure to foreground new surveillance technologies clearly presents difficulties for contemporary analysts keen to understand the technologization of surveillance which has arguably been the most distinctive development in this area in the past half-century.

Certainly, the panopticon is a form of technology, but in concentrating on the play of architecture in establishing systems of visibility, it provides little guidance for examining the place of the new information technologies which are now central to the dynamics of surveillance. Typically, analysts respond to this omission by reading panoptic attributes into the operation of advanced surveillance technologies. However, the specifics of many such technologies are sufficiently unique as to raise their own questions about the dynamics of surveillance which transcend the panopticon. Surveillance is now conducted using sensors, satellites, biometric devices, DNA analysis and chemical profiling. Developments in nanotechnology promise to produce armies of microscopic seeing machines. The operative dynamics of these and assorted other surveillance devices only appear to be tangentially panoptic.

In recent years budget pressures, combined with the high costs of training and maintaining human agents, the inherent unreliability of such agents, and the prospect of efficient inexpensive monitoring technologies has reduced the ratio of human-to-technological monitoring. Moreover, the role of humans increasingly involves monitoring the technologies that scrutinize the behaviours of other people, places and things, which are positioned at considerable distance. Some of these devices display a form of technological agency, automatically initiating responses when they detect motion, heat profiles, sounds, or pre-established informational thresholds and data configurations.

On the one hand, Foucault can be excused for not attending to new surveillance technologies. His empirical focus was on developments in the eighteenth-century; long before any of these devices existed. However, in another sense, Foucault's neglect of contemporary technology cannot be dismissed so lightly. Foucault was not a historian exclusively interested in understanding developments characteristic of a particular time period. His historical preoccupations were part of a project to write the history of the present as a means to detail contemporary power relations. In that respect, he does not have recourse to the historian's justification that recent developments antedate his time period, and are therefore not his concern. Moreover, it is worth noting that the most lasting and prescient image of the place of information technologies in contemporary surveillance was provided by Orwell (1949), who wrote decades before Foucault and the full flowering of new visualizing technologies.

Even if we remain within the realm of surveillance conducted by humans, however, Foucault's panopticon has another limitation. Specifically, what are we to make of the particularities of the agents conducting surveillance? Foucault's concluding comment in his 'Eye of Power' interview (1980: 164) suggests that it might not matter who sits in the central tower, as the effects on the subject of surveillance are identical irrespective of who is doing the watching. This claim can be taken either as a misstatement related to his limited focus on the operational and functional dynamics of the panopticon and his desire to move beyond a sovereign model of power, or it is a simple mistake. In either case the panoptic model provides no sustained account of the role or importance of the watchers.

The myriad manifestations of contemporary surveillance make it abundantly clear that it matters enormously who is actually conducting surveillance. Surveillance of both people and things is typically a component of larger projects associated with a host of potential responses and interventions. The attitudes, predispositions, biases, prejudices and personal idiosyncrasies of the observers can be vitally important in shaping the form, intensity and regularity of those responses. In the surveillance of nature, for example, it matters if wildlife is being monitored by agents of Greenpeace or members of the National Rifle Association. The importance of the subjectivities of the watchers in the surveillance of people is perhaps nowhere more self-evident than in relation to the proliferation of CCTV systems. Ethnographic research on such technologies reveals that their level of intrusiveness, the specifics of how particular groups are targeted, and the precise aims of monitoring, are all shaped by the personal attributes of surveillance agents. So, as Norris and Armstrong (1999) have demonstrated, the racial prejudices of CCTV operators become manifest in disproportionate scrutiny of particular ethnic groups. Moreover, the fact that most operators are male often transforms ostensible security devices into a form of technological gendered objectification. Indeed, Foucault's failure to contemplate the specific characteristics of the operatives conducting surveillance contributes to his notable silence on how a masculine gaze can operate as a mechanism of sexualized objectification. Hence, it is profoundly important whether the people who operate surveillance systems are members of the Canadian Security Intelligence Service, the American Civil Liberties Union or the Ku Klux Klan.

Dynamics of surveillance

The targets of surveillance as depicted in *Discipline and Punish* are largely passive. What little agency they display is directed inward upon themselves in the form of an almost inevitable process of acquiescent 'soul training'. The movement of panoptic principles into new settings is presented as entirely frictionless. Surveillance appears to proliferate because it represents a self-evident increase in the functionality of power. Entirely missing from this account is any sense of a surveillance politics. Focusing exclusively on the panopticon as an idealized model of power, Foucault elides the fact that even in Bentham's day the panopticon was ultimately an unsuccessful political project, with Bentham serving as the failed lobbyist for his utopian architectural dream.

Today a multifaceted surveillance politics operates at different societal levels, and manifests itself in complex forms and dynamics (Haggerty and Ericson 2006). Most obviously, surveillance developments are now routinely counterpoised to some form of privacy rights and civil liberties discourse, with privacy having been institutionalized as a component of the state apparatus. Surveillance politics also includes processes of public claims-making, civil disobedience and more theatrical and artistic interventions designed to eliminate or mitigate the perceived excesses of surveillance (Levin, Frohne and Weibel 2000). Individuals who are intimately aware that they are under scrutiny often respond through a creative politics of space, demeanour and productive resistance which becomes part of their day-to-day routine (De Certeau 1984; Moore and Haggerty 2001; Gilliom 2001). While there are reasons to remain skeptical about the potential for such efforts to seriously challenge the proliferation of surveillance, they nonetheless comprise an important social dynamic and constitute part of the legal and discursive context for the operation and proliferation of surveillance which is outside of the scope of Foucault's analysis.

Foucault stressed the importance that individuals must be conscious that they are under scrutiny, as without such an awareness there is no pressure towards 'soul training'. That dynamic is still operational. That said, many prominent surveillance projects can achieve their goals without fostering such a self-awareness. Indeed, there are often sound political or commercial reasons for not revealing that you are conducting surveillance, the extent of such scrutiny or the categories used in such monitoring. One of the more startling revelations for instructors of courses on surveillance is the degree to which students are routinely unaware of the degree of scrutiny to which they are subjected. This is particularly true in relation to dataveillance, where citizens are typically only dimly cognizant that their consumption practices, movements and communication patterns are recorded, and largely oblivious to the intensity of this monitoring, its precision, or how such information is used.

Normative coding

In his wider body of work Foucault is famously ambiguous about his normative evaluation of the historical transformations in the operation of power/knowledge that he details. His preferred stance is that the developments he analyzes are 'dangerous' rather than being good or bad (Foucault 1983). His discussions of the panopticon, however, abandon such ambiguity in favour of an account that accentuates the disturbing and coercive attributes of panopticism. Most succinctly, he asserts that '[V]isibility is a trap' (Foucault 1977: 200), and refers to the panopticon's 'diabolical' character, suggesting that it amounts to 'a cruel, ingenious cage' (Foucault 1977: 205). Such concerns about surveillance are not unique to Foucault. However, in reproducing and augmenting this normative stance, Foucault further emphasizes surveillance's more dystopian potentials.

Surveillance studies replicate this normative orientation. The approach of many surveillance scholars involves a form of hermeneutics of suspicion whereby new developments are read negatively as involving inevitable and often cunningly devious expansions and intensifications of surveillance in the service of social control. Consequently, surveillance initiatives are routinely presented as raising disconcerting civil libertarian issues. Such studies are important, but in terms of developing an appreciation for the operation of the totality of contemporary surveillance, they are also severely limited. Once we recognize the incredible range of projects in which surveillance is deployed, it is apparent that surveillance studies tend to neglect surveillance practices that might be accepted as a positive development. Hence, there are few studies, for example, of surveillance as part of a global system of infectious disease control or surveillance in parenting, which might accentuate the positive and essential attributes of such scrutiny (Lyon 1994).

One reason why surveillance studies tends to shy away from studying forms of surveillance that might be acknowledged to be a 'good thing' relates to the fact that surveillance scholars are trained in a tradition of critique. Acknowledging and emphasizing the potentially positive uses of surveillance practices risks moving the analysis from critic into advocate and claims-maker on behalf of the system itself.[3]

The hermeneutics of reading Foucault

Originally designed by Bentham, the panopticon is now inextricably linked to Foucault's work. Reference to Foucault pervades surveillance studies, with many analysts having come to this topic through an interest in Foucault's philosophy. This gives the field a considerable degree of theoretical rigour, but it also contributes to some characteristic difficulties in efforts to employ the panopticon to analyze contemporary surveillance.

A by-product of the intense scholarly interest in Foucault has been the development of a voluminous secondary literature of analysis, interpretation and explication. Driven by a desire to foster a more nuanced understanding of Foucault's work, this literature also, paradoxically, can serve as a vehicle for bewilderment. This is due to the familiar dynamic whereby important thinkers routinely spur a series of interlocutors, many of whom produce accounts that the author him/herself would find entirely alien to their intentions or even explicit positions. In the case of Foucault, the quest for novel readings and interpretations has produced a mass of texts that are often in tension with one another or entirely contradictory.

Faced with this unmanageable secondary literature, the temptation is to purify, to filter out the interpretations in an effort to concentrate on the 'pure' Foucault. Rather than encountering such an entity, however, one finds that assembled under Foucault's name are in fact a multiplicity of Foucaults. A host of Foucault's books, articles, interviews, lectures and correspondence provide a sometimes subtle, and sometimes quite dramatic, different gloss on his positions. Rather than helping to bring us closer to Foucault's true meanings, these texts instead offer up a seductive invitation to immerse oneself ever more fully into his wider *oeuvre*.

Consider, for example, my earlier claim that a limitation of Foucault's panoptic model is that it does not contain an image of resistance. A Foucault scholar might correctly respond that resistance is, in fact, a key theme in Foucault's work. While this is undoubtedly the case, it is also true that the issue of resistance arrives comparatively late in Foucault's corpus. His famous statement that 'Where there is power, there is resistance' (Foucault 1978: 95) appears in volume 1 of the *History of Sexuality* which was published several years after his panoptic writings, and was partially a response to the persistent accusation that his prison book often appeared despairing because of a lack of any notion of resistance. The same dynamic is also in operation in relation to my earlier claim that Foucault's panoptic writings contain no suggestion as to the pleasurable aspects of surveillance. While it is certainly true that pleasure becomes an important topic in Foucault's final works, this theme is not evident in his panoptic writings.

For our purposes, this raises the question of whether the panoptic model of surveillance can be found self-contained within Foucault's explicit writing on this topic, or whether it must be informed by insights from his wider *oeuvre*. If it is the former, then it does not seem to entail a model of resistance, pleasure or any of the other phenomena and practices detailed in this chapter. If it is the latter, and the fixation on the panoptic model has adumbrated our relationship with Foucault, requiring us to interpret Foucault's work in the context of his entire theoretical project, this introduces a further layer of interpretive ambiguity due to the characteristically developmental nature of Foucault's thought. Foucault changed his mind; the genealogies differ substantially from the archaeologies and his writings on such key concepts as power, discourse, subjectivity, as well as the relationship among different models of governance, have evolved. Hence, rather than serving as a self-evident means to clarify important points, the strategy of turning to Foucault's wider *oeuvre* suggests many more layers of interpretive openings. Such is clearly the case with his writing on the panopticon and surveillance more generally. Elden (2003) for one, argues that rather than the panopticon being Foucault's definitive statement on surveillance, an examination of his wider *oeuvre* suggests that the panopticon was just one moment in an ongoing and evolving focus on practices of visibility (see also Simon 2005). Alternative models of surveillance are apparent in his works on biopower and in his brief, but suggestive, comments on the menagerie and on plague surveillance in *Discipline and Punish*.

Complicating all of this are the occasional suggestions that translation problems inevitably handicap or thwart English-language readings of Foucault. To truly understand Foucault, this argument goes, one must read the original French texts and ideally have an appreciation for the unique dynamics of the French academy. Indeed, translation issues arise fairly frequently in surveillance contexts when commentators accentuate how the English title *Discipline and Punish* downplays the centrality of surveillance apparent in the original French title *Surveiller et punir*.

Notwithstanding the proliferation of reified one-paragraph summaries of Foucault's panopticon, it is apparent that invoking the panopticon does not easily refer to a self-evident model of surveillance that can simply be applied to different contexts. The more one dwells on the panopticon and immerses oneself in both the original texts and the secondary literature, the more conflicting interpretations one encounters, and the more questions emerge. Foucault's truths on this matter are continually deferred, and often highly contested, accentuating the fascinating complexity and open-endedness of his thought. It also suggests that 'Foucault on surveillance' is a plurality; a series of open-ended texts amenable to multiple creative readings.

These interpretive layers and ambiguities do not in themselves represent a problem that one might hope to rectify, but simply characterize the scholarly relationship with key authors. The importance for surveillance studies, however, pertains to the now common scenario whereby a discussion about surveillance devolves into passionate debate about Foucault himself – what he said, what he meant, and how he should be understood. Such exchanges marshal the full repertoire of interpretive schemata listed above, including appeals to different readings in the secondary literature, illuminating comments made in interviews, pleas for an appreciation for his wider project, differentiating contradictory statements across different texts and advocating for the necessity to read the original French texts. Occasionally accusations that someone has gotten Foucault 'wrong' emerge – a profoundly ironic claim given Foucault's post-structuralist leanings. Such hagiographic battles are often enjoyable and occasionally illuminating. However, there is also a key point in such exchanges beyond which discussion moves from *theorizing surveillance* into a form of Foucault studies.

For my purposes, I am not concerned with unearthing Foucault's final truths, but instead embrace his more pragmatic orientation, encapsulated in his statement that 'I would like my books to be a kind of tool-box which others can rummage through to find a tool which they can use however they wish' (Foucault 1994: 523). Such has been my orientation in evaluating the continuing relevance of the panopticon, suggesting that as an analytical tool it might no longer be well suited for understanding the complexity and totality of contemporary surveillance dynamics.

Discussion

The above analysis indicates that the panopticon is often introduced as a cliché, and in being increasingly reified has nearly exhausted its creative potential as a model for understanding surveillance. Exemplars as firmly entrenched as the panopticon, however, are not displaced in the absence of a new model that helps explain conspicuous anomalies and offer suggestive possibilities for future research and theorizing. In recent years a series of new candidates for understanding surveillance have been proposed, including Bogard's (1996, 2006) emphasis on 'hypercontrol', Lyon's (2003) notion of 'social sorting' as well as the model of the 'assemblage' advanced by Richard Ericson and myself (Haggerty and Ericson 2000). All of these are serious contenders for a successor to the prevailing model for thinking about surveillance. Rather than conclude by championing the model developed by Ericson and myself, however, in the tradition of contrarian thought, and of analyzing complex topics in a complex fashion, I would instead like to offer some reservations about the prospect or desirability of developing a successor model to characterize the operation of contemporary surveillance.

The term 'surveillance' is itself an analytical category, and like all such categories, is a simplifying device. It suppresses a world of specific differences under a broader rubric and involves an implicit claim that, irrespective of individual variations, the instances subsumed under the category are sufficiently similar that they warrant being considered as part of the same grouping. In the case of the analytic category of 'surveillance', however, the boundaries of that classification now risk being stretched beyond all recognition. Hence, I am wary of the prospect of developing a model of surveillance that can usefully be generalized to all or even a considerable number of surveillance contexts. It is already difficult to make confident declarations about surveillance of the type: 'surveillance is used for...' 'surveillance operates by...' or 'the effects of surveillance are...'. All such claims must be endlessly qualified due to the sheer complexity of surveillance, as manifest in the multiplication of its aims, agendas, institutions, operational forms, objects and agents. It has become profoundly difficult to say anything about surveillance that is generally true across all, or even most, instances.

There is, however a potentially useful way forward which is itself inspired by Foucault's larger body of work. In particular, there are connections with the now extensive body of research on governance and governmentality (Barry, Osborne and Rose 1996; Burchell, Gordon and Miller 1991; Dean 1999; Foucault 1991) which have an important place for the study of surveillance. Before such a connection can be entirely forged, however, researchers must reconsider some of the methodological and substantive limitations that governmental theorists have imposed on their own work.

Studies of governmentality are not involved in the study of government, which typically refers to the operation of the formal state apparatus, legislatures and representative bodies. While the state is a key actor in many governmental projects, governance is also enacted and coordinated by extra-state agents such as corporations, non-governmental agencies, international bodies and community groups. Studies of governance also avoid sweeping declarations about the nature of governance characteristic of an entire state or society. Instead, they focus on the particularities of governmental projects, each of which involves characteristic efforts to pattern the behaviour of people in prescribed directions. Each governmental project can, in turn, be analyzed in terms of its specific rationalities and technologies. Governmental rationalities consist of the conscious reflections on the aims and ambitions of governing – how governance is understood from the position of governing agencies. Governmental technologies are the assorted tools used to achieve those governmental ambitions, and can include such varied phenomena as architectural forms, accounting formulas and surveys.

Studies of governance also forgo suggesting that all governmental projects are involved in an inevitable process of social control. In this they are in accord with Foucault's larger body of work which takes an ambivalent normative stance to changes in the dynamics of power. While governance inevitably involves efforts to persuade, entice, coerce or cajole subjects to modify their behaviour in particular directions, the targets of governance are understood to be a locus of freedom, although this freedom is inevitably bounded by various constraints. Nonetheless, the emphasis on subjects as active agents suggests that all governmental projects entail opportunities for resistance, avoidance or subversion.

Even this extremely cursory summary of the governmental approach suggests a number of resonances with the study of surveillance. One of the most important connections relates to the fact that the practice of governance is knowledge dependent. Governing a specific population requires an intricate knowledge of its particularities, tendencies and inclinations. This emphasis on the operation of knowledge, along with an understanding of the importance of different technologies for conceptualizing and executing governmental ambitions, places practices of visibility at the forefront of governmental practices. To be known, objects of governance must be rendered into some representational form, such as image, text or data; phenomena which are central to the concerns of surveillance scholars. Indeed, surveillance in various forms is recognized as being among the most important technologies of governance, as new ways of 'seeing' a population can open up new ways of conceptualizing the aims of governance and its practical possibilities.

The emphasis on particular governmental projects also restrains any desire to conceptualize surveillance *tout court* in favour of examining how particular systems of visibility are deployed in the context of specific governmental ambitions. It allows for a focused consideration of the aims, dynamics and rationalizations of particular surveillance projects. Such a focus can also mitigate the tendency towards forms of dystopian technological determinism that are often apparent in the surveillance studies literature. Combining a normatively ambivalent stance with a focus on particular governmental projects allows for the development of a more refined normative stance towards surveillance. Surveillance is neither good nor bad. We can only develop a meaningful normative position towards surveillance projects that are coordinated and calibrated in light of particular governmental ambitions. Such an emphasis also allows for analysis of the complexities and dynamics of contemporary surveillance politics, as citizens typically do not oppose or resist surveillance in the abstract, but express concerns about concrete manifestations or imaginings of how surveillance is or will be deployed for very specific purposes by particular institutions.

The understanding of citizens as active agents, combined with the frequent suggestion in this literature that governance has political dimensions (O'Malley 2004), suggest a clear place for the analysis of the politics of governance and attendant practices of resistance. However, to date, this line of inquiry has not been embraced, as doing so would entail breaching some of the methodological dictates established by key governmental authors. Having emerged from a Foucauldian framework, governmental studies have concentrated almost entirely on discourse analysis and have been reluctant to explore the nitty-gritty politics of governance or the experience of subjects. Indeed, almost all of these studies have followed Nikolas Rose's admonition that there is no such thing as 'the governed', but instead only 'multiple objectifications of those over whom government is to be exercised' (1999: 40). Rose also proposes that studies of governance should eschew sociological realism in order to concentrate on how authorities have conceived of what it means to govern, and how governance is made possible. Specifically, he suggests that studies of governmentality are exclusively concerned with 'the conditions of possibility and intelligibility for certain ways of seeking to act upon the conduct of others, or oneself, to achieve certain ends' (Rose 1999: 19). In this, governmental studies self-consciously exclude a series of important issues, including the actual operation of systems of rule and the relations among political actors (Rose 1999: 19). Unfortunately, in this quest for a form of methodological and epistemological purity, studies of governmentality inevitably forgo important lines of inquiry into the actual experience of being subjected to different governmental regimes. Studies of surveillance therefore can and should embrace many of the insights about governance advanced within this Foucauldian approach, while also reserving space for modestly realist projects that analyze the politics of surveillance or the experiences of the subjects of surveillance.

Finally, studies of governance also allow for greater reflection on the monitoring of non-human entities. This is apparent in the types of phenomena which are recognized as being subject to governmental ambitions which include a heterodox assortment of such things as pregnancy, universities, pain, and economic life. While governmental authors are only interested in non-human entities to the extent that the governance of things also entails efforts to shape the rationality of human conduct (Dean 1999: 11), there are opportunities to explore whether there is an inevitable relationship between the monitoring of non-human phenomena such as forests, animals and microbes, and efforts to regulate human actions.

Surveillance studies can therefore benefit from embracing a modified governmental approach. It offers a path forward for exploring many of the silences and omissions of the panoptic model, but without falling into the temptation of advancing a totalizing model of surveillance.

Notes

1 I would like to thank Charles Barbour and Karyn Ball for their helpful comments on this article. I would also like to thank David Lyon for the invitation to reflect upon this issue and the participants of the 'Theorizing Surveillance' conference for their excellent comments on a presentation based on an earlier draft of this chapter.
2 Director, Criminology Program, University of Alberta, Department of Sociology, Edmonton, Alberta, Canada, T6G 2H4.
3 One often encounters calls for greater or more intensive surveillance practices directed at powerful interests and institutions such as the police, politicians and corporations. These are typically advanced by political economists and assorted activist communities, rather than from individuals who study surveillance *per se*.

References

Allen, M. (1994) '"See You in the City!" Perth's Citiplace and the Space of Surveillance', in K. Gibson and S. Watson (eds) *Metropolis Now: Planning and the Urban in Contemporary Australia* (Sydney: Pluto), 137–47.

Barry, A., Osborne, T. and Rose, N. (eds) (1996) *Foucault and Political Reason: Liberalism, Neo-liberalism and Rationalities of Government* (Chicago: University of Chicago Press).

Bauman, Z. (1992) *Intimations of Postmodernity* (London: Routledge).

Bentham, J. (1995) *The Panopticon Writing* (edited by M. Bozovic) (London: Verso).

Berdayes, V. (2002) 'Traditional Management Theory as Panoptic Discourse: Language and the Constitution of Somatic Flows', *Culture and Organization*, 8, 35–49.

Bogard, W. (1996) *The Simulation of Surveillance: Hypercontrol in Telematic Societies* (Cambridge: Cambridge University Press).

Bogard, W. (2006) 'Welcome to the Society of Control: The Simulation of Surveillance Revisited', in K.D. Haggerty and R. Ericson (eds) *The New Politics of Surveillance and Visibility* (Toronto: University of Toronto Press), 55–78.

Bousquet, G. (1998) 'Space, Power, Globalization: The Internet Symptom', *Societies* 4, 105–13.

Boyne, R. (2000) 'Post-Panopticism', *Economy and Society*, 29 (2), 285–307.

Burchell, G., Gordon, C. and Miller, P. (eds) (1991) *The Foucault Effect: Studies in Governmentality* (Chicago: University of Chicago Press).

Butchart, A. (1996) 'The Industrial Panopticon: Mining and the Medical Construction of Migrant African Labour in South Africa, 1900–1950', *Social Science and Medicine*, 42 (2), 185–97.

Dandeker, C. (1990) 'Bureaucracy, Surveillance and Modern Society', in *Surveillance, Power and Modernity: Bureaucracy and Discipline from 1700 to the Present Day* (Cambridge: Polity), 1–36.

De Angelis, M. (2004) 'Global Capital, Abstract Labour, and the Fractal-Panopticon', *The Commoner 2001*. Available at: http://www.commoner.uk.org.

De Certeau, M. (1984) 'Walking in the City', in *The Practice of Everyday Life* (Berkeley: University of California Press), 91–110.

De Landa, M. (1991) *War in the Age of Intelligent Machines* (New York: Zone).

Dean, M. (1999) *Governmentality: Power and Rule in Modern Society* (Thousand Oaks, CA: Sage).

Doyle, A. (1998) '"Cops": Television Policing as Policing Reality', in M. Fishman and G. Cavender (eds) *Entertaining Crime: Television Reality Programs* (New York: Aldine de Gruyter), 95–116.

Elden, S. (2003) 'Plague, Panopticon, Police', *Surveillance and Society*, 1 (3), 240–53.

Foucault, M. (1977) *Discipline and Punish: The Birth of the Prison* (translated by A. Sheridan) (New York: Vintage).

Foucault, M. (1978) *The History of Sexuality, Volume I: An Introduction* (translated by R. Hurley) (New York: Vintage).

Foucault, M. (1980) 'The Eye of Power', in *Power/Knowledge: Selected Interviews and Other Writings, 1972–1977* (New York: Pantheon), 146–65.

Foucault, M. (1983) 'On the Genealogy of Ethics', in H.L. Dreyfus and P. Rabinow (eds) *Michel Foucault: Beyond Structuralism and Hermeneutics* (New York: Pantheon), 229–52.

Foucault, M. (1991) 'Governmentality', in G. Burchell, C. Gordon and P. Miller (eds) *The Foucault Effect: Studies in Governmentality* (Chicago: University of Chicago Press), 87–104.

Foucault, M. (1994) 'Prisons et Asiles dans le Mécanisme du Pouvoir', in *Dits et Ecrits, t II* (Paris: Gallimard), 521–25.

Garland, D. (ed.) (2001) *Mass Imprisonment: Social Causes and Consequences* (London: Sage).

Gill, S. (1995) 'The Global Panopticon: The Neo-Liberal State, Economic Life, and Democratic Surveillance', *Alternatives*, 20 (1), 1–49.

Gilliom, J. (2001) *Overseers of the Poor: Surveillance, Resistance, and the Limits of Privacy* (Chicago: University of Chicago Press).

Goombridge, N. (2003) 'Crime Control or Crime Culture TV?', *Surveillance and Society*, 1 (1), 30–46. Available at: http://www.surveillance-and-society.org/articles1/cctvculture.pdf.

Gordon, D. (1990) 'The Electronic Panopticon', in *The Justice Juggernaut: Fighting Street Crime, Controlling Citizens* (New Brunswick, NJ: Rutgers University Press), 438–51.

Haggerty, K.D. and Ericson, R.V. (2000) 'The Surveillant Assemblage', *British Journal of Sociology*, 51 (4), 605–22.

Haggerty, K.D. (2006a) 'Visible War: Information War, Surveillance and Speed', in K.D. Haggerty and R.V. Ericson (eds) *The New Politics of Surveillance and Visibility* (Toronto: University of Toronto Press), 251–68.

Haggerty K.D. and Ericson, R.V. (eds) (2006b) *The New Politics of Surveillance and Visibility* (Toronto: University of Toronto Press).

Haraway, D.J. (1991) *Simians, Cyborgs, and Women: The Reinvention of Nature* (New York: Routledge).

Horwich, P. (1993) *World Changes: Thomas Kuhn and the Nature of Science* (Cambridge, MA: MIT Press).

Hoyingen-Huen, P. (1993) *Reconstructing Scientific Revolutions: Thomas S. Kuhn's Philosophy of Science* (Chicago: University of Chicago Press).

Koskela, H. (2003) '"Cam Era" – The Contemporary Urban Panopticon', *Surveillance and Society*, 1 (3), 292–313. Available at: http://www.surveillance-and-society.org/articles1(3)/camera.pdf.

Koskela, H. (2004) 'Webcams, TV Shows and Mobile Phones: Empowering Exhibitionism', *Surveillance and Society*, 2 (2/3), 199–215. Available at: http://www.surveillance-and-society.org/articles2(2)/webcams.pdf.

Kuhn, T. (1970) *The Structure of Scientific Revolutions* (Chicago: University of Chicago Press).

Leman-Langois, S. (2003) 'The Myoptic Panopticon: The Social Consequences of Policing Through the Lens', *Policing and Society*, 13 (1), 43–58.

Levin, T.Y., Frohne, U. and Weibel, P. (eds) (2000) *CTRL [SPACE]: Rhetorics of Surveillance from Bentham to Big Brother* (Cambridge, MA: MIT Press).

Lynch, M. (1985) 'Discipline and the Material Form of Images: An Analysis of Scientific Visibility', *Social Studies of Science*, 15, 37–66.

Lyon, D. (1994) 'From Big Brother to the Electronic Panopticon', in *The Electronic Eye: The Rise of Surveillance Society* (Minneapolis: University of Minnesota Press), 57–80.

Lyon, D. (ed.) (2003) *Surveillance as Social Sorting: Privacy, Risk and Digital Discrimation* (London and New York: Routledge).

Mann, S., Nolan, J. and Wellman, B. (2003) 'Sousveillance: Inventing and Using Wearable Computing Devices for Data Collection in Surveillance Environments', *Surveillance and Society*, 1 (3), 331–55. Available at: http://www.surveillance-and-society.org/articles1(3)/sousveillance.pdf.

Mathiesen, T. (1997) 'The Viewer Society: Michel Foucault's "Panopticon" Revisited', *Theoretical Criminology*, 1 (2), 215–34.

Moore, D. and Haggerty, K.D. (2001) 'Bring It On Home: Home Drug Testing and the Relocation of the War on Drugs', *Social and Legal Studies*, 10 (3), 377–95.

Nock, S. L. (1993) *The Costs of Privacy: Surveillance and Reputation in America* (New York: Aldine de Gruyter).

Norris, C. and Armstrong, G. (1999) *The Maximum Surveillance Society: The Rise of CCTV* (Oxford: Berg).

O'Malley, P. (2004) *Risk, Uncertainty and Government* (London: The Glass House).

Orwell, G. (1949) *Nineteen Eighty-Four* (New York: Penguin).

Poster, M. (1990) *The Mode of Information: Poststructuralism and Social Context* (Chicago: University of Chicago Press).

Rose, N. (1999) *Powers of Freedom: Reframing Political Thought* (Cambridge: Cambridge University Press).

Rouse, J. (1993) 'Foucault and the Natural Sciences', in J. Caputo and M. Yount (eds) *Foucault and the Critique of Institutions* (University Park, PA: Pennsylvania State University), 137–62.

Simon, B. (2005) 'The Return of Panopticism: Supervision, Subjection and the New Surveillance', *Surveillance and Society* 3 (1), 1–20. Available at: http://www.surveillance-and-society.org/Articles3(1)/return.pdf.

Sweeny, R. (2004) 'Pedagopticon: Beyond *Discipline and Punish* in the Classroom', in *New Forms Festival* (Vancouver, BC).

Thompson, E.P. (1991) 'Time, Work-Discipline and Industrial Capitalism', in *Customs in Common* (New York: New Press), 352–403.

Wacquant, L. (2001) 'The Penalisation of Poverty and the Rise of Neo-Liberalism', *European Journal on Criminal Policy and Research*, 9, 401–12.

Yar, M. (2003) 'Panoptic Power and the Pathologisation of Vision: Critical Reflections on the Foucauldian Thesis', *Surveillance and Society*, 1 (3), 254–71. Available at: http://www.surveillance-and-society.org/articles1(3)/pathologisation.pdf.

Chapter 3

Security, exception, ban and surveillance

Didier Bigo

Critical security studies and surveillance studies have a lot in common, but they rarely interact with one another. Surveillance studies is now a specific field of research in sociology that has been initiated by sociologists such as Gary Marx and David Lyon, which has expanded far beyond its original focus concerning activities of surveillance and control of minorities by police and intelligence services.[1] Surveillance technologies, as well as attitudes towards constant monitoring of activities, have shifted and greatly expanded to become routines of everyday life, rather than exceptional practices. The idea of an Orwellian society in the making, through a 'liberal' agenda, has been much discussed. Michel Foucault uses the term 'panopticon' to describe both the development of the Orwellian society and its transformation, as it moves from a society of discipline to a society of management and monitoring the life of populations encapsulated in a territorial container controlled by the state. Critical criminology has engaged in discussion about the accuracy of using Michel Foucault's 'dispositif'[2] notion of the panopticon, which some authors view as too government-focused, to Deleuze's notion of the 'assemblage' (Haggerty and Ericson 2000). Kevin Haggerty and Richard Ericson have developed the approach of the assemblage, and I have discussed the limits of the Foucaldian notion of the pan-opticon in an earlier piece by proposing the notion of the 'ban-opticon' (Bigo 2005).

The notion of 'ban' originates from international relations (IR) and critical security studies and is on a parallel track with surveillance studies. The ban-opticon deconstructs some of the post-September 11 analysis as a 'permanent state of emergency' or as a 'generalized state of exception',[3] which reinstates the question of who decides about the exception in the heart of the IR debate: who is sovereign, and who can legitimately name the public enemy. The ban-opticon dispositif is established in relation to a state of unease created by the United States and its allies. The United States has propagated the idea that there is a global 'in-security', which is attributed to the development of threats of mass destruction, thought to be derived from terrorist and other criminal organizations and governments that support them. This has led the US to assert the need for a globalized security that would render national borders obsolete and pressure other international actors to collaborate. These developments have created the field of 'unease management', which is the formation of global police networks, policing military functions of combat and criminalizing the notion of war. The governmentality of unease is characterized by practices of exceptionalism, acts of profiling and containing foreigners, and a normative imperative of mobility (Bigo 2005).

The ban attempts to show how the role of routines and acceptance of everyday life protects some over others, or how the protection of these others against themselves as the profound structure which explains the 'moment' of the declaration of exception.[4] It also attempts to reveal the judicial illusion that a specific moment declares the sovereign borders of the political, which is so favoured in many analyses. This view needs to be amended by a sociological stance that takes into account long-term social processes and public acceptance of the routines of surveillance.

Closing the borders and declaring the exception: the sovereign moment of the ban?

In relation to the framing of the ban-opticon, the underlying argument emerging from discussions about September 11 and the notion of the state of exception and the detention of foreigners, is to try to understand that exceptionalism is not only linked with derogatory measures and special laws against presumed terrorists, but also with a specific form of governmentality. The governmentality of unease increases the exception and banalizes it (ELISE 2005). The declaration of an emergency in security by the US, United Kingdom and Australian authorities, and with some nuances in some countries of the European Union, is not

47

the central element of the ban-opticon. Even if these declarations of emergency attempt to change the way we are governed, they do not have the ability to upset the rule of law. A large majority of countries have not 'declared' a 'state of exception', they have merely implemented old and new surveillance technologies, and reinforced control over foreigners without citing any emergency or terrorism activities. Many countries like Austria, Italy, and France have also equated the notion of the criminalization of migration, radical Islam and clandestine organizations[5] with arguments of a struggle against terrorism, organized crime and illegal migration, using the same techniques of dataveillance, of increased checks of identity by different means.[6]

In the US, the 'emergency' has been a way to justify a war against Afghanistan and at the same moment, a militarization of internal security, an enlargement of the role of external intelligence services inside, and a downsizing of the role of police, judges, parliament, and international agreements. The situation in the UK, to derogate from the European Convention of Human rights, is unique in Europe, in that all other countries have not chosen this 'solution'. Also, in the UK, this was not a 'suspension of the law', but specific limited derogations from the rule of law, creating a long struggle between the executive power and the judges to define the boundaries of the right to derogate.[7] In Australia, there is more of a local agenda and an assertion by the Australians about who they really are, or questioning where they belong (are they part of the West?). The unanimity of the EU after September 11 strongly split after the UK and some other states decided to go to war without evidence of the involvement of Saddam Hussein and the strong refusal of the Germans, French, Belgians and Russians to believe the 'information' given by the US and UK on dubious elements. At the EU level, this has reinforced multiple 'lines of flight'[8] and intensified the roar of the battle[9] about autonomy towards the US and solidarity with them. It has also permitted some transnational bureaucracies of the second and third pillars of the European Union[10] to accelerate what they wanted initially 'in the name of the struggle against terrorism' (for example the European Arrest warrant). After the Genoa protest,[11] the European Council of Justice and Home Affairs (JHA) ministers needed a definition that would encompass a very large area. They have, more or less, succeeded in including any large protest of anti-globalization or anti-war campaigns into the definition of terrorism, even if the Belgium presidency has limited the effect of the first draft of the proposal that merely associated the two.

Elements from Schengen, Genoa, and Seville that were originally refused for their danger towards civil liberties, were accepted after

September 11, 2001 and March 11, 2004.[12] Some national derogations were enlarged in their scope and in their justifications such as the French antiterrorists laws, the UK situation in Northern Ireland, and the Italian Vespri Siciliani operations. For some time, resistance was weak from both the parliament, the judges and the NGOs of civil societies. The 'unanimism' of the professionals of politics[13] after September 11 created a specific period for the enunciation of a discourse of necessity of war against terrorism and suspicion against foreigners, ethnic and religious minorities, but it was rooted in previous practices. These previous 'routines' enable the executive, in so-called time of emergency, to use the justification of prolonged derogatory measures (such as indefinite detention, the demand for longer retention of telecommunications traffic data, introduction of new biometric identifiers in visas, passports and ID cards, as well as the use of transnational exchange of passenger name records) with the argument that it is necessary to act to protect people and to reassure the task of collective survival. This political move is embedded in the expansion of resources for control and monitoring opened by the combination of new technologies reconfiguring the relation between space, time, speed and distance and the will of the bureaucracies of control to use them at their maximum.[14]

Therefore, the idea of September 11 as an exceptional event of violence, as 'hyperterrorism', has to be replaced by the one of September 11, 2001, Madrid in March 2004 and London in July 2005 as a series of destructive bombings of varying intensity followed by a backlash to archaic visions of exceptionalism as a solution, either by war or by the dream of a global control of all the individuals on the move around the planet. The combination of the violence of the clandestine organization, the archaism and will to monitor on a global scale and to control the future of the governments has paved the way for a programme which could be laughable if it did not create local tragedies. But this political programme of the perpetual war on terror, or the perpetual emergency situation itself, masks the continuity of the technologically deterministic belief that technology can fix any political problem.

After a while, these technologies are considered so banal (such as ID checks in many countries, military with heavy armaments in public places in France under Vigipirate, and biometric identifiers in documents) that nobody (including the judges) asks for their legitimacy and their efficiency after a certain period of time. Their potential use against a variety of targets is different from the assessment of the political discourse that they will be used only against a specific category (particularly odious and labelled terrorist, organized criminals, traffickers or sexual offenders). These technologies are also forgotten by those who want to reduce the analysis of the situation to a specific state of exception with one sovereign actor, one unique moment, one unique justification (the three prerequisites needed to play the Schmittian shadow theatre).[15]

Against the decisionism and the illusion that the will of power succeeds, the 'routine' of exclusion must be grasped, as well as the 'permanence' or the incrementalization of a so-called 'state of emergency' which, in fact is inscribed into the relationship of the exclusion of the excluded themselves and their capacities to resist and to mobilize. What we need is then to go beyond the debate of the exception as a 'moment' of decision or as the opposite of a 'norm', in following Schmitt and Agamben, and to analyze it as a specific form of governmentality.[16] The ban-opticon is interested not only by the declaration of the executive[17] and its effects on society and democracy but also by the process of tracing the boundaries of (ab)normalization.

Surveillance, legitimacy and September 11: a new era?

The first move of any government that considers its survival threatened is to close its borders and detain foreigners. This is not new. September 11 was a tragic moment but cannot be considered an 'unprecedented event' radically changing the face of the modern world, even if Tony Blair, George Bush and John Howard have said respectively that this date was a turning point in history (Huysmans 2004). The transnationalization of political violence by clandestine organizations is a long process whose roots are as old as the decolonization process of the 1950s, the hijacking of planes by third parties in the 1980s, and the development of killing at distance by remote technologies of bombing, as well as the radicalization of conflicts in Lebanon and Palestine with the rebirth of suicide bombers against French and US armies.[18] What was new with September 11, 2001 was, at the level of the use of violence, the combination of different traditional repertoires of actions (hijacking planes, destroying them, suicide bombers...), the scale of the attacks, and its location in the heart of US territory. However, this is not the birth of a new age of global terrorism *per se*, called hyperterrorism, megaterrorism or third type terrorism, even if some experts on (in)security[19] and some 'fearmongers' have sold the idea with such success that it is still difficult to state what we know and what we do not know four years later.[20] For example, 21 July in the UK seems to be more of a copycat bombing than anything else and one must wonder to what extent Al Qaeda is or is not a unified strategic actor (Heisbourg 2002; Megret 2003). The novelty then, if any, is that some clandestine organizations, not directly related with a mass movement, are perhaps more credible than before in this claim to launch a war with a high level of intensity by using high-technology weaponry.[21]

This possibility of mass destruction by a clandestine organization of less than 20 people is a serious challenge, but, here also, too many voices have used the argument that the successful monopoly of legitimate means of violence over a territory by the state has ended, and the closure of the 'Hobbesian' solution with September 11: to plead for exceptional and global means of unifying police, intelligence services and armies in each nation and obliging them to collaborate strongly at the Western level. This solution has opened the way for an argument in favour of a world empire protecting us from the threat of the 'fanatics'. We have to distinguish between the seriousness of the miniaturization and dissemination of arms, which may have mass effects, and the apocalyptic narrative, which is an overstatement of the situation, and try to justify any 'answer', however disproportionate and unjust (ELISE 2005).

The novelty of September 11 then, and perhaps mainly, is in the disproportionate reactions of some politicians. September 11 is not an exceptional event of violence which reframes the relations of politics; rather, it is the regression of some politicians towards habits that reveal the logic of a form of governmentality which informs deeply what is called liberalism and generates illiberal practices (Bigo 2004, 2002).

The role of the professionals of politics is important in relation to the professionals of (in)security, and their competitions and alliances frame the debate about the capacity to declare the exception and the period of emergency with some success. This element has been developed in detail, analyzing what could be considered as a 'North Irelandization' of the world after September 11.[22] These professionals were afraid (or claimed they were afraid), to such a point that they came back to the old idea of vindication and to the belief that a military war would solve the problem. In just a couple of days, the military path taken by the professionals of politics gave the intelligence services an incredible new role, and justified major breaches of rule of law and democracy by arguing that these attacks were threatening the survival of their nations, that they were a kind of undeclared war and not a criminal act (Huysmans 2004). George Bush's statement on 13 November 2001 declaring 'an extraordinary emergency', as well as what has been known as the Patriot Act I and II, and various executive orders including the decision to create special military commissions with powers to judge any aliens suspected of terrorism, have been justified by the belief in an exceptional situation of violence and threat to the survival of the nation. But the reactivation of border controls after the bombing of September 11 was not the sign of renewed efficiency, it was a sign of a ritual against fear of the unknown, with fewer and fewer people believing in the ritual and now seeing it as a simulacrum.[23]

Yet, it is easier to see this four years after the event. In the immediate aftermath of September 11, few people challenged the idea that the sovereignty and integrity of the body of the US nation were at stake; that the survival of the nation after such a wound was jeopardized. Instead they participated in the creation of a wave of patriotism, an appeal to be more protected and a will to revenge. Nevertheless, from an academic point of view, it is worthwhile to remember the form of evolution taken by political violence in previous decades. This gives a different angle to the question of protecting the population and of the possibility to close the borders against foreign enemies, like in a Maginot line[24] full of electronic gadgets. This history challenges the choice of the professionals of politics to choose war when others strongly resist it, the choice to enhance any form of technological surveillance available, and to use it against foreigners and their own population measures of exclusion and discrimination.

David Cole insists on balancing liberty and security.[25] He claims that the sacrifice of the liberty of others for personal security is not seen as a sacrifice and he has tried to explain that this is one of the main reasons for the lack of protest in favour of civil liberties. I think this is an important argument as long as it is not framed as a rational actor game, and is correlated with the more general structure of surveillance. In terms of civil liberties, the discrimination created between American citizens and non-citizens (including those with permanent residence) has taken considerable dimension, given the fact that the position of the administration is to say that only American citizens can claim access to some of the fundamental principles of civil liberty, such as a fair trial with the right of defence, to know the content of case files, to know when the trial will take place, to have a jury and to know on what legal basis the client is being charged. For detainees in Guantanamo, outside of US territory, these rights are not legally binding on the administration. Also, the possibility to detain people indefinitely without disclosing the charges held against them was finally given approval on 13 November by military order, which, as one recalls, was refused when the vote for the Patriot Act took place on 26 October 2001. This is only the most visible aspect of this problem and led the American government to systematically interrogate more than 5000 nationals from Middle East countries over several days on the sole basis of their nationality. Several of these nationals were arrested and the American government also frequently carried out 'surveys' at the centre of the population being targeted and encouraged allied countries to do the same (such as Saudi Arabia). In addition, the American government implemented a series of practices that are derogatory to accepted international conventions, in a bid to centralize and control IT databases containing the personal data of these foreigners or long-term residents. This has not only played a negative role with regards to civil liberties and individual rights of foreigners in the US, but also to foreigners in Europe, through pressure imposed by the American government regarding laws to be adopted in relation to the fight against terrorism.

If the US was the first to stress this vision of a more globalized surveillance, they were not the only ones. To give but one example of technologies operative at the European level, multiple databases have been put in place to permit the profiling of risks associated with certain individuals. Concerning crime, other than the already aging Interpol database, the Sirene system facilitates the rapid circulation of judiciary documents and the exchange of information.[26] New developments of this system will 'overlook' the possibility for lawyers to see the documents; this will be only for magistrative inquisitions to decide. Since the Amsterdam Treaty and the Tampere meeting, justice follows in step with other security agencies, and does the same thing at a distance via networks.[27] The creation of Eurojust and the forgetting of the *corpus juris* have provoked disequilibrium between the level of judges of instruction and judges of accusation that are able to draw on EU resources, and a defence that is confined within a national frame that has no access to this information. But this point is considered secondary to that of speed and efficiency. The rule of law is viewed as less important than the speed of rising suspicion and the accumulation of information and rumours about predefined categories.

The functions of borders change with the regime (political and economic) over time. It is important to point out that unlike Carl Schmitt and his followers, such as Samuel Huntington, the delimitation between inside and outside is not a natural one; it is not the declaration of exception that frames the boundary between the norm and the exception, but the routines of technologies of surveillance. After September 11 this narrative is coming back to justify the policy of George Bush. Some important writers have given credence to this vision of the exceptional moment of the declaration as the 'moment' transforming history, and giving leaders the right to reframe the boundary of the normal and the exception, to reframe what is law and the rule of law and what is outside of the law in any case. For these authors, the relation of the exception is a relation of the suspension of the law, which gives law its true meaning. The exception is then logically bordering the law, determining what the law is and is not. Even if lawyers' strategies are to create the illusion that the law includes exceptions and circumvents the exception by agreeing with the idea of an arbitrary hole or decisionism controlled by law. But to counter Schmitt's rhetoric, one needs to remember Neuman's arguments about the Roman dictature to save the republic and the importance of liberal thinking by justifying checks and balances, the role of judges, and of limits against the 'supreme' sovereign, the 'führer' (Huysmans 2004). Of course, the black letter law cannot predict the future and 'new' events, but the spirit of the rule of law and habeas corpus has not been endangered by the right of the sovereign to declare (even for a specific period and for a specific object) that he will use derogation in cases of emergency.

The exception has to be reframed into the general principles of the rule of law and cannot trace the boundaries of legality. Torture can never be justified by a theoretical worst-case argument. Pasquale Pasquino explained in detail the liberal vision of the 'Roman dictatorship' and the 'safeguard of democracy' by the 'exceptional moment' to show that the so-called Schmittian solution is a 'fascist' solution by the providential man. He emphasized the difficulty for unwritten constitutions to cope with the moment of exception inside the rule of law, but also the greater flexibility of unwritten constitutions and the specific role of judges there (i.e. the UK). He developed different doctrines of monism and dualism in the moment of exception (Ferejohn and Pasquino 2004). Elspeth Guild has shown that the EU is more protected than the US from this move of the leader to insist that he has the absolute right to reframe law and civil liberties in the name of a new situation, demanding exceptional coercive and intrusive measures never before been seen (Guild 2003b).

I agree with Huysmans, Pasquino and Guild, against the justification of the exceptional moment by the sovereign. For me, in contrast, what is important is essentially that the liberal vision developed by the constitutional lawyers in Germany and France is also one of 'a moment of exception', which is in fact derogation to the law admitted by the law under certain circumstances. I want to make clear that the discussion at the legal level is underpinned by the transformation of technologies of surveillance and control and by the involvement of intelligence services and military personnel inside a country. It is this element which is crucial for our democracies. Military bureaucracies, as well as secret services, cannot be put in charge of the life of the nation by the professionals of politics. The potential threat of catastrophic terrorism and bombings is not a new kind of perpetual war. Civilians may accept that the 'rules' of the military, which are normally reserved for use outside the country, 'invade' the rules of law governing civilians inside, if the territory is invaded. They nevertheless try to maintain control over the military's ends, if not the means. If the war is perpetual, the invasion is always legitimate, as is the connection between the interior and defence ministries when they are backed up by the leaders in a security state. So the discussion about the matter, size and period of exception is thus more one of military involvement inside as means to combat the enemy than a question of jeopardizing the rule of law (Bigo 2004). By focusing too much on the legal aspects rather than the organic or institutional aspects, critics neglect the importance of routines and technologies of control. It is here that surveillance studies are extremely valuable for security studies.

The routines of the technologies of surveillance and control

All these derogatory and emergency measures are supposed to answer the questions haunting security services and politicians. How will it be possible to find the boundaries again, the distinctions between those who are hostile and the 'others' when everybody is inside the country? How can people be protected against those wanting to get in and how can they clarify their motivations? How can somebody anticipate their actions? How can somebody control the fear of others, of all others, including their relatives?[28] It is clear that classical control procedures and the indiscriminate use of IT linked to other identification technologies using digital imprints, photo-numerical systems, iris or genetic imprints, is not the solution. Nevertheless, the narratives of the professionals of politics in the US and Europe, the discourses of the main international bodies and the main world companies repeat again and again that technologies of control are not a solution, but that the solution to terror is in its capacity to trace the movement of people, to recognize patterns of behaviour and to prevent the suspected terrorists or criminals to act.

As for the war, the professionals know that the efficiency of the struggle against clandestine organizations passes by other means, but the large-scale mobilization of money and technology is supposed to convince the people that the government cares about their safety and is doing what needs to be done. Graham Allison eloquently said that for bureaucracies that have a hammer, the world is reframed as a nail;

the narratives that the technology of surveillance is efficient against an unknown enemy are framed by the available solutions, not by the real problem.

It is this element that the professionals of politics refuse to admit. From September 11, the transnationalization of the bureaucracies of surveillance is seen as the alternative to the Sisyphean task to seal the borders at a national level. Global surveillance by coordination of the different services inside and by the different nodes of coordination at the Western level is seen as an 'imperative' which cannot be delayed by any consideration of privacy. Every politician, either in favour of the war or for a more judicial approach, agrees on this view; more centralized and globalized intelligence about people on the move is the key to success against all the evils generated by the freedom of movement of persons.

The main narrative starts with the security of airplanes and the request for air marshals inside planes. The security of airplanes depends on knowing that nobody has brought arms onto the plane under a false name; thus the security of airports relies on the reinforcement the control of luggage and of the identity of the people travelling abroad. As developed by David Lyon:

> to strengthen this security, several countries have proposed to exchange data, under the Personal Name Record programme, to secure their travel documents (visa and passports), to create new national identification card systems, some involving biometric devices or programmable chips. Some have questioned how new, while others have questioned how necessary, are the measures that have been fast-tracked through the legislative process (Lyon 2003).

Along these lines, biometrics have become widespread and are linked by transnational databases; iris-scanners have been developed and justified at airports – now installed at Schipol, Amsterdam, and being implemented elsewhere in Europe and North America as well; CCTV cameras are present in public places, enhanced if possible with facial recognition capacities such as the Mandrake system in Newham, South London; and DNA databanks are used to store genetic information capable of identifying known 'terrorists'. Biometrics have also been implemented not only in visas, passports and resident permits, but also in ID cards and social security cards. In Northern Europe, the American company Printrack International is pushing its services that enable tracking and automatic identification of people crossing borders, whether by cards with digitized fingerprints in ports and airports, or retinal imprints. The goal is to control identities in the most invisible manner possible, and their advertisements signal that this is the best way 'due to the fact that this society of individuals does not like to be affected or slowed down when controlled, but as long as they do not register the act of control, they do not protest'.[29] One can therefore think of generalizing the system in the future not only in airports but in any collective place, in the name of transparency (not to hide from the police) and fear of the future.

The discussion about airport security and safety shows the extent of the US government's unease. The discourse is moving toward more control by the state and public agents in airports and for systematic control over everyone, but social practices are moving massively in the other direction. Privatization is one factor; so is the desire of the rich not to be targeted. If surveillance practices become private, the multiplicity of actors will limit any attempt to have a good system of data protection. In short, controls are always differentiated and carried out under different logic. They articulate more than they integrate. They are unequal and do not target the same people in the same way. They reinforce the advantages of some and the disadvantages of others, even if sometimes they have contradictory and unpredictable effects. These effects come also from multiple technologies and disciplines and are not only confined to border technologies and their locus, but are concentrated there.

It is not the proliferation of these technologies that is surprising, it is the will to de-differentiate them, to interconnect databases and to enlarge their possible use, especially those of police and intelligence services. The development of all these technologies is correlated with the rise of surveillance, from the mid-1980s and especially after the end of bipolarity. These technologies are not at all new, but they are now intensified and globalized. For example, the Schengen Information System (SIS) manages individual dossiers, and functions as a file preventing illegal migrants from returning to the EU. This system is not very effective at managing criminality, but Schengen is now seen as the cornerstone of all security in Europe. In a (not so) amusing way one knows the Schengen system has difficulty working. The sphere of Schengen's application is constantly being enlarged to create uniform visas not only in the EU but now also at the level of GATT (General Agreement on Tariffs and Trade). In the same way, the exceptional possibilities of identity control in border zones generalizes itself in all countries up to 20 kilometres from the border, even in countries where the concept of legitimate suspicion envelops controls very strictly. It is barely contested by the police authorities in question that Schengen institutes immigration police as its priority, even though only five years ago there was great resistance to using it, and there was no focus on the relation between crime and missing persons. This link between criminal and foreigners' files that the SIS puts in place with respect to foreigners reaffirms the suspicion against them and focuses the attention on small acts of delinquency or illegality while making police and customs infractions primary in importance.

Profiling done for Europol files tends to make surveillance more refined and precise, rather than extending its general reach. Europol registers people who are capable of following through on their potential to commit a crime. As distinct from the Interpol databases whose entries are dependent on criminals who are effectively fugitives of justice, the Europol files contain sought-after criminals, suspects who have not yet entered the system of judicial inquiry, lists of possible informants, possible witnesses who might testify about their neighbour or colleague, victims or persons susceptible of being victims. Here it amounts to reconstructing individual or social trajectories, marking territories or borders between populations at risk and others, of analyzing and deciding who is dangerous; here we are at the heart of proactive logic.

It is under this perspective that one must read the US Total Information Awareness Project, renamed in order to disguise the disproportionate ambition: the Terrorism Information Awareness Project. This project was partly blocked by Congress in one of the first acts of opposition to the Bush administration, but relaunched by different 'red' states and a group of private companies at a more local level.

Disciplinarization and exclusion in the name of the protection of the normalized: monitoring the future

In order to be able to manage the individualization of dangers and the complicated borders between the ones to be excluded and the normalized, the job of detective and intelligence had to find a new dimension and become globalized. Fragmentation was answered with the surveillance of these movements at a global scale. This programme of 'mastering' the world and the future, which as one will see, leads to the 'fictionalization of the world'[30] placing it into a 'maximum security' programme, has not benefited from unanimous approval.

In the European Union, the recently adopted database Eurodac contains the digital fingerprints of asylum-seekers, undocumented migrants sent back home, as well as an explication of the motives they have given, and the reasons for which they have been refused entry. The purpose of the database is not only to prevent the overlap of multiple applications from individuals, but also to spot the stereotypical narratives of asylum-seekers – to trace whether or not they are helped by NGOs in cases of false declaration. This system is designed to create profiles permitting prediction of the groups which are potentially using routes or travel agencies considered as 'dubious' in order to block the 'profilees' which look like the previous 'offenders' by refusing their visas or their travel to Europe. It is not clear if the individuals have to pass extra checks or if members of a suspected group will be refused by the consulates without being aware of it. Parallel with Eurodac, a securitized net is being developed to address FADO (False and Authentic Documents) that will function on the basis of information exchange concerning false documents. The idea is that for some series of official passports of 'dubious' origin and/or country, the burden of proof will be on the person submitting the document. Documents without biometrics at the standard required by the EU and the US will be considered as dubious. The principle of suspicion subverts the principle of innocence at both the individual and the state levels.

The work carried out by the research team of Elspeth Guild and Ewelein Brower from Nijmegen University has given full details of these practices in Europe, which are too often forgotten by those who only debate 'internally' in the US. This team has shown the impact in the European Union on demands for asylum, immigrants, tourists, the management of the control of borders, transport management on a global scale, the ways demonstrations are linked to terrorism, as well as on communication via the Internet.[31]

This will to control via the link between databases and biometrics continues to face opposition and has not been able to establish itself as the new programme of truth. It has been forced to make numerous concessions to the traditional view of frontier control by human beings, of war and intelligence against the hostile foreigner. It has done this by infiltration instead of combining statistical data connected with software, enabling profiling of unknown individuals whose actions and behaviour look like previous individuals condemned by the system.

Here the foreign status or abnormality is linked to specific statistical and technological processes, building the profiles of what is normal and what differs from it. It is no longer the foreigner as such who is the one being targeted, but all those, foreigners or not, who have an action profile that behaviouralists establishing the profiles have judged to be a sign of potential danger. For example, buying an outbound airline ticket without purchasing a return ticket, buying a ticket with cash and not with a credit card, buying it from a third city and not from the point of departure, or for having recently viewed films or read books that show an attraction for the East and for Islam, having travelled to those countries, etc. The main advantage of this policy is that it hides itself behind 'technical neutrality': it appears as reasonable and not subjected to classic racism. This policy is also inspired by the science of traceability and aims to anticipate through an in-depth analysis, action sequences in which the computer has no soul and therefore, does not have the human defect of classifying some rather than others according to the colour of their skin.

The 'technical' redefinition of the foreigner does not solve at all the failure to determine the image of the enemy. It is all about a forward escape onto the 'technology' as last resort and far from developing reasonable antiterrorist policies; it drags the politician onto a world of 'fiction'. The foreigner is no longer the non-citizen, he is the one with the strange, bizarre and slightly deviant abnormal behaviour, or the opposite, having such normal behaviour that it seems suspicious. Ericson and Haggerty have insisted on the growth of machines to make and record discrete observations and on the machine/human continuum that I have discussed in my study about the police liaison agents in Europe.[32] They have distinguished between control and discipline; where a single entity has to be modelled, punished, controlled and 'surveillance which commences with a creation of a space of comparison and the introduction of breaks in the flows that emanate from, and circulate within, 'the human body' (Haggerty and Ericson 2000: 612), and the construction of a body/information network. I have borrowed from them this idea about the possible desingularization of the individual and the construction of a fantasmatic collective body of a group that is constructed by social science 'knowledge', which has specific features and patterns of behaviour and is the base or the scale of dangerousness for comparison of each suspect with the pattern.

The ACLU, Statewatch and CHALLENGE have developed a detailed critique of all these programmes reactivated after September 11, 2001.[33] For example, the FBI programme that tries to correlate the health information of the body with a pattern of fear of police and then with a possible terrorist motivation. This programme mixes serialized body information, captured by a discrete machine of surveillance, with a dubious correlation between fear and heat of the body. It uses an old-fashioned behaviourist argument between a feeling and an action in the name of efficiency and the belief in the joining of technology and science, even if, of course, they have not stopped any potential terrorist, only a handful of aliens with falsified documents, and a large majority of pregnant women. Nevertheless, the FBI presents its programme as the most efficient profiling software in the world and pretends that it is a key element in the struggle against terrorists.

The argument of the imminence and danger of the attack is always used to justify a pre-emptive defence in the eyes of the US, because of the irreparable character of the action. This justifies the position of 'not waiting until it is too late', as a website showing the Twin Towers and a nuclear mushroom cloud tried to suggest. The heart of the question about probability in the future and anticipation as fiction is at stake. The belief in the imminent danger of the Apocalypse justifies at the same time 'proactive' policing actions, 'pre-emptive' military strikes, 'administrative and exceptional justice', where anticipations of behaviour are considered as a sufficient element to act. The decisions of those deciding are then based upon the 'belief' they are in a rush, and not upon wisely considered actions backed up by facts. They are based on profiles, on assumptions concerning the possible future, or more exactly the belief that the intelligence services have a grammar of '*futur antérieur*', that they can read the future as a form of the past through their technologies of profiling.[34]

Their selections of data are framed by the 'morphing' of the different virtual paths from the point of departure to the point of arrival. This 'reversal' of time is to prevent events from occurring, by identifying the causes of predictable events. Thus, not everyone is put under surveillance, identified, categorized and checked. This is only the case for what is constructed as a specific 'minority', an 'abnormal' group, a group with virtually violent behaviour, even if this behaviour has never been actualized. The time criterion is created through the artefacts of statistics concerning correlations that occur with a certain regularity and can be anticipated. These statistics may correlate drug use and crime, migrants and crime, asylum-seekers and unemployment or social welfare fraud – they are there to create 'profiles' through a specific knowledge of psychology, criminology and social science. These 'profiles' are important for one main reason: in a liberal regime, surveillance must not be too costly for the global system. So, in a nutshell, globalization is linked with space and time. The control of the global scale is more preventive and proactive than systematic and pinpointed to a specific place. However, this 'economy' is both inefficient and illegitimate.

Of course one could say that the situation requires 'prevention' because, after a catastrophic bombing, it will be too late, and it is not enough to be a good detective after the fact, or to put out fires after crimes occur. It is easy for the professionals of politics to say that they rely on science and teams of 'profilers', who can anticipate before the act, who is potentially going to commit an offence and what their actions will be in the future. Nonetheless this second job is still one of science fiction. One could say, of course, that this evolution is the fault only of the transformation of violence; that we need to try everything to stop the apocalypse. However, the present situation is also the fault of the will to master the world, to try to control some part of it by 'scientifically' discriminating the enemy within, and to believe that technology can do it.

The will to control time and space, present and future, here and there, has an effect that goes beyond antiterrorist policies; it creates a powerful mixture of fiction and reality, of virtual and actual, which merge their boundaries and introduce fiction into reality for profiling as well as it de-realizing the violence of the state and of the clandestine organizations. The anticipation or 'astrological' dimension of the scientific modernity of the combination of biometrics and databases at the transnational level destroys its false pretence to be 'the' solution. The solution lies within the present tension regarding the fight against terrorism and its lawfulness. Many examples can be given of this will to control the future and its dramatic consequences. If the war in Afghanistan has already provoked reactions regarding the way it has been led, it is pointless to distinguish between prisoners of war and enemy combatants; terrorists sent to Guantanamo Bay as well as the war in Iraq, demonstrate the problem of political decisions made on unconfirmed information due to lack of time and on the basis of the fear of acting too late when confronted with a serious but randomized threat, in which the capacity of 'stealth' (in the same way as a stealth aircraft) is great.

One has the opportunity to see, with the Dr Kelly affair and the Hutton inquiry in the UK, how decision-making is founded less and less on facts but instead on beliefs, and how this ends up in a competition among political figures, the media and intelligence services in order to find out who holds the truth. This is not only in a given moment but the other way around, once the temporality of the chain of causality has been reconstructed. To put it differently and more simply: there are not, despite the expectation of American strategists, any ways to foresee the future and to structure it as one would like to. It is not because people believe in the existence of weapons of mass destruction, ready to be used and capable of striking in 45 minutes, that they necessarily exist as such in a certain moment, even if Iraqi plans anticipating such usage had to be found. The phantasm of the virtualization of the real, of the anticipation of action turns into the phantasm of fiction. The film *Minority Report* has undoubtedly had enormous success because it recalls this ambiguity, this uncertainty of political security and more particularly of contemporary antiterrorist policies to try to foresee the future. The dream of security agencies is more to foresee the future and arrest people before they commit a crime.[35]

Conclusion

In conclusion, to focus on governmental antiterrorist policies alone, on Guantanamo Bay and torture in Iraq or elsewhere, without seeing the relationship to the daily treatment of foreigners at the borders and the suspicion concerning any deviant behaviour, is misleading. We need to insist on this normalization of emergency as a technique of government by unease, and on the success of the differentiation between a normalized population which is pleased to be monitored 'against danger' and an 'alienation' of some groups of people considered as dangerous 'others'. The surveillance and monitoring of the movement of each individual is growing, but effective controls and coercive restrictions of freedom are concentrated on specific targets. These targets are constructed as 'invisible and powerful enemies in networks' and the narratives concerning these threats predate September 11 and even the end of bipolarity. Nevertheless, September 11 has reinforced the idea that the struggle against these threats justifies the profiling of certain people's potential behaviours, especially if they are 'on the move'. The political reaction to September 11 justifies a proactive and pre-emptive strategy, which has the ambition to know, and to monitor the 'future'. The call for preventive action creates uncertainty and gathers, inside large transnational databases, to control the judiciary protection of privacy, both solid information about the past, and rumours collected by different sources. They are used to create profiles and trends in order to anticipate the events through social sciences and psychological bodies of knowledge. But in fact, this new technique is mixing the newest technologies (biometrics, databases, DNA analysis) with a kind of astrological discourse of intelligence agencies and of some professionals of politics concerning their capacity to know the future with some certainty. It is driven by a faith in the truth of the body identification as a sign for a predictable pattern of behaviour. And it fails.

Notes

1 See the following: Fijnaut and Marx 1995; Lyon 1994, 2002, 2003; Marx 1988.

2   The meaning and methodological function of the term 'dispositif' was described by Foucault to Neil Brenner as 'a thoroughly heterogeneous ensemble consisting of discourse, institutions, architectural forms, philosophical, moral and philanthropic propositions – in short, the said as much as the unsaid' (Brenner 1994). It is often translated to mean 'system'.

3   The notion of 'state of exception' exists in many European constitutions under this label or the label of state of emergency allowing the government, under special circumstances, to act beyond the rule of law. They often have limits in time, space and object. If these limits disappear in the name of a permanent and invisible threat, then civil liberties are in danger. For a theoretical discussion see Carl Schmitt, Giorgio Agamben, Pasquale Pasquino, Rob Walker, Jef Juysmans, Mike Dillon.

4   See the following: Bhuta 2003; Blanc 2005; Byers 2003; Cohen 2003; Darcy 2002; Dillon 2002; Gartenstein-Ross 2002; Guild 2003a, 2003b; LaFeber 2002; Noll 2003; Schiavon 2003; Schwab 1989; van Ooyen 2002.

5   On the notion of clandestine organizations see Didier Bigo and Daniel Hermant *La Relation Terroriste. Etudes Polémologiques n°37 2/ 1986.*

6   See list of antiterrorist legislations in the European area in CD-ROM ELISE.

7   See the following: Bonner and Cholewinski 2005; Guild 2003a, 2003b.

8   Term by Deleuze.

9   From Nietzche and after Foucault.

10 The European Union Treaties from Maastricht distinguish between a first pillar about common market and leading role of the EC Commission, a second pillar about Common Foreign Security Policy, and a third pillar of Liberty, Security and Justice called before Justice and Home Affairs (JHA).

11 During the Genoa protest against the G8, clashes with police led to the death of two people as well as harassment of hundreds, which created an increase in rage against the practices of maintaining law and order in Italy. At the same time it also caused tough reaction by the government, who wanted to criminalize the protest by including violent protest in the definition of terrorism. See Jan Pierre Masse, Nathalie Bayon.

12 Attacks in the US and in Spain.

13 A label by Max Weber.

14 Of course, to say that is not to downsize the importance to struggle against the detention of suspected terrorists in the name of human rights. It is useful to avoid to have more victims of arbitrariness of the executive and its intelligence agencies, but if the critical discourse limits itself to discuss the proportionality of the measures and the right balance between the two imperatives of freedom and security, it is *de facto* an acceptance of the framing of September 11 as a radically new situation which supposes radically new solutions beyond the previous 'norm' and an acceptance of a legitimate right to go beyond the rule of law to save the rule of law and democracy. It is quite impossible in this framework to answer to the 'legitimate' fear of the population, except by insisting on the universal

necessity to comply to the rule of law when it is an undisputed *jus cogens*. So, in this framing about the right to declare the exception, all the protagonists forget that the origins of the problems are not rooted in whether or not the rule of law is applied fully or not by the government, and with or without good justifications, but on why, how and to whom control and surveillance technologies apply and for what purposes. The legalistic question is important but the debate cannot be limited to the full implementation of the rule of law. In any case, these technologies are often used beyond the limits posed by privacy rights and the rule of law, which often incorporates previous situations of exception which have been routinized.

15 Carl Schmitt, 2003.

16 I use the notion of governmentality following Foucault definition. See below.

17 Montesquieu: three branches of government: executive, legislative and judiciary.

18 See the following: Bigo and Hermant 1988; Campbell and Dillon 1993; Schmid 1993; Tilly 2003.

19 The notion of (in)security means that security is not the contrary of insecurity, the two may develop at the same moment. See Didier Bigo, Mike Dillon.

20 We know that we had an involvement of Bin Laden in the World Trade Center and Pentagon attacks, but not in the anthrax scare. The links between Iraq, Saddam, weapons of mass destruction, and transnational clandestine organizations were alleged but not proven. We still don't know exactly what the relations are between the attacks in New York, Washington, and in Bali, or Sudan, and also have doubt about the seriousness of the relations between the events in the US, Istanbul, Madrid and the UK, even if the so-called Al Qaeda network claimed to have organized these attacks afterward.

21 At least if we can believe the secret services of some Western states and the information given after the Afghanistan war.

22 See the following: Bigo 2002 and Guittet 2004. L'Irlande du Nord devant la CEDH. Entretien avec Me Nuala Mole. *Cultures et Conflits* (56): 63–71. Bigo, Didier, and Emmanuel-Pierre Guittet, 2004. Vers une nord-irlandisation du monde? *Cultures et Conflits* (56): 171–182.

23 Jean Baudrillard, *Simulacre et Simulation*, Paris, Galilée, 1987.

24 The Maginot line was the line of defence of the French in 1940 against Germany. Germany just passed through Belgium to invade France. It is a symbol of a meaningless fortress.

25 David Cole, *Enemy Aliens*, 2003.

26 The Sirene system is the supplementary information required on entry and exit, linked with the Schengen information system used to control the borders of 13 and soon 23 member states of the EU (except partly UK and Ireland).

27 On the European Union development from Amsterdam and Tampere

and their later development, see the websites of the European Union and for more critical voices http://www.statewatch.org, http://www.libertysecurity.org http://www.conflits.org.

28 See the recent play called *Homeland Security* by Stuart Flack, directed by Sandy Shinner.

29 http://www.conflits.org. See Didier Bigo and Elspeth Guild, '*Le visa Schengen*'.

30 To use the formula of Zizeck borrowed from Baudrillard.

31 See: Guild, Brouwer and Catz 2003, p 16. See also the website ELISE www.eliseconsortium.org.

32 Didier Bigo, Polices en réseaux, Paris, FNSP, 1996.

33 http://www.aclu.org, http://www.statewatch.org, http://www.libertysecurity.org.

34 Greg Elmer and Andy Opel (this volume).

35 This is better reflected in the recent movie *Minority Report* than *The Last Castle*.

References

Agamben, G. (1997) *Homo Sacer* (Paris: Seuil).

Baudrillard, J. (1981) *Simulacres et Simulation* (Paris: Galilée).

Bhuta, N. (2003) 'A Global State of Exception? The United States and World Order', *Constellations*, 10 (3), 371–91.

Bigo, D. (2002) 'Reassuring and Protecting: Internal Security Implications of French Participation in the Coalition Against Terrorism', in E. Hersberg and K.W. Moore (eds) *Critical Views of September 11: Analysis from Around the World* (New York: New York Press), 125–51.

Bigo, D. (2005) 'Global (in)security: The Field of the Professionals of Unease Management and the Ban-opticon', *Traces: A Multilingual Series of Cultural Theory*, 4, 34–87.

Bigo, D. and Guillet, E.P. (2004) 'Vers une Nord Irlandisation du Monde?', *Cultures et Conflits*, 56, 171–83.

Bigo, D. and Hermant, D. (1988) *La Relation Terroriste, Analyse de la Violence Politique des Organisations Clandestines dans les Democraties Occidentales* (edited by E. Polémologiques) (Paris: Documentation Francaise).

Blanc, F. (2005) 'Possibilities of Resistance Within a State of Exception? Challenging The Security Debate After 9/11', (Sciences-Po Paris and Northwestern University, Evanston, IL).

Bonner D. and Cholewinski R. (2005) 'Immigration and Asylum Law: The Impact of Terrorism. The case of the United Kingdom: A contrast of the Responses of its Legal and Constitutionnal Orders to the First Gulf War (1990–91) and the Post 9/11 "War" on Terrorism', (ELISE: European, Liberty and Security), 5th PCRD EC Commission.

Byers, M. (2003) 'Letting the Exception Prove the Rule', *Ethics and International Affairs*, 17 (1), 9–16.

Campbell, D. and Dillon, M. (1993) *The Political Subject of Violence* (Manchester and New York: Manchester University Press and St. Martin's Press).

Cohen, W.I. (2003) 'The American Dream: Empire without Tears', *Global Dialogue*, 5 (1/2), 1–11.

Cole, D. (2003) *Enemy Aliens. Double Standards and Constitutional Freedoms in the War on Terrorism* (New York and London: The New Press).

Darcy, S. (2002) 'The Rights of Minorities in States of Emergency', *International Journal on Minority and Group Rights*, 9 (4), 345–69.

Dillon, M. (2002) 'Network Society, Network-Centric Warfare and the State of Emergency', *Theory*, 19 (August), 71–9.

ELISE, 5th PCRD (2005) 'Suspicion et Exception', *Cultures et Conflits*, 58 (1) 312.

Fijnaut, C. and Marx, G.T. (eds) (1995) *Undercover: Police Surveillance in Comparative Perspective* (The Hague and Boston: Kluwer Law International).

Foucault, M. (1977) *Discipline and Punish: The Birth of the Prison* (New York: Pantheon).

Gartenstein-Ross, D. (2002) 'A Critique of the Terrorism Exception to the Foreign Sovereign Immunities Act', *New York University Journal of International Law and Politics*, 34 (4), 887–947.

Guild, E. (2003a) 'Agamben Before the Judges: Sovereignty, Exception, and Anti-Terrorism', *Cultures et Conflits*, 51 (autumn), 127–56.

Guild, E. (2003b) 'Exceptionalism and Transnationalism: UK Judicial Control of the Detention of Foreign International Terrorists', *Alternatives*, 28 (4), 491–515.

Guild, E., Brouwer, E. and Catz, P. (2003) *Immigration Asylum and Terrorism: A Changing Dynamic in European Law* (Nijmegen: CMR).

Haggerty, K.D. and Ericson, R.V. (2000) 'The Surveillant Assemblage', *British Journal of Sociology*, 51 (4), 605–22.

Heisbourg, F. (2002) *L'Hyperterrorisme* (Paris: Odile Jacob).

Huntington, S.P. (2004) *Who Are We? The Challenges to America's National Identity* (New York and Toronto: Simon & Schuster).

Huntington, S.P. (1996) *The Clash of Civilizations and the Remaking of World Order* (New York: Simon & Schuster).

Huysmans, J. (2004) 'Minding Exceptions: Politics of Insecurity and Liberal Democracy', *Contemporary Political Theory*, 3 (3), 321–41.

LaFeber, W. (2002) 'The Bush Doctrine', *Diplomatic History*, 26 (4), 543–58.

Lyon, D. (1994) *The Electronic Eye: The Rise of Surveillance Society* (Minneapolis: University of Minnesota Press).

Lyon, D. (2002) *Surveillance as Social Sorting: Privacy, Risk, and Digital Discrimination* (New York and London: Routledge).

Lyon, D. (2003) *Surveillance After September 11: Themes for the 21st Century* (Malden, MA: Polity Press).

Marx, G. (1988) La Société de Sécurité Maximale', *Déviance et société*, 12 (2), 147–66.

Megret, F. (2003) 'Justice in Times of Violence', *European Journal of International Law*, 14 (2), 327–45.

Noll, G. (2003) 'Visions of the Exceptional: Legal and Theoretical Issues Raised by Transit Processing Centres and Protection Zones', *European Journal of Migration and Law*, 5 (3), 303–41.

Pasquino, P. and Fejenhof Institut des hautes études de la sécurité intérieure (2003) *Sécurité et démocratie: deux objectifs concurrents ou complémentaires?* (Paris: IHESI).

Schiavon, G. (2003) 'The State of Exception', *Il Politico*, 68 (2), 364–6.

Schmid, A.P. (1993) 'Terrorism and Democracy', *Terrorism and Political Violence*, 4 (4), 14–25.

Schmitt, C. (2003) *La valeur de l'etat et la signification de l'individual* (Geneve: Droz).

Schmitt, C. (1985) *Political Theology: Four Chapters on the Concept of Sovereignty* (Cambridge, MA: MIT Press).

Schwab, G. (1989) *The Challenge of the Exception: An Introduction to the Political Ideas of Carl Schmitt between 1921 and 1936* (2nd ed.) *Contributions in Political Science*, no. 248 (New York: Greenwood Press).

Tilly, C. (2003) *The Politics of Collective Violence: Cambridge Studies in Contentious Politics* (Cambridge and New York: Cambridge University Press).

van Ooyen, R.C. (2002) 'The New World of War and the Law: The Need for a Constitutional Regulation of Out-of-Area Bundswehr Operations', *Internationale Politik und Gesellschaft*, 1, 90–110.

Chapter 4

Looking into the future: surveillance, globalization and the totalitarian potential

Maria Los

Si-tien said, 'Someone collected my writings, letters, books, sayings, lectures, parabolas, fairy-stories, obiter-dicta and sketches; then deciphered my alleged soul through them, and was arrogant enough to press me to resurrect myself. So, here I am, back, against my wishes, crippled, maimed and functioning counter to my own intentions' (Podgorecki 1995).

Introduction

In this chapter, I examine a possibility that we are drifting into some form of totalitarianism without knowing it. To address this question, I explore the totalitarian potential of the late modern forms of regulation and surveillance. I am focusing on the conditions and areas of vulnerability that could either facilitate a *deliberate* imposition of a totalitarian domination or have *unintentional* totalitarian effects.

Through my earlier research on the nature of the twentieth century's scientific totalitarianism, embodied in the Stalinist and Nazi regimes, I have established a number of conditions that seemed necessary for its success (Los 2004). They included a monistic centralization of control, social uprooting, atomization and obliteration of the social, as well as the negation (or eradication) of such notions as liberty, truth, ethics[1] and the Self. To a large degree, these conditions were achieved through deliberate processes of ruthless social engineering guided by powerful utopian ideological visions, which were buttressed by self-referential 'scientific' narratives.

Late modernity cannot be understood in isolation from the historical totalitarian experience. Notwithstanding the critical role of totalitarian ideologies, these projects were made thinkable by a modern idea of the centralized state and a strong belief in science and progress. The cultural shift away from grand narratives and concepts of totality, objectivity, necessity, essence and the truth represents a form of anti-totalitarian (magical) thinking. New epistemologies have been promoted to endorse diversity, subjectivity, relativism, local narratives and fragmentation of the self. At the same time, new ethics have emerged that stress the global scope of human condition and obligation. Their versions range from global libertarian individualism to cosmopolitan solidarism (Dower 1998; Burger *et al.* 2000; Gasper 2001; Held 2002).

The importance of business interests notwithstanding, the dread of the totalitarian experience has fuelled – or justified – support for free circulation of people, goods, information and ideas and the drive towards global interdependence and homogenization of the world. A new scientific utopia has been predicated on the belief that with eradication of stereotypes, borders and politics of exclusion, there will be no conflicts, no wars, no discrimination. This open vision of a free-market global society had to be buttressed, however, by new, globally shared, rationalities of risk management and social sorting.

Below, I assess some of the contemporary, late modern, practices of regulation and surveillance for their potential vulnerability, or affinity, to totalizing designs. My discussion is organized around the above-mentioned key conditions that were crucial to the implementation of the twentieth century totalitarian states. I conclude that – albeit through very different means – the late modern epistemologies, surveillance and globalization have contributed to de-traditionalization, de-socialization and atomization of society and a displacement of the Self. These processes have been accompanied by a hollowing out of both the epistemological and ethical normativity through the refutation of relevance of such notions as truth and morality, which, in turn, made room for a new version of extreme, surveillance-driven positivism.

First, however, I address briefly the role of new globalizing surveillance technologies in mimicking some effects of centralization that was typical of totalitarian states.

Globalization, centralization and the totalitarian potential

It is not my intention to paint a dystopian vision of the future or to demonize such aspects of the contemporary world as the intensification and globalization of surveillance. It is important, however, to recognize that *total*itarianism is, by nature (or rather by definition), a global project that cannot be fully accomplished in just one community or one country. Being fuelled by the need to suppress any alternative orders and ideas, it knows no natural limits and is bound to aim at totally dominating everything and everyone (Arendt 1958).

The ultimate feature of the totalitarian domination is the *absence of exit*, which can be achieved temporarily by closing borders, but permanently only by a truly global reach that would render the very notion of exit meaningless. This in itself justifies questions about the totalitarian potential of globalization. Can the logic of globalization be fully separated from the logic of totalization of control? This also begs a question about the value of borders. Is abolition of borders intrinsically (morally) good, because they symbolize barriers that needlessly separate and exclude people, or are they potential lines of resistance, refuge and difference that may save us from the totalitarian abyss?

The question about the future of totalitarianism in the twenty-first century takes us inevitably beyond the national state as the site of total rule. The corollary of globalization is that it undermines familiar political models, forcing both democracy and totalitarianism to seek new ways of political expression and new political institutions with meta-authority. Since multinational integration oversteps the usual democratic mechanisms – as witnessed in the European Union – it ultimately requires supranational, state-like structures to democratize and legitimize itself. Theoretically, if globalization undermines the tested, state-based models of democracy, the world may be vulnerable to a global totalitarian etatization. Consequently, any inquiry into contemporary mechanisms of surveillance has to include their global dimension.

One of the key dimensions of historical totalitarian regimes was centralization. Yet by visualizing totalitarianism as a mono-centric police state, we tend to underestimate the importance of incoherence and maze-like structure of these states. The totalitarian experience of the past century teaches us that to pursue total, monistic domination, the ruling structure cannot be itself monolithic and coherent, yet it must generate a belief in a menacing deeper unity, hidden underneath and perpetuated behind the scenes. The deliberate ambiguity of the power arrangement between the movement (the Party) and the administration (the State), vagueness, shapelessness and duplication of functions and services, all prevent establishment of a stable government that might lose revolutionary zeal. The masses need to acquire a Kafkaesque sense that the true power structure does not lie in the visible maze of offices, but is deeply hidden and profoundly secret (Los 2004). They have to believe that 'the meaning of every law [is] "secret"' (Fuller 1995: 81; see also Podgorecki 1996).

Totalitarianism seems to require a sense of conspiracy and the type of mentality that, to use Arendt's words, 'sees every conceivable action as an instrument for something entirely different' (1958: 409). Nothing can be taken at its face value. There are, therefore, no valid criteria for pragmatic action or even for positioning oneself within the maze. Even the secret services have to be multiplied and set against each other for mutual supervision, surveillance and vigilance, as witnessed in both Stalinist and Nazi regimes (Los 2004).

Various authors have recently stressed that despite the late modern surveillance web becoming ever denser and more pervasive, there is no clear totalizing trend. The contemporary surveillance is often portrayed as neither mono-centric nor predominantly control-focused and dispowering. For example, Lianos (2003) contends that the late modern regulation/surveillance does not even have control as its primary goal. He argues that what looks like control is generally organized around managerial rather than controlling functions. The latter become, however, quietly embedded in institutions as they mediate an increasing range of our choices. Control occurs through the particular conditions that mould relations between those who produce the controlling effect (without necessarily intending it) and those who experience it (without necessarily seeing it as controlling). In this conception, control is viewed as a side-effect of both managerial activities and goals and our willingness to partake in offered choices.

When Haggerty and Ericson (2000) refer to the *surveillant assemblage,* they draw our attention to a multiplicity and heterogeneity of elements that come together and work jointly in the exercise of surveillance. The assemblage lacks a clear centre, boundaries or governmental authorization. While, however, different surveillance systems continue to produce separate flows of information, the increase in such practices as sharing or selling information, inter-institutional networking and creation of multipurpose databases have contributed to their convergence and, as a result, a more comprehensive surveillance capacity and coverage (Haggerty and Ericson 2000: 613).

Nevertheless, Haggerty and Ericson argue that these, ever denser, information linkages do not lead to a centralized control system and they emphasize the diversity of motives that 'now energize and serve to coalesce the surveillant assemblage, including the desires for control, governance, security, profit and entertainment' (2000: 609; also Ericson and Haggerty 1997). The authors use very effectively the rhizome[2] metaphor, borrowed from Deleuze and Guattari, which helps to conjure an image of surveillance as an ingrained, multidirectional maze that expands and regenerates itself continuously in a virtually subterranean fashion. While, however, this metaphor reinforces the polycentric (or non-centric) vision of the contemporary surveillance, it also suggests a hidden deeper structure, which echoes Arendt's observations on totalitarian control. It may, therefore be argued that the rhizomatic maze may have a totalizing effect, especially if there is a growing awareness of being helpless in face of the omnipresent, interconnected and internationalized surveillance.

Also building on the work of Deleuze and a number of other authors, Nikolas Rose (1999) speaks of technologies of *securitization of identity*. To exercise freedom and become included in multiple zones of freedom, we have to present a proof of our legitimate identity, which allows for both individualization and authorization. Rejecting such labels as electronic panopticon or totalizing surveillance, Rose describes the *securitization of the self* in terms of the conditional nature of 'access to circuits of consumption and civility' as we daily pass numerous 'recurrent switch points ... in order to access the benefits of liberty' (1999: 243).[3] Emphasizing the role of management of liberty in contemporary surveillance, Rose and others warn against ascribing to the new technologies of securitization any monistic, totalitarian intent. Yet, as I argue later in this chapter, the development and deployment of these technologies tend to dehumanize liberty by rendering it external to human beings, making it thus potentially more liable to central manipulation.

Globalization has been linked with centralization (through Americanization, Westernization, the 'world government', etc.) as well as with pluralistic cross-fertilization and multiple competing forces, including those related to political culture, market, religion and technology. What is obvious, however, is that the demands of globalizing institutional/managerial logic fuel proliferation of new surveillance technologies, which have to be flexible enough to adapt to the demand for information sharing within the multi-centric web of networks. This provides an element of quasi-centralization as well as a potential for massive deliberate accumulation and manipulation of information by so inclined agencies or forces.

An important feature of the contemporary surveillance, which distinguishes it from state totalitarianism, is that it is conducted by multiple, state and non-state, local and global entities, for a variety of purposes. Yet, the messy appearance of totalitarian power arrangements should warn us that the complexity and apparent chaos of the contemporary world may not be a sufficient guarantee of pluralism and local autonomy. The multi-site governance of security, multiple hierarchies and preponderance of networks may not constitute an effective barrier to totalizing forces. Moreover, contrary to predictions of its disappearance, the Western state continues to be capable of extraordinary mobilization, as witnessed in the aftermath of September 11 and subsequent attacks in Madrid and London (see Lyon 2003a for more detailed discussion of this issue). This capacity may have been amplified rather than diminished by the logic of global coordination.

Before addressing other issues listed at the beginning of this chapter, I want to emphasize the key importance of the concept of *data double*. I agree with those (such as Haggerty and Ericson) who claim that one of the key features of contemporary surveillance is the fact that we are being constantly transformed into bits and flows of information, which are processed into our multiple data doubles. What I argue is that, despite many differences, there may be a significant affinity between the data doubles and *the file* which was at the centre of the last century's totalitarian mechanisms of surveillance.

The file

As someone who grew up and lived for over 30 years in a communist country, I can attest to the central importance of the notion of the file. It was never far from one's mind. Assumed but almost never encountered, the file was envisaged as a secret, central paper folder, somewhere in the Ministry of the Interior, where all the undesirable information about us would almost inevitably end up. We now know that the belief that everybody had a secret file was far from accurate,[4] but the assumption that this was the case was essential to the underlying total control strategy.

If fear can be construed as an inherent condition of totalitarian domination, the file may be its most recognizable symbolic prop. As I elaborated elsewhere (Los 2002), in Soviet-type societies, a normalized fear, which buttressed the regime's stability, resulted in conformity-projecting strategies and the habitual pursuit of invisibility. In these societies, where risks and knowledge surrounding them were highly politicized, people seemed mentally to block out extensive danger areas, relegating them to shadowy, taboo zones. Their world was constructed through a series of taboos, which led to what I have called a *taboo mentality* – a mental attitude that helped people to ritualize their avoidance practices. The taboo mentality was directly linked to the pervasive file awareness. To quote from my earlier article:

> People did not know what exactly would happen if they spoke up, criticized, showed disbelief ... or discussed politics with strangers. They knew, however, that harmful consequences would inevitably befall them. Even when no visible, direct repercussions occurred, they would visualize a new black mark in their *secret file* and wonder what curse this might later bring upon them or their children. (Los 2002: 170; emphasis added).

For those living under a totalitarian regime, the knowledge of oneself (self-knowing) cannot be separated from the image of the file and the surmised process of its compilation. Any suspicion of internal freedom may mark one's file for special attention. Self-discipline is to a large extent directed towards the negative goal of limiting any disclosure of the self, as any information can be a fodder for the file. Furthermore, given the fallibility of self-control and self-censorship, it is prudent to avoid having the kind of self whose disclosure may get one in trouble. For this, one's senses have to be kept in check in order to prevent seeing, hearing or knowing too much. What is not known cannot be accidentally disclosed.

In his analysis of the role of Western databases in contemporary surveillance, Whitaker (2001: 177–9) compares them to files kept by the intelligence services and the police responsible for home security. Given that both databases and intelligence files contain personal information collected with the aim of serving certain purposes, they represent knowledge that translates into power. Noting some structural similarities between them, Whitaker also elaborates three main differences. Firstly, unlike intelligence files, which comprise mostly secretly uncovered information, the ordinary databases, especially in the private sector, are collected mostly through relatively open, consensual processes. Secondly, intelligence files, being secret, are rarely shared with others, unless it is required by joint operations conducted with other services or by well-guarded exchanges of sensitive information. In contrast, databases have become a commodity and their commercialization has created a new type of data market. Thirdly, intelligence files are highly centralized and contained within a hierarchical structure of control, while databases are generally decentralized and linked through horizontal rather than vertical connections. Whitaker observes that historically the secret file served a strong centralized state, while the emergence of databases has coincided with the decentralization and weakening of the state relative to the expansion of commercial power. Nevertheless, with computerization, both types of data are now predominantly in electronic form and are amenable to network connections. Moreover, they tend to be subordinated to two principal concerns: (1) risk evaluation and exclusion, and (2) consumer/client identification and inclusion (Whitaker 2001).

In addition to displaying the same superficial characteristics as its democratic counterpart – surreptitious methods of data-gathering, secrecy and centralization – the totalitarian secret file has certain unique features. It may be postulated that its main function is related not so much to its ability to provide information or answer specific questions but to its general systemic role as a compelling reminder of being watched. The power of the image of the file goes far beyond the specific knowledge these files may contain. Under totalitarian conditions, the image of a comprehensive, secret, centralized, political surveillance seems to be of a greater importance than the actual information collected. For it to succeed, however, people have to *believe* that it is the information and not the psychological effect of the act of surveillance that is of crucial value to the authorities. To make this mechanism more vivid, one can imagine a huge fire that destroys the central archives of a totalitarian country (in the pre-electronic era). Could the regime survive such a disaster? If I am correct about the underlying rules of its operation, the regime would survive, if it were able to prevent its subjects from learning about the destruction. If, however, people realized that their secret files had been erased, they could become dangerously emboldened by this sudden uncoupling of their selves from the all-knowing file.

In general terms, the totalitarian power operates through the individual's awareness of being known and an implicit assumption that this knowledge is inherently perilous. This may seem to resemble Bentham's panoptical mechanism, where the subjects, aware that they are watched, work on themselves to achieve the expected norm. For Bentham, however, the omnipresent watchful eye was to assist individuals to internalize the norm, while in the totalitarian scheme, the system's eyes operate as an instrument of negating individual subjectivity and agency. The totalitarian gaze, which is arbitrary and predicated on fear, aims not at normalization but at infinite malleability and obedience. If there is a norm, it is not a stable, predictable, positive standard of achievement but, rather, a negative standard of eradication of the self or, more accurately, the dissolution of the individual into the collective. This is based on the totalitarian assumption of *tabula rasa* and the ability of the state to create a new breed of essentially *self-less* people.

The data double(s)

Given that the data double phenomenon appears to be a significant feature of the late modern surveillance/control regime, it may be worthwhile to explore whether it can be in any meaningful way compared to the file and its impact on the Self. In comparing these two entities, I will keep in mind their respective roles in historically specific forms of ruling and surveillance.

There is much debate on the question of the extent and nature of surveillance awareness in contemporary Western societies. It seems that there is a high degree of passive acquiescence to some forms of technological surveillance, astounding ignorance about other forms and a good deal of creative engagement with its selected types. Moreover, in contrast to totalitarian surveillance, the effectiveness of much of contemporary surveillance (especially so-called *dataveillance*) does not appear predicated on the awareness of being watched (see Haggerty in this volume on this subject). I expect, however, that as people accumulate illuminating personal experiences of unforeseen effects of surveillance on their life, they will gradually recognize that surveillance is not an abstract feature of environment or culture but has tangible personal consequences that need to be reckoned with.

I am going to exemplify my reference to personal, eye-opening experiences related to surveillance with an event from my own life. After an unfortunate accident – when I fell into an insecurely covered drain hole, sustaining major injuries and, consequently, financial losses – I decided to sue the town authority responsible for the road maintenance. Straight away, I was told by my lawyer that the moment I became a plaintiff, I had to expect to be spied on by the insurance company of the sued party. He warned me that I would have to live for many months or possibly years (until the case was resolved) with the assumption that I may be covertly photographed, videotaped, audio-recorded, and so forth. This awareness stayed with me during the whole process and beyond.

What is more interesting, however, I was requested to sign tens of information release forms that authorized the town's lawyers to obtain personal information about me from all kinds of agencies for up to ten years preceding the accident. In addition to representing a massive and frightful invasion of my privacy, this process gave me an opportunity to encounter my data double – a huge pile of information that various parties collected about me over the years. It comprised copies of all my medical records (including notes taken by doctors), pharmacy print-outs, tax reports, personal files kept by my employer (both at the university and faculty levels), records from banks and insurance companies, and so on. I was struck not just by the sheer amount of information and how swiftly it could be assembled, but also by the startling errors, fictitious information and misleading interpretations.[5] I was thus facing the empirical reality of my virtual clone, the data double that was to become a real presence during my hearings. Needless to say, this experience has affected me beyond the lifespan of the legal case.[6]

Despite a relative ease with which my data double was conjured up in the case at hand, it still required quite a bit of paperwork and even, on the part of some organizations, double-checking whether my consent was genuine. It is realistic to predict, however, that for the sake of efficiency and/or profit-making, this procedure will be, with time, further simplified by a more centralized system of authorization and data double processing for various purposes. It will likely include the already existing, formal and informal, services and amalgamated databases, such as those related to creditworthiness, insurance risk or litigation records.

It was obvious that the data double with which I was dealing represented just one of the endless number of possible combinations and that the fragmented, decontextualized information, collected for many specific purposes, may acquire a multitude of completely different meanings depending on its particular compilation, re-contextualization and application. As well, because of the ramified nature of data networks, it appears practically impossible to correct erroneous or twisted information. In this context, the notion of biographical truth loses any meaning.

It is also noteworthy that doubles are becoming a global entity – a cross-national species (with all the dangers of distortion through translation), perpetually displaced, culturally uprooted aliens that know no borders (especially in view of supranational nature of many banks, insurance companies, employers, security arrangements, databases, etc.). Moreover, the already shaky distinction between commercial databases and intelligence files – the latter being closer in nature to *the file* – is further diminished, when new security threats or crises prompt significant expansion of securitization (as outlined by Bigo in this volume). This normally entails both the expansion of traditional police and intelligence services and a greater inclusion of other private and public agencies in a seamless mesh of surveillance.[7] As a result, the data double acquires some characteristics of *the file* and any resistance to this securitized managerial logic may be increasingly bound by the dominant patterns of surveillance.

The intention of the personal example presented in this section was, first of all, to highlight the reality that increasing numbers of people either have or will personally (or vicariously) encounter their own (or other's) data double(s) and that this experience will likely alter their perception of the meaning of surveillance. This observation, if accurate, would also point to a potential usefulness of the concept of *surveillance-directed* character type in studying the contemporary society.

Surveillance-directed character type

In view of the rising prominence of surveillance in our perception of the contemporary society, it may not be far-fetched to explore its possible influence on what used to be called 'social character' – a socially conditioned individual normative make-up common in a particular place and time. Erich Fromm believed that: 'In order that any society can function well, its members must acquire the kind of character which makes them *want* to act in the way they *have* to act as members of the society or of a special class within it' (Riesman *et al.* 1953: 19). Can we theorize about the surveillance society's character type?

I will approach this issue by revisiting David Riesman's (1953) observations on historical shifts in mechanisms that guide individual choices and help ensure conformity. He believed that in traditional, pre-Renaissance societies, people tended to be *tradition-directed*. They were guided by ritualized behavioural patterns and prescriptions, which aimed at securing external behavioural conformity. 'While behavior is minutely prescribed, individuality of character need not be highly developed ... [B]ut a social character *capable* of such behavioral attention and obedience is requisite' (Riesman 1953: 30). Riesman claimed that with the Renaissance and Reformation people became increasingly *inner-directed*. Greater personal mobility and rapid technological and economic changes presented individuals with unprecedented range of choices, which demanded initiative. Behavioural conformity continued to be important, but it was no longer sufficient and unambiguous. The emerging new mode of life required 'character types who [could] manage to live socially without strict and self-evident tradition-direction ... [T]he source of direction for the individual is "inner" in the sense that it is implanted early in life by the elders and directed toward generalized but nonetheless inescapably destined goals' (Riesman 1953: 30). This inner compass helped people navigate in the new reality without losing their normative grounding and roots, essential to maintaining a sense of fixed integrity. A new awareness of the existence of a variety of traditions led to a conscious recognition of the meaning of tradition as such.

Writing in late 1940s America, Riesman and his co-workers noted another character type emerging in metropolitan centres and new middle classes, likely triggered by advanced levels of capitalism, industrialism and urbanization. The emergence of the *other-directed* character type was explained by the decreasing size and role of families and the increasing role of peer groups, secondary organizations and the mass media. It was marked by 'exceptional sensitivity to the actions and wishes of others' (Riesman 1953: 38). Children were socialized not so much to follow tradition or their inner compass as to look for direction by observing their contemporaries, including those whom they knew only from the media. For other-directed individuals, goals are no longer fixed. What gives them stability is their commitment to 'the process of striving' and 'the process of paying close attention to the signals of others' (Riesman 1953: 37). In short, other-directed people seem to be driven by the need for approval and direction from others (contemporary others, not one's elders or ancestors).

What happens, when in conducting their life and exercising daily choices, people become increasingly attentive to camera surveillance, scanners, data readers, audio-monitoring and so forth, without even visualizing human presence behind these devices and their systems? Are they becoming *surveillance-directed*? If so, what does this mean? Are they simply reacting to certain uses of technology or is something going on here that is deeper, more systematic and/or more profoundly related to the changing nature of social organization? And how does this compare to the social/psychological effects of the (historically specific) totalitarian surveillance?

In my definition, the surveillance-directed type would connote a high level of daily attention paid to diverse forms of surveillance and data-gathering, perceived as a system rather than unconnected acts of surveillance. This system would be visualized as capable of making dispersed bits of information to coalesce around a particular individual, group or subject. Such routine attention could eventually be coupled with a habit of second-guessing the impact that our behaviour, interactions with others, appearance or speech (and their various combinations) would have on our composite data doubles.

At this stage, the surveillance-directed type is a hypothetical construct. As indicated earlier, the awareness or visualization of widespread surveillance may still be relatively low. Yet personal experience, media stories and increased intrusiveness and overlap of surveillance in the war on terrorism and pandemic prevention era are likely to foster an increased recognition of the surveillance systems' implied interconnectedness, agility and potentially decisive impact on one's life.

Surveillance, liberty and the Self

Andrei Sakharov: Behave as if you lived in a free country.
Gabriel Berger: Behave as if Stasi did not exist.
(Ash 1997, paraphrased)

Totalitarian domination depends on a successful negation of the notion of freedom, both as an ideal and a resource for governing and resistance. As I demonstrated elsewhere (Los 2004), any acknowledgement of freedom – such as choice, initiative, spontaneity, privacy – would refute the type of ideology that enabled the all-inclusive, monistic, compulsory politicization of life required by the twentieth century totalitarian regimes.

It is worthy of note that the double I encountered in connection with my legal case was assembled to a large extent from the information which I gave more or less voluntarily to various institutions and their representatives. I also consented to the release of these dispersed data into the hands of the defendant's lawyer. In both cases, I was generally free to refuse cooperation *if* I were prepared to forsake such benefits as gainful employment, travel, health care or, in the case at hand, the right to a due compensation from the negligent party. If I were coerced, this was a special kind of coercion that deserves more systematic theoretical attention.

Various authors have suggested that the new surveillance should not be categorized as anti-liberal, as it actually cultivates and protects certain types of freedom useful for the sort of society we are living in (a consumer society, risk society, cosmopolitan/open society). The securitization of the self and of habitat (Rose 1999), surveillance related to management of choice and risk and surveillance as social sorting (Lyon 2003c), all may be considered to be predicated on and in the service of a certain type of liberty. They are shaped by the demands of social organization that 'depends upon the capacities of free individuals' (Rose 1999: 64), which is obviously contrary to the totalitarian ethos.

81

Freedom becomes a resource for governing and 'a formula of rule' (Barry *et al.* 1996: 8), but the exercise of freedom is conditional on the acceptance of quasi-economic rationality. We exchange our image (data) for access to opportunities that structure the globalizing society and make possible its perpetuation. While this exchange is seemingly voluntary for individuals, a withdrawal from some types of exchange may lead to a blanket exclusion from other exchanges, based on a high risk rating due, for example, to the lack of a credit record, driving record or, more generally, the meagreness (not just ugliness) of one's data double. The question of choice thus becomes moot and the individual resistance is rendered very precarious. The consequences of a meagre double may be likened to the ostracism of a stranger, an unknown wanderer. The fear of surveillant ostracism may lead to interiorization of the imperative to be known and recognizable by multiple surveillance systems. This may clash with the fear of getting too much surveillance exposure that may also trigger a blockage of access.

The current governmental rationalities – in their Foucauldian understanding as 'a part of the fabric of our ways of thinking about and acting upon one another and ourselves' (Barry *et al.* 1996: 7) – appear to be highly focused on individuals trying to maximize their personal choices in a calculated and prudent way. If so, our subjectivity at least to some extent is being shaped, or manufactured, through our concentration on fulfilling external conditions of our freedom. Surveillance plays an ever-growing role in the perception of these conditions. Assuming that our self-knowing increasingly evolves around our imagined and/or encountered self doubles, it is likely that a symbolic interaction with theoretically infinite configurations of surveillance data is becoming an important factor in moulding our subjectivity. This may structure the individual self in ways that accommodate multiple surveillance-oriented 'looking-glass selves', removed from one's interactions with human others. If this is the case, in the process of striving to meet the conditions of (dehumanized) freedom, the human 'other' in the other-directed type would be gradually supplanted by a multitude of virtually possible composite data constructs of our self.

Given, however, rapidly advancing digitalization and integration of diverse surveillance systems, the pursuit of choice and interactions with multiple doubles may soon turn into strategies of avoidance of an automatic blockage of choice across the board. At this level, multiple doubles may gradually mutate into a 'quasi-file'.

One significant difference between the logic of surveillance in the totalitarian and late-modern democratic regimes is that the former is predicated on an explicit refutation of the 'free individual' as an agent of social order and change, while late-modern surveillance principles are linked to the systemic imperative of both cultivating and policing individual agency. Nevertheless, there seem to be some convergence in the way the Self is affected by the denial of freedom and the file-centred surveillance under totalitarianism *and* the late-modern dehumanization of freedom as a resource for governing and surveillant deployment of data double(s).

Finally, and in keeping with Deleuze's (1997) suggestion, by becoming digitalized, the individual ceases to be the basic and indivisible unit of society and the society itself becomes converted into a series of non-social entities such as numerical samples, databases and virtual markets.

Surveillance, trust and sociality

One of the key conditions of totalitarian domination is social atomization. It entails separation of members of society from each other through secret infiltration, ideological obliteration of tradition, criminalization of association and deliberate uprooting schemes such as forced population movements, mass arrests and grandiose industrial or military projects.

As my earlier analyses show (Los 2002, 2004; Los and Zybertowicz 2000), totalitarian surveillance aims at a radical destruction of trust. Its key mechanism involves a conversion of every member of society into a police surrogate for both oneself and others. The penetration of society by the secret police and its collaborators induces pervasive fear, suspiciousness and mistrust. Consequently, each individual not only views all others as potential spies but must also be aware of being similarly viewed by others. This creates painful barriers of fear and humiliation that divide and terrorize society. People have no way of verifying who is a secret agent and have no way of preventing others from suspecting them of being one. The resultant culture of fear and suspicion atomizes society and thwarts social resistance.

One of the central features of late-modern cultural ethos is 'de-traditionalization', which is predicated on breaking with old habits of thinking and concepts of fixed space, time and continuity. This goes beyond questioning particular traditions and scrutinizing their biases or discriminatory potential. By entailing the refutation of tradition as such, the process of de-traditionalization undermines the habitual bases for sustained community bonds, trust and sociality.[8] When social organizing and cooperation based on traditional criteria are rendered suspect, much of the impetus for grassroots associations and 'natural' social niches is lost. Various moral panics and, more recently, the war on terror have focused on the enforcement of the citizens' duty to mistrust each other and to inform authorities about any suspicions they may have. Moreover, a playful, malicious or vigilant use of new surveillance technologies in private and quasi-private encounters adds unpredictability to the contemporary, securitized environment and erodes the necessary quantum of trust needed for a basic sociality and solidarity (see, for example, Staples 1997; Lyon 2003a; 2003b).

Michalis Lianos (2003) points to the profoundly atomizing and de-socializing effects of late-modern institutional control/surveillance. Because institutional practices tend to be focused on inclusion and enticement of 'users', surveillance is applied to identify potentially risky individuals, without burdening people with social/human responsibility for each other. Lianos analyses security devices in terms of their specific applications and their consequences for the conditions and social relations in the given social environment. For example, based on his examination of magnetic tagging of products to prevent theft, he argues that in so far as it replaces human beings, who used to watch customers,[9] it marks a move from social control that had an in-built margin for negotiation towards a control based on binary normativity predetermined by the institution in question.[10] Since these devices are not programmed to differentiate on the basis of social status, their proliferation reduces 'the motivation for acquiring cultural resources that are likely to increase respect, credibility and trustworthiness' (Lianos 2003: 424).

While not all forms of new technologies of surveillance are characterized by social blindness – and Lianos does not claim that they are – it can be argued that traditional, intuitive, informally personalized evaluation of respectability and social standing is rapidly becoming obsolete. The binary codes simply do not reflect the personal effort, sincerity or good will, which can only be accounted for within socially grounded interactions. This reinforces Lianos's claim that institutional surveillance/control is deeply de-socializing as it disengages its subjects (users) from social belonging (2003: 425). Traditionally, social belonging was founded on the aspiration to gain social inclusion and approval through competition for culturally defined social status. It is noteworthy that an important aspect of the Soviet totalitarian strategy of uprooting was an assault on culturally defined criteria of social status/esteem and elaborate attempts to replace them by mechanisms of institutional membership and ritual.

The de-socializing effects of new surveillance technologies do not preclude, however, their tendency to enforce longstanding biases and categories of stratification. Conventional criteria of social evaluation still enter into the picture where the application of a new technology depends on human assessment and mediation (Norris 1999, 2003). Moreover, digitalization of surveillance systems allows for automatic profiling based on whatever categories, codes or algorithms are programmed into the overall data system (Lyon 2003a, 2003b; Norris 2003; Gandy this volume). Yet, this is done at a distance and in separation from any meaningful cultural context and personalized contact.

The new logic of late-modern surveillance, typified by the data double, dehumanization of freedom and de-socialized criteria of sorting, suggests a special form of biographical uprooting, whereby for many people a caring relationship with their peripatetic, de-contextualized virtual double(s) is likely to become a major preoccupation. The realization that even privileged information constitutes a latent piece of our virtual double(s) may also indirectly undermine such traditionally trust-based relationships as those involving medical/caring professions. Moreover, the new intensity of post September 11 securitization campaigns and unprecedented proliferation of surveillance technology markets have introduced new forms of mistrust and suspicion into the social realm. As various authors have noted, a new culture of suspicion recasts citizens simultaneously as spies and suspects (see, for example, Lyon 2003a), a phenomenon eerily familiar to survivors of totalitarianism. Finally, the relocation of sociality into the Internet and other global arenas is being accompanied and shaped by new awareness of being under a virtually infinite, culturally unbound, worldwide surveillance.

Surveillance and normativity

Under historical scientific totalitarianism, individual subjectivity was to be replaced by a compulsory, objective, collective truth that could not be verified outside the ideological, make-believe reality. Individuals had to be purged of any attachment to conventional criteria of truth and falsehood and any notion of individual moral choice.

Truth

The totalitarian experience has shown that a deliberate and systematic fabrication and promotion of falsehood is a powerful tool of total domination. The regime's omnipotence is validated when people can be made to say whatever the rulers want them to say. Breaking subjects' mental and moral integrity is an important step in their subjugation. In the long run, this strategy of ruling strives to erase the very need for distinguishing between truth and lie and discredits any former epistemological, moral and linguistic standards attached to them. By instilling indifference to truth and falsehood, it certifies a make-believe reality of the moment as the only thinkable and sayable reference (Los 2004).

The Western epistemological revolution of the recent decades has resulted in a radical questioning of the validity of common-sense, pre-given rationality criteria and the objective search for truth. The sense of both historical and biographical truth has also been shaken by the new openness to multiple truths, perspectives, chronologies, identities and facts. Various versions of new epistemologies have permeated our culture, unsettling traditional habits of thought and speech. They have served simultaneously to deny the possibility of truth and enforce the correct criteria of truth (through 'political correctness'). By shaking up our ethno-centrism, our reliance on stereotypes and our fixed standpoint, new epistemology movements genuinely moved us to re-examine our prejudices and petrified ways of seeing the world around us. Yet, they also removed cognitive and moral supports related to our upbringing, shared meanings and intuition. This loss needed to be compensated. As Staples suggests:

> [Ours is] a culture characterized by fragmentation and uncertainty as many of the once-taken-for-granted meanings, symbols, and institutions of modern life dissolve before our eyes … Under this circumstance, we turn to increasingly more pervasive, rational and predictable means of surveillance and social control. In essence, we are seduced into believing that subjecting ourselves to more and more meticulous rituals is an unfortunate but necessary condition given the apparent tide of problems we face (Staples 2000: 8).

While the place of surveillance in this epistemological counter-modernization has not been given much attention, it may be postulated that it both exploits and subverts the new epistemological climate. In a relative cognitive vacuum, products of surveillance technologies are increasingly construed as a new form of truth, more real and authoritative than any subjective sense of reality held by individuals. The data double is more real that the person behind it. Yet, even though the veracity of our accounting of ourselves is being constantly checked by various monitoring technologies, the veracity of our virtual doubles is no longer verifiable, correctable or even considered an issue. The notion of individual biographical truth, already weakened by current epistemologies, is further marginalized by pragmatic institutional choices, where both actuarial calculations and data-matching procedures constantly produce real consequences for individuals represented by their ersatz doubles. The very nature of the data double phenomenon indicates that it both functions as truth and, given its multiplicity, versatility and arbitrary constitution, also negates the possibility of truth.

When people become used to living with multiple, vague, conflicting, often contradictory flows of information, there is a danger that the only knowledge that is granted the status of reality will be that which relates to risk/security and comes from intelligence agencies and other risk-managing networks. Given the largely opaque nature of their truth-manufacturing processes and their increasingly global reach, this kind of knowledge is generally not directly accessible to citizens. One of the aspects of this domain of knowledge involves intelligence-based data doubles, whose prominence has been boosted in the present climate of antiterrorist securitization.

Finally, while the new epistemologies weakened the belief in the possibility of truth, the emerging mode of regulation through surveillance undermines the relevance of the moral principle of speaking the truth (being truthful) because the truth/lie is defined and detected automatically regardless of what we say. The surveillance data reduce confession and testimony to the role of a negligible appendage to technical monitoring and verification. Also, increasingly, 'the truth' can be gleaned directly from the body, through various tests, new biometric technologies and digitalization of the body (van der Ploeg 2003), which removes the subjectivity from the truth and nullifies the moral choice of revealing/concealing it. In an interesting twist, this goes against the current epistemological climate which emphasizes the subjective relativity of truth(s).

Morality

There is a noticeable tendency in current modes of social control to displace morality to the margins of evolving technologies and rationalities of governing.[11] When monitoring targets people in their roles as consumers, clients or employees, it is not necessarily programmed to enforce a system of moral values. A moral focus could be easily challenged in a late-modern, uprooted, relativistic, fluid cultural climate. Even more importantly, the prevailing market/managerial rationality is not concerned with the morality of choices made as long as they coincide with the desired dynamics of consumption, efficiency and administrative compatibility. Reiterating Lianos's intuitions (2003), it is useful to visualize this as a process of dislocation of the social through fragmentation and waning of the wide-ranging normative/evaluative grid that was previously crucial to social control. Lianos argues that institutional normativity has a very weak evaluative base as particular institutions and their users share a narrow 'field of consensus' that relates to the effectiveness of their interactions. In a new development, the generalized conformity typical of relational social networks is being replaced by the mediating capacity of specific institutions and systems that serve them (Lianos 2003: 425). This development is part of a larger context that goes beyond deliberate control strategies and involves systems and technologies, including surveillance technologies, which simultaneously and similarly shape interactions between institutions and users in diverse areas.

By displacing morality, surveillance makes itself indispensable. This is well illustrated in the following quotation from Staples:

> [In a school bus], once the camera is in place, no one has to bother teaching children *why* they should behave, it's enough just to get them to do it. This begs the question, How will they act when they are not under the gaze of the camera? Of course, the logical outcome of this 'solution' is to make sure that they are *always* under its watchful eye (Staples 1997: 133).

An important implication is that we should not assume that control continues to be intentionally 'embedded in a project of shaping the self' whereby normative control is achieved through 'injection of values into the subject' (Lianos 2003: 425). The norm assumes new foundations, external to processes of internalization, and liberty is redefined in terms of access and use of systems. This may signify 'the death of the soul' and a major departure from the social control Foucault analyzed.

It can be legitimately argued that in the integrated context of the late-modern culture and institutional (increasingly de-socialized) normativity, the morality and truth are fading away from the make-up of the Self, rendering meaningless the notion of moral integrity. The uniqueness and wholeness of the individual are no longer culturally validated. Neither moral nor bodily integrity can be sustained as a normative ideal, when de-socialized surveillance technologies are prioritized over human communication and interaction. While under these conditions, deliberate totalitarian technologies that break the integrity of individuals become worthless, this unwitting dissolution of integrity mimics the outcomes of more sinister, totalitarian practices. The Self is thus being freed from the conscience-based evaluative criteria and individuals use their externally directed intelligence to pass institutional tests regulating access and choice. The data double becomes a key reference, which allows individuals to assess themselves in the relevant context while by-passing the Self and the socialized *me*.[12]

It may therefore be argued that under very different conditions and through far less brutal means, late modernity produces effects akin to those pursued by the totalitarian technology of control, which strived to purge the Self and nullify the meaning of individual resistance. Unlike the latter, however, contemporary strategies of institutional regulation seemingly leave the decision-making processes in the hands of individuals and are fuelled by the rationality of mutually beneficial consensual exchanges.

Concluding thoughts: surveillance and new positivism

In this section I focus on selected epistemological implications of the new surveillance culture and their relationship to relativist epistemologies of the late twentieth century. In this context, it may be instructive to recall the arguments made by such legal thinkers as Gustav Radbruch and Lon Fuller, who claimed that German legal positivistic tradition had contributed to the eagerness of Germany's lawyers to cooperate in the enforcement of Nazi laws. According to their arguments, the positivistic philosophy, which had dominated the German legal profession, actually facilitated the establishment of the Nazi regime. For Fuller, the core issue was that: 'German legal positivism not only banned from legal science any consideration of moral ends of law, but it was also indifferent to what I have called the inner morality of law itself' (Fuller 1995: 85). The German lawyer was thus peculiarly prepared to accept as law 'anything that called itself by that name...' (Fuller 1995: 85).

It can be postulated that the epistemological revolution triggered by the totalitarian experience of the twentieth century created a normative vacuum, in which a new, extreme form of positivistic truth, generated by surveillance, has found a receptive ground. The technicistic approach that prevails in global surveillance culture and likely affects programmers, managers and users of surveillance systems removes these systems' codes and scripts from the scope of moral reflection. These truncated, de-humanized and de-socialized scripts appear as 'given' and acquire a very positivistic air. This process is also evident in the way many surveillance mechanisms work, whereby any occurrence inconsistent with the formal scripts programmed into them triggers automatic penal/exclusionary reaction.[13] Consequently, a seeming objectivity of surveillance-based processes of control ultimately results in granting an almost unlimited discretion to the forces behind the scenes.

In short, just as legal positivism aims at removing human reflection and discretion from the administration of justice, *surveillant positivism* tends to purge them from the increasingly automated application of new surveillance technologies in the regulation of order, market and security.[14] The emerging prevalence of the 'management at a distance' seems consistent with (legal) positivistic philosophy which assumes that human involvement introduces inherently risky interference because of its subjectivity and arbitrariness. Yet, as the Nazi example may suggest, there is a danger that unreflective, remote systems of regulation, which are not subject to everyday conscious scrutiny by their administrators and subjects, can be more easily reshaped to fit unrevealed designs of a totalitarian/monistic nature. Paradoxically, while anti-positivistic (relativistic) epistemologies have aspired to counter the totalitarian potential of our thoughts, they might have in the end contributed to the rise of an extreme form of technologically enhanced positivism.

Concluding thoughts: taking care of the double and the vanishing self

In what way is the new surveillance constitutive of the subject? Does it encourage individuals to objectify themselves in search of direction or satisfaction of their desires? Does it rely on the individuals' ability to work on their selves? I have argued in this chapter that socio-psychological by-products of new surveillance technologies may share certain characteristics with the deliberately effected conditions of total domination. In this context, I have highlighted growing concern with our double(s), which may resemble some of the psychological correlates of *the file*.

It may be predicted that 'taking care' of our virtual double(s) will develop into a major preoccupation, de-centring the earlier focus on the Self and its image in the eyes of others. The proposed concept of the surveillance-directed type may be helpful in tracing and exploring these processes. If true, these changes would render obsolete the earlier socio-psychological theories on interiorizaton of social control as well as Foucault's ideas on technologies of the self. Indeed, the whole notion of working on our real selves to achieve ethically/socially desirable results is becoming pointless as our care is refocused on a virtual sphere populated by our potential clones.

The data double becomes a key reference, which allows individuals to assess themselves in a relevant context while by-passing the Self and the socialized 'me' (to use Mead's terminology). This 'taking care' of the virtual double is likely to extend far beyond the awareness of our fleeting image being caught by an anonymous camera, our voice being recorded on some unidentified listening device or even our 'identity' being stolen by some criminally inclined individuals or gangs. In this new sense, the surveillance would be seen as an invisible web, or a virtual system, that is constantly gathering, individualizing, differentiating and generalizing enormous amount of personal and conjectural information. Moreover, once the hollowed-out self becomes virtually a mirror for surveillance, *the social* is consumed by whatever system rationality shapes and fuels that surveillance.

Notes

1 In their everyday conversations, members of communist societies tended to complain bitterly about the de-moralization of society and the triumph of the lie. They still point to these features as a lasting legacy of communism.

2 Rhizomes are plant stems that shoot up in various directions from a mass of horizontally interconnected roots.

3 While he concurs with various other authors in noting that this type of surveillance, which depends on continuous refinement of the criteria and processes of inclusion, leads to the multiplication of parallel processes of exclusion, this is not directly relevant to the evaluation of the totalizing potential of contemporary surveillance.

4 In his engaging book *The File*, the British writer Timothy G. Ash (1997) describes his own encounter with the secret file kept on him by the East German Interior Ministry (STASI), which was made available to him after the fall of communist regime in that country. He also notes the disappointment and embarrassment of those former East Germans, who were told that there was no file on them in the vast secret archives: 'Then came the dreadful letter from Authority: so far as we can establish, you have no file. Humiliation. ... [They say:] "It seems that mine was destroyed." ... No one ever says, "I am sure they didn't have one on me." One could describe the syndrome in Freudian terms: file envy' (Ash 1997: 22).

5 What is also noteworthy, inadvertently mixed with my records were numerous pieces of personal information about other people, often identified by name, address, etc.

6 For example, talking to doctors will never be the same again.

7 It has to be noted that a distinction between private and public security sectors has been blurred for some time now. Researchers have repeatedly pointed to their merging and interweaving in the process of pluralization of policing (see Marx 1987, 1988; South 1988; Loader 2000; Garland 2001). New theories emerge that situate this process within a multi-site model

of governance, where multiple 'nodes' related to the state, the market, the voluntary sector, globalization and so forth, constitute together a complex realm of regulation, prevention and enforcement of security (Johnston and Shearing 2003).

8　Merriam-Webster's Collegiate Dictionary (1993) defines sociality as 'the tendency to associate in or form social groups'.

9　See also Jones and Newburn (2002) on the disappearance of many jobs that used to fulfil secondary controlling function (bus conductors, concierges, etc.) and their replacement with new forms of surveillance.

10　This, of course, is true at the level of pre-programmed technology. Either the store/library exit gate sounds the alarm or it does not. But I would argue that a social negotiation process may still follow, when the personnel reacts to the alarm and confronts the culprit. The plea of absentmindedness, for example, is still possible. And the race or age may still play a role.

11　For a differing view, see, for example Hunt (2003).

12　As understood by Mead (1934).

13　See Jones (2000), on the essentially penal nature of 'digital rule' and Haggerty (this volume) on technological agency.

14　See Ogura (this volume) on government as the official biographer, which monopolizes and certifies of who we are. See also his comments on modern/postmodern view of humanity as lying at the root of uncertainty that can only be overcome by making humans more like machines.

References

Arendt, H. (1958) *The Origins of Totalitarianism* (Cleveland and New York: Meridian).

Ash, T.G. (1997) *The File: A Personal History* (New York: Vintage).

Barry, A., Osborne, T. and Rose, N. (1996) 'Introduction', in A. Barry, T. Osborne and N. Rose (eds) *Foucault and Political Reason: Liberalism, Neo-liberalism and Rationalities of Government* (Chicago: University of Chicago Press), 1–17.

Burger, R., Berezovszky, P. and Pelinka, P. (eds) (2000) *Global Ethics. Illusion or Reality?* (Vienna: Czernin Verlag).

Deleuze, G. (1997) 'Postscript on the Societies of Control', in N. Leach (ed.) *Rethinking Architecture: A Reader in Cultural Theory* (London: Routledge), 309–12.

Dower, N. (1998) *World Ethics – The New Agenda* (Edinburgh: Edinburgh University Press).

Ericson, R.V. and Haggerty, K.D. (1997) *Policing the Risk Society* (Toronto: University of Toronto Press).

Fuller, L.I. (1995) 'Positivism and Fidelity to Law – A Reply to Professor Hart', in J. Feinberg and H. Gross (eds) *Philosophy of Law* (fifth edition) (Belmont, CA: Wadsworth), 73–87.

Garland, D. (2001) *The Culture of Control* (Oxford: Oxford University Press).

Gasper, D. (2001) *Global Ethics and Global Strangers – Beyond the Inter-National Relations Framework: An Essay in Descriptive Ethics*, Working Papers Series No. 341 (The Hague: Institute of Social Studies).

Haggerty, K.D. and Ericson, R.V. (2000) 'The Surveillant Assamblage', *British Journal of Sociology*, 51 (4), 605–22.

Held, D. (2002) 'Cosmopolitanism: Ideas, Realities and Deficits', in D. Held and A. McGrew (eds) *Governing Globalization. Power, Authority and Global Governance* (Cambridge: Polity Press), 305–24.

Hunt, A. (2003) 'Risk and Moralization in Everyday Life', in R. Ericson and A. Doyle (eds) *Risk and Morality* (Toronto: University of Toronto Press), 165–92.

Johnston, L. and Shearing, C. (2003) *Governing Security: Explorations in Policing and Justice* (London: Routledge).

Jones, R. (2000) 'Digital Rule: Punishment, Control and Technology', *Punishment and Society*, 2 (1), 5–22.

Jones, T. and Newburn, T. (2002) 'The Transformation of Policing? Understanding Current Trends in Policing Systems', *British Journal of Criminology*, 42, 129–46.

Lianos, M. (2003) 'Social Control after Foucault', *Surveillance and Society*, 1 (3), 412–30. Available at: http://www.surveillance-andsociety.org/articles1(3)/AfterFoucault.pdf.

Loader, I. (2000) 'Plural Policing and Democratic Governance', *Social and Legal Studies*, 9 (3), 323–45.

Los, M. (2002) 'Post-communist Fear of Crime and the Commercialization of Security', *Theoretical Criminology*, 6 (2), 165–88.

Los, M. (2004) 'The Technologies of Total Domination', *Surveillance and Society*, 2 (1), 15–38. Available at: http://www.surveillance-and-society.org/articles2(1)/domination.pdf.

Los, M. and Zybertowicz, A. (2000) *Privatizing the Police State: The Case of Poland* (Houndmills and New York: Palgrave Macmillan).

Lyon, D. (2003a) *Surveillance after September 11* (Cambridge: Polity Press).

Lyon, D. (2003b) 'Surveillance as Social Sorting: Computer Codes and Mobile Bodies', in D. Lyon (ed.) *Surveillance as Social Sorting: Privacy, Risk and Digital Discrimination* (London and New York: Routledge), 13–30.

Lyon, D. (ed.) (2003c) *Surveillance as Social Sorting: Privacy, Risk and Digital Discrimination* (London and New York: Routledge).

Marx, G.T. (1987) 'The Interweaving of Public and Private Police in Undercover Work', in C.D. Shearing and P.C. Stenning (eds) *Private Policing* (Newbury Park, CA: Sage), 172–93.

Marx, G.T. (1988) *Undercover: Police Surveillance in America* (Berkeley: University of California Press).

Mead, G.H. (1934) *Mind, Self, and Society* (Chicago: University of Chicago Press).

Norris, C. (1999) *The Maximum Surveillance Society: The Rise of CCTV* (Oxford: Berg).

Norris, C. (2003) 'From Personal to Digital', in D. Lyon (ed.) *Surveillance as Social Sorting: Privacy, Risk and Digital Discrimination* (London and New York: Routledge), 249–81.

Podgorecki, A. (1995) *One Hundred and One Stories of Si-tien* (Ottawa: Carleton University).

Podgorecki, A. (1996) 'Totalitarian Law: Basic Concepts and Issues', in A. Podgorecki and V. Olgiati (eds) *Totalitarian and Post-Totalitarian Law* (Aldershot: Dartmouth), 3–37.

Riesman, D. with Glazer, N. and Denney, R. (1953) *The Lonely Crowd: A Study of the Changing American Character* (Garden City: Doubleday Anchor).

Rose, N. (1999) *Powers of Freedom* (Cambridge: Cambridge University Press).

South, N. (1988) *Policing for Profit* (London: Sage).

Staples, W.G. (1997) *The Culture of Surveillance: Discipline and Social Control in the United States* (New York: St. Martin's).

Staples, W.G. (2000) *Everyday Surveillance: Vigilance and Visibility in Postmodern Life* (Lanham, MD: Rowman and Littlefield).

van der Ploeg, I. (2003) 'Biometrics and the Body as Information: Normative Issues of the Socio-Technical Coding of the Body', in D. Lyon (ed.) *Surveillance as Social Sorting: Privacy, Risk and Digital Discrimination* (London and New York: Routledge), 57–73.

Whitaker, R. (2001) *Big Brother.com: La Vie Privée Sous Surveillance* (Québec: Les Presses de l'Université Laval).

Part 3

Space and Time in Surveillance Theory

Chapter 5

Surveillance assemblages and lines of flight

William Bogard

Like all machinic and enunciative assemblages, surveillance assemblages are both territorial and cut across by lines of deterritorialization or 'flight'. Indeed, one way to describe the evolution from panoptic to post-panoptic systems is from territorial to deterritorialized forms of social control, for example, from guarded or confined spaces to digital networks. Often, this evolution is depicted in Orwellian terms – no more privacy, no more secrets, universal tracking, perfect customized identification. Deterritorialized controls are far from perfect, however; they produce deterritorialized forms of resistance as a function of their own organization. Networked information is hard to secure and easy to reproduce. This fact of the digital age explains both the power of surveillance assemblages today (the ease with which they gather and share information on us) and their potential weakness or vulnerability. There are even good reasons to see prospects for freedom in surveillance assemblages, since networks make it very hard for power to monopolize the machines that identify and track us, or determine the flow and price of information. Control of information becomes more impossible the closer an information network gets to the model of a 'rhizome', in which every node must connect to every other node in an open structure. Perhaps here we can discover what Guattari describes as a paradoxical 'safety' in the machine, even an Orwellian machine that watches and records everything.

The theme of the machine has concerned me for a long time, but perhaps less as a conceptual than an affective object. I have always been fascinated by the machine, and even remember, as a student at the Sorbonne, ... [being] scathingly opposed to the mechanicist visions of the machine, and thought instead that we could look forward to a kind of safety in the machine. Since then, I have tried to nurture this machinic object, although I admit it is something I cannot control (Guattari 1990).

Technology has run away from the rules. The law has become irrelevant (Internet pirate responding to the new Swedish anti-piracy laws).

This is the end of Capital as we know it (Post on an Internet forum dealing in stolen credit card numbers).

It has never been more imperative than today to think about resistance to global, networked surveillance. It is especially important to focus on modes of resistance that are immanent to how the system organizes itself, not just laws or political reforms, such as better privacy or freedom of information protections. Theories of surveillance society after Foucault have generally framed surveillance as a power/knowledge relation, not simply a juridical or legal matter (Bogard 1996; Davis 1998; Elmer 2003; Foucault 1977; Haggerty and Ericson 2000; Koskela 2000; Lianos 2003; Lyon 1994, 2001, 2002, 2004; Mathiesen 1997; Poster 1990; Virilio 1994, 2000). Still, when it comes to resistance, this is how the problem is usually posed, as if the power of the law were not itself already totally invested in surveillance, or as if political institutions that are themselves fully operationalized by surveillance could somehow effectively regulate it.

In fact, surveillance, as a network of power and knowledge relations, always generates resistance. This is only to restate Foucault's well-known claim that power requires resistance as a force immanent to its action. We need to better understand how such counter-forces are built into the surveillance assemblage itself, how surveillance (normally a means of identification, normalization, deterrence, exclusion, etc.) can become a force against itself (of multiplication, deviation, seduction, inclusion).

To surveil something essentially means to watch over or guard it. Guardianship is not a simple constraint, but an art of control that makes it safe for something to move freely. You keep a close eye on your child playing, or someone deflects a danger close to you before you even sense it. A computer silently screens airline passengers for security risks when they purchase their tickets, weeks before they travel, assuring a free, unrestricted flow of passengers at boarding. Are any of these practices more freeing than any other? Consider the surveillance machine assembled by the photographer Sophie Calle, who discreetly from behind, in secret, takes pictures of a man who is a virtual stranger to her. She follows him for days on end, travels behind him, always watches him from a distance, catches images of his comings and goings and meanderings, until finally one day he notices her watching him and she is forced to abandon her project. What kind of surveillance is this? In his commentary on her work, Baudrillard says there is nothing to suggest Sophie has an interest in controlling this man or verifying his story (Calle and Baudrillard 1983). There is no 'object' of surveillance in the traditional sense, only a complex assemblage consisting of Calle, her photographic and note-taking equipment, the man, her spontaneous desire to follow and observe and record him, all this together producing a certain affective quality or intensity that Baudrillard identifies with seduction, not control (cf. Baudrillard 1990; Calle and Baudrillard 1983: 76). Although she takes secret pictures of him, Calle does not seek to expose her subject to anyone, to find out who he is; and while he is under surveillance, the man does not develop the kind of self-judgemental subjectivity we associate with panoptic surveillance. Sophie does not desire to influence or predict this man's behaviour, to know him in any way; in fact, the whole point of her 'experiment' in watching him is to lose control of the whole situation, to open everything, the whole assemblage, including herself, up to luck. The man, for his part, is not placed under any normalizing or 'individualizing' gaze, but watched from behind by a machine that paradoxically 'cares' for him, and in so doing ultimately seduces him.

For Baudrillard, to be seduced is to lose one's identity, to have the responsibility of being one's self suddenly lifted, and he notes that Calle herself is seduced, loses herself, no less than the man in whose footsteps she blindly follows. The surveillance assemblage here, far from an apparatus of the law or a means of subjectification, is rather in this case a kind of gift or 'gift-assemblage', one that functions 'to watch over another's life without him knowing about it', and Calle's photographic project symbolizes a way of cancelling, through a kind of 'blind' surveillance or guardianship, the debt society makes us owe to our own existence (Calle and Baudrillard 1983: 80–1). It is, from her position as a photographer and an artist, a gift of relieving this man of the reality and truth of who he must be in this world – now, as he enters unwittingly into the assemblage, he is transformed into someone else, someone freer than before.

Like all surveillors, Calle certainly desires to 'extract' an identity from this man, but not in the sense of wanting to identify him. She does not wish to verify or determine who he is. Just the opposite: in following him she must preserve his (and her own) anonymity, within and through the very assemblage that tracks him and organizes her watching. Here is a kind of 'safety' in the machine, an immanent aesthetic and ethical function of the assemblage. State and corporate surveillance today too, of course, is routinely couched in the language of 'safety', but this is the safety provided by police technologies of identification and verification, where everything about you and what distinguishes you from others is known. This is not at all the kind of safety – or freedom – offered by Calle's assemblage. What she offers instead is a kind of freedom from identification, a line of flight that takes the form of 'caring for the other's image' that at the same time leaves him unmarked, a line that is immanent to the assemblage and how it functions from the start.[1]

Calle understands that surveillance must follow something and sustain its resistance, unlike the state, which always tries to lead with surveillance and eliminate resistance in advance. In other words, Calle knows that surveillance must connect to an 'outside' that is immanent to the assemblage, a space of necessary indeterminacy within the system of control itself that she seeks to nurture, not stamp out. Indeterminacy and resistance at first seem inconsistent with surveillance, but they really constitute its core. This is true whether we are talking about panopticons or databases. In the panopticon, power resists the decoding – that is, the visibility – it imposes on everything else; it works by indetermination, hiding its always possible absence behind the walls of a central guard tower. With databases, firewalls, passwords and encryption become our new 'guard towers', and power still resists the decoding it imposes on everything else, only this time, it resists not its own visibility, but its own conversion to information (informationalization). The point is that surveillance, like all power, flees the very thing it produces, flees determination. Unlike state surveillance, however, which reserves freedom to itself, Calle's surveillance has no firewalls or codes to break, no walls to hide behind. She practises surveillance in a way totally consistent with what it demands, that is, a free, open and non-determined flow of information.

Lyon notes that surveillance has a dual function, to both constrain and enable social relations (in information societies, electronic surveillance is a means of control that also generates the 'token' trust necessary for social transactions) (Lyon 1994; Lyon 2001: 27). We can also understand surveillance in terms of capture and flight. Capture involves fixing or arresting a flow – surveillance as a mode of territorialization, determination, verification and identification, normalization, and so on. Surveillance as flight, on the other hand, refers to its role in releasing a flow – escape, deterritorialization, indetermination and resistance. Flight and capture are not opposed terms, however. Deleuze and Guattari note that some lines of flight can become fixed in their direction, speed, intensity, etc. (Deleuze and Guattari 1987: 214–6). Surveillance becomes a police power (in the broad sense) precisely to the extent that it arrests flows of information. In the same way, deterritorialization does not always imply freedom. Post-panoptic surveillance has evolved deterritorialized controls that radically subvert the movement to free societies. Hardt and Negri note, for instance, that deterritorialized information networks are central to the production and organization of global civil war and the global policing of society (Hardt and Negri 2004: 12–32).

On the positive side, flows of information in the global surveillance network are never completely fixed. A network is like a rhizome to the extent that any node in it must connect to any other (Deleuze and Guattari 1987: 7). Ultimately no police power is capable of controlling the deterritorialization of surveillance, because the number of virtual connections in a rhizomatic network always exceeds the number that can actually be monitored (if one path is blocked, another can be found). If surveillance is about control and the police, it also has these 'anti-police', 'anti-control' tendencies too, immanent to its deterritorialization. We see these tendencies at work in resistant practices like file sharing and copying, hacking and cracking, reverse engineering, spamming, identity theft, communications jamming, and many more. Of course, these are police practices too, perhaps originally so, since they are all means of information control. The difference is that the police try to retain exclusive control of them, or block their use by anti-control forces with firewalls, encryption, etc. (themselves resistant technologies). The tendency of surveillance assemblages, information networks, and power relations generally, however, to develop rhizomatic connections, suggests that exclusionary strategies of information control are unlikely to succeed.

The surveillance assemblage

Actually, there are many surveillance assemblages, not just one. Haggerty and Ericson define a surveillance assemblage as a machine 'that operates by abstracting human bodies from their territorial settings and separating them into a series of discrete flows. These flows are then reassembled into distinct "data doubles" which can be scrutinized and targeted for intervention. In the process', they assert, 'we are witnessing a rhizomatic leveling of the hierarchy of surveillance, such that groups which were previously exempt from routine surveillance are now increasingly being monitored' (Haggerty and Ericson 2000: 606).

The notion of a 'rhizomatic levelling' of hierarchies of surveillance at first seems contradictory. On one hand, if this is rhizomatic surveillance, it appears as an expansion and intensification rather than diminution of social control. Surveillance now operates at real-time speeds over global networks, connecting multiple flows of information across a multiplicity of scales from molecular to molar (across the whole range of biopolitical production). In this picture, control hierarchies may be disappearing, but the emerging form of horizontal or 'flat' control seems even more totalizing than before, as surveillance captures ever more phenomena in its gaze. For more discussion on the totalizing potential of surveillance, see Maria Los's chapter in this volume.

By definition rhizomes are nonlinear, non-binary, and non-unitary structures (even the term 'structure' is potentially misleading). How accurate can this model be for a control system that grounds itself in information science? Information science is based on a tree model whose content is articulated in normal (central tendency) probability functions, not on the model of a rhizome. And tree models, as Deleuze and Guattari note, invariably serve closed, hierarchical systems of decision and control – the state, the police, the corporation, and so on (Deleuze and Guattari 1987: 6–7).

On the other hand, if the emerging network of global surveillance is an open system in which each information node can and must connect to every other, then it makes sense to call this system a rhizome.[2] Certainly, surveillance today is more decentralized, less subject to spatial and temporal constraints (location, time of day, etc.), and less organized than ever before by the dualisms of observer and observed, subject and object, individual and mass. The system of control is deterritorializing, and the effects of this are to intensify but also, in a very real sense, to democratize surveillance. The very logic of information networks that information must be free to flow between any part of the system, for surveillance means more ways to observe the observers, bypass their firewalls, access their databases and decode their communications. The question today is whether centres of power – states or corporations – can control the global networks their own information requirements push them to produce. Certainly, they can make some kinds of information very difficult to access, and this is easier for them the more networks are like trees (where all branches emanate from a single trunk or central stem). But if networks are rhizomes, information becomes next to impossible to secure, and no firewall, password or encryption technology works for long. If networks are rhizomes, power based on security or secrecy has good reason to be concerned.

Haggerty and Ericson borrow the concept of an 'assemblage' from Deleuze and Guattari to describe surveillance networks (Deleuze and Guattari 1983: 36; Deleuze and Guattari 1987: 503–5, 510–14; Haggerty and Ericson 2000: 608–9). Assemblages are not discrete objects, but consist of open relations among heterogeneous elements whose only unity derives from the fact that they operate together (and even then it is not exactly right to speak of a unity, since counter-actualizations of the assemblage are internal to it and continuous). Every assemblage is a multiplicity composed of other assemblages that are also multiplicities that together form a functional, ever-changing ensemble (or 'meshwork', to use De Landa's term) (De Landa 1997: 57ff.). The surveillance assemblage consists of all the diverse means available today of gathering, sorting, recalling and processing information (including information blocking or jamming technologies) (Bogard 1996; Der Derian 1992). It encompasses not just monitoring devices in the technical sense (sensors, recording instruments), but a whole matrix of corporeal and incorporeal relations, or power-knowledge relations (Foucault and Gordon 1980). We must consider the surveillance assemblage that is, as having both material and immaterial components, a complex deployment of bodies and machines as well as an order of events, discourses, concepts and formulae.

Deleuze and Guattari define assemblages in the following way, along a double axis:

> We may draw some general conclusions on the nature of assemblages ... On a first, horizontal, axis, an assemblage comprises two segments, one of content and one of expression. On the one hand it is a machinic assemblage of bodies, of actions and passions, an intermingling of bodies reacting to one another; on the other hand it is a collective assemblage of enunciation, of acts and statements, of incorporeal transformations attributed to bodies. Then on a vertical axis, the assemblage has both territorial sides, or reterritorialized sides, which stabilize it, and cutting edges of deterritorialization, which carry it away (Deleuze and Guattari 1987: 504).

We must stress the relative nature of these distinctions. Deleuze and Guattari are not interested in creating a formal typology of assemblages. Just as in Foucault, power and knowledge are never separate in practice, Deleuze and Guattari draw no hard lines between machinic and enunciative assemblages, or between territorializing and deterritorializing functions of assemblages. An assemblage consists of machines and statements, words and things; and stabilizing (fixing, stratifying) and destabilizing (fluid, transformative) events.

We could, alternatively, view an assemblage simply as an ensemble of different machines, using 'machine' in its widest sense to include both material and immaterial processes. If we take Guattari's philosophical machinism as our guide, this ensemble includes materials and energy, semiotic, diagrammatic and algorithmic components (plans, mathematical formulae, engineering calculations), bodies and parts of bodies, individual and collective mental representations, desiring machines and social machines that produce subjectivities adjacent to the material and diagrammatic components of the machine, and finally an 'abstract machine' that connects all these together (Guattari 1995). The panopticon, if we understand it not simply as a formal model but also a material organization, provides an excellent example of a machinic assemblage in Guattari's expanded sense, since it functions both as a kind of diagrammatic or abstract form of control (one that operates autonomously from and organizes a variety of material relations), but also a concrete arrangement of forces for connecting bodies to lines of desire and fitting them to modes of subjectivity and discursive knowledge.

For the moment, however, let us hold on to the original distinction between a machinic and an enunciative assemblage. A machinic assemblage joins or separates diverse material flows. For example, the prison, as Foucault sees it, is a territorial machine that works by enclosing and partitioning space, segregating bodies, or again, by connecting them together into larger functional ensembles, coordinating their collective flows, and so on. This is the 'disciplinary' function of the assemblage (that the surveillance assemblage supports and serves as a means).

The enunciative function of an assemblage, on the other hand, is to produce statements. Such an assemblage, at the risk of oversimplifying a complex process, attaches words to things. It is a collective 'attribution' machine that assigns properties ('incorporeal transformations' or events) to bodies (corporeal flows, embodied actions, passions, etc.). For Foucault, among the most significant attributions the enunciative assemblage makes are 'true' and 'normal' (Foucault 1972; Foucault,

Lotringer and Hochroth 1997; Foucault and Rabinow 1997). The surveillance assemblage, in addition to its disciplinary role, is a 'truth machine' that records, identifies, names, and categorizes material processes, and inserts them into a discourse, into a system of knowledge and judgement.

How surveillance works, from this point of view, is a question about how it is actualized in this 'double' assemblage – that is, as a disciplinary machine and a discursive machine; as a distribution of bodies and material flows, and a distribution of properties that measure the subjective states of those bodies. In the prison, Foucault says, the body becomes a 'delinquent' body, an object of the gaze and subject of knowledge; it is in the asylum that one becomes mad, and so on (Foucault 1965, 1975). The two assemblages are really parts of the same assemblage, yet they run parallel to and relatively independent of each other (for example, different properties may be attributed to the same bodies, while different bodies may come to instantiate the same properties). There is no necessary connection, for example, between delinquency and discipline – the disciplinary apparatus extends beyond the prison and is applied to the correction of many other 'abnormalities' besides delinquency. Words and things are not held together by some natural affinity, but by relations of power.

Haggerty and Ericson's definition of the surveillance assemblage describes a two-stage process of deterritorialization (abstraction from a material or immaterial flow) and reterritorialization (reshaping of abstracted materials into specific forms) (Haggerty and Ericson 2000: 606). Speaking ontogenetically, Deleuze and Guattari sometimes refer to this first stage as 'smoothing', which produces a certain uniformity or regularity of elements (in the way, for example, that iron ore is processed into liquid steel); the second stage is striation (or reterritorialization), the moulding of resulting materials into specific fixed objects (a hammer, a sword) (Deleuze and Guattari 1987: 474ff.; Guattari 1995). Immaterial things can deterritorialize too. Ideas, knowledge, affects and images can all be rendered uniform and smooth, as can subjects, identities and personas. Abstraction is a mode of sorting, in the way, for example, words in languages are sorted, impurities or improper usages filtered out, etc. (Bogard 2000; Laporte 2000). Similarly, immaterial flows can be striated. We can point to the commodification of ideas and knowledge in our societies, or to the commercialization of images and affects, for ready examples of how elements of expression are abstracted and reassembled into new, and highly controlled, forms.

The most important dimension of immaterial production from the point of view of surveillance is the production of a subject. A certain subjectivity always develops alongside this assemblage. The surveillance assemblage functioned in the modern age as a means of 'soul training' or self-correction through processes of individualization and normalization. The diagrammatic form of this assemblage, of course, was the panopticon. With postmodernity, the panopticon has been informationalized (see earlier); what once was organized around hierarchical observation is now organized through decoding and recoding of information. There has been a shift to virtual forms of control (simulation, modelling, profiling, etc.). Deleuze describes this change in the diagram of social control as the production of 'dividuals', or partial information objects, rather than 'individuals' (Deleuze 1992: 4). The individualized soul is replaced by fragmented 'data doubles' whose uniform elements are freely recombinable, 'hybrid subjects' who are little more than computer codes (*proactive normalization*). The individual subject is a relic of a productive system that demanded functional unities – it was a rigid, somewhat static form (the product of a 'mould', as Deleuze says). Today, the global system of capital and control demands fluid, flexible, and heterogeneous subjects – subjects that are not moulded once and for all, but capable of finely graded modulations, like partial frequencies that can be isolated and adjusted to fit a multiplicity of acoustic environments (Deleuze 1992: 4). Adaptability is the key criterion for hybrid subjects.

The consequences of these changes have been enormous. The panopticon, however much it became a general mechanism of control in modern society, remained essentially a territorial machine bound to a central hub and a circular form. Social control today is decentralized and shape-shifting. Longstanding divisions between types of labour – industrial, agricultural, service work – have begun to fade, as have distinctions between spaces and times of labour (the home, the office, the shop) (Hardt and Negri 2000, 2004; Hochschild 1997; Zuboff 1988). This does not mean these types of labour and spaces of control have disappeared, any more than it means panoptic control has disappeared in postmodern societies. What has changed is the way information has become their common mode of organization. Much the way that agricultural production was industrialized in the modern age, so today both agriculture and industry have been informationalized. Computers today connect home and work and play, enabling each to enter and mix freely in the space of the other. They are all deterritorializing in information.

Lines of flight

Deleuze and Guattari note that assemblages are basically territorial, that they 'begin by extracting a territory from a decoded milieu' (decoded in the sense of translatable into a different code, language, structured content, etc.) (Deleuze and Guattari 1987: 510). Each assemblage consists of decoded fragments that it recodes as properties or events (normal, true, delinquent, mad). Every assemblage must be described both in terms of its content (what we have called the machinic assemblage) and its expression (the enunciative assemblage). That is, one must examine not only what the assemblage does but also what it says. The panopticon, in Foucault's view, is not simply an assemblage that organizes a physical space of power relations, but also a field of knowledge and discourse relations where truth as a property is produced, specifically the truth of the subject. The power of Foucault's analysis comes from its ability to describe in the most detailed fashion the operation of this assemblage, both from the point of view of how it controls the actions and passions of the prisoner, and how it produces what can be stated or known about him or her.

Territorialization involves staking out a kind of 'event-space' or 'control surface' on which flows are made to pass in a stable fashion. The surveillance assemblage, for example, as a hierarchy of control, establishes parameters for sorting different kinds of flows (flows of actions, feelings, body fluids, money, signs; essentially whatever moves), determining the state of connection or disconnection between these flows and assigning a rank order to them (this is the panoptic assemblage in its widest sense). The work of the assemblage is to trap or capture lines of flight, arrest flows and convert them into reproducible events, like a tape recorder captures sound, or film captures images.[3] The surveillance assemblage is essentially a 'recording' machine (cf. Yurick 1985). In its more advanced forms, it is like a 'pre-recording' machine that can capture performances 'in advance' (in the same sense clones are like pre-recorded life forms, or profiles are pre-recorded statuses or identities) (cf. Bogard 1996), referred to as the 'future anterieur' tense in surveillance by Genosko and Thompson (this volume).

At the same time, Deleuze and Guattari say, assemblages have edges of deterritorialization, like the fluid edges of crystals. 'Lines of flight' cross the surfaces of assemblages and 'carry them away' (Deleuze and Guattari 1987: 9, 510). Flight refers to how assemblages change as an effect of their own organization. Foucault, as previously stated, views power/knowledge relations as simultaneously relations of resistance. Knowledge 'invents' the secret (Foucault 1975); discipline produces its own unruly bodies. In panoptic assemblages, lines of flight are indocile bodies that won't behave, or ungovernable words whose meanings are hidden or will not stay fixed. Deleuze and Guattari sometimes call such forces 'nomadic singularities' or 'non-formalized functions', even non-sense (as a resistant force within language) (Deleuze and Guattari 1987: 511; Deleuze 1990). In a crucial sense, assemblages as a whole are lines of flight. Older organizations of punishment, such as torture or the spectacle, deterritorialize on the panopticon. The panopticon is a line of flight or resistance in relation to these organized forms, a set of virtual, disconnected practices that will later actualize in a new technology of the body and a new model of visibility (Foucault 1977). What we have called rhizomatic surveillance is a convergence of resistant lines that develop immanently within panoptic assemblages (specifically, resistant to limits on recording imposed by space and time, the need for centralized, hierarchical control, etc.). Finally, there are lines of flight immanent to rhizomatic surveillance that take advantage of the decentralized, non-hierarchical nature of information networks – unruly practices like file sharing, decryption, anonymization, use of 'proxies' and simulated identities/locations, 'sousveillance' (surveillance 'from below'), as well as more conventional political forms of resistance to computer monitoring, etc. (Bogard 1996; Gilliom 2005; Haggerty and Ericson 2000; Mann *et al.* 2003a; Mann *et al.* 2003b; Poster 1990).

Assemblages, in short, operate both through capture and flight, territorialization and deterritorialization. Music captured on digital media, for example, can be played anywhere, anytime, copied, shared, sampled, cut, edited, reformatted, distorted, snapped to grids, cleaned, etc. These are territorializations of decoded flows of sounds – in this case, a musical performance – that are in practice singular, irreproducible and tied to their context. How are these territorializations also forms of resistance? In the same way that copying anything challenges its claim to originality or uniqueness, sharing anything resists its claim to be property, or reformatting anything destroys its content. Surveillance is not just about collecting information, but decoding and recoding it, sorting it, altering it, circulating it, re-playing it. All these are simultaneously modes of deterritorialization or flight.

We need to pose an important question about the assemblage: What does the assemblage as a whole resist, from what does it flee? One answer is that an assemblage simply flees itself, or resists the territorialization it imposes on everything else. The surveillance assemblage converts flows into properties or events. These flows get caught up in the assemblage's 'truth machine', that is subject to verification (like recorded sounds or images can be judged for their fidelity to the original or norm). The assemblage, for its part, flees this production of truth; it resists its own recording and verification (the recording process is not recorded). There is a configuration analogous to this in the panopticon, according to Foucault, where power and resistance to power involve the problem of visibility (Foucault 1977). We immediately see that the panopticon's visibility to the prisoner (in the figure of the guard tower) is of an entirely different order than the prisoner's visibility to it; the panopticon's power derives precisely, as Foucault says, from its un-verifiability, whereas the prisoner is subject to verification at any time, to confirmation or disconfirmation by the constant comparison of his individual case record to the norm. 'Visibility is a trap', Foucault says. But this is only true for the prisoner (at least until he or she learns how to evade the system). Technically, the panopticon is always visible (the guard tower's presence is a constant imposition), yet power escapes visibility by escaping its own means of verification; that is, it eludes being seen and recorded by its own tools. It resists being converted into a verifiable event, even while its façade remains visible. If he wishes to subvert panoptic power, the prisoner must adopt a parallel strategy, i.e. remain visible but unrecorded and unverifiable. And he must take advantage of the same tools and strategies that the system of surveillance uses to verify his presence and status within the system (architectural blind spots, detailed observations, etc.) – not so he can become a surveillor, but rather so he can dismantle the surveillor's control of the relation of visibility to verification (cf. Mann 2003). Somehow, the system of control must evolve a way of deterritorializing visibility so that it is not a trap but becomes a line of flight (like Sophie Calle following her subject).

The surveillance assemblage is just one example of how any machine works; that is, by resisting itself or 'breaking down'. Foucault's writing usually depicts the prison in its territorial functions, but he knows that there are always lines of flight that act in multiple ways to deterritorialize it. Internally, every prison is a meshwork of both territorialized and deterritorialized spaces, stabilized and unstable economies. Every prison controls internal communications, but just as certainly develops informal and secret lines of information that it cannot control and indeed must produce to function normally. Again, the very machine constructed to control delinquents must produce them, and not just in an external sense, but immanently to its operation (Foucault 1977). However much of Bentham's panopticon was designed as a closed system, in fact it connected to a state machine, a war machine, a pedagogical machine, a desiring machine, to a host of assemblages that supplied it with raw materials, food, plans, money, publicity, and so forth. From its inception, the prison was tied to flows that provided the material and immaterial inputs necessary for its development, and it produced material and immaterial outputs for the state and wider society, the working bodies, technologies, information, money, etc., they required to function.

Today, many of these connections of the modern prison have been 'informated', a technical transformation begun in the earliest penitentiaries as observations were already converted into 'data', and one that even then already foreshadowed the extension of panoptic systems to the regulation and control of all areas and levels of life ('carceral society', as Foucault describes it, is precisely this deterritorialization of wider society on the prison, and the prison's deterritorialization on wider society, within the sphere of everyday life, or what Hardt and Negri refer to as 'biopolitical production' (Hardt and Negri 2004: xvi)). We are now at a point where this transformation, at least in terms of information flows, renders the distinction 'inside vs. outside the prison' almost useless. Although this development in one sense has made us all prisoners of the surveillance assemblage, it has also made a prisoner of the assemblage itself by threatening to make its operations more transparent and its efforts to profit from information more difficult. It has to set up machines to flee its own capture (encryption, password protection, firewalls, simulation), but those machines are difficult to secure in a networked society where any information refuses to stay locked up for long. As Foucault understood, the techniques of verification developed in the prison are turned back on the prison, which from the beginning becomes the object of public scrutiny and investigation. When these techniques are informated, and then become widely available to the general population – facilitated by the expansion of electronic networks and growing access to computers – the potential for totalizing control grows, but so does the potential for resistance to that control. Dürrenmatt imagined contemporary society as an electronic nightmare of surveillance, where everyone observes the observer of the observer, everyone is watched and recorded by everyone else, and the entire system of verification is given up to a network – a network, however, that contains no more privileged points of access or escape, no more hierarchical control of observation, no more panoptic structuring of visibility (Dürrenmatt 1988).

Against the Orwellian vision of no escape from the surveillance assemblage, the notion of the assemblage as a line of flight might get us beyond our tendency to articulate the problem of resistance to surveillance in juridical or institutional terms; that is, in terms of the very fields it structures, and consider it more immanently, in terms of the assemblage's own liberatory or even democratic potentials. As part of its normal development, the surveillance assemblage develops lines of resistance that exploit the rhizomatic potential of electronic networks, lines that are self-organizing and have little or nothing to do with those networks' legal or political status.

There are many examples of immanent resistance to surveillance that do not take juridical forms. Corporations and the state may ceaselessly monitor everything about their employees and citizens (like parents increasingly do with their children's digital lives), but they also supply them with the very information gathering, interception, sharing, blocking, and editing tools they need to defy that control. Home recording and broadcast technologies challenge industry's domination of the market in music, film and video; global positioning and satellite imaging technologies can pinpoint centres of information control; firewalls can bar access to many kinds of unwanted intrusion; freely available data mining, mapping, copying and encryption tools, all work both for and against bureaucratic systems of control. Then there are all the extra-legal or illegal means made possible by developments of digital technology by which hierarchical systems of information are deconstructed from within today – hacking, cracking, data piracy and file-sharing, network jamming and spamming, wireless telecommunications interception. Immanent conflicts emerge not only in cyberspace, but over the production and control of genetic information and life forms, and not just in legal settings, but in places like farms, where farmers resist loss of control of their seed stock to bio-tech firms that maintain proprietary rights to genetically modified seed. These conflicts revolve around issues of law to be sure – whether engineered genes are property, whether species can be patented, and so forth – but a focus on legal battles obscures deeper antagonisms in the surveillance assemblage itself, between its encoding and decoding, or territorializing and deterritorializing, functions. Mathiesen (1997) has argued that surveillance systems are both panoptic and synoptic – they are not just about the observation of the many by the one, that is, hierarchical power, but the one or the few by the many, decentralized power. Digital media today allow an unprecedented level of scrutiny of the powerful by the powerless, rulers by the ruled, the rich and famous by 'common' people. There has never been another time when the means of surveillance have been so widely distributed in the general population, by the very powers that depend on them for control. In fact, it is the production of a new deterritorialized 'common' by the global surveillance assemblage that constitutes its dominant line of flight today.

The surveillance common

The new 'common', as Hardt and Negri describe it, refers to the hegemony of 'immaterial production' in the postmodern global organization of labour (Hardt and Negri 2004: xv). Information networks increasingly order all sectors of production in the global economy – manufacturing, agriculture and services. Hardt and Negri do not argue that production today has somehow become immaterial, or disappeared, but rather that immaterial forces structure and connect very different spheres of production, that these forces have become hegemonic 'in qualitative terms and have imposed a tendency on other forms of labour and society itself', hence the term 'common' (Hardt and Negri 2004: 109). Just as 150 years ago economic and social production were organized by the 'industrial model', and all forms of labour had to industrialize even though industry in itself accounted for only a small proportion of global output, today production is structured by the information sector of the economy despite its size relative to global production as a whole. Immaterial production is the production of ideas, knowledge, communication, affects and social relations, and today 'labor and society have to informationalize, become intelligent, become communicative, become affective' (Hardt and Negri 2004: 109).[4]

Ultimately, immaterial production is geared not just to the manufacture of goods or services, but to the production and control of life itself. Hardt and Negri borrow Foucault's concept of 'biopower' to name the form of sovereignty that today rules over the new common (Foucault 1978; Hardt and Negri 2000: 18–25).[5] Biopower is the negative form of the common. It refers to a production of life that simultaneously threatens the planet with destruction and death (war, ecological catastrophe, the annihilation of species). Hardt and Negri often describe the rule of biopower as a state of global civil war, governed by exceptionalism and unilateralism in global politics and economics, high-intensity police actions and pre-emptive strikes, and of course networked surveillance. It is what Virilio has called elsewhere a state of 'pure war', or what Baudrillard has referred to as virtual, simulated war (Baudrillard 1995a; Virilio 1997). Whatever its name, the dominant climate of the new common is fear, however broadly that term is defined, accompanied by the need for safety and security (or the absence of risk) (Beck 1992, 1999). In postmodernity, the need for security replaces defence as the moral justification for global police/surveillance interventions of all kinds, in military matters to be sure, but also in economic, political and cultural affairs, in matters of health, sexuality, education, entertainment, and so on. 'War' becomes the common framework through which all problems are recognized and addressed, both in the relation of states to other states, but of states to their own populations as well. In fact, when it comes to the multiplicity of wars in postmodernity, the old categories of international or intra-national conflict no longer apply. The regime of biopower, like the modern system of penality, has no walls and is truly a global form of sovereignty; it dismantles the old oppositions between public and private spheres, erases the economic and political boundaries between states, and aims at the absolute elimination of risk in advance through the development of sophisticated communications and information gathering and decoding technologies; that is, through networks of surveillance and control. Didier Bigo discusses this at length in this volume.

The new common, however, organized by biopower and subject to the controls of networked surveillance, also has liberatory and democratic potentials, which Hardt and Negri locate in what they call 'biopolitical production', the production of the 'multitude' (which for them has replaced industrial labour as the postmodern force of revolutionary change) (Hardt and Negri 2004). Biopolitical production is not biopower, although it is not the opposite of biopower either. Both engage the production of life and social relations in their entirety, but in very different ways. Hardt and Negri write, 'Biopower stands above society, transcendent, as a sovereign authority and imposes its order. Biopolitical production, in contrast, is immanent to society and creates social relations and forms through collaborative forms of labor' (Hardt and Negri 2004: 94–5). Biopower is the new form of empire, whereas biopolitical production is the new form of resistance to empire. Both are effects of changes in the organization of production brought about by the advent of postmodern systems of control; that is, by transformations in the surveillance assemblage and the expansion of information networks. In arguments reminiscent of Marx that the development of the means of global communication creates the potential for the revolutionary organization of labour, they show how global information systems have destabilized not only traditional forms of private property and have cut across class divisions, but also race, gender and other hierarchies, producing a common 'poverty' from which new forms of democratic participation and social creativity can emerge. It is as if biopower, the system of sovereign control supported by global surveillance and the culture of war and fear, had produced the very communicative and geopolitical conditions necessary for the development of a shared humanity. Hardt and Negri are quick to point out, however, that the idea of a new 'common' does not imply the sameness of its elements or some transcendent identity standing over society, but rather consists of singularities whose differences constitute a heterogeneous multiplicity capable of spontaneous organization and the power to deconstruct the global sovereign regime of biopower (Hardt and Negri 2004: 128–9). Today, despite differences of class, race, gender, nation, occupation, language, religion, age, etc., new forms of resistance are arising grounded in the common subjection of the global population to the imperatives of biopower, and its common transformation of labour into a global network of informated production.

Ironically, the surveillance assemblage has opened a new de-territorialized space of communication that with time may undermine the regime of global biopower. Biopower depends on the control of information, but also on the rhizomatic qualities of networks to facilitate global production and coordinate the global division of labour. These are contradictory ends, but beyond that, they point to a new refuge from power in networks that is absent in panoptic systems. In the latter, one had to find a space within a confined area where one could hide in plain sight. In the former, one can hide in all the multiplicity of ways information provides, and the possibilities of resistance are greatly expanded.

Safety in the machine

According to Guattari, we are today at a kind of crossroads, where the machine is abhorred or seen as a kind of curse that will one day destroy humanity, and which we cannot connect to an ethical project (Guattari 1990). The history of the machine, its use in war and the production of weapons, its effects on the environment, and its uses for social control and discipline, for generating information on us, all these reinforce this view. The question, he asks, is whether we must react to these developments by looking backward for models of how we might somehow regain control of machinic forces and redirect them from a space they do not dominate to more ethical ends; or whether we must begin immanently, within the machinic forces that dominate the present and seek within them potentials for lines of flight or possibilities of resistance.

In *The Question Concerning Technology*, Heidegger challenges the nihilism that both infects and is produced by our technological understanding of Being (Heidegger 1977). The essence of technology he calls 'enframing', which converts the Earth into 'standing reserve' and subjects it to instrumental control. The more the Earth resists this control, because it is not passive in relation to it, the more the forces of technology attempt to master it. In Heidegger's view, technological mastery of the Earth poses an ultimate danger, the destruction of nature. His concern, however, is more ontological than ecological. For Heidegger, the question concerning technology points beyond enframing and its dangers to a 'saving power', a potential for opening that 'in no way confines us to a stultified compulsion to push on blindly with technology or, what comes to the same thing, to rebel helplessly against it'. He promises that 'when we once open ourselves expressly to the essence of technology, we find ourselves unexpectedly taken to a freeing claim' (Heidegger 1977).

For Heidegger, as technology reveals its essence as enframing, it also reveals an ontological power of 'unmasking' within *dasein*. As we come to understand technology, through the very manner in which it reveals itself to us, we gain the power to refuse its domination over us. Heidegger never simply rejects technology. He says:

it would be foolish to attack technology blindly. It would be shortsighted to condemn it as the work of the devil. We depend on technical devices; they even challenge us to ever greater advances … We can affirm the unavoidable use of technical devices, and also deny them the right to dominate us, and so to warp, confuse, and lay waste our nature (Heidegger 1977).

Paradoxically, the technological understanding of being as enframing, which for Heidegger is something that is always already 'given' to us immanently, allows us to step outside that understanding. 'The self same danger is, when it is as the danger, the saving power' (Heidegger 1977). Enframing is also the power of revealing, the bringing into the open of being.

Guattari rejects most of this view in developing his notion of the 'machine', although he retains the idea of a saving power, in the form of an ethico-aesthetic project. The machine, for Guattari, is not equivalent to 'technology'. Technologies are always social products, but machines, at their most abstract level, are simply flows and breaks of matter and energy. Neither are machines 'mechanisms'. Guattari develops a philosophical machinism that is non-mechanist, that would not reduce the idea of a machine to a simple construction *partes extra partes* (Guattari and Genosko 1996). We think that humans control machines, but in fact machines only require humans as catalysts, not as creators. They are not organic or a form of life, although collectively they have a kind of 'non-organic life', a 'self-organization' or 'phylogenetic line of development' different from that of the biomass (cf. also De

Landa 1991). Guattari thus rejects vitalist philosophies that would assimilate the machine to living beings and instead assigns it its own singular status. And although Guattari accepts the idea of machinic self-organization, he does not define this cybernetically as 'feedback'. Finally, as I have said, he departs from philosophical notions of *techné* that link its saving powers to an ontological ground of 'unmasking', as in Heidegger. Throughout all these positions, Guattari proposes a concept of 'machinic heterogenesis' that would attempt to view the machine not from these limited perspectives, but in its complex totality, in its 'technological, social, semiotic and axiological avatars', a project that will involve a basic rethinking of what a machine is (Guattari and Genosko 1996). Ultimately, for Guattari, it is *'flows in their totality, flows and breaks of flows, material and immaterial, that constitute the sphere of the machinic*, distinct from the biosphere', with its own unique modes of self-organization, growth, and development (Guattari and Genosko 1996, emphasis added).

It is from this idea of the machine, as a heterogeneous multiplicity, that the notion of a surveillance 'assemblage' derives. We must understand this as a machinic assemblage, not simply a technology. It has no Heidegerrian 'essence', however much it appears as the perfect example of both enframing (instrumental control) and unmasking. The 'safety' in the machine Guattari refers to is not about its power to unmask. To pose the problem in these terms is to think from the logic of the system of control itself, which promises us safety at the price of our anonymity, security in exchange for revealing every secret, for recording every communication, testing everything for everything. Unmasking is the surveillance assemblage works. If we interpreted Sophie Calle's experiment in surveillance as an example of the saving power of unmasking, however much we thought it differed from the unmasking powers of states and corporations, this would be a very bad interpretation indeed.

Guattari's safety in the machine rather lies in its capacity to deterritorialize. Machines, in other words, are rhizomes – they are not closed systems. Machinic assemblages always have an immanent 'outside', a decoded milieu whose fragments they capture and recode, but which in turn also changes the nature of the assemblage. The question is: what is 'outside' the global surveillance assemblage today? (Anything?). And is there a sense in which we can say this 'outside' is immanent to how the assemblage organizes itself? Once again we come to the problem of networks (cf. Castells 1996, 2004; Hardt and Negri 2004). If an information network is a rhizome, then information must be able to travel in all directions, directly or indirectly, from every node to every other node. And this must be true in practice, not just in theory or in principle. Guattari's claim is that every machinic assemblage can and must, in a practical sense, be an open, self-organizing system. The panoptic assemblage expands from the prison to work, home, school, the street, etc., always a new space, a new outside, to observe and control. When the panoptic assemblage becomes a network, the outside consists of all the virtual connections among nodes the assemblage has yet to identify and monitor.

Virtual relations, Deleuze and Guattari say, are real, not merely possible or imaginary, relations. They are 'available', they can be 'selected' and actualized, and are thus connected to an ethico-aesthetic project. It has been said, 'information wants to be free'. Information, once locked up in physical files, deterritorializes on the network and the new technologies of recording and playback. By the network's own logic, all channels of information must be accessible, and it develops and organizes the means to achieve this. Even the surveillance assemblage – especially the surveillance assemblage – wants information to be free (for itself at least). If surveillance is an ethico-aesthetic project and not merely a technology of control, that project today involves taking advantage of the rhizomatic potential of networks and expanding the range of access to information to everyone, not just the powers that police it. As Lyotard said years ago, power in postmodernity is about access to the data banks (Lyotard 1984).

Free access to data *on* you, but not *by* you, is the goal of police (corporate, state) control of surveillance networks: an impossible task made more impossible by the rhizomatic qualities of the network, which always spawns new paths for information to flow. The surveillance assemblage would like to close itself off from the 'outside', but unfortunately the outside is where it must place its machines. Not only every actual path of information must be monitored, but every virtual one as well. Cameras watching every space (CCTV). A computer for everyone, or better, a computer in everyone! Little data banks in your cells and on your DNA (nanotechnology). Network everything together, connect everything. That's not just the dream but the actual practice of the surveillance assemblage. The 'outside' of the assemblage is everything it does and must connect to – any concept of rhizomatic surveillance, if we are not to conflate it with totalizing control, must include this paradoxical reference to the outside.

Hardt and Negri have another name for the immanent 'outside' of surveillance networks. They call it the sphere of 'biopolitical production', the production of everyday life, the creative energy of the 'multitude' (their word for the new global information common). The multitude is a product of the network, in the same sense delinquency is a product of the prison, and at the same time a force of resistance to it. The network never perfectly captures this energy, just as digital information can never perfectly capture a musical performance. We say rather that the recording deterritorializes on the performance. The recording machine 'opens' to the performance, it changes its organization to (more truly, more 'realistically') capture the performance, evolving from a spatial machine (for example, the acoustic design of the music hall), into a digital machine (sampling and sequencing software, computerized sound). Really, it is the performance – the singularity of the performance – that captures the recording, not vice versa. The entire recording machinery must follow its lead, just like Sophie Calle must follow the lead of her traveller, who in turn flees something else. (Who knows what? His job, his lover, his boredom? It doesn't matter to Calle.) In the process, this man unwittingly captures her, causes her to track him. In the same way, try as it may, a surveillance network cannot capture biopolitical production. Just the reverse, it deterritorializes on it. Biopolitical production, the production of life, causes it to change its organization. No longer workable as a form of hierarchical control, the network has to become a rhizome, like the multitude. But in changing into a rhizome, it is really biopolitical production, the multitude that captures the network. The latter loses its 'police powers'. We could look at it this way: the surveillance assemblage changes from a spatial to a digital form of control (from the panopticon to the network) to more truly capture the complexities of biopolitical production. The assemblage opens into a network to map the rhizomatic qualities of the multitude. And this openness, which has nothing to do with unmasking, is the saving power of the network, and the surveillance assemblage.

We need not be so abstract. Everyone knows that information networks cannot be policed in the old ways, and perhaps they cannot be policed at all. There are too many virtual connections, too many observers of observers, too many points of recording: all products, ironically, of the networks themselves. Information wants to be free. The surveillance assemblage, I argued years ago, was already finding creative ways around the obvious limitations of network control. Networks have too many holes, too many openings; passwords can be cracked, software can be hacked, files shared, data banks raided. Networks have radical potentials to democratize power, to wrest control of information from the state and media, to circumvent hierarchies and laws. The surveillance assemblage, even as a network, has probably outlived its usefulness and is morphing into a simulation assemblage. It is, in other words, no longer deterritorializing on the multitude, but on models of the multitude, models of biopolitical production. Modelling, simulation, as Baudrillard saw, is today the preferred method of the police (Baudrillard 1995b). That is the surveillance assemblage's current line of flight from the network.

Notes

1 It is not surprising that electronic networks today have tremendous potential as both technologies of identification and anonymity. That surveillance may enhance anonymity is not really such a strange idea, if we remember that 'watching over' someone can also mean to shield him or her from another's gaze. I have written in another context (Bogard 1996) how surveillance is a 'jamming' as much as 'sensing' technology, i.e. it blocks information as well as captures it (caller ID on your phone, for example, collects information on a caller in order to screen out unwanted calls, an effective jamming device against advertisers – but of course also a technology used by advertisers to identify and screen their customers).
2 Increasingly, rhizomatic models are used to design Internet file-sharing networks because they are more efficient than tree or arborescent models (cf. Loban 2004) analysis of the relative speed advantage and low failure rate of decentralized networks like Gnutella and Kazaa over eDonkey or OpenNap, which employ centralized distribution systems).
3 I prefer the term 'event' to 'property' since it carries more of a temporal emphasis (e.g. 'delinquent' signifies not just a static feature of something, but a series of actions or passions defined as abnormal).
4 Affective labour, for instance, is labour that produces feelings of comfort, security, excitement, and so on. We can see this labour in the work of service workers, care providers, and other occupations where the attitude and character of employees, as well their communicative skills and 'prosocial' behaviour, are qualifications for work.
5 Although 'biopower' is not equivalent to the surveillance assemblage, the surveillance and simulation of life processes are certainly at its foundation. The control and organization of information are at the root of genetic science, food science, the medicalization of culture, the regulation and commercialization of risk, the control of deviance. This list today is virtually endless as more aspects of life find themselves recorded and translated into models for the production of more life.

References

Baudrillard, J. (1990) *Seduction* (New York: St. Martin's Press).
Baudrillard, J. (1995a) *The Gulf War Did Not Take Place* (Bloomington: Indiana University Press).

Baudrillard, J. (1995b) *Simulacra and Simulation* (Ann Arbor: University of Michigan Press).

Beck, U. (1992) *Risk Society: Towards a New Modernity* (London and Newbury Park, CA: Sage).

Beck, U. (1999) *World Risk Society* (Malden, MA: Polity Press).

Bogard, W. (1996) *The Simulation of Surveillance: Hyper-Control in Telematic Societies* (New York: Cambridge University Press).

Bogard, W. (2000) 'Smoothing Machines and the Constitution of Society', *Cultural Studies,* 14 (2), 269–95.

Calle, S. and Baudrillard, J. (1983) *Suite Vénitienne* (Paris: Editions de l'Etoile).

Castells, M. (1996) *The Rise of the Network Society* (Cambridge, MA and Oxford: Blackwell).

Castells, M. (2004) *The Network Society: A Cross-Cultural Perspective* (Cheltenham and Northampton, MA: Edward Elgar).

Davis, M. (1998) *Ecology of Fear: Los Angeles and the Imagination of Disaster* (New York: Metropolitan).

De Landa, M. (1991) *War in the Age of Intelligent Machines* (New York: Zone).

De Landa, M. (1997) *A Thousand Years of Nonlinear History* (New York: Zone).

Deleuze, G. (1990) *The Logic of Sense* (New York: Columbia University Press).

Deleuze, G. (1992) 'Postscript on the Societies of Control', *October,* 59 (Winter), 3–7.

Deleuze, G. and Guattari, F. (1983) *Anti-Oedipus: Capitalism and Schizophrenia* (Minneapolis: University of Minnesota Press).

Deleuze, G. and Guattari, F. (1987) *A Thousand Plateaus: Capitalism and Schizophrenia* (Minneapolis: University of Minnesota Press).

Der Derian, J. (1992) *Antidiplomacy: Spies, Terror, Speed, and War* (Cambridge, MA: Blackwell).

Dürrenmatt, F. (1988) *The Assignment, or, on the Observing of the Observer of the Observers* (New York: Random House).

Elmer, G. (2003) 'A Diagram of Panoptic Surveillance', *New Media and Society,* 5, 231–47.

Foucault, M. (1965) *Madness and Civilization: A History of Insanity in the Age of Reason* (New York: Pantheon).

Foucault, M. (1972) *The Archaeology of Knowledge* (New York: Harper and Row).

Foucault, M. (1975) *The Birth of the Clinic: An Archaeology of Medical Perception* (New York: Vintage).

Foucault, M. (1977) *Discipline and Punish: The Birth of the Prison* (New York: Pantheon).

Foucault, M. (1978) *The History of Sexuality* (New York: Pantheon).

Foucault, M. and Gordon, C. (1980) *Power/Knowledge: Selected Interviews and Other Writings, 1972–1977* (New York: Pantheon).

Foucault, M., Lotringer, S. and Hochroth, L. (1997) *The Politics of Truth* (New York: Semiotext(e)).

Foucault, M. and Rabinow, P. (1997) *Ethics: Subjectivity and Truth* (New York: New Press).

Gilliom, J. (2005) 'Resisting Surveillance', *Social Text*, 23 (2), 71–83.

Guattari, F. (1990) 'On Machines', *Journal of Philosophy and the Visual Arts*, 6, 8–17.

Guattari, F. (1995) *Chaosmosis: An Ethico-Aesthetic Paradigm* (Bloomington, IN: Indiana University Press)

Guattari, F. and Genosko, G. (1996) *The Guattari Reader* (Oxford and Cambridge, MA: Blackwell).

Haggerty, K.D. and Ericson, R.V. (2000) 'The Surveillant Assemblage', *British Journal of Sociology*, 51 (4), 605–22.

Hardt, M., and Negri, A. (2000) *Empire* (Cambridge, MA: Harvard University Press).

Hardt, M., and Negri, A. (2004) *Multitude: War and Democracy in the Age of Empire* (New York: Penguin Press).

Heidegger, M. (1977) *The Question Concerning Technology, and Other Essays* (New York: Harper and Row).

Hochschild, A.R. (1997) *The Time Bind: When Work Becomes Home and Home Becomes Work* (New York: Metropolitan).

Koskela, H. (2000) '"The Gaze Without Eyes": Video-Surveillance and the Changing Nature of Urban Space', *Progress in Human Geography*, 24, 243–65.

Laporte, D. (2000) *History of Shit* (Cambridge, MA: MIT Press).

Lianos, M. (2003) 'Social Control After Foucault', *Surveillance and Society*, 1 (3), 412–30. Available at: http://www.surveillance-andsociety.org/articles1(3)/AfterFoucault.pdf.

Loban, B. (2004) 'Between Trees and Rhizomes', *First Monday*, 9 (10). Available at: http://www.firstmonday.org/issues/issue9_10/loban/#14.

Lyon, D. (1994) *The Electronic Eye: The Rise of Surveillance Society* (Minneapolis: University of Minneapolis Press).

Lyon, D. (2001) *Surveillance Society: Monitoring Everyday Life* (Buckingham and Philadelphia: Open University Press).

Lyon, D. (2002) 'Everyday Surveillance: Personal Data and Social Classification', *Information, Communication and Society*, 5, 242–57.

Lyon, D. (2004) 'Globalizing Surveillance: Comparative and Sociological Perspectives', *International Sociology*, 19, 135–49.

Lyotard, J.F. (1984) *The Postmodern Condition: A Report on Knowledge* (Minneapolis: University of Minnesota Press).

Mann, S., Fung, J., Federman, M. and Baccanico, G. (2003a) 'PanopDecon: Deconstructing, Decontaminating, and Decontextualizing Panopticism in the Postcyborg Era', *Surveillance and Society*, 1 (3), 375–98. Available at: http://www.surveillance-and-society.org/articles1(3)/PanopDecon.pdf.

Mann, S., Nolan, J. and Wellman, B. (2003b) 'Sousveillance: Inventing and Using Wearable Computing Devices for Data Collection in Surveillance Environments', *Surveillance and Society*, 1 (3), 331–35. Available at: http://www.surveillance-and-society.org/articles1(3)/sousveillance.pdf.

Mathiesen, T. (1997) 'The Viewer Society: Michel Foucault's "Panopticon" Revisited', *Theoretical Criminology*, 1 (2), 215–33.

Poster, M. (1990) *The Mode of Information: Poststructuralism and Social Context* (Chicago: University of Chicago Press).

Virilio, P. (1994) *The Vision Machine* (Bloomington, IN: Indiana University Press)

Virilio, P. (1997) *Pure War* (New York: Semiotext(e)).

Virilio, P. (2000) *The Information Bomb* (London and New York: Verso).

Yurick, S. (1985) *Behold Metatron, The Recording Angel* (New York: Semiotext(e)).

Zuboff, S. (1988) *In the Age of the Smart Machine: The Future of Work and Power* (New York: Basic).

Chapter 6

Tense theory: the temporalities of surveillance

Gary Genosko and Scott Thompson

This chapter extrapolates from grammars of time in language, that is, tense and aspect, in order to investigate the theoretical prospects of questions concerning temporal emphases in the surveillance literature. This chapter does not provide lessons in tense and aspect, however, because the deployment of tense is towards the goal of critically excavating and then soothing tensions. The past, present and future of theorizing surveillance draw on French and English tenses and temporal orientations in order to point out imbalances in the secondary literature, and suggest new directions for thought.

Theory profits from the context of history. Research on surveillance technologies is troubled by the constant development of 'new' technologies, the effect of which, a heavy protentive leaning, has been to displace historical analysis. Nonetheless, it is safe to conclude that much can be learned from the history of surveillance, especially the pre-computerized near past. A critical analysis of the discourses of a pre-computerized near past, meticulously applied in specific locales in the name of an increasingly intrusive and transformative social control, can offer incredibly informative insights into not only the development of current social environments but also to the lasting social threads of surveillance technologies. We will give one example of such a case study of social sorting (Lyon 2003) leading to distorted constitutions of identity in the form of current research we are undertaking on the administrative surveillance of alcohol in Ontario between 1927 and 1962. We would like this to serve as a tool, horizontally embedded across our discussions of the three tenses, with which to turn the idea of the computer as the key technology changing social relations in the society of surveillance towards another, earlier set of infrastructures where individuals and communities met (Bowker and Star 2000: 33).

First, we take up the trouble of apprehending history within certain strains of surveillance literature; then, we turn to the present, a tense fragmented and pulverized into all too fascinating bits – the temporality of the postmodern condition itself – further degraded by ever-increasing technological claims on its so-called reality. Finally, the *futur antérieur* (the future perfect), whose vividness is troubling because it feeds technological determinism and an alarming comprehensiveness, the likes of which have been anticipated in dystopian fiction (Kafka, Orwell, and Dick) and historical studies of total societies, according to Maria Los. We are not alone in this temporal turn, as we find Greg Elmer and Andy Opel (in this volume), among others, probing the political logic of 'pre-emption' at the limits of surveillance.

A (troubled) past

The challenges of history have at times bewitched theorists of surveillance. Surveillance has many symbolic beginnings; I do not want to focus on these. Instead, it is the narrow, winding, etymological trails of key concepts, for example, that provide a preliminary symptom. Take the conceptual innovation of 'datavelliance'. Widely attributed to Roger Clarke (1988, 2003) by many key figures in the field (from Gandy to Lyon and beyond) and claimed as an original coinage by him dating from the mid-1980s, this concept, however, has deeper roots. Clarke's neologism combined data and surveillance in order to describe 'the systematic monitoring of people's actions or communications through the application of information technology' (1988: 500). His key point was that this monitoring had become automated and as a consequence physical surveillance would be supplanted by the ensemble of rapidly accumulating, technologically enabled techniques. But already in 1973 the conceptual innovation of dataveillance was used by Donald R. Davis, then editor of the *Columbia Human Rights Law Review*. Indeed, it appears in the title of the proceedings of the journal's symposium from the same year on 'Surveillance, Dataveillance and Personal Freedoms: Use and Abuse of Information Technology'. The neologism is, however, attributable to Davis himself, since he used it in his contribution. He wrote:

The computer and the related science of cybernetics permit the manipulation and management of vast quantities of disparate bits of information and afford government officials the ability to conduct 'dataveillance' (review presently stored information on a particular subject) for the purpose of retrieving, collating or evaluating those bits of information relevant to the subject of the records check (Davis 1973: 124).

I do not wish to belabour the similarities of concern across the years expressed by Davis and Clarke about how the means of consolidating data furthers multi-purpose electronic monitoring. It is, after all, just a symptom, perhaps, not even the sort one is supposed to enjoy. The fact that we find the coinage already in Davis actually helps us very little because it does not offer an escape from the supposition that dataveillance is a feature of computerization (essentially automated administrative surveillance enabled through techniques integrating data, authenticating transactions, and exercising enforcing functions through file-matching, clustering, factor analyses, etc.), and an evolving creature of IT, focused on both individuals and groups (Gandy 1993: 71), with disciplinary consequences. This symptom of a troubled past is just the sort of disturbance that helps us refocus our attention, despite the traumas of grammar that haunt many of our own personal histories.

Here is a brief description of an historical case study concerning the administration of alcohol in Ontario from 1927 to 1962. From its inception in 1927, The Liquor Control Board of Ontario (LCBO) was primarily concerned with the governmental control of liquor rather than its sale for profit. It is more than evident to us that alcohol and profit do not mix. Moreover, control, ultimately leading to self-control, was a compromise with temperance values. To this end the LCBO created technologies for capturing transnationally generated data at its retail outlets for all purchases of liquor in the province, linking types of products, amounts and frequency of purchase to individual names and addresses. One such technology was the Permit Book, a kind of passport recording details of each purchase of alcohol. One copy of this book was held by the permit holder, another by the vendor (permits were geographic and purchase-type specific) and the third was sent to the Permit Department in Toronto, to be continually updated with any classifications or limitations through the submission of daily records by vendors around the province. There were many different types of permits, each with maximum quantity stipulations, but subject to vendor discretion based on research findings, and in conformity with the overriding dictate of social control leading to self-control. The stamps of individual LCBO employees imprinted on the Permit Books also allowed for the administrative surveillance of staff in case of retail irregularities (gaol supervisors themselves were subject to mutual supervision in the fluid dynamic of power automatically functioning in panopticism, as Kevin Haggerty reminds us in this volume by interrogating the principle of hierarchy in panoptic thought). Tracking and classification of consumers were intensive and continuous. This was both enabling for the purpose of permit renewal, and restrictive, given that the data generated were used to create profiles of drinkers around their fitness *vis-à-vis* income, employment, consumption habits, and/or deviancy. The latter would then be disciplined by being placed on the Interdiction List (known informally as the 'Drunk List' and through its racialization as the 'Indian List'). Files on interdicted persons constituting problem cases contained information gathered from multiple institutional sources; already, then, file matching was at work across different institutions since the LCBO shared files with the provincial police, municipalities and aid organizations. The massive bureaucratic apparatus of investigation, classification and analytic operations undertaken by the LCBO was facilitated by the use of Hollerith punch-card technology. But vendors, too, were subject to surveillance. The purchase order made possible the individual surveillance of vendors at the local level. The original purchase order forms were to be filled out by the staff of the Liquor Control Board stores, signed by the permittee, then stamped 'Endorsed' with an individually numbered stamp, traceable to the local employee who filled the order. The Board issued individualized stamps to all staff who filled orders and kept detailed records of who was 'operating each stamp' as a means of vendor identification (LCBO Circular 557.1928).

The social sorts that interest us in this project are primarily around race, specifically the constructed figure of the 'drunken Indian'. This was a category with dramatic transformative potential since the interdiction of white drinkers could lead to the conversion of their private abodes to public property for the purposes of criminal investigations under the Liquor Control Act, thus 'Indianizing' them by rendering private property into a kind of 'reserve' land. A specific form of alcohol behaviour (pronounced in cases where First Nations' land was adjacent to small towns with LCBO outlets) was produced by provincial and federal legislation; since alcohol had to be consumed on private property, and reserve land was public property, any drinking on the reserve was by definition illegal. Thus, public drinking became common for First Nations persons. However, even after First Nations people were granted the legal right to purchase alcohol in 1951, and before that time, when they technically acquired the right to purchase alcohol by giving up their treaty rights (which was known by the sinister term as enfranchisement[1]), this did not mean they would be served by their local LCBO vendors. Any 'Indian-looking' person was considered suspect and thus by dint of classification a potential problem drinker (which included geography since First Nations persons living in urban centres could be excluded by that fact alone). Individuals and First Nations Bands were required to petition for wet status from the early 1950s into the 1960s.

Engaging in case studies of this kind, we are suggesting, has the potential to revalorize the past in surveillance theory and provide conditions for a reconception of the pre-computer era as a resource of rich data on surveillance systems and technologies. Our preliminary research has already provided insights into many areas of theory, including of course questions concerning temporal emphasis within surveillance literature. We are not claiming that Hollerith technology has been ignored (Elmer 2004) or that social historians working on specific technologies have not at all provided surveillance theorists with rich historical case studies (Torpey 2000).

A (fragmented) present

What of the present then? What lurks there is a vividness, used by Fredric Jameson to describe the depthless, perpetual present of the postmodern moment in which an intensification occurs that isolates the signifier, rendering it more literal and more vivid, yet disconnected from the other signifiers that give it an identity. What we want to regain from Jameson (1991: 24) is his subtle appreciation of the effects of tense, a critical practice he learned from Jean-Paul Sartre. In French, the choice of tense has 'characteristic effects' from which crises of temporal organization may be diagnosed. This occurs when French is transposed into the analysis of English texts where those same tenses either do not exist or only do so in awkward forms. Jameson was actually stronger on the question of the temporal organization of postmodernity than on the spatial analysis for which he is best known.

In a period in which the 'timeless time' of the network (Castells 2000: 494) and the immediacy of 'real time'[2] dominate our technological languages, Jameson's diagnosis seems out of step. But thinking of surveillance today in the present means confronting the broken, stranded presents of a temporal disunity, shining with an eerie glossiness, in every claim on immediacy and contemporaneity in the temporal return of a 'real' whose most salient feature is its utter constructedness. A modifier like 'real' draws attention to the non-reality of the very thing it purports to ground, as in 'time' or 'TV' (Poster 2001: 78–9).

The temporal disunity of the postmodern present is explained semiologically by Jameson in terms of the breakdown of the means by which meaning is generated. Jameson focuses on the relationship between signifiers whose value is based solely on what each is not, that is, in terms of their negative, differential, interdependencies (namely, syntagmatic or linear chains of signifiers). Meaning is an effect produced in the passage from signifier to signifier; the meaning effect is the signified generated through interdependent difference. When the very source of a signifier's identity is torn asunder, when it is no longer linked in a chain of signifiers, the meaning effect is no longer projectable, and the signifieds (concepts) of language thus wane. What emerges in their passing are signifiers in isolation. A new intensity accrues to these stranded signifiers as they assume a 'pure materiality' and begin to hum and glow with a strange power. Jameson (1991: 27) describes them as 'pure unrelated presents in time'. These unrelated presents are incapable of solidifying and unifying a past and future, which under normal conditions of language and the hermeneutic circle is an active function. When the temporal horizon suddenly contracts and the present breaks apart, it becomes separated from understanding (tradition, anticipation, etc.): 'thereby isolated, that present suddenly engulfs the subject with indescribable vividness, a materiality of perception properly overwhelming, which effectively dramatizes the power of the material – or better still, the literal – signifier in isolation' (Jameson 1991: 27). Such vividness is described in aesthetic terms as 'affective', 'hallucinatory', or 'mesmerizing'. In negative terms these effects are schizophrenizing and terrifying; yet positively they produce euphoria and exhiliration. What Jameson proceeds to do is derive a new aesthetics of postmodernism from them in which the 'vivid perception of radical difference is in and of itself a new mode of grasping what used to be called relationship: something for which the word collage is still only a very feeble name' (Jameson 1991: 31).

Let us turn to our early pre-computer liquor control example. Previously in Ontario when a liquor permit holder went to purchase liquor, a purchase order form was required to be filled out. This form contained a formal declaration of a request for liquor that had to be signed by the permit holder and listed the type of liquor requested, amount of liquor requested, the date and the individual's permit book number. These forms were reviewed by the store vendors or permit endorsers along with an individual's liquor permit, and if approved, the order would then be filled, and the original purchase order form was filed at the LCBO head office in Toronto (LCBO Circular 851.1929).

Here, in the LCBO's purchase order form, the present is frozen and broken out of time; dated, signed and stamped. The actions of both the purchaser and the vendor were recorded within these forms and filed for later review, to be retrieved as needed by the Board. From these simple documents almost nothing can be understood of either the permittee's purchase behaviour or the vendor's selling behaviour; all depth and identity of the present is lost in this fragmented version of events. However, the Board saw these fragments of the present as the only means of identifying those involved in sales 'irregularities' (LCBO Circular 557.1928). In these cases the future anterior is introduced, though the event was not captured as such, that is, it remains known, but not visible, outside the frame. The fragment can be understood as a 'pregnant' clue, to which meaning is given after the event. The Board consistently used these forms when they needed to recreate the 'meanings' behind purchase behaviour. The 'single frames' of the purchase form allowed the Board to use these limited fragments of the present as a kind of flip-book of 'evidence against the purchaser' or a means of protection for themselves 'should a complaint be lodged' (LCBO Manual to Vendors 1951).

Now consider the 'fragmentation' of the present, as it is exemplified in our LCBO example, as an insight into the theoretical understanding of 'real time'. Real time conjures the event through so-called revolutions in immediacy and directness, in tele-presence or rather fragmented tele-presents. Real time observation or coverage takes place in the 'present tense, moment-by-moment, deleting ... any sense of a criticizable or even interpretable history of past events' (Murri 2002: 496). Real time is a pollutant, a by-product of the infosphere's speed (Virilio 1996). It causes a condensation of the past and future in a strange durationlessness. Real time kills '"present time" by isolating it from its here and now, in favour of a commutative elsewhere that no longer has anything to do with our "concrete presence" in the world,' as Paul Virilio puts it (1997: 10–11). For Virilio, real time hammers the final nail in the coffin of the present: 'Defining the present in isolation is tantamount to murdering it' (Virilio 1993). The ubiquitous nowness of tele-presence is an affront to lived, phenomenological time. If there is a parallel aesthetics of real time, Virilio simply suggests that presentification is the vivid sameness of commutable nows rather than a perception of difference, but it is a new perception nonetheless. Like Jameson, Virilio associates this predicament with strangeness and mystery, and considers it not to be the source of a new aesthetics (the paradigm of video art as the postmodern form) but, rather, a kind of subjugation of embodied subjectivity.

For the LCBO, understanding only comes after the implication of a user, or after the threat of an accuser. It is from these actions that 'meaning' is returned to the fragmented present. Other examples of this can be found in the widespread exploration of the aesthetic dimensions of the surveillance camera by artists and theorists engaging the future anterior as aesthetic style (Pauleit 2002: 474). In these cases 'presents' (sometimes called stills or videograms) are extracted or cut from a surveillance recording and visibly maintain their time and place signatures. The stills used by Jamie Wagg of the toddler James Bulger shows one of the older boys, eventually convicted of his murder, taking the younger boy's hand (ultimately leading him to his death); Princess Diana passes through the revolving doors of the Hotel Ritz on her way to the car in which she would meet her death (Pauleit 2002: 471). The completed future floods into an image in which there is nothing yet wrong (safety) and that is still stamped with a specific, fragmented present (Cousins 2002: 487): 'The "time" of the security camera lies always in the future of itself; in the role it will play after an event' (Cousins 2002: 488–9). Security as the perfected future displaces the safety of the visible present. But the completed future is the unsafe sense of the video image.

A future (past)

Finally, we go back to the future. One of the most important dimensions of post-panoptic theory has involved the use of the French *futur antérieur*, the expression of a future about which one can speak definitely because it is already past. This tense has helped a diverse range of thinkers to fuse simulation and surveillance through such ideas as the anterior finality (a perfected future) of the code and front-loaded data generating scenarios in advance of their actual occurrence. Indeed, new media artists have also referred to this tense in explicating the 'fertile moments' in CCTV evidence around traumatic events not themselves recorded but, in a way, telescoped in rewind. This is the most advanced, that is, the most inflected, temporal thought at play in surveillance today and it has vivified its theoretical outlook.

Like many of Jean Baudrillard's richest concepts, simulation is a phenomenon of absorption – the primary absorption being that of the edifice of representation in the passage from the second to the third order of simulation. Relationality or referentiality, formerly the foundation of seminal critical distinctions between signs and objects, questions and answers, is neutralized and dissipated. The shift into the third order emphasizes the modulated differences of codes. 'Modulation is ultimately more fundamental than serial reproducibility, distinctive oppositions more than quantitative equivalences, and the commutation of terms more than the law of equivalences,' writes Baudrillard (1993: 56). There is in Baudrillard's description an extreme semiosis of social control, in an almost totally cyberneticized society: control proceeds by models, in other words, by the anterior finality of codes in an anticipatory register. Further, signification is superseded by signaletics, signals generated tactically by the codes. 'Social control,' Baudrillard explains, 'by means of the end ... is replaced with social control by means of prediction, simulation, programmed anticipation ... all governed, however, by the code' (1993: 60). This was already theorized and worked through in a variety of analyses of consumer society and critiques of structuralism by Baudrillard in the late 1960s and early 1970s.

The connection between simulation and surveillance was not explored in depth until Bill Bogard's (1996) elegant analyses appeared 20 years later (Baudrillard published his orders in 1976). Again underlining the anteriorty and hyperreality of diagnostic profiles, fully front-loaded verifications preceding identification, Bogard understands simulation in a 'future-past' projected as 'already over' (1996: 34). This fantasm of completeness has a tendency to send one into fictive universes (recently, though, Bogard has introduced the idea of the deterritorialization of information on the immanent plane of the panoptic machinic assemblage such that the illusion of the totality of the future past is called into question by the flight of data beyond the reaches of the network). However, the temporality of the anticipatory already over, conceived tactically, can point to contemporary simveillance environments like casinos. The more abstract the tense, then, the greater its applicability to the challenges of research on specific sites of the network society (perhaps this echoes Lyon's conundrum: the least panoptic system generates the greatest docility, while the most panoptic generates the greatest resistance). This does not solve the problem of how to study these environments; this is not the world of *Ocean's Eleven* where one can simply stand around and leisurely case the joint. Immobility is a violation of the social control of flows, right down to the level of the gesture. However, simveillant casino environments (places without natural light or timepieces) are promising examples of modulated, that is, tactically scripted, pre-scenarios by means of which 'winning' is rendered a calculable percentile of payout against projected models of the house's take and exterior obligations to municipalities in case of donations, contributions to addiction programmes, free lunches for seniors, etc. Players are integrated into the network in which the house is nothing more than a precession of models. Recent tests of face recognition systems at casinos in Ontario are micro-instances of pre-programmed lists of known launderers and cheats inserted into the matrices of codes which define simveillance complexes in which there is no more Dostoyevskyan pathos, only the delivery of social welfare by the strange seduction of the foregone conclusion: 'the house always wins'.

In our LCBO example calculating profit was not the matter; rather, the issue was temperance by other means (Genosko and Thompson 2005). Control was needed to maintain the support of a strongly temperate voting population, and so the LCBO could not be seen as generating profit through the exploitation of addicts or the ruination of families (Willison 1924; Ferguson 1926). As surveillance apparatuses of the LCBO gathered more and more vivid information on liquor users, their exclusive sorting revealed the need to expand the 'drunk' list to those who, given the collected data, would 'abuse the permit privilege' (LCBO 904, 1930). In 1930 the Board started to issue what it called 'preventative cancellations': these were 'intended to prevent some unsuitable party obtaining a permit' and what the Board argued would be the inevitable 'warrant collection and forwarding of his permit' (LCBO 904, 1930). In the order delivered to the individual it was explained that: 'this notice is sent as a preventative of your exercise of the permit privilege, because of non-confidence in your proper observance of the law' (LCBO 904, 1930). Here tense conceptualization at the LCBO shifts from previous liquor control methods as the intemperate moments of the future, that previously had to be discovered through investigation, to now become a predictable part of the known future-past. Fiction meets prediction at the liquor store.

Recipients of these 'preventative' cancellations would be added to the 'drunk list', and would have no conceptual or legal distinction from those who were listed for criminal convictions or sentenced by a judge. Pre-eliminated individuals of the 'prohibited list', like their interdicted or convicted counterparts, were then subject to increased disciplinary surveillance as well as barred from Legions, Union Halls and other licensed establishments (Liquor Control Act R.S.O.1927. 17 George V c.257). The preventative cancellations of this 'prohibited list' were originally designed to target those receiving financial aid (state benefits) and those who were suspected of driving under the influence of liquor. But in a short time the list was expanded to include the

Board's three main historical targets: those who 'abused liquor', those who 'from the amount of their purchases and from their standing and circumstances are likely to be supplying bootleggers', and those whose financial standing 'is such that the sales must be followed by a diminution of the comforts of life in the family' (LCBO 1766, 1936).

The future past also reveals the protentive leanings of the literature and it exposes a rather heavy reliance on deviating from degraded futures in which predictions are not so much forecasted as foregone. We can see this in the use of conditional constructions, what are called if–then statements, with regard to the degree of vividness of the futures already fulfilled. In simple conditionals, the future that will be fulfilled is a future real or *future-more-vivid*; in an unreal conditional, the future that would be fulfilled is a future unreal or *future-less-vivid*. The idea of vividness that waxes and wanes according to the degree of implicative force and/or doubt expressed in the conditions tempering the fulfilment of the main clause may be used to question a widespread practice in writing on surveillance. What we are suggesting is that a future-more-vivid is hyperrealized in the passage into simulation because its conditions of real fulfilment are superseded by a future that will have already been fulfilled. We consider the future-more-vivid to be under the reign of simulation as a *future-too-vivid*, as hyperreal. This leaves the future-less-vivid, which then acquires a certain urgency.

Surveillance theorists struggle with these conditionals because they are commonly used to express the vicissitudes of technological determinism in the spread of computerization, the rise of the society of surveillance, and in the rhetorics of 'beyonds' of surveillance theory that regularly arise in calls to get beyond the latest model (Genosko 2003). Technically, the degree of vividness depends on the implications contained in the 'if' clause – no alternance equals more-vivid; some potential for some alternance equals less-vivid. The choice is between the former hyperreal and the latter, another real. The greater the vividness, the greater the control; the greater the vividness, the more intractable the problem of determinacy and the grip that the future anterior has over surveillance theory, and hence appearance and frequency of calls to get 'beyond' this model. For instance, David Lyon (2004) evokes a future-less-vivid in a complex if–then statement:

> If local moral panics produce public interest in video surveillance in streets deemed to be dangerous at night, or on a national level, attacks such as the sarin gas assault on the Tokyo subway in 1995 lead to surveillance crack-downs, then global panic regimes such as that generated by the attacks on the World Trade Center and the Pentagon will have similar effects (136).

133

To make the future less technologically vivid is a counterclaim that surveillance theorists feel compelled to make against the more-vivid imaginaries of technocrats whose solutions to public nuisances and terrorism are found in new technologies, in lieu of policy development and diplomacy. Making less-vivid involves injecting doses of ambiguity (Lyon 2003: 13) and uncertainty, yet this is often done alongside the mining of the hyperreal vividness of the future anterior. Mined and turned, for the point is that 'interest' in surveillance, while it may not blossom into an anti-surveillance social movement, may arise in response to the infrastructures put into place after micro- or macro-panics. Those who call for futures-less-vivid, either praising, cultivating or practising anti-surveillance, thinking spaces of confrontation or even amelioration, often do so in the guise of a call to go 'beyond' existing theoretical models. But in order to go there one has either to abandon the future-too-vivid of the future anterior, and thus risk reducing the temporal sophistication of one's theorizing, or find a way to shift it towards a less vividly theorized outcome.

Conclusion

A note on modulation is in order. It is widely reported that Gilles Deleuze, in going beyond Foucault, announced the displacement of disciplinary societies based on confinement by control societies that capitalize on the breakdown of institutional sites with 'free-floating', open systems based on modulations (alterations according to circumstances) rather than moulds (firmly set and into which one must be made to fit). Modulations entail continuous assessment, postponement of every end, passwords that allow coded 'dividuals', as Deleuze (1995) called them (including post-private dividuals like Paris Hilton), to move from one complementary institution to another or, conversely, fall between them. No container moulds, only modulations: 'like a self-transmutating moulding continually changing from one moment to the next' (Deleuze 1995: 179–80). Deleuze's emphasis was on continuity and linked databases of institutions sharing and generating information amongst themselves and with other interested third parties. Modulation is short-term and flexible; it undulates, like a snake. Deleuze's innovation, what is sometimes referred to as his 'corrective to the Foucauldian panopticon' (Elmer 2004: 43), was already forecast by Baudrillard using the very same terminology of modulation and code, circularity, cybernetic loops, and the effects of the tactical management of differences. Baudrillard's theoretical interests were in giving an account of consumer society based on differentiation through affiliation with models and in developing a description of simulation. Baudrillard's modulatory code circa 1976 and Deleuze's turn to this language in 1990 share an important feature: the degree of determination of digital codes. Both Baudrillard and Deleuze saw in digitality a new figure of social control: for Baudrillard digitiality included binarity as the 'true generative formula' (Baudrillard 1993: 73) that heralds the breakdown of all meaningful differences; for Deleuze digitality may not be binary at all and is the flexibility to continuously change and adapt. Data dividuals with their access codes and passwords pass from one system to the next, until a blockage occurs, either introduced intentionally (to fix a position, for example) or otherwise (Deleuze 1995: 181–2). Deleuze's vision was of the future-less-vivid in which resistance could arise, whereas Baudrillard's sense of the code's 'all pervasiveness' (Hegarty 2004: 56) remains all too vividly hyperreal.

The question we are asking is not about the applicability of the tenses of the digital age of surveillance to the pre-computer, proto-digital era of punch cards and sorting machines. To be sure, we take seriously the prospect that a good place to begin to grasp the panoptic sort is the sorting machine and the social tabulations it made possible under a variety of political conditions ranging widely from conservative Ontario to Hitler's Germany. If we were asked whether our example of the LCBO's preventative listing of targeted populations, namely, First Nations and Inuit, fits neatly into the discussion of the future anterior and of too-vivid scenarios, we would say yes, but race politics must also be considered. The future-past of the pre-selected were those for whom self-control was thought to be, by inheritance, impossible. Surveillance theory has not ignored race, as anyone familiar with the urban studies of Mike Davis (1990) or John Fiske (1998) will attest. Indeed, we note that Mariana Valverde's (2003) attempt to stage a 'backwash' theory in reading the race specificity of liquor laws in Ontario in terms not of their obviously overt racism against First Nations but for how they constitute the ontology and epistemology of whiteness. Our overall focus has been to accept the fundamental orientation of this 'backwash' approach but to look at the categorizations, technologies and classifications at work in a complex informatics of subjugation within the framework of surveillance theory, here illustrating the more abstract problems of temporal orientation.

To end, let us pose the question of resistance against the LCBO that is central to our note on modulation and the move toward a less-vivid future. We know that many persons shared permits, thus deploying opportunities for anonymity and identity adoption as a way to slip under the radar of transactionally generated personal data. Of course, the tried and true way to buy alcohol, as almost any teenager knows, is to have somebody of the legal drinking age buy it for you. Purchasing alcohol for one another was and remains a widespread counter-practice to administrative zealousness. Finally, on the supply side, as it were, vendors were known to mutilate (by damaging or rubbing off digits) their endorsement stamps so that their personal identifiers could not be readily decoded. This was one way for supervisors to escape supervision by intentionally introducing ambiguity.

Notes

1 'Enfranchisement was the voluntary or involuntary loss of Indian status'. Individuals who were enfranchised gained 'certain benefits, which varied over time according to changes in the Indian Act. Early major benefits were full Canadian citizenship and ownership of a parcel of reserve land. A later benefit was the one-time payment of the individual's shares of band funds and annuities.' Researching Your Aboriginal Ancestry at Library and Archives Canada. Canadian Genealogy Center.
   http://www.collectionscanada.ca/genealogy/022-607.002.01.01.18-e.html
2 Magical anticipation of continuous exchanges arising from constant connection, as theorized by Andreas Kitzmann, among others, in terms of electronic self-documentation (Kitzmann 2004).

References

Baudrillard, J. (1993) *Symbolic Exchange and Death* (translated by I. H. Grant) (London: Sage).

Bogard, B. (1996) *The Simulation of Surveillance: Hypercontrol in Telematic Societies* (Cambridge: Cambridge University Press).

Bowker, G.C. and Star, S.L. (2000) *Sorting Things Out: Classification and Its Consequences* (Cambridge, MA: MIT Press).

Castells, M. (2000) *The Rise of the Network Society* (Oxford: Blackwell).

Clarke, R.A. (1988) 'Information Technology and Dataveillance', *Communications of the Association of Computing Machinery*, 31 (5), 498–512.

Clarke, R.A. (2003) 'Dataveillance – 15 Years On', Available at: http://www.privacy.org.nz/media/Roger%20Clarke.pdf.

Cousins, M. (2002) 'Jamie Wagg, "History Painting"', in T.Y. Levin, U. Frohne and P. Weibel (eds) *CRTL [SPACE]: Rhetorics of Surveillance from Bentham to Big Brother* (Cambridge, MA: MIT Press), 486–91.

Davis, D.R. (1973) 'Police Surveillance of Political Dissent', in *Surveillance, Dataveillance and Personal Freedoms: Use and Abuse of Information Technology* (Fair Lawn, NJ: RE Burdick), 113–54.

Davis, M. (1990) *City of Quartz: Excavating the Future of Los Angeles* (New York: Verso).

Deleuze, G. (1995) 'Postscript on Control Societies', in M. Joughin (trans) *Negotiations 1972–1990* (New York: Columbia University Press), 177–82.

Elmer, G. (2004) *Profiling Machines: Mapping the Personal Information Economy* (Cambridge, MA: MIT Press).

Ferguson, H. (1927) 'The Prime Minister, on the Second Reading of the Liquor Control Bill in the Legislature, March 15th 1927' (Toronto: Archives of Ontario).

Fiske, J. (1998) 'Surveilling the City: Whiteness, the Black Man and Democratic Totalitarianism', in *Theory, Culture and Society*, 15 (2), 67–88.

Gandy, O. (1993) *The Panoptic Sort: A Political Economy of Personal Information* (Boulder: Westview).

Genosko, G. (2003) 'Baudrillard and Surveillance', in V. Grace, H. Worth and L. Simmons (eds) *Baudrillard West of the Dateline* (Palmerston North, NZ: Dunmore), 37–56.

Genosko, G. and Thompson, S. (2005) 'LCBO: Profits versus social duty', *Toronto Star*, Monday 25 July, A17.

Hegarty, P. (2004) *Jean Baudrillard: Live Theory* (London: Continuum).

Jameson, F. (1991) *Postmodernism or, The Cultural Logic of Late Capitalism* (Durham, NC: Duke University Press).

Kitzmann, A. (2004) *Saved From Oblivion: Documenting the Daily from Diaries to Webcams* (New York: Peter Lang).

Liquor Control Act (1927) R.S.O. 17 George V c. 257.

Liquor Control Board of Ontario (1927–1986) 'LCBO Circulars to Vendors', in *Administrative Records of the General Manager of the Liquor Control Board of Ontario, Ontario Government Record Series RG-41-3* (Toronto: Archives of Ontario).

Lyon, D. (2003) 'Surveillance as Social Sorting: Computer Codes and Mobile Bodies', in *Surveillance as Social Sorting: Privacy, risk, and digital discrimination* (London: Routledge), 13–29.

Lyon, D. (2004) 'Surveillance as a Global Phenomenon: Comparative and Sociological Perspectives', in *International Sociology*, 19(2), 135–149.

Murri, S. (2002) 'Chris Petit - Surveillance', in T.Y. Levin, U. Frohne and P. Weibel (eds) *CTRL [SPACE]: Rhetorics of Surveillance from Bentham to Big Brother* (Cambridge, MA: MIT Press), 496–7.

Pauleit, W. (2002) 'Video Surveillance and Postmodern Subjects: The Effects of the Photograhesomenon – An Image-form in the "Futur antérieur"', in T.Y. Levin, U. Frohne and P. Weibel (eds) *CTRL [SPACE]: Rhetorics of Surveillance from Bentham to Big Brother* (Cambridge, MA: MIT Press), 465–79.

Poster, M. (2001) *The Information Subject* (Amsterdam: Gordon and Breach).

Torpey, J. (2000) *The Invention of the Passport: Surveillance, Citizenship, and the State* (Cambridge: Cambridge University Press).

Valverde, M. (2003) 'Racial Masquerades: White Inquiries into "the Indian Style of Life"', in *Law's Dream of a Common Knowledge: The Cultural Lives of Law* (Princeton, NJ: Princeton University Press), 193–221.

Virilio, P. (1993) 'The Third Interval: A Critical Transition' Available at: http://www.georgetown.edu/grad/CCT/tbase/viriliotext.html.http://www.georgetown.edu/grad/CCT/tbase/viriliotext.html.

Virilio, P. (1996) 'Speed Pollution: Interview by James Der Derian', *Wired* (May). Available at: http://www.wired.com/archive4.05/virilio.html.

Virilio, P. (1997) *Open Sky* (translated by J. Rose) (New York: Verso).

Willison, J. (1924) 'Alberta Liquor Act: One Woman's View', *Ottawa Journal*, 5 September.

Chapter 7

Pre-empting panoptic surveillance: surviving the inevitable war on terror

Greg Elmer and Andy Opel

With the successive introduction of electronic tabulation and counting machines, followed by mainframe computers, databases, spreadsheets, and a phalanx of data visualization programmes, generations of public and private sector infonauts have gazed at their new flickering lights, screens, and interfaces, and uttered the mantra for our time-travelling age: 'What if ...'. And while Wall Street investment firms warn investors against taking 'forward looking statements' as fact – albeit in small print – such new technologies have seemingly provided a compelling, consequence-free vision of the future. In other words, in advance of acting or making key organizational, political or economic decisions, we can now ponder computer-generated answers to our questions about the future: What if we reduce taxes? What if we increase production? What if we lay off half our workers? What if ...

Today answers to such visionary questions draw upon complex computer algorithms and technological networks. The ability to accurately answer 'what if' questions requires stable real-time data flows and surveillance systems to construct a history of information that subsequently suggest possible continued relationships, patterns and risks (Elmer 2004). However, since the devastating attacks on September 11, and the subsequent invasions of Afghanistan and Iraq, conventional 'what if' wisdom has seemingly gone out the window. With the non-discovery of weapons of mass destruction in Iraq almost every political player in the US – including top administration officials themselves – have called into question the reliability of surveillance and foreign intelligence-gathering programmes. In this murky fog of war for hearts and minds, one question is seldom posed in public: What if the United States is attacked again?

In this chapter we revisit theories of surveillance and social control in light of the ongoing 'War on Terror' and specifically the American doctrine of pre-emption. We question how the pre-emptive requirement to act in advance of intelligence/evidence, through police, law enforcement, or military action, questions the role of surveillance and intelligence gathering. While Foucault's panoptic thesis suggested an automatic form of surveillance and intelligence gathering of the *past* to control future behaviour, we argue that a more cynical, pre-emptive form of social control and discipline posits an inevitable *future* – specifically continued terrorist strikes in the US – as the overarching rationale for privatizing public debate over law enforcement and military action.

In the first half of the chapter we discuss the renewed importance of survival as a central discourse and civic duty in the dangerous, inevitable future. And while discourses of survival serve to highlight the passive role that citizens are asked to play in a dangerous inevitable future, surveillance technologies continue to spread and increase in power. What few and already feeble government safeguards remain over ubiquitous and unregulated surveillance and wiretapping by US law enforcement have now been declared unnecessary by the Bush administration as a consequence of inevitable attacks and the war of terror. In an attempt to further highlight our thesis, though, we turn in the last section of the chapter to a discussion of relatively novel techniques for collecting both public and private opinions on the war on terror. Given the failure of surveillance and intelligence-gathering technologies and programmes of the past, we discuss the growing influence of 'insider trading' markets, as intelligence-gathering technologies that, in keeping with the tenets of the survivor society (privatization of public debate, inevitable futures, etc.), encourage citizens to join secretive, nefarious 'insiders' (CIA, Pentagon, FBI, and possibly terrorists themselves) in placing bets on the time and place of inevitable terrorist strikes.

When, not if

In the contemporary 'War on Terror' what-if scenarios are being reconfigured by 'when, then' scenarios, i.e. 'when the terrorists strike again then we can mitigate the effects.' The difference between the two approaches is quite striking: the 'what if' scenario is a preplanning strategy that draws upon histories of consumption, travelling, voting and other behaviours, to construct psychographic and demographic profiles (groups of so-called 'likeminded', and geographically clustered individuals). Such profiles, or market segments, are in turn used to predict likely future behaviour. Answers to 'what if' questions, subsequently, put one on the offensive, in the driver's seat. 'What if' answers proffer a back to the future-like advantage in the present. As a consequence, the ability to get informed 'what if' answers affords power and control and an ability to position oneself to encourage and privilege certain future outcomes.

Popular culture is, of course, littered with tales of time-travelling protagonists battling dubious corporate and governmental agents for access to the future. Contemporary science fiction is particularly rife with technologies that enable various quasi-privatized agents to view or otherwise travel to the future. Such fictional visions, where the present somehow sees the future, often resemble 'what if' forecasts or stories that are told over and over about probable futures and outcomes, 'pre-meditating' our collective imagination. For instance, discussing the aftermath of September 11 in the United States, Richard Grusin, argues that 'the anthrax scare became an obsession of the media not for the damage it had done but for the damage it could do in the future, for the threat it might become' (2004: 23).

Yet, in contrast to the 'what if' or 'premediated' perspectives, where possible futures are pondered, explored and mediated in the present, we have also noted stories, again typically from science fiction, where a desperate fatalism reigns, that is where the future looks back at the present. The third instalment of Governor Schwarzenegger's *Terminator* franchise, for example, sends back in time the hulking emissary to preserve the inevitable future. The Terminator succeeds in his mission as the puppet-like protagonists merely survive the planet's inevitable nuclear Armageddon, the apocalyptic 'Judgement Day'. As we detail in this paper, this 'when, then' logic invokes – indeed requires – a shared fatalistic assumption, a futility that collectively moves us to an inevitable future, so as to rhetorically 'gaze backward' in an effort to control the future.

Part of our interest in interrogating 'when, then' scenarios and diagnostic techniques in the post-September 11 context is theoretical. As others in this volume have also noted (particularly Bigo, Bogard, Genosko and Thompson, and Haggerty), while the Foucauldian panopticon continues to dominate much theoretical debate amongst surveillance studies scholars, its iconic, metaphoric, and diagrammatic status has been increasingly challenged by advances in technology, recent trends in post-structural thought (in particular those articulated by Deleuze, Guattari, Baudrillard and others), and for some the political and rhetorical aftermath of September 11. While we avoid wading into the minutiae of some of these arguments, we would like to situate our chapter within contemporary debates that these and other scholars have forwarded.

Many of those explicitly pushing or pulling surveillance studies away from its Foucauldian roots are arguing for more nuanced theories that might explain inverted, contested, or intensified cases of surveillance. Bigo, however, stands out in his contribution herein, for his de-coupling of the 'pan' from contemporary optics of power, perhaps taking a cue from Mathiesen's (1997) influential 'synoptic' arguments about the many watching the few. In so doing, Bigo succeeds in moving outside of the panoptic walls of punishment, to question the optics and governmentality of detainment, a questionable legal tactic used in the war on terror. Moreover, by embracing Agamben's notion of the 'state of exception', the 'no man's land between public law and political fact' (2005: 1), Bigo questions a fundamental pillar of Foucualt's panopticism – the demise of sovereign forms of power: For Agamben, Carl Schmitt has perceived what Foucault has not: he has seen the sovereign moment, he has an understanding of the 'real' political moment with the declaration of exception (Bigo, this volume).

While Agamben and Schmitt locate this state of exception within laws that in effect lay to waste the central tenets of liberal democracy during times of crisis (or 'exceptions'), Bigo also subtly reintroduces the power of political rhetoric, specifically the declaration of exception (for example, the war on terror), that subsequently enacts the suspension of certain rights and laws. We are equally convinced that theories of surveillance and control must begin to recognize the rhetorics of sovereignty, power and exception. A pivotal part of this equation and argument though must remain historical. Bigo takes us only so far beyond Foucault; he is able to rearticulate the politics of space, boundaries and bio-political containment, yet he too falls back into a certain 'what-if' forecasting/profiling mode of inquiry: 'The political reaction to September 11 justifies a proactive and preemptive strategy, which have the ambition to know, and to monitor the "future"' (in this volume). Gary Genosko helpfully refers to such musings on the search for the future as an instance of 'tense theory' in surveillance studies, in short a predilection for the future anterior (for example, 'I will have finished this paper tomorrow'). Like Bigo, though, Genosko, seemingly stops one step short of tackling the declarations and discourses of inevitability ('when–then') and pre-emptive politics, arguing that the dominant 'if–then' tense of inquiry in surveillance studies is a commonly shared trope by the sometimes divergent arguments of David Lyon and William Bogard.

By comparison, in this chapter we question the rhetorics of 'action' over simulations, models or other studies, and inevitable futures over conditional or even probable ones. As a consequence, perhaps implicitly, we are looking to expand the common definition of optics to include not only 'seeing' but also being 'sighted': 'that is, discovered, localized, identified in order to be hit or struck' (Weber 2005: 8).

Thus, as media scholars, we are particularly mindful of the long history of Pentagon- (and other military-) funded research into new information and communication technologies (GPS, the Internet, etc.) and the increasingly close ties and collaborative projects between Hollywood and the military (Der Derian 2001). As a consequence, we believe that the innovative – yet decidedly provocative – programmes and public campaigns developed by the RAND (research and development) corporation and the American Defense Department's Defense Advanced Research Projects Agency (DARPA) offer significant visions and models for post-September 11 security, defence and political order, just as they did in the mid-twentieth century during the height of the Cold War. We discuss how such programmes represent an integral logic of the 'war on terror' – specifically within the context of the expansion of pre-emptive policies both at home and abroad (in the form of the war against Iraq, and the interrogation and arrest of 'pre-protestors'). Considering the Bush administration's argument that threats must be eliminated before they even materialize,[1] this chapter seeks to reconfigure the significance of forecasting models and theories of surveillance within a political culture that seemingly requires little to no proof of threats for military intervention, arrests, incarceration, interrogation, etc.

This chapter is therefore primarily concerned with techniques of social control and more broadly the reconfiguration of a democratic political culture. The latter is much less explicit in the work of Foucault and Deleuze (or should we say surveillance and control society theses), in part because they are typically concerned with collecting information for the purposes of managing populations and markets in real-time and the future. By comparison, we are intrigued by contemporary political discourse because government and various other sectors of society have increasingly told the population that the future is inevitable, specifically that the collective security of the United States will be breached. In an environment of already made, or pre-made decisions, in 'response' to inevitable events, we believe there is a need to rethink theories of social control that have evolved out of the pervasive use of surveillance and other intelligence-gathering techniques. Moreover, to return to the point about democracy, we argue that if a future is known or easily knowable, that certain events are inevitable, there is little need for public deliberation and debate (saying nothing of dissent). As we detail in the beginning of our chapter, in such a state of affairs inevitable events not only initiate premeditated and pre-empted military conflicts (obviously the case in Iraq), they also domestically cultivate a politics of survival.

Pre-emption and the inevitable future

Pre-emption invokes a predetermined inevitable future that requires military and police action. Through the pre-emptive lens the future becomes an inevitable series of events, elevating 'fate' to an agent of historical evolution. Rational free will, as a motivating factor in social and political change, by comparison, is not only futile, it becomes potentially life threatening. Pre-emption then becomes a new (old) superstition, a courting of fates and furies in an attempt at one and the same time to know a determined future and to be able to reshape that determination in a god-like fashion. The ethics and politics of such visionary pre-emptive actions are of course compelling fare for Hollywood. *Minority Report*, the Philip K. Dick-inspired Steven Spielberg film, for instance, offers a holy trinity of mutated humans or 'pre-cogs' with the ability to see the future. The pre-cogs are enslaved by a privatized police state, kept alive in stasis in a special chamber called 'the temple' where their visions of the future are recorded and then used to prevent crimes before they occur. Citizens are routinely arrested before they commit murder, convicted on the recorded visions of the three pre-cogs. And while the film goes to great lengths to chronicle an epic battle between fate and human agency, its title, *Minority Report*, also expresses a decidedly democratic tension that highlights the hidden disputes among the pre-cogs about the clarity of their visions and intelligence.

Yet, as in *Minority Report* – where evidence is akin to dreams and visions – a mystical state (or perhaps an apparatus) of faith is required to justify and privilege the deployment of police violence, domestically and internationally. Similarly, while Philip Dick's fictional future is known by semi-comatose humans who act as a type of oracle, in what we call the *survival society* the marketplace becomes the new oracle. Moreover, as we see later in the case of DARPA's 'terrorist futures markets' (a Wall Street-inspired model that encourages 'investors' to wage or place bets on the likelihood of future terrorist attacks), its visionary power is predicated upon the absence of social, political or ethical critique. And ironically, in the shadow of Enron, Nortel, World Comm (and the list goes on), such futures markets are designed to encourage bets from insiders, including possible terrorists themselves.[2]

In the survivor society, inevitable attacks and gathering threats are invisible to the body public (who are called upon to trust their leaders). Evidence of potential threats has been consistently cloaked in classified documents that must be trusted – a faith-based politic that has been called into question with the missing weapons of mass destruction and lack of Iraq–Al Qaeda connections. Moreover, unlike *Minority Report* where inevitable futures were shown to be mutable, the real-world drama of global foreign policy and domestic security continues to be driven by inevitability and the pursuant response of pre-emption. The age of enlightenment and the invisible hand of a marketplace driven by the rational choices of individuals have been replaced by a predetermined future with inevitable outcomes that can only be known by an elite class of sacred bureaucrats. The pre-cogs of *Minority Report* become 'intelligence' under the Bush Doctrine, both of which justify the doctrine of pre-emption. 'The concept is not limited to the traditional definition of pre-emption – striking an enemy as it prepares an attack – but also includes prevention striking an enemy even in the absence of specific evidence of a coming attack' (Brookings Institution 2002: 3). Thus, as the public in *Minority Report* is left to trust the visions and unanimity of the pre-cogs, we must trust the 'intelligence' produced by government, intelligence that is increasingly inaccessible as freedom of information is constrained in the name of security. Even the 'absence of specific evidence' serves as justification for action, reinforcing the need for faith as opposed to evidence.

At first glance, the Bush administration's domestic and foreign policies and its calls to arm, police, and secure are, similarly, predicated upon the apparent need for surveillance and intelligence. Such impatience with monitoring and watching in favour of decisive action is all too apparent in the White House's National Security Strategy: 'In the new world we have entered, the only path to peace and security is the path of action' (Government of the United States of America 2002). To suggest that surveillance techniques and technologies are on the decline under a pre-emptive worldview, that acting has altogether supplanted watching and monitoring would, however, be a mistake. Late in 2005, it was widely reported in the US and through global news outlets that President Bush had authorized the National Security Administration to begin a new programme of warrantless domestic wiretapping and monitoring of phone and computer-based communication (Risen and Lichtblau 2005). Even after *The New York Times* (NYT) waited for over a year to publish this story, President Bush met with NYT publisher Arthur Sulzberger and executive editor Bill Keller in the Oval Office in an attempt to suppress the story (Alter 2005). Although the full extent of the story is still to be uncovered, a deeply controversial, pre-emptive reconfiguration of American surveillance programmes was already apparent. Under President Nixon the surveillance of known terrorists all too easily led to the routine monitoring of civilian groups and individuals. Public outrage over such domestic spying programmes led to the Church Commission and the establishment of the Foreign Intelligence Surveillance Act (FISA) of 1978. While Bush and others in his administration have argued that the United States must be free to act quickly to track and capture terrorists, the FISA record of declining wiretaps would not seem to pose much of a hindrance. Since 1979, the FISA court has rejected just four out of over 17,000 applications for warrants (EPIC 2005). What is more, before the scandal over Bush's warrantless wiretaps came to light, his administration was already working under a pre-emptive form of surveillance, where law enforcement could wiretap first, and later (up to 72 hours) ask for a legal permission to do so.

Thus, as the American executive branch of government continues to question the need for documented threats, intelligence, laws and international agreements, political discourse takes on a renewed importance in the survivor society (unlike the surveillance and control society theses that tend to focus on the automation and networking of technologies such as databases, biometrics, face-recognition cameras and software, etc.). For example, while various US government departments and agencies claim that attacks are preventable and/or not inevitable (published in policy documents freely available to the public), flagrant and unequivocal claims of inevitable attacks in the future, by comparison, are commonplace and routine in public statements broadcast in the media. In May of 2002, for example, FBI Director Robert Mueller told a National Association of District Attorneys conference that more suicide bombings in the US were 'inevitable', 'We will not be able to stop it. It's something we all live with.' The first Homeland Security Director, Tom Ridge, was similarly quoted in public saying that it was 'Not a question of if, but when', a specific phrase repeated on television punditry programming by Vice President Cheney and Don Rumsfeld (Noah 2002). Former Democratic Senator Bob Graham, a vocal critic of the Bush administration in Washington, however, offered US citizens and residents a much more optimistic perspective: 'There is a likelihood almost to the point of certainty that over the next say, three to five years, that there will be another terrorist attack inside the US (CNN. com 2002b).'

While key members of the Bush cabinet continue to warn against impending attacks, the administrations own 'National Security Strategy' document (2002) suggests that such attacks can be prevented and that the war on terror is finite, that global terrorism can be defeated (Government of the United States of America 2002: 5). Yet again, the terms of success in this epic battle are not transparent: 'The struggle against global terror is different from any other war in history. It will be fought on many fronts against a particularly elusive enemy over an extended period of time. Progress will come through the persistent accumulation of successes – some seen, some unseen' (Government of the United States of America 2002: 5).

By comparison, the notion of a preventable future or at least an unsure future is in fact a common theme in the influential White House document 'National Security Strategy of the United States of America' (September 2002). Surprisingly, time and again the document refers to the prevention of attacks, a common theme within a series of post-September 11 government documents. For example, one of the central goals of the administration, as articulated in its Security Strategy, is to: 'Strengthen alliances to defeat global terrorism and work to prevent attacks against us and our friends' (Government of the United States of America 2002: 5). Similarly, the US government's high-profile Department of Homeland Security, specifically its 'Ready Campaign' document 'Individual Preparedness and Response to Unconventional Terrorist Attacks', exclaimed that 'The likelihood of such terrorist attacks is highly uncertain' (Government of the United States of America 2002: xiii). Most striking, however, was the departing statement made by Bush partisan and former Attorney General John Ashcroft. Just a few weeks after the American presidential electoral campaign – which saw countless 'inevitable attack' warnings from Vice President Dick Cheney and other administration allies – Ashcroft wrote in his resignation letter to President Bush that: 'The objective of securing the safety of Americans from crime and terror has been achieved'.[3]

Literally, coming out of the mouths of senior government officials, repeated warnings of inevitable attacks made for compelling television programming. Such unequivocal pronouncements, however, mask the underlying debate over the best way to address security issues, institutionally and rhetorically. While journalists often point to competing interests, intelligence reports and political agendas as sources of internal governmental contradictions, in this case we see that public officials – as opposed to government bureaucrats who wrote the previously cited government reports and position papers – are much more inclined toward espousing inevitable futures. As we see next, such is also the case with the private and quasi-public entities, DARPA and the RAND Corporation. Moreover, in both examples we also see programmatic examples of 'what-if' forecasting campaigns and techniques reconstituted in light of the survivor society.

The genesis of survivability: DARPA and RAND

I thought that there was nothing more appropriate than having a DARPATECH at Disneyland. Disneyland is a land full of dreams and fantasy becoming reality, and that is what DARPA does and does well (Dr Tony Tether, Director, *DARPA*).

While one might find some differentiation between the public discourse of inevitable terrorist attacks and the public documentation of 'preventability' at one level, one finds no such contradictions or equivocations at the level of homeland security, specifically with regards to readiness and terror preparation campaigns. Such campaigns at best suggest diligence, at worst – particularly as they work in concert – promote a climate of fear and a sense of a population under siege. Moreover, such programmes place survivability of the individual as their ultimate goal. Survivability has always served as a central trope of the network age and of course before that the nuclear age. In many respects, contemporary discourses of 'survivability' are an attempt to rearticulate domestic Cold War doctrine, replete with flourishing book publishing[4] and home security industries. For many new media scholars and historians in particular, the nuclear and networking age intersected during the early 1960s with the collaboration of two venerable American 'think tanks', the American Defense department's amorphous 'Defense Advanced Research Project Agency' (DARPA) and the RAND Corporation – both institutions that have played pivotal roles in establishing American political, economic and military priorities and programmes. RAND, DARPA and the US military have collaborated in a number of projects dating back to the Cold War, typically focusing on the technological dimension of warfare and security hardware. While promoting itself as non-partisan, RAND, of course, promotes a distinct brand of neo-liberal ideology, highlighted in its philosophy of research and development. In a publication highlighting its 50 years of collaboration with the US Air Force, the RAND Corporation (1996) notably includes an entire chapter on its conceptual and philosophical contribution to American society:

> Perhaps the highest aspiration of the joint venture that initiated RAND was to explore the frontiers of knowledge. Thinking 'outside the box' – or daring to think imaginatively – has been a consistent feature of RAND throughout its 50-year association with the Air Force. As with any frontier ventures, not all of the ideas proved prophetic or helpful. Some reached too far or misjudged the unfolding future, but enough hit their mark to encourage the persistence of RAND researchers and the patience of their Air Force sponsors (DARPA 1996: 11).

Over 50 years after its founding the RAND Corporation continues to be a key political player and military-governmental adjunct in the United States. As a 'think tank' the corporation has made significant contributions to policies, campaigns and documents for homeland security issues. Moreover, the corporation's work has played a central role in promoting active preparedness on the part of all Americans, as was articulated by President Bush soon after the September 11 attacks: 'Our Security will require all Americans ... to be forward-looking and resolute' (Ponte 2002). The RAND Corporation also replicates the administration attempts to forcefully remind Americans about the devastation and emotional upheaval created by the September 11 attacks. A series of RAND's featured homeland security publications,[5] for example, all include the same curious graphic depicting a small crowd of individuals gazing skyward (in clear reference to the numerous media shots of Manhattans gazing up at the burning twin towers), juxtaposed against glass skyscrapers and construction cranes.

The primary goal of RAND's homeland security documents, particularly its featured publication 'Individual Preparedness and Response to Unconventional Terrorist Attacks' and accompanying shorter texts, is to reinforce individual decision-making as a potential life-or-death moment. As such, the number one priority for an 'individual's strategy' is to 'Act first to ensure your own survival' (Davis et al. 2003a: xxii). In addition to inaction, risky behaviour is also defined as social awareness: 'it will be important for an individual to act with a set of clear priorities because an individual's instincts may be wrong. Stopping to help others or acting to contact family and friends is a natural reaction. However, such actions could put an individual's own survival at risk'.[6] To help remind Americans of such counter-intuitive thinking, RAND's quick guide to terrorist survivability includes a series of reference cards – very similar to cards produced by Health Management Organization's (HMO) and other agencies to help doctors diagnose their patients. In fact, the use of RAND's cards was clarified for subscribers of the Internet Medical Journal (presumably doctors, medical researchers, and other health care professionals): 'The Quick Guide and the reference card are designed to be read by ordinary citizens as a part of personal safety preparation. The reference card can be easily carried in a pocket, purse or bag or can be set on a desk at work or shelf at home' (The Internet Medical Journal 2003). There are five reference cards in total. Four of the cards refer to a specific type of attack: chemical, radiological, nuclear, biological, while the last card provides a summary of preparatory actions to be undertaken 'ahead of time'. In addition to outlining 'response actions' to each respective attack, the cards also provide a bizarre description of 'What you will experience'. For example, for the chemical attack: 'You will know that you are in a chemical attack because you will see many people who are nauseous, have blurred vision, and have difficulty breathing or because you see many sick or dead animals' (The Internet Medical Journal 2003). The description of a nuclear attack clearly resonates with President Bush's October 2002 pre-Iraq invasion speech that 'Facing clear evidence of peril, we cannot wait for the final proof – the smoking gun – that could come in the form of a mushroom cloud' (CNN.com 2002). According to RAND's nuclear attack reference card, 'You will know you are in a nuclear attack by the loud explosion, widespread destruction, intense heat, strong winds and the rising of a mushroom cloud' (Davis *et al.* 2003b).

While the impact and reach of such cards and documents are questionable, their message is entirely consistent with the post-millennial burgeoning survivalist industries: all Americans should prepare and play their part in the war against terror. Above all else their duty is to survive. Faced with a deluge of public warning about inevitable terrorist attacks, the public is encouraged to dispel their social impulses for a hyper-individualistic, survivalist position. Indeed, RAND's cards collectively speak to individuals in the first person as survivors of lethal attacks, calling upon the very corporality of their senses to imagine the unimaginable.

Insider markets, evacuating critique

The American Defense Department's amorphous 'Defense Advanced Research Project Agency' (DARPA) is of course now a well-known staging ground for imaginative research, what they and RAND refer to as 'thinking out of the box' doctrine and innovation. In an age of absent evidence, justifications and threats, DARPA provides the prototypical organizational schematic for the survivor society. According to a recent (February 2003) 'Strategic Plan': 'DARPA's mission is to maintain the technological superiority of the US military and prevent technological surprise from harming our national security by sponsoring revolutionary, high-payoff research that bridges the gap between fundamental discoveries and their military use' (DARPA 2003: 1). Equally as important for DARPA though, and clearly its workers, is its innovative organizational structure. During the welcoming speech to the 2002 DARPATECH conference, Director Tony Tether made light of DARPA's distinctiveness within the American public sector: 'We don't hire people for jobs at DARPA. There are no jobs. We hire people for their ideas. PMs come into the agency with an idea. We squeeze it out of them, drain them, then throw them out, and get another one' (Tether 2002).

In many respects DARPA's de-centred, collaborative and ephemeral structure personifies the agency's most successful invention, the ARPANET, the precursor to the Internet. And as many scholars have noted, Paul Baran, in his RAND Corporation research paper entitled 'On Distributed Communications Networks', was among the first, and now among the most cited early network papers, to articulate the benefits of a communications 'array' in the Cold War – a distributed network of computers without central command and control. In short, Baran's work sought to quantify degrees of network survivability assuming the nuclear destruction of various nodes in the network. The research constituted Baran's own 'what if' research agenda (Baran 1962).

While DARPA's research continued to forward defence technologies and network protocols, nearing the end of the millennium its work increasingly turned to questions of intelligence and information gathering. Post September 11, DARPA has proposed a series of controversies with projects such as the Orwellian sounding 'Total Information Awareness' programme whose mystical logo (see below) depicted an eye positioned at the apex of a pyramid peering over the earth.[7]

Another example of this new mystical form of intelligence gathering received decidedly more criticism. On 28 July 2003, the Pentagon announced the formation of the DARPA-backed Policy Analysis Market (PAM) or 'terrorist futures market' as it came to be known. The programme was designed for cultures, regions and nations where the US had little to no intelligence-gathering mechanisms, limited surveillance techniques, or obvious allies. To an extent, the betting system was meant to act as intelligence in lieu of surveillance techniques which have proven problematic in an age where American enemies are publicly named and threatened (as seems to be the case with Bush's pre-emptive doctrine). Thus while the American military has been called upon to smoke out terrorists and 'insurgents', PAM's market logic proposed the establishment of an insider trading market. To use police terminology, the programme attempted to create its own legion of 'informants'.

In short, the programme would allow online, real-time betting on the likelihood of the next terrorist attack (among a host of other security-related issues). The US Defense Department noted that 'Research indicates that markets are extremely efficient, effective and timely aggregators of dispersed and even hidden information' (BBC news 2003). The Policy Analysis Market was based on the efficient market hypothesis, the central premise being that collective thought, and in particular insider knowledge, is more accurate than individual opinion or policy analysis from a distance. This model has been used to predict a range of future outcomes, from elections to commodity harvests. 'Some studies have showed it does better than pollsters at predicting election results. Similarly, the orange juice futures market is better than the National Weather Service at predicting Florida weather' (Said 2003). Under the PAM proposal, the Pentagon was to act as 'the House', setting the odds on 'literally millions of possible scenarios' (Coy 2003). In a contradictory and somewhat confusing attempt to both harness the power of market incentive while limiting the potential to profit from terror and manipulate the markets, bets were to be limited to $100. This price cap was also said to be a way to minimize the cost to the government as they expected to lose money to well-informed investors.[8] This cost was seen as a small price to pay for accurate information (Coy 2003).

The programme was quickly criticized on the floor of the US Senate, with Hillary Rodham Clinton calling the programme a 'futures market in death' (Pethokoukis 2004). This prompted an intense debate in Washington and on cable news. The programme was attacked as 'morally repugnant and grotesque' and criticized as a potential venue for terrorists to bet for or against their own efforts and potentially profit from their actions (Hulse 2003). A week later the Pentagon scrapped the idea. Shortly after the programme was shut down, though, a chorus of economists began to articulate the rationale behind the Policy Analysis Market, chiding critics for injecting morality into a prediction modelling tool that was designed to prevent future attacks. CNN financial commentator and columnist Lou Dobbs (2003), for one, accused the critics of PAM of 'asserting the all-too-familiar orthodoxy of both Washington and New York, the capitals of politically correct-inspired conformity'. As details of the programme emerged after its demise, the coupling of insider 'prediction' or intelligence and market forces became clear. George Mason University economics professor, Robin Hanson, the scholar behind the model, defended the programme as a way to 'pay people for information about bad things' (Said 2003).

While the semi-public version of PAM was scrapped, a privatized version soon reappeared from Net Exchange, an original partner on the DARPA-led project. The programme was defended as a viable alternative to surveys and a new tool for gaining potentially valuable information. Yet, its reliance upon potential dubious insiders was clear in a 2003 presentation to the Microsoft Research department, where a representative of Net Exchange (2003b) discussed possible 'investors' in the market: 'Mossad agent thinks Hamas mil. [sic] wing will not disband – buys ~B @$0.50'. Net Exchange president Charles Polk explained it this way: 'One way to look at the use of a market-type process is that it provides a filter at the very front [it provides] the incentive to concentrate on those things that they actually know something about' (Edmonson 2003).

Thus while PAM and its privatized version were criticized on moral grounds – for betting on terror, and to a lesser extent 'paying out' to questionable sources, its economic logic received much less derision in the recent American presidential election. However, unlike the insider model of PAM and Net Exchange, 'Futures markets have proven themselves to be good at predicting such things as elections results; they are often better than expert opinions' (Hulse 2003). The Iowa

Electronic Markets run by the University of Iowa's Business School for example, has accurately predicted the results of the last four presidential elections better than polling data (Coy 2003).

Throughout the media discourse over the virtues or moral failings of the policy analysis markets, broader questions about the possibility of individuals 'knowing' anything new was never addressed. The problem of citizens producing 'accurate' information under the social conditions of consolidated media implicated with defence contractors is clearly problematic. With the dominant US news media issuing a series of *mea culpa* explanations for their failure to investigate governmental claims about weapons of mass destruction (WMD) and Iraq Al Qaeda connections leading up the start of the Iraq war, coupled with scandals about forged documents, non-investigative journalism and a US presidential election campaign dominated by discussion of television ads over social issues, the possibility of a well-informed electorate making accurate forecasts of terrorist activity was unlikely and rather circular – people betting on possible events based on information disseminated from the government seeking insights from the general public. Nevertheless, proponents of PAM assailed the critics as being 'politically correct' and injecting morality into an amoral (sic) process. What we are left with is a call to embrace a market system that is driven, not by rational judgement and intelligence, but rather fuelled by the emotion of fear. Morality, dissent, criticism and analytical thought must be evacuated for the market to perform smoothly. Citizens turned gamblers take part in homeland (in)security by wagering money on potential terror outcomes, based on information provided by a media that reproduces government allegation as fact. As we saw in the height of the Wall Street Technology insider-driven bubble of the late 1990s, there was no need for analysis of a business balance sheet, it could be assumed that a 'new economy' had emerged. Decisions were made based on an inevitable future where evidence and balance sheets were replaced by optimism. In this case, the market is driven by pessimism, the fear of what will happen.

Conclusion

In the lead-up to the presidential election of 2004, the Bush administration repeatedly defended the strategy of pre-emption and the actions taken against Iraq with statements that 'the world is safer'. This rhetorical turn exemplifies the language of the survival society, where statements are beyond proof and evidence is no longer necessary. Most Americans have no way to either refute or to affirm the central question raised: are we safer? Indeed in the face of so many troubling unknowns and such fearful uncertainties, facts fall by the wayside. Thus, in many respects the survivor society is sustained by a suspension of disbelief. Morality, critical thinking and dissent actively inhibit the smooth functioning of society. As inevitability becomes the dominant trope, individual agency is redirected toward survival, a hyper-individualism that evacuates the possibility of critical exchange in the public sphere. Critical exchanges, dissent, hindsight and re-evaluation are said to support the enemy and undermine the pre-emptive efforts. Citizens are then called upon to continue shopping and maintain 'normal' behaviour because to do anything less would disrupt the flow of consumer goods and services and weaken a fragile economy.

Theoretically speaking, we need to continue to question how surveillance functions in an environment where evidence is not needed to justify state violence, arrests, incarceration, etc. (America's pre-emptive policy at home and abroad). We have characterized this as a shift in reasoning, from 'what-if' simulation models – where surveillance intelligence fuels forecasting models, to 'when, then' thinking where the future is deemed inevitable (i.e. 'not if but when terrorists will attack'). The RAND and DARPA terrorist preparation programmes and terrorist futures market examples demonstrate that 'when, then' reasoning is not as much about tracking and monitoring behaviour as it is evacuating the possibility of social critique and political debate. According to DARPA and other 'betting' proponents, rational thought and ethical questions about the market disable their predictive powers. Thus, in the survivor society social control is achieved through distancing the need for evidence and installing forecasting technologies that by their very nature must function critique-free.

The discursive contours of the survivor society offer stark contrasts to those of the Cold War era and the emerging surveillance society. During the Second World War, the US government implored citizens to sacrifice for the collective good, initiating everything from recycling programmes to gardening as a way to conserve resources and boost food production. 'Victory gardens' became a symbol of civic participation, where individual actions were directed toward a collective good. These programmes were materially based and discursively centred around active participation in the war effort. Alternatively, the war on terror has elicited calls for a hyper-individualism that focuses on the immaterial – faith, wagering and the primacy of individual survival. Civic participation is equated with maintaining (or increasing) consumer debt, participating in the privatized 'marketplace of ideas' futures markets and avoiding any temptation to inject morality, dissent, criticism or analytical thought because these aid and abet the enemy and interfere with the smooth functioning of predictive markets.

This new rhetoric of the survivor society is amplified through an increasingly monolithic commercial televisual media system. Although policy documents offer more nuanced predictions about the war on terror, public statements by a host of government officials, broadcast repeatedly as sound bites, describe a stark, inevitable future of unending terror threats. The contradictions between the written documents and the public statements suggest a wilful attempt to harness the immediacy (and uniformity) of network and cable news outlets to distribute and maintain an atmosphere of fear and emotion that encourages participation in the new regimes of hyper-individualism.

For those who resist these new regimes, choosing to dissent, ask for evidence, or request public documents, their actions are met with increased hostility and accusations of irrationality. Moreover, the foundational concept of pre-emption, predicated on an inevitable future that must be intervened, undermines the possibility of dissent. If a future is inevitable, to question that future is to question reality and becomes a mark of irrationality or worse. Debate, deliberation and reflection are by-passed by a discourse of inevitability, leaving dissent among the ranks of the delusional. Thus the new victory garden grows from the seeds of fear, fed by emotion, and harvested as a fragmented populace devoid of transparency and cut out of the democratic process. Members of the survivor society are asked to prepare themselves (as individuals) through a series of purchases and by remaining vigilant, all without any request for collective sacrifice or coordination. The neo-liberal model becomes embodied in a new response to war, a privatization of self-preservation with the possibility of becoming your own war profiteer as you wager on future catastrophes.

Notes

1   As anti-war demonstrators in the US have increasingly found, 'gatherings' now constitute a *de facto* threat in need of action.
2   In a PowerPoint presentation entitled 'Forming a Core Trader Group for The Policy Analysis Market', Net Exchange euphemistically refers to these dubious insider traders as 'practitioners'. Cf. http://hanson.gmu.edu/PAM/reports/Trader-Solicitation-6-5-03.pdf (Accessed 28 July 2005).
3   http://www.cnn.com/2004/ALLPOLITICS/11/09/ashcroft.text.ap/
4   Senator Bill Frist, the Republican's majority leader in the Senate, for one, took it upon himself to offer the reading public a 'Family Survival Guide' in his book *When Every Moment Counts*.

5 The bold graphic dominates the front of a series of publications instructing Americans on how they can prepare for various sorts of terrorist attacks, including the 'Pocket Edition Survival Guide' of 'What You Should Do to Prepare for and Respond to Chemical, Radiological, Nuclear, and Biological Terrorist Attacks' (Davis *et al*. 2003b).

6 Comparatively, similar anti-terror readiness programmes in Canada encourage individuals to seek out emergency information from local schools and community organizations. Nevertheless, the Canadian government still acknowledges its minor role when it entitled its Public Safety and Emergency Preparedness document: 'Self-Help Advice for Families and Individuals: Preparing for the Unexpected' (Government of Canada 2003).

7 The logo was removed soon after the programme received criticism from privacy advocates. Cf. http://www.thememoryhole.org/policestate/iao-logo.htm.

8 http://www.biz.uiowa.edu/iem/markets/pr_Pres04_VS.html.

References

Agamben, G. (2005) *The State of Exception* (Chicago: University of Chicago Press.

Alter, J. (2005) 'Bush's Snoopgate', *Newsweek*, 21 December 2005. Available at: http://www.msnbc.mcn.com/id/10536559/site/newsweek/.

Baran, P. (1962) 'On Distributed Communications Networks', Santa Monica, CA: RAND Corporation. Available at: http://www.rand.org/pubs/papers/2005/P2626.pdf.

BBC News (2003) 'Pentagon Axes Online Terror Bets', 29 July 2003. Available at: http://news.bbc/co.uk/2/hi/americas/3106559 stm.

Brookings Institution (2002) Brookings Policy Brief, no. 113, December 2002. Available at: http://www.brook.edu/comm/policybriefs/pb113.pdf (Accessed 1 July 2005).

Bogard, W. (1996) *The Simulation of Surveillance: Hypercontrol in Telematic Societies* (Cambridge: Cambridge University Press).

Coy, P. (2003). 'Betting on Terror: PR Disaster, Intriguing Idea', *Business Week*, 25 August 2003, 41.

CNN.com (2002a) 'Bush: Don't Wait for Mushroom Cloud', 8 October 2002. Available at: http://archives.cnn.com/2002/ALLPOLITICS/10/07/bush. transcript/ (Accessed 15 October 2004).

CNN.com (2002b) 'Terrorists may Target Tall Apartment Buildings', 20 May 2002. Available at: http://archives.cnn.com/2022/US/05/20gen.war. on.terror/index.html.

Davis, L., LaTourrette, T., Mosher, D.E., Davis, L.M. and Howell, D.R. (2003a) 'Individual Preparedness and Response to Chemical, Radioloical, Nuclear, and Biological Terrorist Attacks', Santa Monica, CA: RAND Corporation.

Davis, L., LaTourrette, T., Mosher, D.E., Davis, L.M. and Howell, D.R. (2003b) 'What you Should do to Prepare for and Respond to Chemical, Radiological,

Nuclear, and Biological Terrorist Attacks – Pocket Edition Survival Guide', Santa Monica, CA: RAND Corporation. Available at http://www.rand.org/pubs/monograph_reports/2005/MR/MR1731.2.pdf.

Defense Advanced Research Projects Agency (DARPA) (1996) *Project Air Force: 1946–1996*. Available at www.rand.org/publications/PAFbook.pdf. (Accessed 10 December 2004).

Defense Advanced Research Projects Agency (DARPA) (2003) *Strategic Plan 2003*. Available at: http://www.darpa.mil/body/pdf/DARPAStrategicPlan2003.pdf (accessed on 5 April 2005).

Der Derian, J. (2001) *Virtuous War: Mapping the Military-Industrial-Media-Entertainment Network* (Boulder, CO: Westview).

Dobbs, L. (2003) 'Deep-Sixing a Bright Idea', *U.S. News and World Report*, 11 August 2003, 32.

Edmonson, G. (2003) 'Mideast Futures Market Scheduled to Start in March', *Atlanta Journal-Constitution*, 18 November 2003, 4D.

Electronic Privacy Information Center (EPIC) (2005) 'Foreign Intelligence Surveillance Act Orders 1979–2004'. Available at: http://www.epic.org/privacy/wiretap/stats/fisa_stats.html.

Elmer, G. (2004) *Profiling Machines: Mapping the Personal Information Economy* (Cambridge: MIT Press).

Frist, B. (2002) *When Every Moment Counts: What You Need to Know About Bioterrorism from the Senate's Only Doctor* (Boulder: Rowman and Littlefield).

Government of Canada (2003) 'Self-Help Advice: Preparing for the Unexpected', Ottawa, ON: Public Safety and Emergency Preparedness Canada. Available at: http://ww3.pseps-sppcc.gc.ca/info_pro/self_help_ad/pdfs/uxpected_e.pdf.

Government of the United States of America (2002) *The National Security Strategy of the United States of America*, September 2002. Available at: http://www.whitehouse.gov/nsc/nss.html.

Grusin, R. (2004) 'Premediation', *Criticism*, 41 (1), 17–39.

Hulse, C. (2003) 'Threats ands Responses; Plans and Criticisms; Pentagon Prepares a Futures Market on Terror Attacks', *New York Times*, 29 July 2003, A1.

Mathiesen, T. (1997) 'The Viewer Society: Michel Foucault's "Panopticon Revisited"', *Theoretical Criminology*, 1 (2), 215–34.

Net Exchange (2003a) 'Forming a Core Trader Group for the Policy Analysis Market', Arlington, VA, 5 June 2003. Available at: http://hanson.gmu.edu/PAM/reports/Trader-Solicitation-6-5-03.pdf (Accessed on 28 July 2005).

Net Exchange (2003b) 'The Policy Analysis Market: "Market in Death" Or Your Next Decision Support Tool', Presentation to Microsoft Research, Redmond, WA, 9 September 2003. Available at: http://www.nex.com/whitepapers.htm (Accessed 10 December 2004).

Noah, T. (2002) 'Crisis Over: Now that anti-Bush 9/11 recriminations have died down, so too, can the imminent risk of terrorist attack', *Slate.com*. (Accessed 20 September 2004).

Pethokoukis, J.M. (2004) 'All Seeing All Knowing', *US News and World Report*, 30 August 2004, 54.

Ponte, L. (2002) 'Preemptive Politics', *Frontpage Magazine.com*, 5 June.

Risen, J. and Lichtblau, E. (2005) 'Bush Lets us Spy on Callers Without Courts', *New York Times*, 16 December 2005, A1. Available at: http://www.commondreams.org/headlines05/1216-01.html.

Said, C. (2003) 'Pentagon to Start Futures Market for Terror Attacks; Wagering concept is based on a legitimate theory.' *San Francisco Chronicle*, 29 July 2003, A1.

Tether, A.J. (2002) 'DARPA State of the Union: DARPATech 2002' speech given 30 July 2002, Anaheim, CA. Available at http://www.dapra.mil/body/news/2002/DirectorSpeechDT2002.pdf.

The Internet Medical Journal (2003) 'Rand Advises Individuals on Actions to Protect Themselves in a Terrorist Attack', Community Forum, 10 September 2003. Available at: http://www.medjournal.com/forum/archive/index.php/t-876 (Accessed 5 December 2004).

Weber, S. (2005) *Targets of Opportunity: On the Militarization of Thinking* (New York: Fordham University Press).

Part 4

Subjects and Contexts of Surveillance

Chapter 8

'The other side of surveillance': webcams, power and agency

Hille Koskela

Introduction

There are more and more sites on the Internet which include visual representations of material, 'real places'. Some of the so-called webcams promote the images of cities being an increasingly important place marketing tool. The most iconic tourist cities especially provide images that aim to give these material places new meaning in the virtual space. Other sites include privately run 'home webcams' which present the daily lives of individuals. Furthermore, there is a range of webcams presenting various semi-public spaces; one can click into hairdressers' saloons, bars and cafes, taxi cars driving around, zoos, or have a look at nature reserves, beaches, slalom resorts, etc. (see Koskela 2004). Apart from being part of the virtual realm, webcams give new meanings to real places, add to them a new layer of interpretations, and link the virtual and material worlds in a fascinating way, and they are yet to be fully understood (e.g. Knight 2000; Jimroglou 2001; Terranova 2001; Burgin 2002; Campanella 2004).

Nevertheless, this phenomenon seems to have largely fallen between two stools as a subject for academic research. Technology studies emphasize new possibilities provided by technology, or users' abilities and experiences. Internet studies, including geographical work which has aimed to develop further the concept of 'virtual space', often focus on the virtual realm as such (see, however, Graham 1998; Nunes 2001). The interaction between 'virtual space' and 'material space' has been studied less, and rarely, when this connection is made has it been through visual images. For example, the discussion on 'digital cities' where 'virtual agoras' work as metaphors for a public sphere (see Crang 2000) has emphasized the 'service portal' nature of these sites, without connections to possible visual city images. Criminological surveillance studies largely seem to pass over the question of worldwide circulation of images and the 'side uses' of surveillance cameras. Globalization is discussed in terms of global data flows (Lyon 2001) and the wide-ranging 'surveillance assemblage' (Haggerty and Ericson 2000). However, webcams, which represent globalization through visual images, are not an amply discussed theme among the researchers of surveillance.

My background as a researcher of video surveillance has led me in this somewhat unexpected direction. Instead of tracking the other forms of surveillance combined with cameras, I have persistently continued to look at 'the pictures' themselves. This extraordinary path has led me to conceptualize what I here call 'the other side of surveillance'. Some changes in contemporary societies make it essential to increase our understanding of this phenomenon. First, the amount of visual representations has multiplied. Despite increasing critique, we have already reached the point where cameras can be literally anywhere. I have called this era of endless representations 'the Cam Era' (Koskela 2003). Second, the roles of these representations have multiplied. The visual material is circulated through various channels and often runs out of the control of those responsible for the original purpose of surveillance. Surveillance cameras have been 'tamed and domesticated by being part of everyday life' (Lyon 2001: 62). Perhaps more than anything else, the Internet representations show that the images literally flee from any organized control. This condition of 'over-production' and increasing circulation of images will mean that there is need for conceptual understanding of the new forms of seeing, looking, presenting and circulating images.

From the wide range of different representations, I have chosen two types of places for closer examination: public urban space with 'citycams' and private space with 'home webcams'.[1] My purpose is to track the dialogue of public(ness) and private(ness) which seems to be essential in surveillance studies, but changes to something different when webcams come to be considered. Furthermore, representations of public and private space open up interesting questions relating to privacy, power and agency – again central themes among surveillance scholars. Since one of my main purposes is to conceptualize the new kind of space which this phenomenon produces, the 'fringes' of spatial scale – the combination of public and private realms – give important information for developing understanding of this.

In theoretical understanding, webcams create an interesting tension by challenging the contemporary concepts of space: they seem to fall 'in between'. Although it is possible to focus on representations of public or private space, these very representations seem to form a new kind of space which is neither of the ones they show. In having connections to both virtual and material realms, webcams contribute to the 'blurring of our perception of different levels of reality' (Bernard 2000: 27). Webcams form somehow ageographic places, simultaneously with and without attachment to the geographies we know. There clearly is 'a transference ... of mental geographies developed in the material world onto cyberspace' (Boys 1999: 188). It has been noted that electronic media have radically reorganized space and that cyberspace can be understood as a new sphere of public space (Frohne and Katti 2000). Also it has been claimed that some webcams represent public exposure of private lives (Knight 2000). Internet representations traffic between physical and mental space, private and public space, material and virtual space. However, I claim that the understanding of what kind of space they actually produce is still vague.

The connection between traditional surveillance and the Internet presentation opens up a wide range of questions. Is what follows a 'democratization' of surveillance? Or increased and more random control? How do the real-time representations change social practices? What kind of new problems do they create surrounding the issues of privacy and civil liberties? How should we reconceptualize surveillance theories and develop our understanding?

The Internet – idealistically/skeptically

From its very early times, the Internet – initially without live cameras – has been claimed to be an arena for interactive democracy, critical expression, as well as a site of new identity formation (Featherstone and Burrows 1995; Shade 1996; Wertheim 1997; Higgins *et al.* 1999, to name but a few). First, it was somewhat naively assumed that the virtual realm would replace essential parts of the physical one. It would, as Bernard describes the early optimism, create 'a seamless place where we can all coexist and be treated equally' (2000: 29). Later, these idealistic notions were questioned and it was pointed out that the prejudices of physical life are reflected in the virtual life. The electronic space is 'not unbiased by definition, but socially conditioned' (Frohne

165

and Katti 2000: 10; see also Graham 1998). As Higgins and others have accurately pointed out, 'the electronic frontier has a history, geography and demography grounded firmly in the non-virtual realities of gender, class, race and other cultural variables that impact upon out experiences of the technological' (1999:111). Further, the Internet provides a channel of extensive surveillance and control of the individuals and moves 'surveillance integration' to a new level (Lyon 1998).

Although the public often goes along with the 'hype' surrounding new technologies, critical attitudes can also be found. This applies to the visual representations shown on the net. A survey conducted in Helsinki concluded that although the respondents were quite pro-surveillance in general, their attitudes were more negative when asked about Internet use of surveillance camera footage (Koskela and Tuominen 2003). The respondents seemed to rely on the authorities who were responsible for surveillance and had access to the tapes. In contrast to this, the Internet representations were seen as a threat to privacy: only 2 per cent of the respondents thought that surveillance material should be allowed to be placed on the Internet. However, when people 'surf' the net and view webcams they do not necessarily perceive them as surveillance cameras.[2]

The question is, why should webcams be discussed within the field of surveillance studies? Why should they be an issue in the first place? The main reason is that the difference between a webcam and a surveillance camera is blurring, sometimes not existing (Koskela 2004: 204). The city of Joensuu in eastern Finland provides a good example of this. In 1997 the Police Department of Joensuu decided to install three surveillance cameras to view the city marketplace. Their purpose was to promote the feeling of safety and curb crime. A follow-up survey was conducted between the years 1998 and 2000 to find out how the cameras fulfil their purpose (Koskela 2001). Originally, there was no plan for worldwide circulation but now these cameras are used as webcams showing images from the marketplace of Joensuu on the Internet.[3] The follow-up survey concluded that the cameras were actually not effective in crime control and, hence, 'place promotion' may eventually become their main purpose. There is no binary opposition between surveillance camera/webcam: the difference is semantic, not functional. Nevertheless, most of the theories on surveillance and surveillance cameras seem to fit poorly into the context of webcams.

'Citycams': glorifying clichéd landscapes

Next, I will take a closer look at the visual representations of public urban space – the citycams. They clearly contribute in 'transforming the landscape of cities into new *imagescapes*' (Boyer 2001: 36). Webcams are by no means 'innocent' illustrations of material urban space. Rather, Internet sites, as well as films, photographs, city plans, etc., 'provide selective representations of the city and shape the metaphors, narratives and syntax which are widely used to describe the experience of urban living' (Balshaw and Kennedy 2000: 4). The city of Jyväskylä in central Finland gives a telling example of what citycams can be like. While the pictures from Joensuu show a general bird's-eye view of the marketplace being almost like an electronic postcard, Jyväskylä provides closer-looking, exceptionally detailed real-time videos on its site.[4] The camera is 'interactive' in the sense that the audience can pan and zoom with it in real time. Faces of the people walking in the city centre pedestrian area are clear, and people can literally be recognized. At the moment, these types of cameras are rare, but I predict that they are 'pioneers' rather than exceptions.

The citycam sites provide different visual images ranging from still images to video and the interactive cameras described above.[5] Both the practices of presentation and regulation vary country by country. In some places the circulation of surveillance camera material is strictly regulated and it is illegal to place it on the Internet. Nevertheless, quite often the same cameras are used for surveilling and for circulating images – and for promoting places, in which the Internet plays a growing role. In countries where public space surveillance is not forbidden, it is practically impossible to regulate the Internet circulation of images. Even in places where surveillance of public space is illegal in principle, it is difficult to control. The case of Berlin illustrates this point. There is an interesting tension between law and practice: the surveillance of public space is illegal in principle, yet, there is an Internet site which provides representations of Berlin. As Balshaw and Kennedy argue, 'televisual space may or may not be the visual space of our urban futures, but it is an increasingly powerful mode of representation of the urban present' (2000: 11).

Boyer's (1992) historical research gives a deeper perspective to the roles of representations. She writes about the nineteenth-century dioramas and panoramas which were popular entertainment at that time, and argues that 'the real city' was never actually displayed but 'the city's image became the spectacle itself' (Boyer 1992: 186). The iconography of citycams produces a quite obvious image of the cities

167

in the picture. Most often, what is shown is the central market square, downtown pedestrian areas, or the places that attract tourists. While webcams create 'real interest on a real place' adding to them 'a whole new stratum of cultural space' (Campanella 2004: 59), they do not necessarily provide any surprises. Rather, they 'glorify' the clichéd, most apparent landscapes. What is shown is a little piece of urban landscape – 'a particular reframing of urban reality' (Boyer 1992: 187). The choice may look haphazard but most often is actually quite tendentious, as I will discuss in the next section where place marketing and tourism promotion are examined. Following Weibel (2002: 214), who argues that the real has become 'a copy of its image', it can be argued that in citycams 'the image is a copy of an image of the real'. What we see on the Internet is a *picture of a picture of a city*.

Place marketing, place identity and new moralities

Citycams have roles that surveillance cameras apparently do not. They have both deliberate and unintended consequences. Often citycams and their images are used as place-marketing tools. When the competition among cities intensifies, it becomes ever more important for each city to 'promote' its image (see e.g. Gold and Ward 1994; Ward 1998). As Boyer states, 'we seem to be witnessing in the contemporary city a proliferation of fictions and simulations ... scenographic visions relying on an art of verisimilitude' (1992: 187). Image-making is often based on conscious strategies which aim to attract companies and investments, as well as inhabitants. Further, the tourist industry plays a key role in why place promotion has become so trendy. Produced city images are used as instruments for adding market value to a place. The Internet forms 'a competitive realm of the virtual in which image-city competes against image-city' (Ward 2004: 250). Citycams are part of this development. When competition intensifies and cities must market themselves, 'their "imageability" becomes the new selling point' (Boyer 1992: 193). In some cities the original purpose for opening a website with a live view may have been to elevate tourism; in others the cameras installed for surveillance purposes are also presented on the Internet. As the example form Joensuu showed, place promotion can replace the original crime-control purpose. What follows is a range of problems and open questions concerning privacy, the ethics of watching, and the 'copyright' of the surveillance material.

Citycams may also have an influence on sense of place and local identity. Despite the notion that citycams do not necessarily produce any surprising images but, rather, represent the most apparent landscapes, they may have a role in strengthening the sense of place. They can create a feeling that 'our city' has its position in the global flow and, thus, support place identity. While the phenomenon becomes more common, the visual representations become less and less 'original'. However, it is exactly their 'real-time-ness' that makes it possible to keep up the idea that they describe something that is original in this particular place. Citycams make places memorable and imageable and, simultaneously, support the sense of belonging among their residents (cf. Boyer 2001: 40). In their function as an everyday device, 'locality and virtuality go hand in hand' (Ward 2004: 252). Residents can be 'proud' of their city. Local presence and 'tele-presence' (Virilio 2002: 109) melt into each other, forming a new experience of place. Hence, these shared images clearly have roles that are different from – or even opposite to – social control. This illustrates how citycams can be empowering in a way surveillance cameras never could. Nevertheless, this does not mean that citycams would not also enable new forms of control.

The virtual representations of material space may create new social practices or change old ones. The citycam Internet sites 'function not simply as tourism portals but as multi-service city information systems' (Ward 2004: 248). For example, the citycams enable parents to watch out for their teenage children who 'hang around' in the city centre or marketplace. This is likely to make those teenagers who do not want to be seen, or watched over, flee from the central places. The 'socially differentiated nature of targeting' (Norris and Armstrong 1999: 201), discussed in relation to video surveillance, applies also to citycams intensifying the stigmatization of youth. But, on the other hand, citycams can also help the teenagers (especially those who belong to the computer-oriented subcultures) in gathering at a particular street corner, etc. and, hence, create new ways of behaving. The Internet is fostering 'a complex web of semi-legitimate, oppositional and alternative subcultures' (Higgins et al. 1999: 117). These forms of socializing overcome the distinction of 'virtual' and 'material' space (see also Massey 1998). These practices are essentially different from the surveillance practices of the authorities. They are more creative and more on the 'grassroots' level, and support active agency among the citizens – the webcam network can be understood as a kind of 'grassroots telepresence project' (Campanella 2004: 61). Nevertheless, there is also a risk that they create new problems surrounding the issues of privacy and civil liberties.

Furthermore, it is possible to use citycams as surveillance tools in many traditional but also new unexpected ways. As Crang (2000) claims, the metaphors through which cyberspace is understood reflect a range of anxieties and desires for urban life. Accordingly, the actual uses of the Internet – especially through webcams – have connections to anxious encounters and conflicts on the street. The possibility to view urban space on the Internet might be helpful for the police, the vigilant audience or potential witnesses of crime. While this may sometimes be helpful from the crime-prevention perspective, it may also create serious security risks yet to be understood. It is by no means clear whether the virtual representations of material space promote or decrease security. The security issues in question are highly complex. It is likely that citycams will also create new moralities and new kinds of social control. They contribute to 'the social construction of suspicion' (Norris and Armstrong 1999: 117). The 'vigilant audience' may have multiple roles and multiple motives for their watching. An ironic mundane example of this is provided by the server Geocities, where the place-marketing slogan for the city of Oulu in Northern Finland goes: 'Oulu Market Place: See who's most drunk!'.[6]

Lately, there has been a lot of discussion about exclusion and urban space. As Hubbardt has pointed out, 'this "exclusionary urge" has been most vividly demonstrated in the way that city space, often regarded as democratic and open, has become increasingly regulated', resulting in 'groups and individuals whose lifestyles are viewed as incompatible with so-called "normal" ways of behaving have had their access to urban space limited' (Hubbardt 2000: 248). The role of traditional video surveillance in this exclusionary control is apparent (see Lyon 2001; Norris 2002; Coleman 2004, to name but a few). There is a growing 'fear of darkened spaces' which are 'zones of disorder' (Foucault 1980: 153) and are not to be tolerated since they constitute a threat. Surveillance has, indeed, become a mechanism which aims to guarantee purity and to exclude feared strangers: 'the Other' in a literal as well as metaphorical sense (see Koskela 2000). However, how the visual representations on the Internet might relate to this is less obvious.

Two contradictory arguments have been presented. It is possible to aim for a renewed public realm in cyberspace which explicitly evokes an 'open city' (Crang 2000). Digital communications offer 'the promise of an open space of equal exchange based upon a nonhierarchical structure … space without physical boundaries' (Bernard 2000: 26). But on the other hand, it has been pointed out that cyberspace extends a general urban problem of the commodification and closure of public space (e.g. Featherstone and Burrows 1995).

After the examples from 'non-sexy' small cities in Finland, I will make a brief exploration of Times Square, New York, one of the most iconic landscapes in the world. After the renovation and new regulation of Times Square, it has perhaps become the most famous example of 'purified space' – a piece of urban land which is 'as clean and pure as a whistle' (Boyer 2001: 31). New York's zero-tolerance policy has been used to exclude the marginal and 'deviant' groups from (previously) public urban space. Since maintained by the Times Square Business Improvement District (BID), Times Square has been 'an autonomous security zone' (Sussman 1998: 34). The BID is a private company which regulates basically everything that goes on on the square: public behaviour, garbage handling, environmental aesthetics, crime prevention, and exclusion of the homeless (Sussman 1998). The 'exclusionary urge' has certainly changed the nature of the place, making it become a business-led, 'disneyfied' space (Bell 1998).

At present, Times Square has ten interactive real-time citycams, which show general views as well as more detailed pictures of people passing by.[7] While there are many other cameras in New York presenting the symbolic points – such as the Empire State Building Cam or the Ground Zero Cam[8] – these ten cameras around Times Square are the greatest amount of webcams presenting one square. The Internet presentation seems to complement the development in material space. As Times Square itself 'has been transformed into a simulated theme park for commercial entertainment' (Boyer 2001: 49), where 'land values are tied to moral values' (Sussman 1998: 39), it seems somehow 'natural' that this simulation is present in the virtual world. As Terranova claims, 'the society of spectacle, simulation and virtual reality can be seen to collapse into each other' (2001: 130).

I do not claim that webcam presenting would be the 'reason' for purification nor the other way round. There is no causal relationship. Yet, they seem to have some kind of relationship – they somehow support each other. If Times Square was not 'purified' in the first place, it would most likely not have been chosen for such an intense Internet circulation. Hence, purification was an essential prerequisite of the installation of the citycams. The place as it previously was – with the homeless, prostitutes and drug users wandering around – would not have given a place image glorious enough to be circulated. Only the purified urban space is worth presenting. And since it is now seen worldwide, this can be used as (an additional) justification for further purification. It becomes ever more important to keep the place 'impressive'. In this sense, webcams have an unexpected link to the practices – as well as theories – of surveillance and social control. Indeed, the representation of places in the virtual realm contributes to the production of space in the material realm.

'Home webcams' and the construction of post-cyborg identities

There is some voyeuristic fascination in looking, but, reciprocally, some exhibitionist fascination in being seen. As Tabor writes: 'the very idea of surveillance evokes curiosity, desire, aggression, guilt, and, above all, fear – emotions that interact in daydream dramas of seeing and being seen, concealment and self-exposure, attack and defense, seduction and enticement' (2001: 135). While being seen may be unpleasant for some, others are eager to increase their visibility (Groombridge 2002: 43). The popularity of home webcams demonstrates this clearly. No longer is surveillance necessarily interpreted as a threat but rather 'as a chance to display oneself under the gaze of the camera' (Ernst 2002: 461). Private non-commercial webcams, which promote nothing but the existence of the person presenting oneself – and perhaps her/his belonging to a certain (virtual, global) community – differ a lot from traditional surveillance cameras. Further, they also differ greatly from citycams. Nevertheless, they are worth studying for increasing our conceptual understanding of presenting and hiding, power and control, hegemonies and resistance. In contrast to being targets of the ever-increasing surveillance, people seek to play an active role in the endless production of visual representations. I claim that they seek *active agency* – a condition where they can be subjects rather than objects (of surveillance). In doing this, they 'reclaim the copyright of their own lives' (Koskela 2004: 206).

As Haggerty (this volume) notes, to be seen (as well as to see) can be 'fun' – experienced as pleasurable. Exposing oneself can be connected to identity formation. The structure of home webcam sites resembles that of web blogs, which have lately become popular. They often include personal diaries, archives of pictures, as well as e-mail or chat connections which enable the viewers to communicate with the target of their gaze. It is quite apparent from these sites that the person on the cam wants to be known. That is what 'the very structure of these sites indicates' (Knight 2000: 23). What seems to be essential to identity formation – and different from the surveillance contexts of being seen – is that the home webcam owners have agency in their project. These people may be a continuation to what (Los this volume) calls 'surveillance-directed individuals' – the ones who are not just reacting to new technologies but, rather, show 'creative engagement'. Webcams are individual projects where there are 'no outside editors, directors, or producers to decide who gets how much airtime' (Knight 2000: 24).

Many questions surrounding private space home webcams remain unanswered. How do the home webcams modify their owners' identity? What are the motives behind installing the equipment? Why do people 'voluntarily' make themselves visible? How does it feel to be seen by a global unknown audience? Webcams fuse exhibitionism and solitude (cf. Burgin 2002). They link individuals to global communities. As Knight points out, 'those involved in this type of production develop a sense of community' (2000: 21–2). People with cameras communicate with their viewers or others who are present. They sometimes face risks or receive threats (see Adam 2001; Burgin 2002) but, nevertheless, are willing to 'take the risk'. This seems quite radical in the era when the 'culture of fear' dominates and personal risk-taking is close to a taboo (Furedi 2002). Simultaneously, they question our conceptual understandings of presenting and hiding, hegemonies and resistance.

A home webcam can be interpreted as a component in an integration of body and technology, an object embedded in a 'post-cyborg subjectivity' (Koskela 2004). In this integration, 'the camera moves from a recording instrument to an integral aspect of the subjects' lives' (Knight 2000: 24). Webcams seem to be opening up radically new subjectivities. They describe how new technologies do not only serve surveillance but liberation, resistance and 'escape' (Bogard this volume). While it is evident that the Internet does not provide such an idealistic open, democratic forum that was previously thought, it still has a role in creating and organizing resistance and forming new identity politics. The virtual world was once thought to bring us to an era which could be called 'post-gender' (Higgins *et al.* 1999: 111). It was supposed to be a realm where identities could be hidden, where gender-switching would become possible and 'misrepresentations of self' could be understood to be an opportunity rather than a morally precarious action (Wertheim 1997; Roberts and Parks 2001). In the initial stage of virtual space it was assumed that 'the "gaze" was removed' (Boys 1999: 190). Home webcams contribute in turning this development up-side-down by bringing back the bodily subjects – or, more precisely, their visual representations. They generate a re-embodiment of subjects, and break the distinction between 'pure human beings' and 'simulated disembodied post-humans' (Featherstone and Burrows 1995: 11). Some ostensibly minor changes in the conventional code of what can and what cannot be shown hit deeply in our understanding of looking and being looked at. They reveal cultural tensions surrounding epistemological conceptions of vision, gender and identity and raise questions regarding the role of technology in the representation and construction of subjects (Jimroglou 2001: 286).

Ripping up 'the straitjacket of otherness'

The field of vision, most often, seems to have a gendered dimension (see e.g. Wilson 1995; Ainley 1998; Koskela 2002). Private visual representations on the Internet are often explicitly connected with sexuality. Most webcams that are installed by women exaggerate sexuality, even those which are not commercialized. There are two parallel explanations that go hand-in-hand in this. First, it seems to be popular among women (especially young women) to present themselves as sexual beings. Second, the 'top ten' lists, etc., on the Internet make sure that the sexualized cameras are the ones that are promoted, and thus, become 'more visible' than the non-sexualized ones.[9] So easily, the body becomes 'idealized – and therefore a commodity' (Knight 2000: 22). The female body is an object of a gaze in a different way than the male body. The heterosexual context is the dominating one; subcultures, however, having their own strong iconography as well.

It can be argued that it is 'more radical' for women to install home webcams than for men. The cultural meanings of obscuring gestures are deeply gendered. Women are constantly reminded that an invisible observer is a threat. In crime-prevention advice, for example, women are recommended to keep their curtains tightly closed whenever it might be possible for someone outside to see inside (Gardner 1995). This advice presents the potential observer as male. Conventionally, 'concealing' goes along with being a woman and the 'exposure' of a female body is easily interpreted as exploitation. Hence, it is obvious that women's home webcams rupture our understandings of the field of vision and the production of gendered subjects.

These points are not to be simplified: women can be perpetrators as well as objects of the gaze. Wilson has argued against the reproduction of a condition in which 'women are stuck forever in the straight jacket of otherness by the Male Gaze' (1995: 69). In the context of home webcams, gender relations become complex. Indeed, the female body is presented as 'something to be seen', yet within the conditions set by the one who is seen, not the viewer, as is the case in surveillance or harassing looks on the street. It can be a way of creating a female subject that is able to 'require and yet simultaneously resist certain traditional readings of female embodiment' (Jimroglou 2001: 288–9). By presenting intimate pictures of private life, home webcam owners rebel against the modesty and shame embedded in the conception of the private. They 'refuse to be humble' (Koskela 2004: 210).

In the context of safety, 'being seen' connotes either with being safe and secured or with being threatened, depending on who is the perceived 'viewer' (Koskela 2002). In the context of surveillance, 'being seen' connotes either with being 'under control' or with giving up privacy. I argue that home webcams challenge both of these notions. Being seen connotes with something else, something new. Obviously, the idea of home webcams is not to increase 'control', in a traditional sense. Nor to 'give up privacy', in a traditional sense. We will need to understand the meaning(s) of being seen differently.

A surveillance camera represents total one-way-ness of the gaze by making it impossible to look back. There is no 'mutual' gaze. It would feel ridiculous to try to flirt with a surveillance camera (Koskela 2003: 298). Its objects are constantly seen but with no possibility to 'respond' or 'oppose' the gaze. Webcams, on the other hand, are filled with flirt. They can be interpreted as a form of confrontation, surveillance turned into spectacle – a form of resistance. Webcams clearly support active agency. What, how and when is presented is controlled by the person(s) whose images are circulated. They have 'access to both means of production and, through the Internet, the means of distribution' (Knight 2000: 21). Who will then see these pictures, runs out of control. This, however, is exactly the point: to understand revealing as a political act and to reject the traditional understanding of objectification.

Concluding comments: a new kind of 'space in-between'?

What I have tried to describe in this chapter can be called 'the other side' of surveillance: people do not submit to the passive role of 'the observed' that surveillance offers them but, instead, play various active roles with 'surveillance' equipment. Webcams are 'liminal devices' (Campanella 2004: 58) which contest our conception of the old-fashioned surveillance devices. They represent resistance which is immanent to the system of visibility (Bogard this volume). With them, 'ordinary' people are able to take possession of positions they previously did not have. Webcams can be 'liberating and confidence-bolstering' (Knight 2000: 25), unlike surveillance cameras, which are often perceived as suppressing and objectifying.

As surveillance was linking local realities to global practices, webcams do it far more intensively. While surveillance was 'placeless and faceless' (Koskela 2002), webcams create new meanings to places, hence, 'bringing back' places – and faces. They multiply the audience(s) and increase further the 'information overload'. Webcams can also be argued to contribute to the 'democratization' of surveillance, not however, being able to overcome the digital divide.

Webcams challenge some of the very basics of surveillance theory. As Haggerty (this volume) has argued, the 'panoptic model' has dominated surveillance theory and, in this domination, suppressed other forms of understanding. Webcams undermine many of the connections which have been essential in panoptic thinking (Koskela 2004). Their function comes closer to processes of 'synopticism' (Mathiesen 1997) than panopticism. However, the most theoretically challenging question is not formed around the amount of watchers but, rather, around the motivations of the watched. It is the deliberate exposure of the self – whether of cities or individuals – that shifts the surveillance model (Knight 2000). Willingness to be seen has thus far been largely left without theoretical understanding and the theories which are based on the principles of the panopticon are certainly not helpful in developing it.

It is possible to identify at least four modes of thinking which were central to the panoptic model but do not apply when webcams come into focus. First, webcams contest the Foucauldian connection between visibility and power, the idea of power which considers those who can see being more powerful than those who are seen. Webcams seem not to show people as less powerful even if they deliberately make themselves visible. Second, the phenomenon undermines the idea of internalization of control. People who present pictures of their private lives refuse to internalize the rules of hiding and concealing. These rules conventionally relate to the private realm and, by doing so, ensure submissiveness. Third, the panoptic idea of normalization where desire to 'cure' is the purpose of surveillance does not apply here. Webcams do not function as normalization devices, but rather support peculiarities. And fourth, while webcams undoubtedly break some old power relations, there is no purpose to increase control, rather, to blur the lines of control. The 'empowering role' of webcams shows that power and control are two different things and should therefore also be treated as two different concepts within surveillance theory.

Webcams, offering visual representations of both private and public space, show that power operates in complex ways. Anyone can observe but is not necessarily able to exercise power or control in the sense that the 'official' observers were. The 'overseers' turn into 'viewers'. Power has at least two forms which contest the conceptual understanding of surveillance: first, power works through moralities and social control, as the part on public space citycams showed; and second, resisting power works through the empowering nature of home webcams in private space.

The development of the concept of space has been the focus of much theoretical research, where space is understood to be socially produced (starting from Lefebvre 1991). Previously, I have described how some of the power relationships embedded within increased surveillance have changed the nature of urban space (Koskela 2000, 2003). Webcams open up interesting theoretical challenges to be examined in relation to a new kind of social production of space. Space, as it is conventionally conceptualized, has four categories: public, semi-public, private and virtual. There is a wide range of reasoning around all these, and all four concepts have also had a lot of critical attention. Webcams, however, seem to create space that is beyond all previous categorizations. This space is not private, in a traditional sense: even the most private corners become public since they are to be seen by anyone, anywhere, anytime. However, it is not public space either, since it is impossible to (physically) reach. Yet, this space is also different from virtual space if virtual space is, as usual, defined as something beyond bodily presence. Through the cameras the virtual becomes embedded with 'real'.

What kind of space is being created in this 'in-betweenness' of material space and virtual space? How does it differ from the concept of virtual space where visual representations of material space or individuals had no role? How does it differ from concepts of material space, public urban space and private space where people can meet as bodily individuals? To be able to comprehend this phenomenon, we would need to create a new kind of understanding of space. As the binary categories of subject/object, sexualized/non-sexualized and virtual/embodied are questioned, so are the binary categories of space. To understand the 'in-betweenness' of material space and virtual space is a conceptual challenge.

There is a continuum, from the panopticon to the development of video surveillance, again to the development of digital video devices, and from there again to the Internet representations of these videos. A lot has changed along the way. Just to give an example, the conceptualization of space has changed from Foucault's (1977: 141) idea of 'distribution' of individuals in (material) space (as a basis for the exercise of power), to the point where we would need to understand what happens when space is socially produced in the 'in-betweenness' of material and virtual worlds and when, simultaneously, the representations of places in the virtual realm contribute in the production of space in the material realm. We certainly are 'beyond' the panopticon.

Notes

1 My methodological outline is to focus only on non-commercial webcams and I have extended this to cameras which aim to sell something. The cameras that present semi-public spaces are often of commercial nature. I have also excluded those private webcams whose owners charge the viewers.
2 It must be noted that, methodologically, there is a significant difference depending on what the research context is and how the questions are formed. In this case, the 'frame' was a questionnaire which dealt specifically with surveillance, not the Internet as such. Hence, the respondents perceived the question to be in relation to surveillance and placed the images they had in mind into the surveillance context. If the survey had been on Internet pages, the responses would most likely have been different.
3 http://www.jns.fi/webcam.html.
4 http://media.keskisuomalainen.fi/webcam/index.html.
5 see for example http://www.webcamword.com.
6 http://www/geocities.com.
7 http://www.earthcam.com/usa/newyork/timessquare/.
8 The Ground Zero Cam, indeed, is a symbol for 'rebuilding America' after the September 11 attack: while it was a site of disaster, the authorities were not eager to circulate any kind of pictures of it. Since the rebuilding project started, their attitudes turned upside-down. It became important that the site 'is seen'. http://www.earthcam.com/usa/newyork/groundzero/index.php.
9 see for example http://www.camville.com/toptenwebcams.php.

References

Adam, A. (2001) 'Cyberstalking: Gender and Computer Ethics', in E. Green and A. Adam (eds) *Virtual Gender: Technology, Consumption and Identity* (London: Routledge), 209–24.
Ainley, R. (1998) 'Watching the Detectors: Control and the Panopticon', in R. Ainley (ed.) *New Frontiers of Space, Bodies and Gender* (London: Routledge), 88–100.
Balshaw, M. and Kennedy, L. (2000) 'Introduction: Urban Space and Representation', in M. Balshaw and L. Kennedy (eds) *Urban Space and Representation* (London: Pluto Press), 1–21.
Bell, J. (1998) 'Times Square: Public Space Disneyfied', *The Drama Review,* 42 (1), 25–33.
Bernard, C. (2000) 'Bodies and Digital Utopia', *Art Journal,* 59 (4), 26–31.
Boyer, M.C. (1992) 'Cities for Sale: Merchandising History at South Street Seaport', in M. Sorkin (ed.) *Variations on a Theme Park: The New American City and the End of Public Space* (New York: Hill and Wang), 181–204.
Boyer, M.C. (2001) 'Twice-Told Stories: The Double Erasure of Times Square', in I. Borden, J. Kerr, J. Rendell and A. Pivaro (eds) *The Unknown City:*

Contesting Architecture and Social Space (Cambridge, MA: MIT Press), 30–53.

Boys, J. (1999) 'Positions in the Landscape? Gender, space and the "Nature" of Virtual Reality', in Cutting Edge (eds) *Desire by Design: Body, Territories and New Technologies* (London: I.B. Tauris), 183–202.

Burgin, V. (2002) 'Jenni's Room: Exhibitionism and Solitude', in T.Y. Levin, U. Frohne and P. Weibel (eds) *CTRL[SPACE]: Rhetorics of Surveillance from Bentham to Big Brother* (Cambridge, MA and London: MIT Press), 228–35.

Campanella, T.J. (2004) 'Webcameras and the Telepresent Landscape', in S. Graham (ed.) *The Cybercities Reader* (London: Routledge), 57–63.

Coleman, R. (2004) *Reclaiming the Streets: Surveillance, Social Control and the City* (Cullompton: Willan).

Crang, M. (2000) 'Public Space, Urban Space, Electronic Space: Would the Real City Please Stand up?', *Urban Studies*, 37 (2), 301–17.

Earth Cam. (2001) 'Ground Zero Cams'. Available at: http://www.earthcam.com/usa/newyork/groundzero/index.php.

Earth Cam. 'Times Square Cams'. Available at: http://www.earthcam.com/usa/newyork/timessquare/.

Ernst, W. (2002) 'Beyond the Rhetoric of Panopticism: Surveillance as Cybernetics', in T.Y. Levin, U. Frohne and P. Weibel (eds) *CTRL[SPACE]: Rhetorics of Surveillance from Bentham to Big Brother* (Cambridge, MA and London: MIT Press), 460–3.

Featherstone, M. and Burrows, R. (1995) 'Cultures of Technological Embodiment: An Introduction', in M. Featherstone and R. Burrows (eds) *Cyberspace/Cyberbodies/Cyberpunk* (London: Sage), 1–19.

Foucault, M. (1977) *Discipline and Punish: The Birth of a Prison* (London: Penguin).

Foucault, M. (1980) 'The Eye of Power', in C. Gordon (ed.) *Power/Knowledge: Selected Interviews and Other Writings 1972–1977 by Michel Foucault* (Sussex: Harvester), 146–65.

Frohne, U. and Katti, C. (2000) 'Crossing Boundaries in Cyberspace? The Politics of "Body" and "Language" After the Emergence of New Media', *Art Journal*, 59 (4), 9–13.

Furedi, F. (2002) *Culture of Fear: Risk-Taking and the Morality of Low Expectation* (London: Continuum).

Gardner, C.B. (1995) *Passing By: Gender and Public Harassment* (Berkeley: University of California Press).

Geocities. 'Oulu, Finland'. Available at: http://www.geocities.com.

Gold, J.R. and Ward, S.V. (1994) *Place Promotion: The Use of Publicity and Marketing to Sell Towns and Regions.* (Chichester, UK: John Wiley and Sons).

Graham, S. (1998) 'Spaces of Surveillant Simulation: New Technologies, Digital Representations, and Material Geographies', *Environment and Planning D: Society and Space*, 16, 483–504.

Groombridge, N. (2002) 'Crime Control or Crime Culture TV?', *Surveillance and Society*, 1 (1), 30–6. Available at:http://www.surveillance-and-society.org/articles1/cctvculture.pdf.

Haggerty, K.D. and Ericson, R.V. (2000) 'The Surveillant Assemblage', *British Journal of Sociology*, 51 (4), 605–22.

Higgins, R., Rushhaija, E. and Medhurst, A. (1999) 'Technowhores', in Cutting Edge (eds) *Desire by Design: Body, Territories and New Technologies* (London: I.B. Tauris), 111–22.

Hubbardt, P. (2000) 'Policing the Public Realm: Community Action and the Exclusion of Street Prostitution', in J.R. Gold and G. Revill (eds) *Landscapes of Defence* (Harlow: Pearson Education), 246–62.

Jimroglou, K.M. (2001) 'A Camera with a View: JenniCAM, Visual Representations and Cyborg Subjectivity', in E. Green and A. Adam (eds) *Virtual Gender: Technology, Consumption and Identity* (London: Routledge), 286–301.

Joensuu, Finland. Web Cam. Available at: http://www.jns.fi/webcam.html. Keskisuomalainen.

Jyväskylä, Finland. Web Cam. Available at: http://media.keskisuomalainen.fi/webcam/index.html.

Knight, B.A. (2000) 'Watch Me! Webcams and the Public Exposure of Private Lives', *Art Journal*, 59 (4), 21–5.

Koskela, H. (2000) '"The Gaze Without Eyes": Video Surveillance and the Changing Nature of Urban Space', *Progress in Human Geography*, 24, 243–65.

Koskela, H. (2001) *Joensuun Torialueen Kameravalvonnan Vaikutus Kaupunkilaisten Turvallisuuteen*, Joensuun kihlakunnan poliisilaitos, Joensuun keskustakehittämisyhdistys.

Koskela, H. (2002) 'Video Surveillance, Gender and the Safety of Public Urban Space: "Peeping Tom" Goes High Tech?' *Urban Geography*, 23 (3), 257–78.

Koskela, H. (2003) '"Cam Era": The Contemporary Urban Panopticon', *Surveillance and Society*, 1 (3), 292–313. Available at: http://www.surveillance-and-society.org/articles1(3)/camera.pdf.

Koskela, H. (2004) 'Webcams, TV Shows and Mobile Phones: Empowering Exhibitionism', *Surveillance and Society*, 2 (2/3), 199–215. Available at: http://www.surveillance-and-society.org/articles2(2)/webcams.pdf.

Koskela, H. and Tuominen, M. (2003) *Kakspiippunen Juttu: Ttutkimus Helsinkiläisten Suhtautumisesta Kameravalvontaan* Research Reports of the Helsinki Urban Facts, 2003 (3).

Lefebvre, H. (1991) *The Production of Space* (Oxford: Blackwell).

Lyon, D. (1998) 'The World Wide Web of Surveillance: The Internet and Off-World Power-Flows', *Information, Communication and Society* 1 (1), 1–9.

Lyon, D. (2001) *Surveillance Society: Monitoring Everyday Life* (Buckingham: Open University Press).

Massey, D. (1998) 'The Spatial Construction of Youth Cultures', in T. Skelton and G. Valentine (eds) *Cool Places: Geographies of Youth Cultures* (London: Routledge), 121–29.

Mathiesen, T. (1997) 'The Viewer Society: Foucault's "Panopticon" Revisited', *Theoretical Criminology*, 1, 215–34.

Norris, C. (2002) 'From Personal to Digital: CCTV, the Panopticon, and the Technological Mediation of Suspicion and Social Control', in D. Lyon (ed.) *Surveillance as Social Sorting: Privacy, Risk and Digital Discrimination* (London and New York: Routledge), 249–81.

Norris, C. and Armstrong, G. (1999) *The Maximum Surveillance Society. The Rise of CCTV* (Oxford: Berg).

Nunes, M. (2001) 'Ephemeral Cities: Postmodern Urbanism and the Production of Online Space', in D. Holmes (ed.) *Virtual Globalization: Virtual Spaces/ Tourist Spaces* (London: Routledge), 57–75.

Roberts, L.D. and Parks, M.R. (2001) 'The Social Geography of Gender Switching in Virtual Environments on the Internet', in E. Green and A. Adam (eds) *Virtual Gender: Technology, Consumption and Identity* (London: Routledge), 265–85.

Shade, L.R (1996) 'Is There Free Speech on the Net? Censorship in the Global Information Infrastructure', in R. Shields (ed.) *Cultures of Internet: Virtual Spaces, Real Histories, Living Bodies* (London: Sage), 11–32.

Sussman, M. (1998) 'New York's Facelift', *The Drama Review*, 42 (1), 34–42.

Tabor, P. (2001) 'I am a Videocam', in I. Borden, J. Kerr, J. Rendell and A. Pivaro (eds) *The Unknown City: Contesting Architecture and Social Space* (Cambridge, MA: MIT Press), 122–37.

Terranova, T. (2001) 'Demonstrating the Globe: Virtual Action in the Network Society', in D. Holmes (ed.) *Virtual Globalization. Virtual Spaces/Tourist Spaces* (London: Routledge), 95–113.

TopTenWebCams.com. Available at: http://www/camville.com/toptenwebcams.php.

Virilio, P. (2002) 'The Visual Crash', in T.Y. Levin, U. Frohne and P. Weibel (eds) *CTRL [SPACE]: Rhetorics of Surveillance from Bentham to Big Brother* (Cambridge, MA and London: MIT Press), 108–13.

Ward, J. (2004) 'Berlin, the Virtual Global City', *Journal of Visual Culture* 3 (2), 239–56.

Ward, S.V. (1998) *Selling Places: The Marketing and Promotion of Towns and Cities 1850–2000* (London: E. and F.N. Spon).

Webcamword.com. Available at: http://www.webcamword.com.

Weibel, P. (2002) 'Pleasure and the Panoptic Principle', in T.Y. Levin, U. Frohne and P. Weibel (eds) *CTRL [SPACE]: Rhetorics of Surveillance from Bentham to Big Brother* (Cambridge, MA and London: MIT Press), 207–23.

Wertheim, M. (1997) 'The Pearly Gates of Cyberspace', in N. Ellin (ed.) *The Architecture of Fear* (New York: Princeton Architectural Press), 295–302.

Wilson, E. (1995) 'The Invisible Flâneur', in S. Watson and K. Gibson (eds) *Postmodern Cities and Spaces* (Oxford: Blackwell), 59–79.

Chapter 9

Telemonitoring of cardiac patients: user-centred research as input for surveillance theories

Lynsey Dubbeld

Introduction

Healthcare has increasingly become suffused with high-tech applications, in particular, systems based on information and communication technologies (ICTs). As Brown and Webster noted in their book on 'new medical technologies':

> Today, maintaining the body is a problem of technological apprehension or capture requiring the production of new systems for codification, storage, accessibility and distribution. The object of maintenance and care then is no longer simply the individual body, but representations or traces of the body in globalized systems of information and data management. (Brown and Webster 2004: 80–1).

Current studies of surveillance suggest that the globalization of personal data is in fact one of the core trends in contemporary surveillance practices (e.g. Lyon 2003b). Hence, the present-day use of healthcare technologies that imply transnational processing of sensitive information, such as telemedicine and e-health systems, calls for an analysis of its surveillance implications.

This chapter discusses a number of ideas developed in contemporary user studies that contribute to understanding the surveillance aspects of emerging high-tech healthcare practices such as telemedicine. In order to demonstrate that present surveillance studies will benefit from adopting these insights, an empirical case study of telemonitoring is introduced. The central question addressed in this chapter is: In what ways do ideas that have become available in user-centred research contribute to developing surveillance theories that are well equipped for understanding and analysing surveillance aspects of telemonitor-ing?

A case study of telemonitoring of arrhythmias, introduced in the next section, serves as a first step towards answering this question. Then, I briefly discuss some of the views and concepts developed in surveillance studies that are relevant to the case of telemonitoring. Subsequently, a number of insights developed in studies of user–technology interactions are described and their relevance to surveillance theories explored. The last section summarizes in which ways the notions that I discussed will be of benefit to surveillance studies.

Background

Telemedicine, defined here as the delivery of healthcare services and the exchange of healthcare information across distances via ICTs, is currently on the rise (e.g. Rigby *et al.* 2000; Van Rijen *et al.* 2002; Wootton, 2001). Telemedicine is expected to realize cost-effective, or even cost-reductive, healthcare provision (Bauer and Ringel 1999: 7; Emery 1998: 13; Wootton 2000: 19), and to contribute to, amongst other things, improving quality of care and access to healthcare services (Craig 1999: 13; Donaldson and Lohr 1994: 61–2; Eriksson and Terenius 2005: 26; Louis *et al.* 2003: 584; Roberts *et al.* 2000: 4).

One area of innovation where the benefits of telemedicine for patient care are considered to be particularly promising is telemonitoring of the chronically ill, such as patients with high blood pressure (HeartCenter Online 2004). Increasingly, telemedical systems have also been developed for cardiac patients (Buckles *et al.* 2004; Roth *et al.* 2001; Zimetbaum and Josephson 1999; cf. Holter 1961; Louis *et al.* 2003). For example, at the moment, several types of so-called ambulatory electrocardiogram (ECG) recorders are available for diagnosing palpitations and monitoring heart failure: portable devices that allow for patient-activated recording of heart rates. Although privacy and surveillance are regularly discussed as (potential) issues of concern in the literature on telemedicine (e.g. Hentenaar 2003; Ligtvoet 2004; Rodriguez and Cabrera 2004), rather little is known about the surveillance implications of recent developments in telemonitoring (e.g. Cabrera 2004; Owen 2000; Van Rijen *et al.* 2002).

Theory

The adequacy of the concept of the panopticon for describing contemporary surveillance has been challenged considerably, for instance in view of its tendency to produce dystopian, totalizing accounts (e.g. Bannister *et al.* 1998; Gandy 1993; Lyon 1994; Haggerty this volume; Norris 2005). A growing number of theorists have attempted to adapt the panopticon paradigm to make it better suited for addressing current issues in surveillance (e.g. Bigo this volume; Mathiesen 1997; Poster 1990). Others have proposed alternative perspectives that aim to move beyond the panopticon metaphor (e.g. Bogard 1996, this volume; Deleuze 1992; Haggerty and Ericson 2000).

Therefore, surveillance theories have witnessed the emergence of a range of positions and concepts, all of which aim to discuss contemporary surveillance-enabling technologies, either with or without resorting to the panopticon paradigm. But it is uncertain whether these theories are well suited for developing an understanding of the surveillance implications of current telemedicine practices, or, more specifically, the use of telemonitoring systems in the field of cardiology. For example, analyses based on the panopticon tend to produce dystopic accounts, and fail to allow for a nuanced position on the implications of surveillance. And theories of the surveillance society are underdeveloped with respect to explaining their methodologies and theoretical underpinnings.

In this chapter, I introduce a case study of the use of telemedical devices for diagnosis and monitoring of cardiac patients in order to illustrate a set of notions that are derived from the field of science and technology studies (STS). As I argue, these ideas contribute to analysing current trends in telemedicine without resorting to problematic concepts and positions such as those based on the panopticon or the surveillance society.[1] Moreover, the STS insights discussed in this chapter hold the promise of furthering the development of surveillance theories that aim to describe and address surveillance implications of contemporary telemedicine practices.

Methods

The analysis in this chapter builds on a case study of two types of ambulatory ECG recorders for diagnosing palpitations and monitoring heart failure.[2] In addition to a literature review of innovations in telemedicine in the field of cardiology, the case study involved a detailed empirical study.

The fieldwork, conducted in the period between April 2004 and February 2005, consisted of interviews, questionnaires and observations. Because the empirical study was informed by the multiple-use perspective, it included interviews and surveys across a range of different actors involved in cardiac telemonitoring. Interviews were held with managers of two Dutch companies that offer telemonitoring services to cardiac patients; three cardiologists; two general practitioners (GPs) prescribing ambulatory ECG recorders; two consumer groups concerned with the treatment of cardiac diseases; two Home Care offices that delivered telemonitoring devices to patients; and eleven patients who had made use of ambulatory ECG recorders during April and/or May 2004. These patients were interviewed in semi-structured, in-depth interviews that ranged from one to one-and-a-half hours.

In addition, 54 patients (a response rate of 65 per cent) filled in a questionnaire shortly after they had stopped using the ambulatory ECG recorder. Also, questionnaires were sent to eleven GPs who prescribed ambulatory ECG recorders in April–May 2004, seven of which (64 per cent) were returned. In January 2005, I visited a call centre handling calls from patients using ambulatory ECG recorders. During two days I observed the call centre physicians, talked to call centre employees, and made notes on incoming phone calls by patients.

Case study

At the time of study, two types of ambulatory ECG recorders were available on the Dutch market. The first type is a transtelephonic continuous loop recorder, which consists of a small device connected with electrodes to the patient's body that needs to be carried continually and can be activated when arrhythmias occur. Upon activation, several minutes of heart rate are recorded, which can subsequently be transmitted via a regular telephone or mobile phone to a telemedical service centre, where doctors register and interpret the ECG. The ambulatory ECG recorder is designed to aid physicians in making efficient, quick and cost-effective diagnoses of arrhythmias in patients with infrequent, vague, low-risk cardiac complaints. For patients, these telemonitoring services promise to help them avoid waiting times for specialist care, and to allow diagnosis of arrhythmias to be carried out at home with reassuring, around-the-clock telemedical supervision.

A newer type of cardiac telemonitoring system uses an ECG recorder that is integrated in a mobile phone. This so-called cardiophone does not need to be carried continuously. Instead, the phone can be pressed onto the chest area when the patient feels palpitations. The phone allows for an immediate recording of the heart rate, with the data being transmitted directly to a service centre. Some cardiophones are also equipped with emergency buttons, which allow patients to press a button in emergency situations. They are directly connected to a service centre, which, based on the GPS coordinates transmitted through the network, can identify the location of the caller. Cardiophones are prescribed by cardiologists who wish to monitor patients' heart rates at a distance and with little involvement. For patients such as those with chronic heart failure or those who have had recent cardiac surgery, the cardiophone is meant to provide a sense of reassurance in a range of locations outside the home.

In the following, I discuss primarily the first type of ECG recorder, as it has been by far the most widely used type in the Netherlands. Cardiophones so far have only figured in a limited number of pilot studies involving a small number of patients. As I am interested in the everyday use and workings of telemonitoring, a device which has become firmly embedded in actual use practices is more suitable as an object of study than one which figures solely in a small range of test situations.[3] Therefore, the case descriptions in this chapter are based primarily on the use of ambulatory ECG recorders, but in some specific, explicitly mentioned instances reference is made to cardiophones.

Surveillance theories and the case of telemonitoring

At first sight, telemonitoring of cardiac patients might not seem to produce remarkable levels of surveillance. Yet, as a number of studies on new medical technologies and contemporary health surveillance suggest, telemedicine applications in fact involve the operation of discrete surveillance. First, several scholars have discussed the use of telemedicine in terms of a digitization of the body which underpins what Foucault (1973) called the 'clinical gaze' (Mort *et al.* 2003: 275). In this sense, telemedicine is viewed as one of the technologies of inspection and enumeration that are found in contemporary clinics (Mort *et al.* 2003:

276; cf. Brown and Webster 2004: 89). From this perspective, cardiac telemonitoring implies that individuals are surreptitiously surveilled in their homes and day-to-day whereabouts. For instance, from reading transmitted ECGs, telemedical call centres are able to deduce data about users' personal lives, such as when and in which circumstances heart rates were recorded. Also, as was mentioned above, cardiophones allow telemedical service centres to register users' GPS coordinates and therefore collect so-called 'location data' (European Commission 2002).

Secondly, telemedicine applications are a crucial element in an historical shift towards medical objectification, as healthcare steps outside of the hospital and takes medical practices into the wider community (cf. Armstrong 1995). In this view, telemonitoring permits the territorial expansion of technologies of clinical surveillance (Mort *et al.* 2003: 276), acting like a type of global electronic panopticon (Brown and Webster 2004: 1–2).

As the case discussed here reveals, ambulatory ECG recorders produce a variety of data flows, including collection of personal data, exchange of health information among different (public and non-public) organizations, and even transnational processing of medical data. For instance, the telemedical service centre that catered for ambulatory ECG recorders kept paper and electronic records on its patients, and data contained in these files are transferred to GPs and several organizations inside and outside the healthcare sector.

The use of ambulatory ECG recorders thus produces various sorts of surveillance processes. Nevertheless, it is unclear to what extent we can make sense of this type of surveillance on the basis of existing surveillance theories. As I argue in the following two sections, the major theoretical resources and concepts that are currently available in the field of surveillance studies are of limited value.

Panopticon

As mentioned above, telemedicine and other ICTs in the field of e-health have sometimes been interpreted as electronic versions of the panopticon prison. However, the panopticon notion is of limited relevance to the case of telemonitoring: the typical characteristics of the panopticon prison, and of other locations or mechanisms that theorists inspired by the panopticon idea have discussed in terms of panoptic surveillance, do not adequately describe the actual use practices of cardiac telemonitoring. Traditionally, in particular in Michel Foucault's interpretation (Foucault 1991), the disciplinary powers of the panopticon design were associated with the spread and institutionalization of normalizing principles, and with the distinct physical architecture of the observing gaze. Yet, ambulatory ECG recorders constitute rather modest elements in the emerging and transitory development of telemedicine and e-health. As the case study and literature on the use of ICTs in the healthcare sector suggest, the implementation and long-term use of telemedicine is problematic, uneven and subject to considerable, ongoing negotiations (e.g. Berg 2001; Wootton 2000). Moreover, the kind of surveillance that telemedicine systems produce is no longer tied to the physical architecture of a panopticon-like hospital or to the central enactment of a disciplinary gaze (Brown and Webster 2004: 89).

More recent perspectives that draw upon the concept of the panopticon have not identified surveillance solely with established, governmental institutions. Instead, they hold that surveillance operates through dispersed electronic networks (e.g. Deleuze 1992; Poster 1996) or rhizome-like structures (Haggerty and Ericson 2000), implying that its disciplinary effects are magnified and intensified by the aggregation of discrete elements. However, ambulatory ECG recorders can hardly be said to operate as 'surveillance assemblages' (Bogard this volume). Of course, telemonitoring devices produce links and data flows between different locations and actors, thereby creating a network configuration that is intimately tied to the production of medical knowledge (cf. Brown and Webster 2004: 84). But it is unlikely that the emergence or increase of these information exchanges significantly augments or intensifies levels of surveillance, or profoundly transforms the previous state of affairs. In fact, the majority of relations that can be discerned in the use of ambulatory ECG recorders (such as those between GPs and Home Care offices) were already in existence prior to their introduction. Furthermore, patients are able to exert considerable control over disclosure of information about themselves, for instance by withholding information from doctors, taking off the ECG recorder when it feels uncomfortable, or not using the recorder at all (see below).

Therefore, concepts and theories drawing upon the panopticon paradigm overestimate the intensity of surveillance produced by telemedical technologies. Even theories that have moved beyond the traditional Benthamite and Foucauldian approaches fail to provide a balanced, non-dystopic account of surveillance that takes into account the locality and particularity of surveillance-enabling devices, and the agency of surveillance subjects. Hence, the panopticon notion is ill-equipped to provide an empirically valid description of telemonitoring practices.

Surveillance society

David Lyon's proposals for new avenues in surveillance theories (e.g. Lyon 2001) have aimed to move beyond the panopticon paradigm – and indeed they make possible a more balanced approach to surveillance than positions drawing on the panopticon. What is more, some of the conceptual tools provided by Lyon's analyses are well suited to describe surveillance aspects of telemonitoring practices. For one, telemonitoring of cardiac patients is an example of what Lyon called monitoring everyday life (Lyon 2001; cf. Staples 2000). From this perspective, ambulatory ECG recorders serve as inconspicuous devices that are capable of unobtrusively, routinely, remotely monitoring day-to-day, apparently trivial aspects of individuals' personal lives. Also, the use of telemonitoring could be described with reference to what Lyon called the two faces or Janus face of surveillance (Lyon 1994), such that it offers palpable benefits (in this case, consumer health services) while also opening up possibilities for constraining, intrusive surveillance and data collection (processing of medical data). As Brown and Webster concluded in their recent book, many patients experience new medical technologies, such as telemedicine, as offering the promise of cure and treatment, while simultaneously creating new risks and uncertainties (Brown and Webster 2004: 179; for a general account of the Janus face of technology, see Latour 1987).

Ideas such as 'everyday surveillance' and 'Janus-faced surveillance' have strong descriptive appeal with respect to theorizing contemporary surveillance practices such as telemedicine, and provide welcome alternatives to the doom scenarios implied in many invocations of the panopticon. However, Lyon does not provide specific ideas about methodologies for conducting surveillance studies that are based on his perspective. For example, in the concluding chapter of *Surveillance Society*, Lyon puts forward a new approach to surveillance, which stresses the importance of affirming the value of embodied persons and care for the other (Lyon 2001: 151–4). Yet the reader does not get a clear idea of how to take into account these values in theory or practice, or how to apply them in empirical studies of surveillance. In other words, theories of the surveillance society are underdeveloped with regard to methodologies for studying the surveillance implications of telemonitoring devices.

Current surveillance theories thus have a number of shortcomings when it comes to describing and analysing the empirical realities of telemonitoring practices. Contrary to what is suggested in theories inspired by the panopticon, telemonitoring devices are generally applied in discrete settings, which allow patients to exert considerable control over the execution of surveillance and data-processing. Therefore, the panopticon paradigm does not allow for a balanced discussion of the surveillance aspects of ambulatory ECG recorders. Perspectives on the surveillance society do allow for more nuanced accounts of surveillance, but they have little to say about how to conduct empirical studies that will contribute to examinations of telemedical practices. Therefore, what surveillance theory needs is a set of theoretical and methodological notions that allow for recognition that the use of surveillance-enabling devices is changeable rather than inherently negative, and a number of methodological starting points for conducting balanced studies of surveillance practices. As I suggest in the next section, user research in the field of STS provides insights that enable such analyses.

STS perspectives

In my opinion, the following approaches that have been put forward in current studies of user–technology interactions contribute to studies and theories of surveillance.[4]

Insights derived from STS

One of the basic tenets of user studies is the *co-construction* of users and technology (Smit and van Oost 1999). Simply put, this tenet holds that studying user–technology interactions starts with the idea that users do not simply passively consume products and services, but are also capable of actively appropriating, modifying, reconfiguring and resisting technologies. As Brown and Webster argued in their study of new medical technologies, 'we are far from passive in our consumption of novel and innovatory techniques for body maintenance' (Brown and Webster 2004: 82). Indeed, 'people are actively involved in interpreting and recoding technology, often in entirely unexpected and unintended ways' (Brown and Webster 2004: 82–3).

At the same time, technological designs and material artefacts are able to influence user behaviour and impact what users can (and cannot) do (see most notably, Latour 1993; Woolgar 1991; cf. Winner 1986).[5] Applied to the context of ICTs in the healthcare sector, this means, for instance, that the design of electronic patient records or other formal tools such as progress forms does not simply represent existing work practices but also shapes, or even transforms, the organization of healthcare professionals' work (e.g. Berg 1997). Therefore, although user behaviour can be steered through material artefacts, humans are not powerless victims subjected to the whims of technological systems. Rather, the actual operation of technologies implies a process of mutual shaping between human actors and technical objects (e.g. Kline 2003).[6] Hence, studying the ways in which technology is used in practice requires paying attention to 'what users do with technology' and 'what technologies do to users' (Oudshoorn and Pinch 2003b: 2).[7]

Secondly, current studies of the use of technology have put forward a *multiple-user perspective* on socio-technical practices and the social implications of technologies (Oudshoorn *et al.* forthcoming; cf. Friedman and Conford 1989). This perspective employs the idea that different types of users have different capacities for use (Oudshoorn and Pinch 2003b: 6), and therefore proposes to take into consideration the views, interests and actions of a range of heterogeneous actors when analysing the operation of technological systems and artefacts (Cowan 1987; cf. Brown and Webster 2004: 4). For instance, Brown and Webster showed that telemedicine-based communications 'are highly flexible and are worked out in quite different and unpredictable ways according to variations in context and who uses them' (Brown and Webster 2004: 88).

Thirdly, social studies of the use of technologies have shown that both *use and non-use* matter (Oudshoorn and Pinch 2003a; Wyatt 2003). In analysing socio-technical practices, attention should be paid not only to actors involved in the actual use of technologies, but also to those who are (sometimes actively and purposefully, sometimes unintentionally) excluded from involvement (e.g. Star 1991; Oudshoorn *et al.* 2004). In this view, the exclusion of individuals or groups from technological applications is not simply a consequence of the deficiencies of users but also relates to the design of technologies. That is, 'specific practices of configuring the user may lead to the exclusion of specific users' (Oudshoorn and Pinch 2003b: 10).

The three theoretical approaches summarized here share a focus on detailed empirical research into day-to-day practices for the study of technology–society interactions (cf. Latour and Woolgar 1979; Suchman *et al.* 1999). In fact, STS literature is dominated by the discussion of a wealth of empirical case studies (see for an overview, e.g. Jasanoff 1995). In sum, from a user perspective, surveillance theories benefit from conducting empirical case studies in order to explore the multiple use and the non-use of technological applications. Taking into account the processes of mutual shaping between human and non-human actors is considered a basic premise of these analyses.

STS perspectives applied to the case of telemonitoring

In order to make clear the impacts of the aforementioned perspectives in studies of surveillance practices, this section discusses the notions of co-construction, multiple users, and non-use with reference to issues coming to the fore in the case study of cardiac telemonitoring.

Co-construction

Applied to the case of telemonitoring of cardiac arrhythmias, the notion of co-construction means on the one hand that by using ambulatory ECG recorders patients are induced to self-disciplining and self-monitoring conduct. Because arrhythmias tend to occur infrequently and unexpectedly, patients have to make sure to carry the ECG recorder at all times, even during the night. Moreover, ECGs need to be recorded under 'normal' conditions, such as, whenever patients feel palpitations without having gone through unusual exercise or stress. Therefore, the use of ambulatory ECG recorders requires patients to pay close attention to how they feel, and to keep track of the type of activities they undertake, situations that are experienced as stressful, etc. One of the patients that I encountered when doing observations in the telemedical service centre reported taking his pulse regularly, in order to detect irregularities in the heart rate and decide about recording an ECG (observation, telemedical service centre no. 2).[8]

On the other hand, the application of ambulatory ECG recorders does not entirely determine patients' conduct or freedom of movement.[9] For example, in interviews, patients regularly admitted taking off the recorder when going to sleep, because wearing the device on the body would be uncomfortable. Also, some patients did not make recordings when they were outside their homes, because it made them feel self-conscious about the recorder (which makes a rather loud noise when registering an ECG).

In a similar vein, even though cardiac telemonitoring devices in principle allow for detailed tracking of individuals' lives through collecting and storing patient data, patients were able to make real choices regarding the disclosure and use of their personal data. For example, patients calling the telemedical service centre to transmit their ECGs were able to decide for themselves which additional information they wished to share with the responding doctor. Upon receiving a phone call, the physicians in the service centre ask for the patient's ID number (assigned to the patient by the service centre after registration for the telemonitoring services) and name, and sometimes also inquire about the patient's experiences and physical pains during the recording of the ECGs. Then the ECGs are transmitted and stored on the service centre's PC. In many cases, patients would not disclose elaborate medical details about themselves when talking to the physician (although some patients that we interviewed admitted to discussing their medical problems with the physician, who was viewed as lending an empathic ear to their predicament). As one of the patients we interviewed said: 'I transmitted the ECGs, nothing more and nothing less' (interview, patient, male, 25). Also, as a result of data protection legislation and regulations regarding healthcare professionals' duty of confidentiality, those using ambulatory ECG recorders had a right to have their medical records changed or removed, and to refrain from giving consent to data collection. Many patients were aware of these rights, and were willing and able to invoke them (Dubbeld 2005).

To conclude: whereas the panopticon paradigm overestimates the surveillance capacities of ICTs, the perspective of co-construction makes clear that users are not passively subjugated to technological domination or disciplinary surveillance. Hence, in contrast with theories endorsing the panopticon concept, studies paying attention to processes of mutual shaping between humans and non-humans in telemedicine practices allow for a balanced discussion of technological applications and their surveillance consequences.

Multiple use

The multiple use perspective on contemporary technologies provides useful starting points for doing empirical studies of surveillance. As the case description provided here suggests, analyses that focus on the multiplicity of users contribute to detailed explorations of the surveillance capacities of telemedical systems.

At first sight, cardiac patients' use of telemonitoring devices for registration of ECGs may seem to involve only a small number of actors, most notably the patient, ECG recorder, and telemedical service centre. Yet as the scheme shows, several others actors, including various individuals, professionals and organizations, play a role in telemonitoring practices as well. Although the heterogeneity of actors involved in the operation of cardiac telemonitoring can be considered in a sense unsurprising and trivial, with a view to addressing surveillance implications the diversity is far from inconsequential.

For instance, different users tend to have different interests in data protection, privacy, and confidentiality of personal information (cf. Raab and Bennett 1998), and different capacities for influencing levels of protection afforded. The case study results suggest that patients using ambulatory ECG recorders were likely to express an interest in and preference for protection and confidentiality of their personal information (for a more elaborate discussion, see also Dubbeld 2005). But at the same time they conceded that healthcare professionals would need to have access to sufficient patient data.

> L: Do you know if the telemedical service centre keeps a medical record on you?
> P: Yes, of course they have everything on the computer. I think that's great! If something goes wrong with me, then maybe my GP will be able to request some information from them. (interview, patient, female, 81)

Physicians, specialists and doctors employed by the telemedical service centre demanded easy access to accurate patient information, but they were also bound by a duty of confidentiality that prohibited them from disclosing medical information without the patient's consent. In contrast, health insurers had an interest in obtaining medical data on their clients, and the telemedical services company aimed to collect a variety of patient-related data with a view to serving its business interests.

The extent to which cardiac telemonitoring produces surveillance depends on the specific constellation of various actors and their interrelations, such as, on 'the sort of network configuration that is found in a medical field of research and practice' (Brown and Webster 2004: 43). More specifically, surveillance is related to the ways different actors are able to demand and enforce privacy protective measures and to regulate (if not obstruct) data flows. That is, one of the ways that surveillance implications of cardiac telemonitoring can be analyzed and discussed is through studying the ways in which its practical use involves different actors' approaches to data-processing practices and data protection arrangements.

In the case of ambulatory ECG recorders, techniques that were employed to ensure an agreed level of confidentiality included (but were not limited to): the use of forms asking patients' consent for transfer of information, the design of protocols laying down the tasks and responsibilities of GPs who prescribed telemonitoring services, and instructions structuring the work of personnel in the telemedical service centre. Given these protective efforts, surveillance of patients through cardiac telemonitoring was curbed and regulated to the extent that excesses were minimized, or at least could be subjected to control and negotiation.

One advantage of this kind of multiple user perspective is that it allows for a discussion of the arguments of those conducting or promoting surveillance, revealed as one-sided, biased, or executive views. All too often those managing or advocating telemedicine systems claim that patients are unconcerned about privacy and surveillance. Yet when asked, patients do in fact express considerations illustrative of or related to these issues, such as the desire to be able to give (or withhold) consent, to have insight into who has access to data systems, or to have a say in secondary use of information. For example, patients did not object to their medical data being exchanged among healthcare professionals, but they were suspicious of other parties, such as health insurers or marketing businesses, getting access to their personal data.

If it would be solely for marketing purposes, I would first want to know and be able to say yes or no [to data use]. In that case I would want to be well informed. (interview, patient, female, 56)

Look, if it's for medical purposes, my GP or someone like that, then I think it's OK [for data to be transferred from the telemedical service centre to other organizations]. But other than that, it's not desirable. (interview, patient, female, 57)

As these examples suggest, paying attention to patients' views enables the surveillance implications of medical data-processing systems to be discussed and problematized in ways that are likely to differ radically from the stories of empowerment and patient benefit that those involved in the management and promotion of telemedicine tend to put forward. Therefore, taking into consideration the diversity of actors (and their views and actions) that play a role in surveillance-enabling telemonitoring practices allows for a balanced analysis of surveillance produced in actual socio-technical practices.

Use and non-use

In addition to the multiple use perspective, the notion of non-use of technological artefacts provides an analytical point of departure for studying surveillance in the context of cardiac telemonitoring. In the case of ambulatory ECG recorders, non-use of technical artefacts comes to the fore in several ways. First, some categories of patients were explicitly excluded from use, primarily because they were considered incapable of using ambulatory ECG recorders. This was the case in particular with elderly people, who tended to be viewed as incompetent with respect to new technologies (survey, GP no.8), or as difficult to talk to over the phone, especially if they were hard of hearing (observation, telemedical service centre no. 2).[10]

Secondly, some potential users were implicitly excluded from the practice of ambulatory ECG recorders. For instance, youngsters were generally not viewed as patients at risk of (serious) cardiac disease, and therefore were unlikely to receive a doctor's prescription. Also, currently, telemedicine, especially in the field of cardiology, is reimbursed only by a small number of health insurers in the Netherlands, which means that the majority of patients needed to pay for the services themselves. Given the considerable costs of ambulatory ECG recorders, only well-off patients would be able to afford them. Therefore, the promise that telemedicine will enhance patient access to healthcare services is rather controversial in the context of ambulatory ECG recorders. A number of distinct groups of patients were – perhaps against their knowledge or will – constructed as non-users. In user research, exclusion of specific users (especially if it is based on a biased view on gender differences, ethnicity or age and if it concerns exclusion from – presumably or potentially – beneficial services) has generally been viewed as undesirable, or as a deficiency to be remedied (Oudshoorn *et al.* 2004; cf. Institute of Medicine 2001: 53).

With respect to the surveillance implications of telemonitoring, the evaluation of non-users' positions is more complex (cf. Wyatt 2003). On the one hand, the non-use of telemonitoring devices means that patients will not be subjected to surveillance, which could be considered 'a good thing', meaning that there will not be any processing of their personal health data, decreasing the risks of privacy invasions. On the other hand, the exclusion of particular categories of patients, such as those with lower incomes, could mean that telemonitoring is closely allied with processes of social sorting – one of the issues that theorists of surveillance have considered particularly worrisome with regard to contemporary surveillance technologies (e.g. Lyon 2003a; cf. Gandy this volume). In addition, patients who are unwillingly excluded from telemonitoring practices are at a disadvantage because their non-participation means that they cannot experience the (potential) benefits of telemedicine.[11]

However, if the actions (both explicit and implicit, deliberate and indirect) among those involved in telemonitoring that lead to non-use are closely studied, making it possible to examine the particular constellation of the socio-technical practice, and to identify the background, nature and degree of non-use. This examination then serves as an input for the discussion of surveillance in terms of 'social sorting' or digital discrimination (e.g. Lyon 2003a).

In sum, the co-construction perspective on technology use enables a balanced, empirically sensitive discussion of the operation of telemedical surveillance technologies, because it avoids the assumption that technical artefacts applied for surveillance purposes (or capable of enactment of surveillance) will inevitably have a disciplinary influence on the lives of those involved in surveillance practices. What is more, if we take seriously mutual shaping processes involved in socio-technical practices, the position of technological determinism – which is often implied in panopticon inspired accounts of surveillance – becomes simply untenable. An additional advantage of a user approach to surveillance is that it provides a nuanced set of theoretical notions and methodological tools for conducting studies of surveillance. Close-range empirical analyses that take into account configurations of multiple use and non-use contribute to an analysis and critique of surveillance practices as a Janus-faced socio-technical phenomena.

Conclusion

I have argued that theories of surveillance benefit from taking into account a number of theoretical and methodological ideas developed in STS. Insights into processes and issues of technology use derived from user-centred research provide a number of useful starting points for analyzing surveillance aspects of telemedicine practices.

Put briefly, surveillance theories benefit from starting with the assumption that the surveillance implications of telemedicine are the result of the involvement (and lack of involvement) of a heterogeneous set of actors, both human and non-human, in socio-technical practices in which telemedical devices figure. Using this approach, methodologies for conducting close-range empirical studies that are based on the idea that analyses of contemporary surveillance-enabling ICT systems need to take into account processes of co-construction, multiple use, and non-use of technological artefacts.

Based on these theoretical considerations, a methodological framework guiding future research in surveillance studies would then look somewhat like the following. The idea of co-construction of technology and its use is taken as a general presumption that needs to be accounted for (either implicitly or explicitly) in studies of surveillance. The notions of multiple use and non-use serve as points of departure for analyzing processes of co-construction, and provide methodological starting points for conducting empirical studies. The scheme below (Scheme 1), mapping various actors and their relationships with respect to data processing, illustrates this approach. In addition, practices of use and non-use are identified through empirically exploring the ways in which different actors are involved in socio-technical practices and the everyday use of technologies.

It is my contention that the ideas drawn from STS discussed here provide input for developing balanced, empirically valid analyses of contemporary surveillance for two main reasons.[12] First, the notion of co-construction avoids pessimistic views of surveillance – primarily because it refrains from assuming the kind of technological determinism that tends to produce dystopies. Instead, it allows for a consideration of the processes through which technologies become used in practice, including not only the tendencies of technological artefacts to shape users' behaviour but also users' capacities to influence their operation. In this respect, discussions of the positive and worrisome implications of surveillance benefit from ideas provided by analyses that adopted a co-construction view.

Second, the multiple-use and non-use perspectives contribute to research designs that aim to take seriously the actual use of technological applications in socio-technical practices. In this way, a one-sided, executive view on the social implications of surveillance – for example, one that downplays the (potential) negative impact of surveillance on the lives of the surveilled – can be avoided, and a balanced discussion of the social benefits and costs of telemedicine promoted.

Attention for the multiplicity of use and non-use of technologies therefore provides input for, amongst other things, an exploration of the discriminatory tendencies of surveillance. For example, identifying participation and non-participation in socio-technical practices contributes to gaining an overview of those who are excluded, categorized, or 'orchestrated' (Lyon 2001) in the operation of surveillance technologies. In this sense, research methodologies that are based on a consideration of the use and non-use of technological systems are appropriate tools to develop empirically informed discussions of the pros and cons of socio-technical practices that enable or produce surveillance. Hence, some of the ideas developed in user studies contribute to an exploration of both constraining and productive elements in the operation of surveillance, a discussion of individuals' capacities to shape the use of surveillance-enabling technologies, and an assessment of the extent to which surveillance discriminates. It is my hope that theorists of surveillance take up the challenge to adopt and develop these insights in future studies of contemporary high-tech surveillance practices.

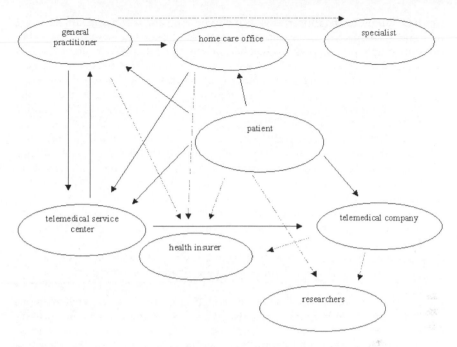

Scheme 1: Flows of personal data produced by the use of ambulatory ECG recorders.

Black arrows indicate routine data flows, dotted arrows refer to data flows that are possible but rarely occur. Please note: data flows are only indicated when they concern processing of personal data, as understood in EU data protection law (EU Directive 95/46/EC, article 2)

Notes

1 In the past few decades, STS research has developed a wealth of insights into the dynamics of interactions between technological artefacts and everyday use practices. Because surveillance theories tend to be concerned with the social implications of contemporary technological systems, it will come as little surprise that STS could be a fruitful repository of ideas that will be of benefit to their future development.

2 The study focuses on an exploration of privacy and security issues, risks, and solutions in cardiac telemonitoring practices (for a more elaborate case description, see Dubbeld 2005). It is part of a larger research project conducted within the Centre for Studies of Science, Technology and Society at the University of Twente, which is concerned with exploring the social implications of telemonitoring and telemedicine in the healthcare sector. I would like to thank Ivo Maathuis and Nelly Oudshoorn for their contribution to the research that is at the basis of this chapter.

3   Admittedly, cardiophones have come to be used at a larger scale in, amongst others, Germany, Switzerland and Israel. Yet these practices are remarkably different from the system studied here, as they are set up as consumer services rather than a doctor-prescribed treatment, as is the case in the Netherlands.

4   It should be noted that the ideas that are discussed here are not uncontroversial, or uniformly accepted in the heterogeneous STS discipline. For example, research on technology use is part of a fragmented, diverse field of enquiry that includes a range of disciplines and perspectives (Oudshoorn and Pinch 2003b). In this chapter, I have highlighted some of the theoretical and methodological principles that promise to be most relevant to surveillance studies, but I do not wish to suggest that they are illustrative of all strands in STS, or that they will be widely endorsed, or that they are usually presented in the way that I have here.

5   Some STS scholars have conceptualized the capacities of non-human actors to shape human actors' conduct in terms of the notion of a script (Akrich 1992; Latour 2000).

6   The notion of co-construction builds on the symmetry requirement developed in early work in STS, which refers to the idea that both successful technologies and those that failed need to be studied (Bloor 1976; cf. Latour 1996). The notion of symmetry has later been extended so as to include the tenet that both humans and non-humans need to be taken into consideration when studying the workings of artefacts (Latour 1991, 1992). The agency of artefacts is, sometimes somewhat implicitly, endorsed in the co-construction perspective on technology. In this chapter, I will assume that both human and non-human actors play a role in telemedicine practices. I would like to note here that adoption of the co-construction perspective also means that it is problematic to talk about the 'effects' or 'consequences' of technology (Van der Ploeg 2003), because technologies and their uses are involved in a complex development process (Berg 2001) rather than a causal linear process. Therefore, I will avoid using such terms, at most referring to the implications of technologies.

7   The term 'users' employed here should not be conceived of as referring to individual persons only, but also to social groups (e.g. Bijker 1995).

8   In a similar vein, several respondents to our questionnaire indicated that they would not want to use the ambulatory ECG recorder for a longer period of time than they had, because it made them feel anxious and worried about their physical condition and potential disease (survey, patient no.41, patient no.56, patient no.60, patient no.61, patient no.63, patient no.71).

9   Some of its proponents even hold that telemedicine will empower patients, because it allows them to have control over healthcare services and delivery (e.g. Bauer and Ringel 1999). In a similar vein, Norman Holter, who invented the first type of ambulatory ECG recorder, was primarily concerned with improving cardiac patients' freedom of movement and freedom from constraining therapies (Holter 1961).

10 In a discussion of the benefits and disadvantages of ambulatory ECG recorders used for cardiac medical services provided by an Israeli company, 'children and incapacitated individuals' were also considered incapable of using the device 'appropriately' (Roth et al. 1997: 2246).

11 For example, the company that is involved in putting cardiophones on the Dutch market holds the view that patients with specific personality traits, the so-called Type-D personalities (Denollet 1997; de Fruyt and Denollet 2002), should be excluded from cardiophone services (interview, management telemedical company V). Because these type of patients suffer from negative emotions, the use of cardiophones is expected to make them feel distressed and depressed about their heart disease. Yet it could be said that it is precisely this group of patients that could benefit from cardiac telemonitoring, as it may make them feel more reassured about their medical treatment and give them a more active role in coping with their disease.

12 I think that the analysis in this chapter also contributes to future studies of surveillance in another respect. So far, telemedicine and e-health have not been major themes in the field of surveillance studies, even though a number of other developments in healthcare technologies have been addressed to some extent (e.g. Armstrong 1995; Brin 1998; Poudrier 2003; Rose 2001). By revealing the surveillance implications of telemonitoring, this chapter may enhance researchers' interests in telemedical technologies, and other innovative ICT applications in the healthcare sector, as sites of surveillance.

References

Akrich, M. (1992) 'The De-scription of Technical Objects', in W.E. Bijker and J. Law (eds) *Shaping Technology/Building Society: Studies in Sociotechnical Change* (Cambridge, MA: MIT Press), 205–24.

Armstrong, D. (1995) 'The Rise of Surveillance Medicine', *Sociology of Health and Illness*, 17 (3), 393–404.

Bannister, J., Fyfe, N.R. and Kearns, A. (1998) 'Closed Circuit Television and the City', in C. Norris, J. Moran and G. Armstrong (eds) *Surveillance, Closed-Circuit Television and Social Control* (Aldershot: Ashgate), 21–40.

Bauer, J. and Ringel, M. (1999) *Telemedicine and the Reinvention of Healthcare* (New York: McGraw-Hill).

Berg, M. (1997) 'Of Forms, Containers, and the Electronic Medical Record: Some Tools for a Sociology of the Formal', *Science, Technology and Human Values*, 22 (4), 403–33.

Berg, M. (2001) 'Implementing Information Systems in Health Care Organizations: Myths and Challenges', *International Journal of Medical Informatics*, 64, 143–56.

Bijker, W.E. (1995) *Of Bicycles, Bakelites and Bulbs: Toward a Theory of Sociotechnical Change* (Cambridge, MA: MIT Press).

Bloor, D. (1976) *Knowledge and Social Imagery* (London: Routledge and Kegan Paul).

Bogard, W. (1996) *The Simulation of Surveillance: Hypercontrol in Telematic Societies* (Cambridge: Cambridge University Press).

Brin, D. (1998) *The Transparent Society: Will Technology Force us to Choose Between Privacy and Freedom?* (Reading, MA: Perseus Books).

Brown, N. and Webster, A. (2004) *New Medical Technologies and Society: Reordering Life* (Cambridge: Polity).

Buckles, D., Aguel, F., Brockman, R., Cheng, J., Demian, C., Ho, C., Jensen, D. and Mallis, E. (2004) 'Advances in Ambulatory Monitoring: Regulatory Considerations', *Journal of Electrocardiology*, 37, 65–7.

Cabrera, M. (2004) 'Editorial: ehealth and the Ageing Society', *The IPTS Report*, 81, 2–3.

Cowan, R.S. (1987) 'The Consumption Junction: A Proposal for Research Strategies in the Sociology of Technology', in W.E. Bijker, T.P. Hughes and T.J. Pinch (eds) *The Social Construction of Technological Systems: New Directions in the Sociology and History of Technology* (Cambridge, MA: MIT Press), 261–80.

Craig, J. (1999) 'Introduction', in R. Wootton and J. Craig (eds) *Introduction to Telemedicine* (London: Royal Society of Medicine Press), 3–15.

de Fruyt, F. and Denollet, J. (2002) 'Type D Personality: A Five-Factor Model Perspective', *Psychology and Health*, 17 (5), 671–83.

Denollet, J. (1997) 'Personality, Emotional Distress and Coronary Heart Disease', *European Journal of Personality*, 11, 343–57.

Deleuze, G. (1992) 'Postscript on the Societies of Control', *October*, 59, 3–7.

Donaldson, M.S. and Lohr, K.R. (eds) (1994) *Health Data in the Information Age: Use, Disclosure, and Privacy* (Washington: National Academy Press).

Dubbeld, L. (2005) 'Privacy and Security Issues in Telemonitoring of Cardiac Patients', in P. Brey *et al.* (eds) *Computer Ethics: Philosophical Enquiry. Ethics of new information technology* (University of Twente, Enschede), 165–80.

Emery, S. (1998) *Telemedicine in Hospitals: Issues in Implementation* (New York: Garland).

Eriksson, H. and Terenius, L. (2005) 'Sweden – A Test Ground for Telemedicine/ Telecare', in K. Dean (ed.) *Thought Leaders: Essays from Health Innovators* (Cisco Systems), 26–36. Available at http://www.cisco.com/web/about/downloads/ guest/c644/ccmigration_09186a0080270105.pdf.

European Commission (2002) 'Directive 2002/58/EC on the Processing of Personal Data and the Protection of Privacy in the Electronic Communications Sector' (Directive on Privacy and Electronic Communications) (Brussels: European Commission).

Foucault, M. (1973) *The Birth of the Clinic* (London: Tavistock).

Foucault, M. (1991) *Discipline and Punish: The Birth of the Prison* (London: Penguin Books).

Friedman, A.L. and Conford, D.S. (1989) *Computer Systems Development: History, Organisation and Implementation* (Chichester: John Wiley and Sons).

Gandy, O.H. (1993) *The Panoptic Sort: Towards a Political Economy of Personal Information* (Boulder, CO, San Francisco and Oxford: Westview).

Haggerty, K.D. and Ericson, R.V. (2000) 'The Surveillant Assemblage', *British Journal of Sociology*, 51 (4), 605–22.

HeartCenterOnline (2004) 'At-home blood pressure readings effective', Thursday 30 December 2004. Available at: http://www.heartcenteronline.com/myheartdr/ home/researchdetail.cfm?reutersid=4972&nl=4 (accessed 4 January 2005).

Hentenaar, F. (2003) *Patiënten Over Fouten in Medische Informatie Overdracht: Een Verkennend Onderzoek* (Amsterdam: NIPO).

Holter, N.J. (1961) 'New Method for Heart Studies', *Science*, 134 (3486), 1214–20.

Institute of Medicine (2001) 'Crossing the Quality Chasm: A New Health System for the 21st Century', Institute of Medicine, Committee on Quality of Health Care in America.

Jasanoff, S.E. (ed.) (1995) *Handbook of Science and Technology Studies* (Thousand Oaks, CA: Sage).

Kline, R. (2003) 'Resisting Consumer Technology in Rural America: The Telephone and Electrification', in N. Oudshoorn and T.J. Pinch (eds) *How Users Matter: The Co-Construction of Users and Technologies* (Cambridge, MA and London: MIT Press), 51–66.

Latour, B. (1987) *Science in Action: How to Follow Science and Engineers Through Society* (Cambridge, MA: Harvard University Press).

Latour, B. (1991) *Nous N'avons Jamais Été Modernes* (Paris: La Découverte).

Latour, B. (1992) 'Where are the Missing Masses? The Sociology of a Few Mundane Artefacts', in W.E. Bijker and J. Law (eds) *Shaping Technology, Building Society: Studies in Sociotechnical Change* (Cambridge, MA and London: MIT Press), 225–58.

Latour, B. (1993) *La Clef de Berlin* (Paris: La Découverte).

Latour, B. (1996) *Aramis, or the Love of Technology* (Cambridge, MA: Harvard University Press).

Latour, B. (2000) 'When Things Strike Back: A Possible Contribution of "Science Studies" to the Social Sciences', *British Journal of Sociology*, 51 (1), 107–23.

Latour, B. and Woolgar, S. (1979) *Laboratory Life: The Social Construction of Scientific Facts* (Beverly Hills, CA: Sage).

Ligtvoet, A. (2004) 'Electronic Health Records: A Key Enabler for ehealth', *The IPTS report*, 81, 21–6.

Louis, A.A., Turner, T., Gretton, M., Baksh, A. and Cleland, J.G.F. (2003) 'A Systematic Review of Telemonitoring for the Management of Heart Failure', *The European Journal of Heart Failure*, 5, 583–90.

Lyon, D. (1994) *The Electronic Eye: The Rise of Surveillance Society* (Cambridge: Polity).

Lyon, D. (2001) *Surveillance Society: Monitoring Everyday Life* (Buckingham and Philadelphia: Open University Press).

Lyon, D. (2003a) *Surveillance after September 11* (Cambridge: Polity).

Lyon, D. (2003b) 'Surveillance as Social Sorting: Computer Codes and Mobile Bodies', in D. Lyon (ed) *Surveillance as Social Sorting: Privacy, Risk, and Digital Discrimination* (London and New York: Routledge), 13–30.

Mathiesen, T. (1997) 'The Viewer Society: Michel Fouacult's "Panopticon" Revisited', *Theoretical Criminology*, 1 (2), 215–34.

Mort, M., May, C.R. and Williams, T. (2003) 'Remote Doctors and Absent Patients: Acting at a Distance in Telemedicine', *Science, Technology and Human Values*, 28 (2), 274–95.

Norris, C. (2005) 'The Bifurcation of Surveillance: Theorizing the British Criminal Justice System', presentation given at Theorizing Surveillance: The Panopticon and Beyond, 12–14 May 2005, Queen's University, Kingston ON.

Oudshoorn, N., Brouns, M. and van Oost, E. (forthcoming) 'Diversity and Agency of Users in the Design of Medical Video-Communication Technologies', in H. Harbers (ed.) *Inside the Politics of Technology: Agency and Normativity in the Co-Production of Technology and Society* (Amsterdam: Amsterdam University Press).

Oudshoorn, N. and Pinch, T.J. (eds) (2003a) *How Users Matter: The Co-Construction of Users and Technology* (Cambridge, MA: MIT Press).

Oudshoorn, N. and Pinch, T.J. (2003b) 'Introduction: How Users and Non-Users Matter', in N. Oudshoorn and T.J. Pinch (eds) *How Users Matter: The Co-Construction of Users and Technology* (Cambridge, MA: MIT Press), 1–25.

Oudshoorn, N., Rommes, E. and Stienstra, M. (2004) 'Configuring the User as Everybody: Gender and Design Cultures in Information and Communication Technologies', *Science, Technology and Human Values*, 29 (1), 30–63.

Owen, J.W. (2000) 'Introduction', in M. Rigby, R. Roberts and M. Thick (eds) *Taking Health Telematics into the 21st Century* (Abingdon: Radcliffe Medical Press), xxiii–xxviii.

Poster, M. (1990) *The Mode of Information* (Cambridge: Polity).

Poster, M. (1996) 'Databases as Discourse; or, Electronic Interpellations', in D. Lyon and E. Zureik (eds) *Computers, Surveillance and Privacy* (Minneapolis and London: University of Minnesota Press), 175–92.

Poudrier, J. (2003) '"Racial" Categories and Health Risks: Epidemiological Surveillance Among Canadian First Nations', in D. Lyon (ed.) *Surveillance as Social Sorting: Privacy, Risk and Digital Discrimination* (London and New York: Routledge), 111–34.

Raab, C.D. and Bennett, C.J. (1998) 'Distribution of Privacy Risks: Who Needs Protection?', *The Information Society*, 14, 263–74.

Rigby, M., Roberts, R. and Thick, M. (eds) (2000) *Taking Health Telematics into the 21st Century* (Abingdon: Radcliffe Medical Press).

Roberts, R., Rigby, M. and Birch, K. (2000) 'Telematics in Healthcare: New Paradigm, New Issues', in M. Rigby, R. Roberts and M. Thick (eds) *Taking Health Telematics into the 21st Century* (Abingdon: Radcliffe Medical Press), 1–14.

Rodriguez, C. and Cabrera, M. (2004) 'Location-Based Healthcare Services', *The IPTS Report*, 81, 12–20.

Rose, H. (2001) *The Commodification of Bioinformation: The Icelandic Health Sector Database* (London: City University and Gresham College, The Wellcome Trust).

Roth, A., Bloch, Y., Villa, Y., Schlesinger, Z., Laniado, S. and Kaplinsky, E. (1997) 'The CB-12L: A New Device for Transtelephonic Transmission of a 12-lead Electrocardiogram', *Pace*, 20 (9), 2243–47.

Roth, A., Malov, N., Golovener, M., Sander, J., Shapira, I., Kaplinsky, E. and Laniado, S. (2001) 'The "SHAHAL" Experience in Israel for Improving Diagnosis of Acute Coronary Syndromes in the Prehospital Setting', *American Journal of Cardiology*, 88, 608–10.

Smit, W.A. and van Oost, E.C.J. (1999) *De Wederzijdse Beïnvloeding van Technologie en Maatschappij: een Technology Assessment-Benadering* (Bussum: Uitgeverij Coutinho).

Staples, W. (2000) *Everyday Surveillance: Vigilance and Visibility in Post Modern Life* (Oxford: Rowman and Littlefield).

Star, S.L. (1991) 'Power, Technologies and the Phenomenology of Conventions: On Being Allergic to Onions', in J. Law (ed.) *A Sociology of Monsters: Essays on Power, Technology and Domination* (London and New York: Routledge), 26–56.

Suchman, L., Blomberg, J., Orr, J.E. and Trigg, R. (1999) 'Reconstructing Technologies as Social Practice', *American Behavioural Scientist*, 43 (3), 392–408.

van der Ploeg, I. (2003) 'Biometrics and Privacy: A Note on the Politics of Theorizing Technologies', *Information, Communication and Society*, 6 (1), 85–104.

van Rijen, A.J.G., de Lint, M.W. and Ottes, L. (2002) '*Inzicht in e-health: Achtergrondstudie Uitgebracht Door de Raad Voor de Volksgezondheid en ZorgB Bij Het Advies e-health in Zicht* (Zoetermeer: Raad voor de Volksgezondheid en Zorg).

Winner, L. (1986) *The Whale and the Reactor: A Search for Limits in an Age of High Technology* (Chicago: University of Chicago Press).

Woolgar, S. (1991) 'Configuring the User: The Case of Usability Trials', in J. Law (ed.) *A Sociology of Monsters: Essays on Power, Technology and Domination* (London and New York: Routledge), 57–102.

Wootton, R. (2000) 'The Development of Telemedicine', in M. Rigby, R. Roberts and M. Thick (eds) *Taking Health Telematics into the 21st Century* (Abingdon: Radcliffe Medical Press), 17–25.

Wootton, R. (2001) 'Recent Advances: Telemedicine', *British Medical Journal*, 323, 557–60.

Wyatt, S. (2003) 'Non-Users Also Matter: The Construction of Users and Non-Users of the Internet', in N. Oudshoorn and T.J. Pinch (eds) *How Users Matter: The Co-Construction of Users and Technologies* (Cambridge and London: MIT Press), 67–79.

Zimetbaum, P.J. and Josephson, M.E. (1999) 'The Evolving Role of Ambulatory Arrhythmia Montoring in General Clinical Practice', *Annals of Internal Medicine*, 130 (10), 848–56.

Chapter 10

The role of confession in reflective practice: monitored continuing professional development (CPD) in health care and the paradox of professional autonomy

Mark Cole

Introduction

Francis Ford Coppola's film *The Conversation* (1974) hinges around the surreptitious taping and photographing of a couple in a busy city square. The lead character, Harry Caul, is the acknowledged expert who undertakes this assignment; his knowledge of surveillance makes him a guarded and deeply private man, traits that early in the narrative make him appear paranoid.

Caul is concerned about the use to which the taped conversation of the couple might be put by those who have commissioned the surveillance. It is stated in the film that a previous assignment led to the deaths of several people. It might be argued that Caul's Catholicism is a filmic, shorthand way of explaining his sense of responsibility and, more particularly, guilt about those events – and his anxiety about his current work.

In fact, the character's faith also serves to throw into sharp relief the question of surveillance in its widest possible sense. Caul's worldly life is dominated by technology – he attends a major convention where listening devices and CCTV systems are being marketed, and later boasts at a party (with unabashed technophile relish) about the microphones that he used on his most recent assignment – but his spiritual life is also surveilled.

Specifically, quite early in the movie, we see Caul in the confessional, speaking to the priest who sits hidden behind the grille. This scene is a useful reminder, particularly to those who take a Foucauldian view of the question of surveillance studies, that confession – in both its religious and secular manifestations – is an important aspect of the philosopher's thinking about power and, in particular, the constitution of the subject.

This chapter uses Foucault's later observations about technologies of the self to review the current context of continuing professional development (CPD) among health care professionals in the UK. Insofar as these practitioners are obliged to engage in CPD in order to maintain their professional status, this analysis is patently timely; moreover, there are similar stipulations in health care throughout the developed world. Importantly, the definition of CPD used by the professional and regulatory bodies that monitor and control these professions actively promotes engagement in a 'confessional' activity called reflective practice.

To undertake this analysis, the chapter initially reviews the way in which Foucault developed his understanding of surveillance and power in the course of his intellectual development. It then discusses the current CPD expectations of health care professionals, using the Foucauldian concept of 'technologies of the self' in order to make some sense of this context. In particular, the issue of how these developments affect professional autonomy in respect of the state is acknowledged. Finally, the chapter seeks to disarticulate that which, from the distinctive theoretical position taken, is positive about the expectations around CPD for professions, which entails a return to pre-Christian understandings of such technologies of the self.

Foucault, surveillance and power

In thinking about his own work, Foucault was moved to observe the following:

> I would like to say, first of all, what has been the goal of my work during the past twenty years. It has not been to analyze the phenomenon of power, nor to elaborate the foundations of such an analysis. My objective, instead, has been to create a history of the different modes by which, in our culture, human beings are made subjects (Foucault 1982: 208).

This may at first appear to be a surprising statement. After all, in respect of the question of surveillance, Foucault's central contribution has traditionally been seen to be his mobilization of the concept – borrowed from Bentham – of the panopticon as a design that facilitates permanent surveillance – or that, more importantly, creates a sense of permanent surveillance (Foucault 1991/1975). As an idea (as opposed to an architectural design), it plays a major part in explaining the writer's description of a shift at the time of the Enlightenment from sovereign to disciplinary power.

The latter is seen to inhabit the systems and structures of a range of disciplinary institutions – the prison, the factory, the hospital, the school – that aim to induce social compliance. Dreyfus and Rabinow suggest that 'to achieve this dream of total docility (and its corresponding increase of power), all dimensions of space, time, and motion must be codified and exercised incessantly' (1982: 154). For Foucault, the panopticon concept serves to facilitate what he describes as 'the automatic functioning of power' (Foucault 1991/1975: 201).

Hence, the expectation that a subject – whether a prisoner or a school student – will be in a particular place, at a precise time, and doing things prescribed elsewhere is distinctive of power as realized in this disciplinary society. Implicit therein is a further expectation, namely that the subject will undertake this without express coercion. Rouse extends this argument by noting that 'these practices of surveillance, elicitation and documentation constrain behaviour precisely by making it more thoroughly knowable or known' (2005: 99).

This observation reveals the key character of Foucault's crucial observation about the complex interrelationship between the idea of power and that of knowledge. The disciplinary society also sees power coursing through its channels as a direct result of the scrutiny and subjectification of individuals therein. Foucault has emphasized the role played by medicine, in particular, in terms of this power/knowledge formulation (Foucault 1989/1963). Johnson observes that:

> The rapid crystallization of expertise and the establishment of professional associations in the nineteenth century was directly linked to the problems of governmentality – including the classification and surveillance of populations, the normalization of the subject-citizen and the discipline of the aberrant subject ... Far from emerging autonomously in a period of separation between state and society, the professions were part of the process of state formation (1995: 11).

It should be noted that Foucault is far from considering power to be a negative thing in these discussions. He argues that this power:

> makes individuals subjects. There are two meanings of the word subject: subject to someone else by control and dependence, and tied to his own identity by a conscience or self-knowledge. Both meanings suggest a form of power which subjugates and makes subject to (Foucault 1982: 212).

Indeed, it is this type of observation which has generated considerable criticism of his position from writers on the political left. For example, Dews is moved to remark that 'since the autonomous subject is, for Foucault, already the product of subjection to power, the aim of political actions cannot be to enhance or expand this autonomy' (1984: 90).

The panopticon in Foucauldian thought has been central to surveillance study. But his view is not uncontested: Boyne (2000) has argued for the abandonment of the concept for a number of reasons, not least because of the difficulty in demonstrating the effectiveness of panopticism in developing docile subjects. The author notes 'That failure is announced in many places: prison riots, asylum sub-cultures, ego survival in the Gulag or concentration camp, retribalization in the Balkans. Such examples make exploration of other forms of subjectivation of considerable importance' (Boyne 200: 302).

Elsewhere, Armitage has reviewed studies undertaken into the effectiveness of CCTV – a surveillance system that is often observed to be an electronic panopticon – and concludes that it 'appears to have no effect on violent crimes, a significant effect on vehicle crimes and it is most effective when used in car parks' (Armitage 2002: 5).

Foucault's intellectual inquisitiveness actually led him to anticipate some of these criticisms. He reflects on his development in this regard when he notes that:

> This was my modus operandi in my previous work – to analyse the relations between experiences like madness, death, sexuality, and several technologies of power. What I am working on now is the problem of individuality – or, should I say, self-identity in relation to the problem of 'individualizing power' (Foucault 2004/1979: 300).

Hence, in this section of the chapter, we return to where we began, at the question of how human subjects are made subject by their inscription in power. And, in order to address this topic effectively, it requires us to think more broadly about the nature and outcome of surveillance in helping to make the subject.

At this juncture, then, it is useful to borrow another Foucauldian idea, one that the philosopher developed in light of his thinking about the history of sexuality. We should begin to talk about 'technologies of the self' and, in order to do so, it makes sense to explore this idea through a practical circumstance, namely the increasing scrutiny of health care professionals by regulatory authorities in the UK with an associated expectation that they will engage in activities such as reflective practice and clinical supervision.

Learning as a technology of the self

To appreciate how the engagement in learning among health care professionals might be considered a technology of the self in Foucauldian terms, it is necessary to outline the current context. Specifically, it is important to understand the expectation that exists in this respect among the relevant regulatory authorities in the UK. And, similarly, it is important to appreciate the nature of reflective practice and the way in which, as a concept and action, it has acquired significance to health care.

The obligation to continually professionally develop

Across the health care professions in the UK, it is demanded that practitioners – in order to maintain their state registration and hence the right to practise – should engage in continuing professional development (CPD). To be clear as to what is meant by this term, the following definition – derived from the Professional Associations Research Network (PARN) – is useful:

> CPD is any process or activity of a planned nature that provides added value to the capability of the professional through the increase in knowledge, skills and personal qualities necessary for the execution of professional and technical duties, often termed competence (PARN 2000).

In health care, the requirement for professionals to undertake CPD is becoming increasingly explicit. For example, as Bruce *et al.* observe,

> In the United Kingdom, a doctor's licence to practise is secured by registration with the General Medical Council. Periodic

210

revalidation, to start in Spring 2005, will be regular demonstration by doctors that they remain fit to practise ... The UK approach will be to link revalidation with continuing professional development through annual appraisal or an independent route (2004: 687).

Meanwhile, the Nursing and Midwifery Council (NMC), the body that regulates the largest of the staff groups in the health sector, makes expressly clear to its members in their code of professional conduct that 'You must keep your knowledge and skills up-to-date throughout your working life. In particular, you should take part regularly in learning activities that develop your competence and performance' (NMC 2004a: 9).

Similarly, the Health Professions Council (HPC), which maintains the state register for 13 health care professions in the UK from physiotherapy through to podiatrists, has just undertaken an extensive consultation with its membership to determine how CPD should be undertaken. For example, it proposes to introduce rules which state that 'A registrant must undertake continuing professional development in accordance with the standards specified by the Council ... and maintain a written record (including any supporting documents or other evidence) of the continuing professional development he has undertaken' (HPC 2004: 6).

The expectation that a professional person would endeavour to remain comprehensively and constantly well informed seems entirely reasonable. For example, most would find it unacceptable if an airline pilot announced over the tannoy as the plane hurtled along the runway towards take off that they had little or no experience or understanding as to how to fly this particular model.

Hence, it seems appropriate to imagine that continuing development is an implicit part of professional status and, perhaps more importantly, of working competently as a professional. Nevertheless, a good number of professional associations across the whole spectrum of professional work now feel the need to make express this requirement with a commensurate loss of professional autonomy for the individual practitioner.

Furthermore, a good many seek to scrutinize their members' engagement in this activity: in the PARN sample of 162 such bodies in the UK, it was found that 87 per cent monitored CPD in some fashion, with 46 per cent of the sample having systems of sanction in place for non-compliance (PARN 2000).

Monitoring and sanction (often in the form of denial of the right of access to the official register which allows people to practise in the profession) is especially evident in health care. The NMC requires its members to re-register every three years, on the basis of a notification of practice (NOP) form, which requires the member to declare that they have met the NMC's two post-registration and practice (PREP) requirements. One of these states that 'You must have undertaken and recorded your continuing professional development over the three years prior to the renewal of your registration' (NMC 2004b: 4).

Similarly, the HPC is proposing that it will introduce audit arrangements wherein it will monitor its standards for CPD which include that 'A registrant must ... maintain a continuous, up-to-date and accurate record of their CPD activities ... [and] ... present a written portfolio containing evidence of their CPD upon request' (HPC 2004: 8).

Hence, the current context is one in which health care professionals in the UK – and, it should be noted here, in other parts of the developed world – are now obligated to demonstrate expressly and to an overseeing authority – that they are engaging in a practice that might well be deemed to be implicit in their professional status and practice. Here, then, is an intimation of the surveillance framework that has developed in and around health care practice.

Dandeker reminds us, in his analysis of the connection between surveillance and modernity, that:

> The exercise of surveillance involves one or more of the following: (1) the collection and storage of information (presumed to be useful) about people or objects; (2) the supervision of the activities of people or objects through the issuing of instructions or the physical design of the natural and built environments ... (3) the application of information gathering activities to the business of monitoring the behaviour of those under supervision, and, in the case of subject persons, their compliance with instructions (Dandeker 1990: 37).

On the basis of this codification, the systems of regulating health care professionals would appear quite straightforwardly to be examples of surveillance. The fact that the regulatory bodies that undertake this surveillance are entitled so to do by licence of the state reinforces this view. By the same token, it can be argued that this new regime of regulation derives from concern over the autonomy of health care professions in light of a number of high-profile cases that revealed a failure on their part to regulate themselves appropriately.

Indeed, the report on the terrible shortcomings of cardiac care at Bristol Royal Infirmary, UK, expressly recommended that 'CPD, being fundamental to the quality of care provided to patients, should be compulsory for all health care professionals' (Bristol Royal Infirmary Inquiry 2001: 447). In this case, checks and balances on medical practice were simply non-existent. Surgeons at this large hospital in a city in the southwest of England undertook procedures on heart patients that were seen to lead to higher than normal mortality rates. However, they failed to acknowledge the shortcomings of their techniques: moreover, their action was not scrutinized by the authorities at the hospital or any of the other health care professionals – medical and otherwise – with whom they worked.

However, within the expectation that health care professionals will engage in educational activity and be able to demonstrate that involvement, there is an even more interesting development. As part of this developing discourse, there has been strong emphasis on reflective practice as a technique that staff should embrace. The exploration of this idea that follows will view this through a Foucauldian prism, particularly in respect of addressing it as a technology of the self.

Reflective practice: the confession of competence?

For most health care professionals, the idea of reflective practice is precisely that: a practical activity in which they are increasingly expected to engage. Few will have given much thought to the philosophical underpinnings of the idea, which can be said to derive from the work of Dewey and Habermas (Morrison 1995; Cole 2000). Some may have a passing acquaintance with the work of Donald Schön (1990, 1995), whose writings truly gave shape to reflective practice as it is now understood.

In essence, Schön observed that, while most preparation for professional work concentrates on equipping the individual with technical and rational skills, their practice takes place in conditions of uncertainty and contingency. In trying to understand how professionals manage in such circumstances, he suggests that, in the course of any professional activity, a practitioner is constantly acting, reflecting on those (and past) actions, and re-acting. Schön describes this as reflection-in-action.

However, he went on to argue that the professional may also engage in reflection-on-action. This entails a more formal retrospective review of a previous episode in professional life with the clear intent of deriving learning and hence enhancing expertise. Pietroni (2001: 9–11) breaks this into three simple practical phases: remembering and recollecting a learning experience; thinking about how the experience made you feel; and re-evaluating the experience. It is, in essence, this idea of reflection that has colonized health care and which now has come to be generally described as reflective practice.

Associated with the idea of reflective practice is the view that health care professionals should participate in 'clinical supervision', a practice that 'aims to bring practitioners and skilled supervisors together to reflect on practice, to identify solutions to problems, to increase understanding of professional issues and, most importantly, to improve standards of care' (NMC 2002).

It is not the intention of this chapter to critique Schön's schema, although suffice to say that it is contested in terms of both theory (Eraut 1994; Greenwood 1998; Clegg 1999; Fenwick 2001) and practice (Mackintosh 1998; Carroll *et al.* 2002). Instead, the link between what Foucault called technologies of the self – particular techniques of caring for the self and developing oneself as a subject – and the prevalence of reflective practice in health care will be explored.

That is not to say, of course, that reflective practice is the exclusive preserve of that particular sector. It is noteworthy that reflection has a considerable and longstanding presence in the field of education: just recently, for instance, the Further Education National Training Organisation (FENTO) in the UK published a set of standards for teaching at this level. One of the eight standards relates exclusively to reflection, stating that 'teachers should recognize the importance of, and engage in, critical reflection upon professional practice, within the context of the internal and external factors influencing [further education]' (FENTO 1999: Standard G).

In producing a manual for reflection in Higher Education, Reed and Koliba (2002) of the University of Vermont provide us with a useful starting point:

> The term 'reflection' is derived from the Latin term *reflectere* – meaning 'to bend back'. A mirror does precisely this, bend back the light, making visible what is apparent to others, but a mystery to us – namely, what our faces look like. In service learning, we look to develop processes that allow people doing service to bend the metaphorical light of their experiences back onto their minds – to make careful consideration about what their experience were (sic) all about (Reed and Koliba 2002).

Importantly, this formulation foregrounds a crucial element in reflective practice, namely, the need to access and acknowledge something that, in normal circumstances, remains hidden. It is important insofar as it allows us to situate this practice of reflection within a broader discourse of confession that has been extensively explored by Foucault, who notes that:

> The confession became one of the West's most highly valued techniques for producing truth. We have since become a singularly confessing society. The confession has spread its effects far and wide ... One confesses – or is forced to confess. When it is not spontaneous or dictated by some internal imperative, the confession is wrung from the person by violence or threat; it is driven from its hiding place in the soul, or extracted from the body ... Western man has become a confessing animal (Foucault 1990/1976: 59).

Foucault's 'technologies of the self'

The character of this confessional practice, according to Foucault's thinking – for which he deploys the term technology of the self, particularly in respect of his work on sexuality – has two manifestations: a Greco-Roman concern with caring for the self and a Christian approach that focuses on its redemptive qualities. Indeed, Foucault observes that:

> there has been an inversion between the hierarchy of the two principles of antiquity, 'take care of yourself' and 'Know thyself'. In Greco-Roman culture knowledge of oneself appeared as the consequence of taking care of yourself. In the modern world, knowledge of oneself constitutes the fundamental principle (1988/1982: 22).

This is a vitally important distinction, for the purposes of thinking about reflective practice. The pre-Christian techniques of the self required the individual to 'retire into the self to discover – but not to discover faults and deep feelings, only to remember rules of action, the main laws of behaviour' (Foucault 1988/1982: 34).

It is, then, an approach that sees the individual practising a number of mental and physical exercises – including a reflection at the start of the day to come and an assessment at the close of the day that has passed (Foucault 1990/1984: 51). Key to these exercises was the maintenance of written accounts – notebooks of observations from life and learning – which come under the general term of *hupomnemata* (Foucault 1997).

However, as Foucault opines about the individual caring for themselves, 'he is not a judge who has to punish; he is, rather, an administrator who, once the work has been done or the year's business finished, does the accounts, takes stock of things, and sees if everything has been done correctly' (Foucault 1999/1980: 165). The individual is, in essence, a 'stock-taking administrator' (Foucault 1988/1982: 33).

These Greco-Roman techniques of the self are aimed at developing an understanding of the self that, in turn, helps the individual to remind themselves of the way in which things should be done; effectively, it is a means of recapitulating and appreciating rules of action. Importantly, the idea of guilt – a sense of shortcoming or wrongdoing – and (to an extent) the sense of something hidden that needs to be mined and revealed by these practices is absent at this point.

However, the same cannot be said for Christian technologies of the self. Foucault points out that:

> Christianity belongs to the salvation religions. It's one of those religions that is supposed to lead the individual from one reality to another, from death to life, from time to eternity. In order to achieve that, Christianity imposed a set of conditions and rules of behaviour for a certain transformation of the self. Christianity is not only a salvation religion, it's a confessional religion. It inflicts very strict obligations of truth, dogma and canon, more so than do the pagan religions (Foucault 1988/1982: 40).

Significantly, however, Foucault suggests that confession was not initially a feature of penance. Penitence, he argues, was an issue of status; one became a penitent, rather than did penance. And, as with the action of sovereign power on the body on a miscreant – the torturing, the branding, the dismemberment – so this original state of penitence was something taken up by the body through, for example, the wearing of sackcloth and self-flagellation. Foucault takes up the theological term *exomologesis* to describe these practices (Foucault 1999/1980: 171–2).[1]

Latterly, it is argued, 'Christianity appropriated two essential instruments at work in the Hellenistic world – self-examination and the guidance of conscience. It took them over, but not without altering them considerably' (Foucault 2004/1979: 310). This shift from penitence as a status to confessional practice is summarized thus:

In the Christianity of the first centuries, there are two main forms of disclosing self, of showing the truth about oneself. The first is *exomologesis*, or a dramatic expression of the situation of the penitent as sinner which makes manifest his status as sinner. The second is what was called in the spiritual literature *exagoreusis*. This is an analytical and continual verbalization of thoughts carried on in the relation of complete obedience to someone else. This relation is modelled on the renunciation of one's own will and of one's own self (Foucault 1988/1982: 48).

It should be noted that this perceived discursive shift, wherein confession gradually comes to occupy a key place in the expression of Christian faith, is blighted somewhat by the ahistoricism which so often characterizes Foucault's thought and, more importantly, his distinctive genealogical methodology. Where he does attempt something akin to a periodization of this development, it creates a sense of intellectual suspicion because it is rendered in such broad-brush strokes (Foucault 2003: 171–4).

This observation creates an interstice in our exposition in which to note some shortcomings of Foucault's approach to this topic. Primarily, there is something of a sense that the writer contrived to make circumstances fit to his theoretical approach. Peters makes a passing observation in a footnote that 'Foucault's friend and colleague at the College de France, Pierre Hadot, professor emeritus of the History of Hellenistic and Roman Thought, on whom Foucault relies for so much his interpretation of classical texts in his last years, takes Foucault to task for his reading of "care of the self"' (Peters 2003: 220).

Perhaps of greater concern are those criticisms levelled by Elden (2005) in a substantial theoretical review of Foucault's work in this respect, wherein he notes that Foucault's theological understanding can be seen to be faulty: Foucault focuses on particular episodes in religious history – but it is far from clear that the import that he ascribes to these events is in any way justified (Elden 2005: 38). It should be noted that Elden's critique is a sympathetic one. He sees this as an aspect of an overall failure to give cohesive shape to the intellectual concerns that governed Foucault's later life. However, he takes the view – very strongly – that this was a productive failure that allowed the philosopher to explore all manner of unintended and unexpected avenues.

To an extent, this is symptomatic of a larger theoretical blind spot, namely, Foucault's willingness to extrapolate extremely localized events into more generalized ideas. For example, his work on disciplinary power is often critically viewed because of the way in which he explores particular French experience to make a global observation. In the specific

217

concerns of this piece, there is a strong sense that Foucault is viewing wider developments through the prism of French Catholicism.

However, a key commentator on this area of Foucault's work presciently observes 'If we accept that Foucault is not concerned with the Christian confession but with the techniques of "truth" within Christianity, then his study is freed from being weighed down by specific chronologies of history' (Carrette 2000: 39). This feels a little like an act of theoretical prestidigitation, but it usefully directs us to the important point that the ideas to which Foucault gives voice patently derive from his genealogical approach to historical events – but they are not necessarily intrinsically linked to those events. In historiography, the events are pre-eminent and need to be accurately recounted; in Foucault's genealogy, it is ideas themselves – and their application and implications – that are primary.

With these observations made, I take licence to continue with this exploration of reflective practice by reference to one of Foucault's own observations in respect to his methodological practice:

> The history of ideas involves the analysis of a notion from its birth, through its development, and in the setting of other ideas which constitute its context. The history of thought is the analysis of the way an unproblematic field of experience, or set of practices which were accepted without question, which were familiar and out of discussion, becomes a problem, raises discussion and debate, incites new reactions, and induces a crisis in the previously silent behaviour, habits, practices, and institutions (Foucault 2005/1983: 28).

To underscore this point, it is useful to observe that Carrette moves on to argue that it is precisely the way in which the techniques of which Foucault speaks produce a subject that is significant; in fact, confessional practice 'subjugates, subjectifies and forms a subject of knowledge' (Carrette 2000: 40). By this is meant that the practice of the confessional exercises control over the confessant, encourages them to identify themselves in reflexive fashion, and converts them into packets of knowledge. It is the action of these techniques – rather than their provenance – that is truly significant when one deploys a Foucauldian approach.

There is an important observation threaded into Carrette's formulation, namely, that the act of confession is not – as we might ordinarily be led to believe – something that brings us liberation; it is, instead, something that inscribes the confessant in power, by the subjection implicit in the process. In this respect, O'Leary notes that 'in the Christian confession it is the confessing individual who is compelled to speak by a confessor who not only has the power to impose an obligation to speak, but who also interprets and judges the proffered speech' (2002: 32).

This inscription in power is seen in sharp relief when we consider the pre-Christian provenance of these techniques, of which Foucault notes that 'when, in the practice of the care of the self, one appealed to another person in whom one recognized an aptitude for guidance and counselling, one was exercising a right' (1990/1984: 53). In the confession, of course, the confessant cannot choose whether to have a confessor or not, nor – broadly speaking – can they choose from a population other than from those who have been ordained.

The precise nature of the exchange that might actually occur is important here. The pre-Christian technologies of the self saw individuals engaging in practices and ways of thinking for their own personal developmental benefit. Any attempts at delusion in the midst of such practice would be self-delusion. However, the Christian confession – whilst personal and redemptive – has an expectation of truthfulness sown into it. Of course, a cynical argument might be that this expectation is premised not on an individual desire to purge oneself candidly but on the somewhat negative assumption that an omniscient God will detect any departure from veracity.

Interestingly, Foucault explored the question of truth telling in a series of lectures that he delivered at Berkeley in 1983. Here, he used his understanding of the Hellenistic period – and, in particular, its literature – to investigate the practice of *parrhesia*, which he defined as:

A kind of verbal activity where the speaker has a specific relation to truth through frankness, a certain relationship to his own life through danger, a certain type of relation to himself or other people through criticism (self-criticism or criticism of other people), and a specific relation to moral law through freedom and duty. More precisely, parrhesia is a verbal activity in which a speaker expresses his personal relationship to truth, and risks his life because he recognises truth-telling as a duty to improve or help other people (as well as himself) (Foucault 2005/1983: 5).

The person engaging in *parrhesia* – the *parrhesiastes* – is seen to have a personal duty to speak truth to power. They voluntarily speak candidly and honestly in circumstances where they stand to lose something – up to and often including their life. And, interestingly, this articulation has two important features: first, the status of the *parrhesiastes* is based upon recognition by others of that person's definite moral quality; and, second, the truth (in a patently pre-positivist world) is defined by the recognition and articulation of it by that individual. In essence, the truth acquires its veracity through the *parrhesiastes* giving voice to it; there is no expectation that the validity of these truth claims would be tested.

In contrast to the *parrhesiastes*, the Christian confessant is obligated – by their wider religious conviction tied to a belief in the supposed omniscience of God – to tell a personal truth about themselves to another. This is a redemptive act, rather than an act of challenge, with loss confined to the purging of sin. The Christian confessant does not speak truth to power; power compels of them that they surrender some personal truth within the confines of the confessional.

In this respect, Foucault notes that, within the practices of the Christian confession, the person confessing 'has something to say and he has to say a truth. Only what is this truth that the person led to the truth has to say, what is the truth that the person directed, the person lead by another to the truth, has to say? It is the truth about himself' (Foucault 2005/1982: 362–4).

In turn, this leads Bernauer and Mahon to observe that 'these practices produced a unique form of subjectivization in the human being. The self is constituted as a hermeneutical reality, as an obscure text requiring permanent decipherment' (2005: 154). In contrast, of course, *parrhesia* involves public articulation and personal risk, while Christian confession is a private act of guided self-interpretation and personal surrender.

Reflective technologies of the self

All of this brings us back to the question of reflective practice – as currently constituted in the broader practice of health care – and its position as a technology of the self. More specifically, it can be seen as a technique that owes more to the Christian confessional at this time than the Greco-Roman approach to caring for the self. In essence, the health care professional has seen reflection subtly drift from being a personal practice to one that is inscribed in power.

Foucault makes a powerful remark in respect of parallels in terms of development of governmentality, one that resonates with the circumstance that this chapter is considering: 'at a time when states were posing the technical problem of the power to be exercised on bodies and the means by which power over bodies could effectively be put to work, the Church was elaborating a technique for the government of souls' (Foucault 2003: 177).

In the state's stipulation that health professionals should be engaged in CPD, with a clearly stated requirement that this should be evidenced through detailed documentation, and in the interpretation by professional and regulatory bodies that this should include active involvement in reflective practice, it would seem as though these two technical questions of governmentality fold into one another and resolve.

It is not solely in regard to health care professionals that this observation holds. In fact, it might be suggested that the development of a closer scrutiny of professionals in health care is part of an overall regime of workplace surveillance. Findlay and Newton apply a Foucauldian approach to performance appraisal while simultaneously critiquing that position at what they see as its weak points. These authors suggest that:

It is easy to see the panoptic power of appraisal in the plethora of appraisal methods ... All such measures are designed to refine the observational assessment of the appraisee, to provide an unfettered gaze upon their job performance and, particularly, to identify any inabilities they may have in meeting expected norms ... However appraisal is about more than surveillance since it is not just about monitoring 'sub-standard' performance, but knowing why it occurred. Answering this question requires an ability to gaze upon the subjectivity of the worker, to know her feelings, anxieties, her identity and her consciousness (Findlay and Newton, 1998: 214).

So, the express requirement that health care professionals should engage in CPD, record those activities formally, demonstrate evidence of that active and constant engagement to a regulatory authority, and include within that broad expectation of development a practical commitment to reflect systematically, needs to be seen as part of a broader complex of power within the workplace. It is in the requirement to reflect, however, that a qualitative difference exists for these professionals, in terms of their inscription in power, which turns precisely on the requirement that they actively reflect.

Clouder (2004) notes how reflection, as a specified approach and defined activity in health care, has insinuated itself across the piece; it has extended surreptitiously into the pre-qualification curricula of nursing and the other professions. In the Republic of Ireland, Nicholl and Higgins (2004) detail how there is an explicit expectation from the regulatory authorities that the curriculum should include reflection. Even medicine, perhaps the most sceptical of the health professions, is beginning to engage with the concept of reflection (Mamede and Schmidt 2004).

Of particular interest to our discussions here, Nelson and Purkis (2004) have critically explored the post-2000 shift in nursing towards a regulatory regime in Ontario, Canada, wherein practitioners experience a mandatory requirement to assess their competence through reflective practice. The authors argue that this expectation means that:

> the nurse is brought under a regime of subjective development – one that shifts his or her understanding of professional practice and resituates the locus of professional development as an exercise in interiority. Thus, as the tool of choice by regulatory authorities, reflective practice provides the mechanism whereby nurses internalize the new professional ethos of self-government. It is the rehearsal of new values and the displays of required attributes that *can* be successfully audited by the processes established by the Canadian regulatory authorities. Clearly, nurses are under surveillance by the registration authorities to make sure this reconstitution of the nurse is achieved and revealed (Nelson and Purkis 2004: 250).

This is an exciting analysis, but it falters slightly because of its 'zero-sum' approach to the issue of power: the authorities here 'have' power, while the surveilled nurses are simply the object of that action of that power. Similarly, an early exchange on the confessional aspects of reflective practice in health care can also be seen to be flawed.

Gilbert (2001) took up a Foucauldian approach to reflective practice, arguing that it was indeed a technique of surveillance. The analysis went further, arguing that it had a vicarious effect in terms of surveillance of the populations served by the reflective professional. The author declared that:

> In the process of managing professional activity these technologies achieve two different but interrelated functions. First, they make individual practitioners 'visible' and through this visibility subject to modes of surveillance. Second, these practices can be located with a range of techniques of ethical self-formation, which have emerged in the late twentieth century (Gilbert 2001: 201).

For Gilbert, the shift perceived from a situation in which health care professionals work in a routine or habitual way to one where they are practising reflectively is not emancipatory. Instead, it is argued, 'it involves the exchange of one form of subjectivity for another, as both are equally the products of the effects of power' (Gilbert 2001: 202).

Within a Foucauldian schema, this is logically consistent, but it stands as a decidedly contentious observation that this chapter would wish to contest. Gilbert's position certainly reflects Foucault's view of power – which is pithily and adroitly analyzed by Wolin (1988) – as a quality that exists within the fullest possible range of social relationships rather than as a commodity that may be possessed by one and denied to another.

In responding to Gilbert in a broadly supportive manner, Clouder and Sellars (2004) usefully seek to emphasize the positive aspects of reflective practice for health care professionals. Certainly, they argue, it represents a surveilling technology of the self, but it is further suggested that the autonomous professional experiences close observation by a good many people – including, most importantly, their clients – and should expect this level of scrutiny, not least because of a lack of public accountability: 'rights and power that come with professional status also come with attendant responsibilities' (Clouder and Sellars 2004: 265).

However, there is something paradoxical about this position. It is not that the authors are seeking to reclaim the positive aspects of reflective practice; instead, they are simply accepting of the need for such surveillance to be in place in order that the accountability of professions can be enhanced. For at least one commentator, this is counterintuitive: 'the pursuit of ever more perfect accountability provides citizens and consumers, patients and parents with more information, more comparisons, more complaints systems; but it also builds a culture of suspicion, low morale, and may ultimately lead to professional cynicism, and then we would have grounds for public mistrust' (O'Neill 2002: 57).

Conclusion: reframing reflective practice

An argument has been developed in this chapter that the regulatory frameworks which govern the practice of health care professionals are becoming increasingly formalized. In part, this may be seen as a *dispositif* (Brenner 1994) that corresponds with the burgeoning of a discourse where professional autonomy is being circumscribed by a greater requirement for public accountability. This, in turn, hints at a general trend towards greater governmentality in the health care sector.

These regulatory mechanisms – specifically, for our purposes, the requirement that health care professionals engage (and are patently seen to engage) in CPD – can be seen to be clear manifestations of surveillance by the state through its proxies. As we have seen, the licence to practise in a given field may be withdrawn if a professional fails to provide (written) evidence of their engagement in this enforced learning. Some of these professions have periodic re-registration systems; others look set to sample their total registered membership on a fairly arbitrary basis.

In this regard, then, the actions of practitioners are being closely scrutinized – or are being undertaken in the knowledge that such surveillance may take place. This arrangement hints at the 'automatic functioning of power' that is seen to be the key outcome of a panopticon. By this action, it can be suggested that the autonomy of those professionals is somewhat delimited. In making this observation, no judgement is intended as to whether this circumscription of professional freedom is a positive outcome or not.

Beyond this simple analysis, however, lies the more sophisticated issue of what should be made of the developing expectation across the health care professions – to a greater or lesser extent, depending on the group in question – that they should engage in reflective practice and clinical supervision. This chapter has taken a Foucauldian position in reviewing this, suggesting that this activity is a technology of the self.

In Foucault's work, a distinction is made between Greco-Roman and Christian practices that the author groups under this heading. The precise nature of the differences in those two approaches is important: in considering the later Christian colonization of the Classical approach to care of the self, Foucault is moved to note that 'here obedience is complete control of behaviour by the master, not a final autonomous state. It is the sacrifice of the self, of the subject's own will. This is the new technology of the self' (Foucault 1988/1982: 44–5).

He is concerned also to point out that 'the modern hermeneutics of the self is rooted much more in those Christian techniques than in the Classical ones' (Foucault 1999/1980: 169). By this he means that the physical and mental exercises of the ancients, designed to hone the person and their day-to-day practice, have been supplanted by confessional regimes wherein a hidden truth is to be revealed by giving voice, invariably to another to whom one is in a somewhat obedient relationship.

It is easily possible, of course, to see reflective practice very much in these terms, as a confessional activity and relationship that is richly threaded through with power. Yet, if disarticulated from the broader *dispositif* that creates the physical circumstances of the discourse of surveillance within health care, critical reflection can be repositioned as a practice that has a good deal in common with the pre-Christian technologies of the self.

Specifically, it has the potential to enrich the autonomy of the professional through providing them with a personal means of enhancing what they do. In this sense, outwith the regulatory expectations, critical reflection can contribute to practitioners being better professionals. To return to an earlier theme, reflexivity should be seen as an implicit part of professional practice, as Gustafsson and Fagerberg (2004) sought to demonstrate in the case of nursing.

Even more importantly, as Schön (1990, 1995) originally intimated, reflective practice continues to be a potential challenge to the dominant technical and rational discourse(s) that have given (and continue to give) shape to health care practice. Findings from a study of reflection in service settings by Mantzoukas and Jasper indicates that:

> The ward culture considered reflective practice as an invalid method of knowledge acquisition ... This did not arise from the fact that reflection actually was invalid and not normal for practice. The nurses used, and indeed acknowledged, that reflection was both powerful for developing practice and was also a tool for revealing the totality of their professional knowledge and input in patient incomes. This demarcation was imposed by powerful groups, ostensibly in the name of evidence-based practice, and reflected the basis of the struggle between groups of differing power (2004: 931).

Hence, reflective practice might usefully be said to have a two-fold effect. As a technology of the self, particularly with its confessional overtones, it is part of a regulatory framework that can be seen to be an assemblage of surveillance. However, critical reflection also represents – in the way that the pre-Christian techniques did – a means of caring for the self.

In pursuing that parallel, it is noteworthy that Phillips speaks effusively about the virtue of engaging in some of these Classical practices, with the specific observation:

> I see *hypomnemata* as a technique for a self-study critiquing where power resides, how discourses inflict the unconscious and conscious acts of self, and as a study of speech acts … Hypomnemata examines the splices of moments, that which can be seen and that which is silent and has potential for implication and liberation at the contested site of self (Phillips 2002: 280).

Connecting reflective practice to the ideas and practice of Classical technologies of the self and breaking it away from its confessional implications, such activities potentially represent an emancipatory tool that has the potential to yield professional and personal benefits for those who practice it. Moreover, the idea of *parrhesia* allows us to acknowledge the public role that professions have – given their relative autonomy from the state – to speak truth to power.

The final observation, however, is a paradoxical one: the health care professional, in utilizing reflective practice and hopefully realizing these emancipatory benefits, is simultaneously being surveilled through their engagement in those techniques. This seems a persuasive – and decidedly Foucauldian – way to think about the way in which power, thought of as a quality rather than a commodity, resides in all social relationships.

Note

1 Those familiar with Swedish film-maker Ingmar Bergman's classic *The Seventh Seal* (1956) will no doubt be able to recall the band of medieval penitents, moving from village to village at a time of plague, whipping themselves. These images – which this author has always found deeply harrowing and distressing – give a clear sense of what is meant when *exomologesis* is discussed.

References

Armitage, R. (2002) *To CCTV or not to CCTV? A Review of Current Research into the Effectiveness of CCTV Systems in Reducing Crime* (London: NACRO).

Bernauer, J.W. and Mahon, M. (2005) 'Michel Foucault's Ethical Imagination', in G. Cutting (ed.) *The Cambridge Companion to Foucault* (2nd edn) (Cambridge: Cambridge University Press), 149–75.

Boyne, R. (2000) 'Post-Panopticism', *Economy and Society*, 29 (2), 285–307.

Brenner, N. (1994) 'Foucault's New Functionalism', *Theory and Society*, 23, 679–709.

Bristol Royal Infirmary Inquiry (2001) *Final Report: Learning from Bristol: The Report of the Public Inquiry into Children's Heart Surgery at Bristol Royal Infirmary 1984-1995* Command Paper: CM 5207. Available at: http://www.bristol-inquiry.org.uk/final_report/ (accessed 31 March 2005).

Bruce, D., Phillips, K., Reid, R., Snadden, D. and Harden, R. (2004) 'Revalidation for General Practitioners: Randomised Comparison of Revalidation Models', *British Medical Journal*, 328 (7441), 687–91.

Carrette, J.R. (2000) *Foucault and Religion: Spiritual Corporality and Political Spirituality* (London: Routledge).

Carroll, M., Curtis, L., Higgins, A., Nicholl, H., Redmond, R. and Timmins, F. (2002) 'Is There a Place for Reflective Practice in the Nursing Curriculum?', *Nurse Education in Practice*, 2 (1), 13–20.

Clegg, S. (1999) 'Professional Education, Reflective Practice and Feminism', *International Journal of Inclusive Education*, 3 (2), 167–79.

Clouder, L. (2004) 'Key Points and Future Developments in Reflective Practice Within the Education of Health Professionals', in S. Tate and M. Sills (eds) *The Development of Critical Reflection in the Health Professions* (London: Higher Education Academy), 101–8.

Clouder, L. and Sellars, J. (2004) 'Reflective Practice and Clinical Supervision: An Interprofessional Perspective', *Journal of Advanced Nursing*, 46 (3), 262–9.

Cole, M. (2000) 'Learning Through Reflective Practice: A Professional Approach to Effective Continuing Professional Development Among Health Care Professionals', *Research in Post-Compulsory Education*, 5 (1), 23–38.

Dandeker, C. (1990) *Surveillance, Power and Modernity: Bureaucracy and Discipline from 1700 to the Present Day* (Cambridge: Polity Press).

Dews, P. (1984) 'Power and Subjectivity in Foucault', *New Left Review*, 144 (March–April), 72–95.

Dreyfus, H.L. and Rabinow, P. (eds) (1982) *Michel Foucault: Beyond Structuralism and Hermeneutics* (Brighton: Harvester).

Elden, S. (2005) 'The Problem of Confession: The Productive Failure of Foucault's *History of Sexuality*', *Journal for Cultural Research*, 9 (1), 23–41.

Eraut, M. (1994) *Developing Professional Knowledge and Competence* (London: Falmer).

Fenwick, T.J. (2001) *Experiential Learning: A Theoretical Critique from Five Perspectives*, Information Series No. 385 (Columbus, OH: ERIC/Ohio State University).

Findlay, P. and Newton, T. (1998) 'Re-Framing Foucault: The Case of Performance Appraisal', in A. McKinlay and K. Starkey (eds) *Foucault, Management and Organization Theory: From Panopticon to Technologies of Self* (London: Sage), 211–29.

Foucault, M. (1982) 'The Subject and Power', in H.L. Dreyfus and P. Rabinow (eds) *Michel Foucault: Beyond Structuralism and Hermaneutics* (Brighton: Harvester), 208–26.

Foucault, M. (1988/1982) 'Technologies of the Self', in L.H. Martin, H. Gutman and P.H. Hutton (eds) *Technologies of the Self: A Seminar with Michel Foucault* (Amherst: University of Massachusetts Press), 16–49.

Foucault, M. (1989/1963) *The Birth of the Clinic: An Archaeology of Medical Perception* (London: Routledge).

Foucault, M. (1990/1984) *The Care of the Self: The History of Sexuality*, volume 3 (London: Penguin).

Foucault, M. (1990/1976) *The Will to Knowledge: The History of Sexuality*, volume 1 (London: Penguin).

Foucault, M. (1991/1975) *Discipline and Punish: The Birth of the Prison* (London: Penguin).

Foucault, M. (1997) 'Writing the Self', in A.I. Davidson (ed.) *Foucault and his Interlocutors* (Chicago: University of Chicago Press), 234–47.

Foucault, M. (1999/1980) 'About the Beginning of the Hermeneutics of the Self', in J.R. Carrette (ed.) *Religion and Culture by Michel Foucault* (Manchester: Manchester University Press), 158–81.

Foucault, M. (2003) *Abnormal: Lectures at the Collège De France 1974–1975* (New York: Picador).

Foucault, M. (2004/1979) 'Omnes et singulatim: Toward a Critique of Political reason', in M. Foucault and J.D. Faubion (ed.) *Michel Foucault, Power: Essential Works of Foucault 1954–1984*, volume 3 (London: Penguin), 298–325.

Foucault, M. (2005/1983) 'Discourse and Truth: The Problematization of Parrhesia (Six lectures given by Michel Foucault at Berkeley, Oct–Nov 1983)'. Available at: http://foucault.info/documents/parrhesia/ (accessed 2 September 2005).

Foucault, M. (2005/1982) *The Hermeneutics of the Subject: Lectures at the College de France 1981–1982* (New York: Palgrave Macmillan).

Further Education National Training Organization [FENTO] (1999) 'Standards for Teaching and Supporting Learning in Further Education in England and Wales', Available at http://www.fento.org/staff_dev/standards.html (accessed 19 February 2005).

Gilbert, T. (2001) 'Reflective Practice and Clinical Supervision: Meticulous Rituals of the Confessional', *Journal of Advanced Nursing*, 36 (2), 199–205.

Greenwood, J. (1998) 'The Role of Reflection in Single and Double Loop Learning', *Journal of Advanced Nursing*, 27 (5), 1048–53.

Gustafsson, C. and Fagerberg, I. (2004) 'Reflection, the Way to Professional Development?' *Journal of Clinical Nursing*, 13 (3), 271–80.

Health Professions Council (HPC) (2004) *Continuing Professional Development – Consultation Paper* (London: Health Professions Council).

Johnson, T. (1995) 'Governmentality and the Institutionalization of Expertise', in T. Johnson, G. Larkin and M. Saks (eds) *Health Professions and the State in Europe* (London: Routledge), 7–24.

Mackintosh, C. (1998) 'Reflection: A Flawed Strategy for the Nursing Profession', *Nursing Education Today*, 18, 553–7.

Mamede, S. and Schmidt, H.G. (2004) 'The Structure of Reflective Practice in Medicine', *Medical Education*, 38 (12), 1302–8.

Mantzoukas, S. and Jasper, M.A. (2004) 'Reflective Practice and Daily Ward Reality: A Covert Power Game', *Journal of Clinical Nursing*, 13 (8), 925–33.

Morrison, K. (1995) 'Dewey, Habermas and Reflective Practice', *Curriculum*, 1 (2), 82–94.

Nelson, S. and Purkis, M.E. (2004) 'Mandatory Reflection: The Canadian Reconstitution of the Competent Nurse', *Nursing Inquiry*, 11 (4), 247–57.

Nicholl, H. and Higgins, A. (2004) 'Reflection in Preregistration Nursing Curricula', *Journal of Advanced Nursing*, 46 (6), 578–85.

Nursing and Midwifery Council (NMC) (2002) *Supporting Nurses and Midwives Through Lifelong Learning* (London: Nursing and Midwifery Council).

Nursing and Midwifery Council (NMC) (2004a) *The Nursing and Midwifery Council Code of Professional Conduct: Standards for Conduct, Performance and Ethics* (London: Nursing and Midwifery Council).

Nursing and Midwifery Council (NMC) (2004b) *The PREP Handbook* (London: Nursing and Midwidery Council).

O'Leary, T. (2002) *Foucault: The Art of Ethics* (London: Continuum).

O'Neill, O. (2002) *A Question of Trust: The BBC Reith Lectures 2002* (Cambridge: Cambridge University Press).

Professional Associations Research Network (PARN) (2000) 'Continuing Professional Development', Available at: http://www.parn.org.uk/cpd/pp/cpd_res.pdf (accessed 24 March 2005).

Peters, M.A. (2003) 'Truth-Telling as an Educational Practice of the Self: Foucault, Parrhesia and the Ethics of Subjectivity', *Oxford Review of Education*, 29 (2), 207–23.

Phillips, D.K. (2002) 'Speaking what I Speak, Speaking Words not my Own: Hypomnemata in Practice', *Reflective Practice*, 3 (3), 279–91.

Pietroni, R. (2001) *The Toolbox for Portfolio Development: A Practical Guide for the Primary Healthcare Team* (Abingdon: Radcliffe Medical Press).

Reed, J. and Koliba, C. (2002) *Facilitating Reflection: A Manual for Leaders and Educators*, Available at: http://www.uvm.edu/~dewey/reflection_manual/ (accessed 29 August 2002).

Rouse, J. (2005) 'Power/knowledge' in G. Cutting (ed.) *The Cambridge Companion to Foucault* (2nd edn) (Cambridge: Cambridge University Press), 93–122.

Schön, D.A. (1990) *Educating the Reflective Practitioner: Towards a New Design for Teaching and Learning in the Professions* (San Francisco: Jossey-Bass).

Schön, D.A. (1995) *The Reflective Practitioner: How Professionals Think in Action* (Aldershot: Arena).

Wolin, S.D. (1988) 'On the Theory and Practice of Power', in J. Arac (ed.) *After Foucault: Humanistic Knowledge, Postmodern Challenges* (New Brunswick: Rutgers University Press), 179–201.

Chapter 11

Supplementing the panoptic paradigm: surveillance, moral governance and CCTV

Sean P. Hier, Kevin Walby and Josh Greenberg

Introduction

Following the London subway bombings in July 2005, closed-circuit television surveillance (CCTV) became an international object of political and public interest when images of the bombers were broadcast around the world. What was particularly striking about the media coverage on public CCTV surveillance was the shift in crime control discourses from prevention to capture. That is, CCTV surveillance was not represented primarily as a technology capable of preventing or deterring crime, as it had been for years, but rather it was identified as the central means by which criminals/terrorists could be identified, targeted and, if they remained alive, apprehended.

As the merits of CCTV surveillance continue to be debated internationally – from Toronto to Tokyo – it is necessary to rethink dominant theoretical explanations for the establishment of public video surveillance schemes. In this chapter, we conceptualize public CCTV surveillance in the context of interrelated changes taking place in the politics and the dynamics of contemporary crime control. We argue that, although recent sociological contributions have displaced the traditional reliance on panopticism with mechanisms of consumer seduction/responsibilization, they have not fully broken from the determinism associated with the panoptic paradigm.

Intending to supplement the displacement of panopticism with a less essentialist framework, we use insights from the sociologies of risk and of moral governance to avoid the determinism that, however inadvertently, continues to characterize the literature. Agreeing with Haggerty's assertion that 'surveillance studies can benefit from a modified governmental approach' (Haggerty this volume), we find that the sociologies of risk and governance better enable us to appreciate the complexity involved in the establishment of CCTV surveillance programmes beyond consumer responsibilization strategies and social ordering techniques. Our purpose is not to substitute one explanation for another, but rather to offer theoretical alternatives for future research.

Displacing the panoptic paradigm

As Hier *et al.* (2006) explain, one of the most common sociological explanations for CCTV surveillance has sought to understand the effects of video monitoring by using the metaphor of panopticon (e.g. Davis 1990; Fyfe and Bannister 1996). The panopticon is an architectural design that was proposed by Jeremy Bentham in the late eighteenth century to facilitate the supervision of prisoners from a centralized location. The idea of the panoptic prison consisted of an inspection tower surrounded by a semicircular structure that housed inmates in separate cells. Each cell was to be made available to the uni-directional gaze of the inspectors, and the utility of panoptic supervision was based on assumptions of uncertainty. It was believed that, because prisoners would not be aware of when inspectors were watching, a state of uncertainty induced by the visible – but unverifiable – expression of power ensured the normalization of discipline and self-control.

The physical structure of CCTV surveillance understandably invites comparisons to panoptic supervision, but ethnographic research in CCTV control rooms has called into question the extent to which the panoptic paradigm can be applied uncritically and in a totalizing manner. With a wider interest in understanding the application of CCTV systems in the context of the social construction of technology, one of the most important arguments against using the panoptic metaphor has been that CCTV does not function as a mechanism to maintain a state of complete 'societal visualization', but rather it contributes to the selectivity of social monitoring and exclusion (Norris and Armstrong 1999; McCahill 2002). Sociological investigations of CCTV control room activities reveal that, far from the comprehensive asymmetrical gaze of the panoptic prison, where the privileged or select few watch over the undifferentiated masses, the surveillance gaze overwhelmingly falls upon individuals occupying morally laden categories of suspicion: youth, homeless persons, street traders and black men (Norris and Armstrong 1999).

Whereas ethnographic research has documented empirically the routine daily applications of CCTV systems, a second line of inquiry has sought to understand the processes involved in the establishment of CCTV monitoring schemes. Drawing from a critical body of literature that theorizes how the panoptic paradigm has been displaced by mechanisms of consumer seduction as the leading principle of social order (Bauman 1998), critics have analyzed the material and ideological processes involved in the uptake of CCTV surveillance. Representative of this perspective is Coleman and Sim's (2000) argument that the establishment of CCTV surveillance in Liverpool involved the social construction of 'moral visions' oriented towards reconstructing deviant images of the city (Coleman and Sim 2000: 629). They explain how the promotion of Liverpool's CCTV camera network involved 'primary definers', associated with the City Centre Business Partnership, formulating definitions and constructions of 'urban risk'. Conceptualized in terms of neoliberal patterns of consumption and leisure, the establishment of Liverpool's CCTV surveillance programme, they contend, was predicated on elite interests oriented towards counteracting the negative image of the city. This was accomplished by expelling those individuals deemed undesirable to the imaginary vision of the urban landscape. For Coleman and Sim, this sequence of processes functioned as 'social ordering strategies' involving the responsibilization of the prudent individual/consumer.[1] Drawing primarily from media coverage based on representations forged through elite partnership networks, they conclude that a 'consensual world-view' (Coleman and Sim 2000: 636) pertaining to the implementation of no less than 40 surveillance cameras in Liverpool's city centre was consolidated through moral visions of urban renewal (see also Coleman 2003).

Coleman and Sim's analysis effectively displaces the panoptic paradigm by exploring the discursive processes through which CCTV schemes are consolidated. In doing so, it also offers an alternative approach to theorizing CCTV surveillance by examining the uptake of monitoring programmes through neoliberal/entrepreneurial responsibilization strategies and social ordering techniques. What is problematic about their argument, however, is that it remains contingent on a 'leap of faith' concerning the extent to which a singular (consumer) subject position was constituted in light of what may conceivably have been perceived by the public as the erosion of personal privacy and infringements on the right to enjoy the unobstructed use of public space (Hier 2004).

By relying on the explanatory purchase of the claims-making activities of primary definers, they invest power in the specific ideological contents of elite/media discourses. Not only does this reproduce the same kind of subject determinism found in asymmetrical conceptions of the exercise of panoptical power, but it also ignores the significance of possible counter-discourses, acts of resistance, and, ultimately, the potential failure of responsibilization strategies to consolidate and maintain high levels of 'public consent'. The theoretical outcome is thus a circumscribed conceptualization of power relations through which hegemony operates as a deterministic articulation of social control based on elite class interests of urban consumerism and profitability (Hier 2004). This argument also suggests dubious allusions to the perfection or completion of interpellation through elite-engineered media discourses, and it restricts the extent to which their insights can be generalized to diverse social, cultural and material settings.

Supplementing the panoptic paradigm

In addition to the problems associated with subject determinism, exclusive reliance on responsibilization strategies and social ordering techniques to explain the uptake of CCTV surveillance schemes presents further difficulties along at least three levels of analysis. First, on a material level it privileges the ideological contents of claims-making activities pertaining to urban or city-centre CCTV surveillance programmes *vis-à-vis* consumer responsibilization while failing to account for the rise of monitoring programmes that exist outside urban areas of consumption. It follows, second, that it also fails to provide a conceptual framework to account for the national and international diffusion of CCTV surveillance into cities with diverse cultural, economic and political infrastructures. Finally, and most importantly for our purposes, it fails theoretically to supplement the displacement of the panoptic paradigm with other, less deterministic and more comprehensive, explanatory possibilities (cf. Boyne 2000).

Recent contributions to criminology and surveillance studies have started to yield several lines of argumentation that, with certain amendments, are able to supplement the functional biases found in the sociological literature concerned with the uptake of CCTV surveillance. With certain amendments, too, recent contributions are able to provide a general conceptual framework that better explains the international diffusion of CCTV surveillance beyond relying solely on the articulation of a single governmental rationality or the merits of the technological object (the actual camera) to explain contemporary crime control techniques.

In one of the most comprehensive syntheses of contemporary crime control processes, David Garland (2001) identifies two broad, interrelated sets of changes taking place in contemporary modes of criminal justice administration. The first pertains to changes in the political culture of crime control. He contends that the last few decades have been marked by an increase in the 'emotionalization' of crime, characterized by discourses of victim-centredness and 'social defence', as well as the prioritization of situational crime prevention as predominant rationalities for crime control and criminal governance. For Garland, higher crime rates have become accepted as a normal 'social fact' of everyday life in most Western societies (2001: 106), and a more generalized 'crime complex' has developed, involving new ways of acting on claims to high levels of crime, fear of crime and public safety concerns.

Interlaced with changes to the politics of crime control have been transformations in the dynamics involved in the development of crime control policy. This is the second major change Garland identifies. He explains that, since 1970, the motif of 'fear of crime' (see also Altheide 2002) has taken on a new discursive and bureaucratic importance, to the extent that it is now regarded as a problem in and of itself. He contends that older forms of penal welfarism sought to explain criminality on the basis of social deprivation and volitional theories of crime, but that contemporary law-and-order politics embody new social interests that increasingly prioritize preventative crime control strategies. For Garland, the dynamics of contemporary crime control policies are increasingly oriented towards reducing fear of crime rather than actual crime, and they rely to an increasing extent on populist discourses of potential victims, symbolic politics, and public/community safety initiatives in the production of social order and social control.

Garland's general insights are useful in conceptualizing the emotional and discursive dimensions of the establishment of CCTV monitoring programmes, insofar as they abstract the locus of explanation from the specificity of individual monitoring programmes and relocate it in a broader politico-cultural context. Not only does his argument help to address the political dimensions in the diffusion of CCTV surveillance for preventative/situational crime control, but it also speaks to the necessity of theorizing the dynamics involved in the proliferation of public CCTV surveillance schemes internationally.

The difficulty to emerge in Garland's explanation, however, is that it reproduces a theoretical framework that prioritizes top-down responsibilization strategies and the ability of elite partners and security experts to 'interpolate the citizen as a potential victim' (Garland 2001: 125) through media reporting and elite-engineered publicity campaigns. It also articulates a rather circumscribed conceptualization of emotion and its place in crime control culture as a primarily 'reactive' phenomenon. Crime discourses not only presuppose negative emotions by providing a mechanism for channelling anger, raising feelings of grief or loss, providing a target for outrage and indignation, and constructing shame; they also have the capacity to generate positive feelings toward others (solidarity, love, respect and trust) that can motivate alliances and lead to action on behalf of others (see Jasper 1998). Thus, rather than inquiring into the complex dynamics involved in the social construction of disorderly social space – as his commentary on situational strategies suggests – Garland relies on the explanatory purchase of elite-initiated discourses to consolidate citizen compliance with elite interests. Despite his claims to the contingency of the 'historical present' (Garland 2001: 1–26), therefore, he unwittingly reproduces a functionalist account of social control processes by insisting on the determinism of punitive social ordering strategies.

To avoid the functional unity found in explanations of late-modern crime control (Garland 2001) or the new/neoliberal authoritarian state (Coleman and Sim 2000; Coleman 2003), we draw from developments in the sociologies of risk and of moral governance to elaborate on the complex dynamics involved in the establishment of public CCTV surveillance systems. While we do not wish to minimize the significance of the valuable insights found in late-modern or neoliberal conceptions of law-and-order politics, their generalizability is nonetheless limited by a shared reliance on top-down explanations for the elite responsibilization of the citizenry. This is problematic because, in many respects, it reproduces the common liberal-modernist dichotomy that conceives of emancipation or liberty as the antithesis of regulation, whereby law-and-order politics are explained in terms of a repressive trade-off between declining personal liberties and increasing public securities (Mathews 2002).

As Garland, Coleman and others (see, for example, Haggerty 2003) have argued, however, a series of interrelated changes have transformed the structure of liberal-modern criminal governance, and these collective changes to techniques of crime control and perceptions of crime itself suggest that emancipation can no longer be blindly conceptualized as antithetical to regulation, but rather that emancipation is commonly sought through the intensification of regulatory (surveillance) mechanisms. These processes are neither predicated exclusively on top-down interpellations initiated by elite partnerships – however much elite partners participate in, or support, promotional efforts – nor necessarily punitive in their nature. They involve, rather, a variety of interests originating from diverse social locations, and they are motivated by a number of material, ideological, emotional and discursive factors which signal wider concerns about risk, safety and social disorder in public space.

CCTV surveillance and moral governance

In an influential set of contributions to the literature on moral governance, Hunt (1999, 2003) argues that, while all forms of moralization involve one group of people acting on the conduct of others, those who become the focus of moralizing discourses and how they are represented changes across economic, social, political and cultural domains. Processes of moralization are restricted neither by time nor space, and moralization does not involve coherently formulated short-term 'strategies' or episodes that can be measured on the basis of their success (cf. Hunt 1999). Moralization as a routine feature of social life is not so much 'strategic' as it is procedural; it involves a myriad of discourses, symbols, feelings, actors, and truth claims that are always rationally 'productive' in the sense that they continually generate ways of thinking about oneself and others.

To better explain the dynamics involved in moral governance, Hunt conceptualizes governance in terms of dialectical constructions of self and other. He contends that, as a growing number of everyday activities become moralized in the form of dialectical judgements pertaining to what is deemed to be 'right' and 'wrong' or 'good' and 'bad', processes of moral governance find expression in hybrid configurations of risk management and harm avoidance. Although the contents of moralizing discourses are neither fixed nor stable, one of the central features of contemporary moral governance is that individuals are called upon to engage in ethical forms of risk management, and these forms of self-conduct exist in tension with collective subject positions of 'harmful others' (Hier forthcoming). What this implies conceptually is that moral governance entails discourses calling for individuals to assume responsibility to manage risk (e.g. prudent public/consumer behaviour) that are dialectically counterposed to collective images of the harmful, irresponsible actions of general others (e.g. unruly youth).

Hunt's insights into the ways in which contemporary moral governance projects find expression through the proxies of risk and harm provide a conceptual foundation that accounts more fully for the dynamics involved in the moral formation of the self. They also offer a richer framework for explaining the normalizing dimensions of 'neoliberal responsibilization techniques' in terms of intersecting discourses, emotions and processes of self-formation. As Hier (forthcoming) explains, the insecurity brought forth through the discursive mediation of risk-based problems can be understood to generate, on the one hand, emotions associated with the 'potential victim' (e.g. fear associated with random crime). These emotions are generated through discursive images of a corresponding collective subject position of harmful others (e.g. 'muggers'). On the other hand, risk-based problems always offer chances for self-fulfilment, or the realization of safety/security, through prudent choice; to be 'at risk' is to possess the information and the capacity to reduce the possibility of harm through responsible self-conduct (e.g. not walking alone in 'risky' areas) (Hier forthcoming). In other words, processes of neoliberal or prudential self-governance involve a dialectic that pits individualized risk-management techniques against collective images of harmful others. These processes are also amenable to conceptualizations of emotion as entailing both 'affective' and 'reactive' dimensions, and a dialectical relationship between them.

The dynamics of the promotion of CCTV surveillance schemes involve a reconfigured nexus of emotions and values. Processes of moral governance are characterized by a continual cycle of responsible decision-making and the 'normalization' of neoliberal subjects. But CCTV surveillance schemes are often additionally characterized by the deployment of volatile, short-lived moralizing discourses more akin to moral panics (Hier 2002, forthcoming). As more direct interruptions in processes of moral governance, the individualizing and collectivizing tendencies found in processes of moral governance can become inverted by temporarily removing responsibility for harm reduction from the prudent individual by attributing responsibility for harm to others. Given that volatile moralization is immediate and short-lived, risk factors are made known in order to be received as a legitimate form of political action requiring decisive and timely regulatory intervention to secure against harm; that is, they are individualized and made transparent through the acute articulation of a specific dimension of harm.

Risk, moral governance and CCTV: the case of London, Ontario

For purposes of illustration, consider the dynamics involved in establishing the City of London's (Ontario, Canada) Downtown Camera Project. The City of London (population: 430,000) is located in southwestern Ontario, situated between the Canada–US border at Detroit and the city of Toronto (approximately 200 km each way). The Downtown Camera Project was implemented on 9 November 2001, ostensibly to provide and maintain a safe environment in the downtown core, by improving the ability of police to respond to crime and other 'anti-social' behaviour and thereby increasing economic activity (e.g. shopping). The city of London is responsible for the operation of the Downtown Camera Project – Canada's largest public monitoring system which includes 16 cameras. The establishment of London's monitoring programme, however, was foremost a citizens' initiative.

The downtown camera project was energized by the stabbing murder of 20-year-old Michael Goldie-Ryder on 16 January 1999. The murder came to symbolize social disorder in the downtown area and led to the formation of 'Friends Against Senseless Endings' (FASE), a grassroots/citizens organization devoted to resisting community violence through education, awareness and legislative change. Spearheaded by family and friends of Goldie-Ryder, the public presence of FASE was instrumental in raising the necessary funds and levels of community support to launch the Downtown Camera Project. For example, following Goldie-Ryder's death, FASE visited numerous London-area high schools; persuaded the Federation of Canadian Municipalities to endorse a motion to increase criminal penalties for crimes involving knives; and rallied the City of London's Community and Protective Services to cover outstanding costs for the monitoring programme. In conjunction with a London-area school board, members of FASE also organized a 'walk against violence' in May 2001 in which more than 800 London residents protested against rising violence in the city. What has since become the annual 'Goldie-Ribbon' Campaign, the original campaign initially raised $10,000 to support CCTV surveillance in the downtown core (Miner 2001). By August 2001, FASE had garnered enough publicity to raise the funds and levels of community support necessary for the city to launch the Downtown Camera Project.

The symbolic role that FASE played in the ascension of CCTV surveillance in London indicates that the establishment of monitoring programmes is not always a top-down initiative involving strategies for the responsibilization of prudent consumers. Indeed, local officials initially resisted calls for a camera programme in response to Goldie-

Ryder's murder. For example, Sgt John O'Flaherty of the London Police Service declared: 'The downtown, other than that area [where Goldie-Ryder was murdered], is a safe place to be' (Somerville 1999). Councilor Joe Swan, Chair of the City Hall Committee to Revitalize Downtown London, stated: 'This is not about location but a violent act that took place in our society' (Brown and Yasvinski 1999). And London's then mayor, Dianne Haskett, responded to the murder by rallying the federal government to tighten penalties for carrying concealed weapons, using the Criminal Code of Canada, rather than pushing for the implementation of CCTV surveillance in the downtown core (Brown and Yasvinski 1999). Despite these initial reactions from police, community and city representatives, however, the momentum gathered by FASE was strong enough to consolidate support for the Downtown Camera Project within three years of Goldie-Ryder's murder.

The 'cycles of responsibilization' that emerged through the establishment of London's Downtown Camera Project require more elaborate theorization of the nuances involved in how discourses, values and emotions configure to signal risk and disorder in social space. As we explained above, contemporary processes of moral governance entail continual, long-term cycles of responsible decision-making. They also entail the 'normalization' of prudent subjects through a series of discourses that invite individuals to make responsible choices to reduce harm and manage risk. The establishment of the Downtown Camera Project, by contrast, entailed the deployment of a more fleeting, short-lived set of discourses that reconfigured the individualizing and normalizing dimensions of calls for increased surveillance. Following the murder of Goldie-Ryder, a volatile set of political and media discourses unambiguously allocated responsibility and blame to his murderer, who was eventually sentenced to life in prison. As an acute articulation of the harm posed by a specific, 'irresponsible' other, harm was individualized and responsibility attributed to a 'known' person. Rather than inducing technologies of self-formation through flexible, long-term responsibilization techniques to secure against a collective or general subject position of harm, the volatile articulation of harm at once articulated a moment of problem (moral/legal transgression) and resolution (legal action/restitution). For the Downtown Camera Project to be received as a legitimate form of political intervention to secure against future (potential) harm, therefore, the scope of problematization had to be expanded beyond the specificity of Goldie-Ryder's murder.

Conceptually, this occurred through the dialectical articulation of two types of problems: grievance and risk (cf. Eide and Knight 1999). As a form of complaint, the grievance levied against Goldie-Ryder's murderer functioned in a reactive, direct and diagnostic manner and as a response to an already existing problem. Unlike the future-oriented character of risk-based problems, the purpose of which is to individualize responsibility and induce ethical forms of self-conduct to avoid or reduce the likelihood of harm, the purpose of grievance-based problems is to eliminate or mitigate a specific harmful activity. To suffer a grievance is to suffer a moral condition that situates aggrieved against transgressor, and the purpose of resolution is to restore a sense of stability and social order to the contingencies encountered in the everyday world (Edie and Knight 1999). In this regard, the dynamics involved in grievance-based problems are conceptually different from the dynamics involved in risk-based problems. Whereas grievance-based problems articulate a specific action in response to a specific (real or perceived) transgression, the latter articulate an unspecified moment of resolution that stimulates technologies of self-conduct to secure against possible future victimization (see also Hier 2004; forthcoming).

Despite the conceptual distinction between grievance-based and risk-based problems, however, it remains a paradox that the dialectic of problem and resolution in the articulation of the grievance against Goldie-Ryder's murderer only became amenable to politicization through the articulation of risk-based problems. Following Goldie-Ryder's murder, the specific articulation of harm associated with the grievance against his murderer quickly transformed into a series of discourses, articulated primarily but not exclusively in the press, that laid claim to risk factors afflicting the downtown area. The *London Free Press*, for example, linked the murder to a 'rash of killings' (Sher 1999), to 'an escalating situation' (Herbert 1999) and to an immediate need to 'clamp down on violence in the downtown core' (Beaubien 1999). The grievance against Goldie-Ryder's murderer was extended to risk factors such as bank robberies, purse-snatching and random assaults (Beaubien 1999) – particularly facing women and the elderly (Herbert 2001) – and Goldie-Ryder was consistently referenced to signify social disorder and public risk in the core.

This brief illustration suggests that the dynamics involved in the establishment of London's Downtown Camera Project can be explained within neither the parameters of neoliberal responsiblization strategies nor an undifferentiated moral governance framework. As Hunt (1999) has argued, all forms of moralization involve one group of people acting on the conduct of others, but those who become the focus of moralizing discourses and how they come to be thought about, experienced, represented and 'made known' are often case-specific. Understanding moral governance in terms of a continuous sequence of attempts to negotiate social life requires insight into the ways in which certain people/groups are subjected to the practices and processes involved in moralization at particular historical and political moments; it requires insight into the ways in which harm is attributed to certain people/groups; and it requires insight into how the self and others are represented, experienced and acted upon.

Moral governance does not necessarily involve specific agents of authority acting on the conduct of non-official individuals in the wider interests of social control. While this form of moral governance does occur, we are suggesting that it is sociologically problematic to explain moral governance exclusively on the basis of the actions of authoritative state agents. We have also highlighted the importance of attending to the role of emotion in signalling and mobilizing support for more intensified forms of public surveillance. Grassroots organizations like FASE illustrate that emotions not only become a part of the reaction to trigger events that accelerate calls for greater surveillance, but can also help to shape the goals of collective action and are 'deeply tied to moral values', arising from 'perceived infractions of moral rules' (Jasper 1998).

Conclusion

In this chapter, we have demonstrated how theoretical explanations for the rise of public CCTV surveillance programmes have hitherto failed to fully avoid the determinism found in the panoptic paradigm. Progressive contributions to the establishment of CCTV surveillance schemes have displaced the panoptic metaphor, but they have not supplemented the logic of panoptical power with other, less deterministic and more comprehensive explanatory alternatives. While contributions to surveillance studies have explored the nuances of synopticon (Mathiesen 1997; Hier 2003), empirically informed theoretical insights capable of supplementing the panoptic paradigm remain largely absent from the literature. Developments in the sociologies of risk and of governance, we have demonstrated, offer fruitful theoretical alternatives to rethinking the empirical contingencies of public CCTV surveillance beyond the panoptic metaphor.

Although our analysis is theoretical in nature, its implications for understanding how support for CCTV surveillance programmes is consolidated are also significant for resisting proposals for, and the establishment and expansion of, CCTV surveillance systems. As Walby (2005a,b) has recently argued, open-street CCTV surveillance

241

programmes in Canada are generated from at least three general social positions that he conceptualizes in terms of governance from above, from the middle, and from below. He conceptualizes governance from above as 'some hierarchal political or administrative body'; from the middle as 'business entrepreneurs'; and below as 'citizens [who] themselves seek out regulatory measures for their own communities through moral entrepreneurship' (Walby 2005a: 669). While the three social positions are used for primarily heuristic purposes in Walby's analyses, they help us to think about the complex influences involved in the rise of public video surveillance systems. This matters because a more comprehensive explanatory framework capable of addressing the complex set of relations involved in CCTV surveillance helps to avoid the determinism reminiscent of panopticon, as well as the Leviathan image of political practice still prominent in the social sciences. The general diffusion of camera surveillance should not be conceptualized simply as the imposition of increasingly strict controls on social life from elite social positions. This conceptual understanding is empirically narrow and it leads to a narrow politics of resistance. Instead, we encourage interested parties to think about how the diffusion of camera surveillance and other surveillance technologies is always socially constituted, involving the body politic taking its own members as fields of action for problematization, for regulation, and for resistance.

Note

1 Garland defines responsibilization strategies as 'a way of thinking and a variety of techniques designed to change the manner in which governments act upon crime' (2001: 124). Responsibilization strategies, in Garland's assessment, involve a sequence of activities designed to encourage citizens to take responsible for their own safety and security by addressing them as potential victims and by creating a sense of duty to act on the conduct of oneself. From neighbourhood watch programmes to closed, or gated, communities, Garland theorizes a shift away from rehabilitation and state-based regulation to a more individualized form of crime management.

References

Altheide, D. (2002) *Creating Fear: News and the Construction of Crisis* (New York: Aldine de Gruyter).

Bauman, Z. (1998) *Globalization: The Human Consequences* (New York: Columbia University).

Beaubien, R. (1999) 'Cameras urged for 16 sites downtown: Anti-crime surveillance plan goes to council next month for OK', *London Free Press*, Friday 17 December, A3.

Boyne, R. (2000) 'Post-Panopticism', *Economy and Society*, 29 (2), 285–307.

Brown, M. and Yasvinski, D. (1999) 'Victim dies from stab wound', *The Gazette*, Wednesday 20 January 1999, 92 (63).

Coleman, R. (2003) 'Images from a Neoliberal City: The State, Surveillance and Social Control', *Critical Criminology*, 12, 21–42.

Coleman, R. and Sim, J. (2000) 'You'll Never Walk Alone: CCTV Surveillance, Order and Neoliberal Rule in Liverpool City Centre', *British Journal of Sociology*, 51 (4), 623–39.

Davis, M. (1990) *City of Quartz* (London: Vintage).

Eide, M. and Knight, G. (1999) 'Public/Private Service: Service Journalism and the Problems of Everyday Life', *European Journal of Communication*, 14, 525–47.

Fyfe, N.R. and Bannister, J. (1996) 'City Watching: Closed Circuit Television Surveillance in Public Spaces', *Area*, 28 (1), 37–46.

Garland, D. (2001) *The Culture of Control: Crime and Social Order in Contemporary Society* (Chicago: University of Chicago Press).

Haggerty, K.D. (2003) 'From Risk to Precaution: The Rationalities of Personal Crime Prevention', in R.V. Ericson, and A. Doyle (eds) *Risk and Morality* (Toronto: University of Toronto Press), 193–214.

Herbert, J. (1999) 'Police Chief Plans Call for Action on Core Violence', *London Free Press*, Monday 25 January, A1.

Herbert, J. (2001) 'Walking the Walk: Is There Enough Policing in the Core', *London Free Press*, Saturday 8 December, B4.

Hier, S.P. (2002) 'Conceptualizing Moral Panic Through a Moral Economy of Harm', *Critical Sociology*, 28, 311–44.

Hier, S.P. (2003) 'Probing the Surveillant Assemblage: On the Dialectics of Surveillance Practices as Processes of Social Control', *Surveillance and Society*, 1 (3), 399–411. Available at: http://www.surveillance-and-society. org/articles1(3)/probing.pdf.

Hier, S.P. (2004) 'Risky Spaces and Dangerous Faces: Urban Surveillance, Affective Governance & CCTV', *Social and Legal Studies*, 13 (4), 541–54.

Hier, S.P. (forthcoming) 'Thinking Beyond Moral Panic: Risk, Governance, and the Politics of Moralization', *Theoretical Criminology*.

Hier, S.P., Greenberg, J., Walby, K. and D. Lett (2006) 'Beyond Responsibilization and Social Ordering: Media, Communication, and the Establishment of Public CCTV Surveillance'. Unpublished Manuscript.

Hunt, A. (1999) *Governing Morals: A Social History of Moral Regulation* (Cambridge: Cambridge University Press).

Hunt, A. (2003) 'Risk and Moralization in Everyday Life', in R.V. Ericson and A. Doyle (eds) *Risk and Morality* (Toronto: University of Toronto Press), 165–92.

Jasper, J. (1998) 'The Emotions of Protest: Affective and Reactive Emotions in and Around Social Movements', *Sociological Forum*, 13 (3), 397–424.

Mathiesen, T. (1997) 'The Viewer Society: Michel Foucault's "Panopticon" Revisited', *Theoretical Criminology*, 1 (2), 215–34.

Matthews, R. (2002) 'Crime and Control in Late Modernity', review of *The Culture of Control: Crime and Social Order in Contemporary Society*, by Garland, D. *Theoretical Criminology*, 6 (2), 217–226.

McCahill, M. (2002) *The Surveillance Web: The Rise of Visual Surveillance in an English City* (Cullompton: Willan).

Miner, J. (2001) 'Walk against violence raised $10,000', *London Free Press*, Thursday 17 May, A2.

Norris, C. and Armstrong, G. (1999) *The Maximum Surveillance Society: The Rise of CCTV* (Oxford: Berg).

Sher, J. (1999) 'Councilors at Odds Whether Knifings Hurt Core's Revival', *London Free Press*, Monday 18 January, A3.

Somerville, B. (1999) 'Stabbings Incite Police Concern, Safety Review', *The Gazette*, 19 January, 92 (63).

Walby, K. (2005a) 'Open-Street Camera Surveillance and Governance in Canada', under submission to *Canadian Journal of Criminology and Criminal Justice*, 47 (4): 655–83.

Walby, K. (2005b) 'Watching the Nation: CCTV in Canada', Master's thesis, University of Victoria.

Part 5

Security, Power, Agency and Resistance

Chapter 12

Surveillance, urbanization, and the US 'Revolution in Military Affairs'

Stephen Graham

Introduction: the neglect of military power within surveillance studies

The recent upsurge of critical social scientific analyses of surveillance has been overwhelmingly dominated by attempts to theorize and analyze the complex relations between surveillance, citizenship, social control, governmentality and social relations. Whilst the emerging discipline of surveillance studies has built on this foundation to theorize the connections between globalization, new technologies and social and political power within contemporary civil societies, it has strikingly neglected another extremely important domain of political and social power. This neglect is especially problematic because this domain of power has been a prime, perhaps even dominant, force in imagining, bringing in to existence, and normalizing new surveillance techniques, technologies and practices since the origins of modern societies. This domain, of course, is that of military power.

Such a lacuna within surveillance studies might be partially explained by the effects of the academic division of labour within the Western academy (Bishop and Clancey 2004). This division has traditionally worked to undermine links between spheres of work conventionally deemed 'sociological' – those centring largely on civil domains, domestic scales, social disorder and non-political violence within nation states – from the larger-scale 'political' domains centring largely on international relations, international politics, geopolitics, military power and violent conflict involving formal state militaries. Whilst critical and interdisciplinary work linking military power, technology, geopolitics and surveillance is starting to emerge (see Gray 1997; Blackmore 2005), it is, not surprisingly, a struggle to cut across the diverse theoretical, scalar and epistemological traditions of the many silo-like disciplines.

This situation helps explain why, for example, the promising theoretical work of writers such as Paul Virilio (1998), Mackenzie Wark (2002), Manuel de Landa (1991) and James Der Derian (1990, 2001), who have done so much to theorize and problematize the links between the projection and imagination of military power and techniques and technologies of surveillance, has not been more influential in sociologically oriented surveillance research. Eric Toepfer and colleagues (2005) thus correctly diagnose a failure within the emerging sub-discipline of surveillance studies to back up such theoretical openings with critical empirical work. Whilst 'studies of military surveillance exist within International Relations and studies of warfare and espionage' (Toepfer *et al.* 2005), they argue that:

> these remain disconnected from studies of surveillance across other disciplines. However, methods and technologies developed for military purposes are deeply embedded in contemporary 'civil surveillance societies', as, for instance, cornerstones of the digital universe of geographic information, CCD chips in modern CCTV cameras, or C3I centres as next generation of police control rooms (Toepfer *et al.* 2005).

In such a context, this chapter develops one detailed case study of a particular intersection of surveillance and contemporary military power: that linking United States military forces and processes of global urbanization. In what follows, I seek to problematize the ways in which the discursive and technological aspects of US military surveillance are currently being reworked to address the purported impacts of rapid urbanization across the geographical areas of the Middle East and global south that US military theorists see as their *de facto* future battlespaces. Analysis is centred particularly on how urbanization processes are being imagined and represented by US military theorists as processes which significantly undermine the American military and their technoscientific hegemony that derives from their unrivalled powers of digital surveillance.

The chapter falls in to three parts. The first describes the ways in which global south cities are perceived to interrupt and frustrate wider military strategies of transglobal surveillance and power projection surrounding the so-called 'Revolution in Military Affairs' (or 'RMA'). The second analyzes the way in which key actors within the US military-industrial complex are suggesting deeply technophiliac 'solutions' to this purported erosion of US geostrategic power through global south urbanization. The final part of the chapter attempts to draw theoretical and research conclusions for understandings of surveillance from the preceding discussions.

Fantasies frustrated: urbanization and the US 'Revolution in Military Affairs' (RMA)

> For Western military forces, asymmetric warfare in urban areas will be the greatest challenge of this century ... The city will be the strategic high ground – whoever controls it will dictate the course of future events in the world (Dickson 2002: 10).

Western military theorists and researchers are increasingly preoccupied with how the geographies of cities and processes of global south urbanization influence both the geopolitics and the technoscience of post-Cold War political violence. Indeed, almost unnoticed within 'civil' urban geography and social science, a large 'shadow' system of military urban research is quickly being established. Funded by Western military research budgets, this research is quickly elaborating how such effects are allegedly already becoming manifest, and how the global intensification of processes of urbanization will deepen them in the future.

Fuelled by the growing realization that the scale and significance of contemporary processes of urbanization throughout the world might significantly reshape the geopolitics, doctrine and realities of post-Cold War Western military strategy, this research is generating a crucial set of technomilitary discourses. Within and through such discourses, attempts are currently being made to reconstitute dramatically the structure, orientation and technoscience of Western military power to directly reflect the alleged implications of such urbanization.

The widening adoption of such 'urban warfare' doctrine follows centuries of Western military planners preaching Sun Tzu's mantra from 1500 BC that the 'worst policy is to attack cities'. This shift follows a Cold War period marked by an obsession with massive, superpower-led 'Air–Land' engagements within and above the spaces between bypassed city-regions. When cities were addressed through such Cold War doctrine, the United States' forces, in the euphemistic language so typical of military forces, 'approached the urban area by rubbling or isolating the city' (Grubs 2003: iii). That is, they either ignored or sought to systematically annihilate urban places.

As the global military hegemon, the military forces of the United States provide the most interesting and important example of how, after three decades concentrating on global surveillance and power projection, discursive constructions of 'urban terrain' in global south cities are now being used to justify the 'transformation' of the technologies, tactics and strategies of national military intervention more broadly.

The military strategies to project, sustain and deepen the US military hegemony in the post-Cold War period rest on the exploitation of a 'transformation' of US military power through what has been termed a 'revolution in military affairs' (see Pieterse 2004; Duffield 2002). Centring on the technologies of 'stealth', 'precision' targeting and satellite geopositioning, the RMA has widely been hailed amongst US military planners as the means to sustain US dominance in the post-Cold War world (Stone 2004).

Central to the RMA is the notion that 'military operations are now aimed at defined effects rather than attrition of enemy forces or occupation of ground' (Cohen 2004: 395). Through the interlinkage of the 'system of systems' of US military technologies, RMA theorists argue that a truly 'network-centric warfare' is now possible. Through this, US forces can continually dominate societies deemed to be their adversaries by utilizing their increasingly omnipotent surveillance and 'situational awareness', devastating and precisely targeted aerial firepower, and the suppression and degradation of the communications and fighting ability of any opposing forces (Arquilla and Ronfeldt 2001). Thus, RMA theorists imagine US military operations to be a giant, integrated, 'network enterprise' – a 'just-in-time' system of post-human, cyborganized warriors that utilize many principles of logistics chain management and new-technology based tracking that are so dominant within contemporary management models (Duffield 2002; Gray 2003).

Importantly, however, such technophiliac discourses depicting an RMA ushering new, relatively reduced-risk, 'clean' and painless strategy of US military dominance assumed that the vast networks of sensors and weapons that needed to be integrated and connected to project US power would work uninterruptedly. Global scales of flow and connection have thus dominated RMA discourses. Technological mastery, omnipotent surveillance, real-time 'situational awareness', and speed-of-light digital interactions have been widely portrayed as processes which, intrinsically, would usher in what US military planners term 'full spectrum dominance', on a planetary scale, irrespective of the geographical terrain that was to be dominated.

RMA discourses have, in this sense, been notably ageographical. Crucially, from the point of view of the current chapter, little account has been taken of the geographical specificities of the spaces, or geographical terrains inhabited by the purported adversaries of the US in the post-Cold War period (or how they are changing through processes of urbanization and globalization). A key axiom of RMA rhetoric has been the idea that the US was now able to prosecute its global strategies for geopolitical dominance through a 'radical non-territoriality' (Duffield 2002: 158).

RMA discourses have also been obsessively inward-looking; they have centred almost exclusively on how the Cold War strategies and military systems of the US military can be 'transformed' using new technology. 'The enemy never really figured very much in the RMA debate', writes Eliot Cohen (2004: 397). While 'American theorists and foreign imitators spoke in abstract terms of 200-mile by 200-mile boxes, sensor-to-shooter links and dominant battlefield awareness' Cohen (2004: 397), they completely ignored the complex processes of urbanization that were substantially undermining the possibility of realizing their dreams of dominance.

In an attempt to address these weaknesses, and driven by the ongoing horrors of the urban insurgency which has followed the US invasion of Iraq, RMA theorists and military research and development establishments have recently tried to 'urbanize' the RMA. That is, they have sought to change the focus of theory, along with research and weapons development, so that the RMA transforms the US military into a fighting force whose primary mission is to control and destroy urban insurgencies in global south cities. Two key emphases have emerged here.

First, emphasis is placed on the ways in which the sheer three-dimensional complexity and scale of global south cities allegedly undermine the United States' expensively assembled and hegemonic advantages in surveillance by targeting and killing through 'precise' air and space-based weapons systems (Graham 2003; Davis 2004). Many US military theorists now argue that the urban terrain in poor, global south countries is a great leveller between high-tech US forces and their low-tech and usually informally organized and poorly equipped adversaries (Gregory 2004; Graham 2004a). Such perceptions have been strengthened dramatically by the horrors of the Iraqi occupation and urban insurgency. The complex and congested terrain below, within and above cities is thus widely viewed by US military commanders and theorists as a set of physical spaces which limit the effectiveness of high-tech space-targeted bombs, surveillance systems, and automated, 'network-centric' and 'precision' weapons. The US defence research agency, DIRC, for example, argue that 'the urban environment negates the abilities of present US military communications equipment resulting in dead spots, noise, signal absorption, propagation problems which severely undermine the principles and technologies of "network-centric warfare"' (DIRC 1997).

Second, it has been widely assumed that the purported effects of urban landscapes on US military systems will directly and causally lead to an increasing tendency amongst the United States' political adversaries to take refuge within urban areas. 'The long term trend in open-area combat', writes the leading US 'urban warfare' commentator, Ralph Peters, 'is toward overhead dominance by US forces'. As a result, he predicts that 'battlefield awareness [for US forces] may prove so complete, and "precision" weapons so widely available and effective, that enemy ground-based combat systems will not be able to survive in the deserts, plains, and fields that have seen so many of history's main battles' (Peters 1996: 6).

Fantasies reclaimed? From pre-emptive war to 'Persistent Area Dominance'

> The time has come to change the perception that the high-tech US war machine fights at a disadvantage in urban areas (Houlgate 2004: 17).

The RMA is being fundamentally reworked because of the widespread perception that the intensifying urbanization of the parts of the global south that the US military envisages being their dominant areas of operation is radically undermining the US' broader efforts at technoscientific transformation. With the urban insurgency in Iraq as an ongoing fulcrum war, a 'transformation' based on the technophiliac celebrations of the death of geography through new technologies is, ironically, being transformed into a major technoscientific effort to develop and experiment with surveillance, communications and targeting systems that are specifically tailored to the fine-grain physical and human geographies of global south cities.

It is now widely argued within US military strategic organizations and think-tanks that the RMA needs to be reconfigured to address the challenges of tightly built global south cities. Along with that, new bodies of 'urban' research are being built up to try and understand how to use military violence to deliver precise 'effects' in such cities. And finally, it is widely argued that the doctrine, weaponry, training and equipment of US forces need to be comprehensively redesigned so that urban military operations are their *de facto* function. Major Lee Grubbs (2003: iii–5) of the US Army argues that US forces need to be redefined so that their main purpose is to:

> create operational shock in the urban environment. Operational shock as an urban operational concept depends on selective influence ... The utility to selectively influence depends on a deep understanding of the battlespace to identify causality between critical point, action, and effect achieved. The level of situational understanding within the infinite relationships of any enemy system and the urban area requires a variation on the doctrinal development of an understanding of the city and operational design ... Operational design and a process for understanding the city becomes critical for the selection of critical points to destroy, control and influence ... The challenge is the development of an executable operational concept for achieving systematic, across the entire system, effects within the urban environment through the selective use of force (Grubbs 2003: 4).

A large output of conceptual, technoscientific and research and development material has been created by the 'urban turn' of the RMA, especially since the Iraq invasion (see Grubbs 2003; Houlgate 2004). The overwhelming rhetoric in such efforts emphasizes that new military technoscience, specifically developed to address cities, will turn global south urban environments into areas that US forces can completely dominate, using their technological advantages, with minimum casualties to themselves. The widespread effort to tailor the RMA to support US forces' goal of dominating global south cities falls into two complementary areas of work.

Technophiliac unveilings of global south cities: dreams of 'real-time situational awareness'

The first involves programmes designed to saturate such cities with myriads of networked surveillance systems. The dream of US military theorists is that this can be done to such an extent that any target can be automatically identified at any time and in so doing be exposed to the high-technology tracking and killing powers of 'network-centric' weapons. Such visions imagine pervasive and interlined arrays of 'loitering' and 'embedded' sensors as overcoming all the limits and interruptions that megacity environments place in the way of successfully implementing network-centric warfare. Ackerman (2002), for example, suggests that such sensor suites will be designed to automatically trace dynamic change rather than constantly soaking up data from unchanging environments: observing 'change' rather than observing 'scenery', as he puts it. In other words, algorithms will be designed to function only when definable changes occur. They will thus identify purported notions of 'normality' against the 'abnormal' behaviours and patterns that can then be assessed as 'targets'.

One major example of such a development is the tellingly titled 'Combat Zones That See' (CTS), a project led by the US Defense Advanced Research Projects Agency (DARPA). Launched at the start of the Iraq insurgency in 2003, CTS 'explores concepts, develops algorithms, and delivers systems for utilizing large numbers (1000s) of algorithmic video cameras to provide the close-in sensing demanded for military operations in urban terrain' (DARPA 2003: 4). Through installing computerized CCTV across entire occupied cities, the project organizers envisage that, when deployed, CTS will sustain 'motion-pattern analysis across whole city scales' (DARPA 2003: 4). These will be linked to the tracking of massive populations of individualized cars and people through intelligent computer algorithms linked to the recognition of number plates and scanned in human facial photos.

It is envisaged that, once CTS has been developed by 2007, it 'will generate, for the first time, the reconnaissance, surveillance and targeting information needed to provide close-in, continuous, always-on support for military operations in urban terrain' (DARPA 2003: 6). It will be designed to specifically address the 'inherently three-dimensional nature of urban centres, with large buildings, extensive underground passageways, and concealment from above' (DARPA 2003: 7).

The central challenge of CTS, according to DARPA, will be to build up fully representative data profiles on the 'normal' time-space movement patterns of entire subject cities so that algorithms could then use statistical modelling to 'determine what is normal and what is not' (quoted in Sniffen 2003). This will be a purported aid to identifying insurgents' activities and real or potential attacks, as well as warning of the presence or movement of target or suspect vehicles or individuals. The report states that the CTS project will:

include ... analysis of changes in normalcy modes; detection of variances in activity; anomaly detection based on statistical analyses; discovery of links between places, subjects and times of activities; and direct comparison and correlation of track data to other information available to operators. Predictive modelling, plan recognition, and behaviour modelling should alert operators to potential force protection risks and hostile situations. Forensic information (where did a vehicle come from, how did it get here?) should be combined and contrasted to more powerful 'forward-tracking' capabilities (where could the vehicle go?, where is the vehicle going?) to allow operators to provide real-time capabilities to assess potential force threats (DARPA 2003: 13).

After a stream of protests from US civil liberties groups, DARPA stressed that, whilst the initial test of mass, urban tracking will take place at a US army base within the United States (Fort Belvoir, Virginia), the deployment of CTS will only take place in 'foreign urban battlefields' (Defense Watch 2004).

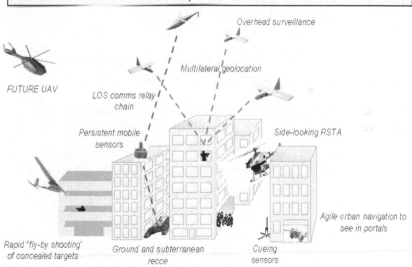

Figure 1 DARPA urban 'Reconnaissance, Surveillance and Target Acquisition' (RSTA) platforms as envisaged by its HURT Programme (DARPA 2004).(LOS = Line of Sight, RSTA = Reconnaissance, Surveillance and Target Assessment, UAV = Unmanned Aerial Vehicle)

Saturating occupied or target cities with microscale and even nanoscale sensors and cameras is also being investigated by the CTS programme and an associated programme labelled HURT (Heterogeneous Urban Reconnaissance, Surveillance and Target Acquisition Team). This programme centres on the development of a wide range of 'persistent' and unmanned surveillance and weapons platforms tailored to the demands of global south urban environments (Figure 1). DARPA's HURT and CTS programmes are, in turn, being backed up by major virtual simulations of wide-scale future urban wars in cities like Jakarta (an exercise known as 'Urban Resolve'). In these, future suites of surveillance systems, like those under development in HURT, are inputted into the simulations to assess their likely effectiveness.

Increasingly, the wide-scale automated CCTV systems being developed through CTS and HURT are being merged with the geospatial simulation systems discussed above. They provide simulations of global south cities which also include real-time surveillance of the tracks and locations of purported 'targets'. One system, for example, labelled 'video flashlight', uses software to 'paint' in simulations of the details of occupied cities based on data fed in by CTS-like CCTV systems and other radars and sensors. 3D virtual models of subject cities can thus be created, allowing viewers to 'fly' through them, exploring the real-time tracks of known or suspected 'targets'. 'Our goal is to get to where I can model a small town in six hours' reports Steve Hsu, an employee of RCA Labs who work on the project. 'Such speed is critical for jobs like rapidly installing video surveillance on an urban battlefield' (Perkins 2004: 72).

'Persistent area dominance': towards robotic killing systems in urban warfare

This leads neatly to the second main area of defence research and development to help assert the dominance of US forces over global south cities: a shift towards robotic air and ground weapons. When linked to the persistent surveillance and target identification systems just discussed, these weapons will be deployed to continually and automatically destroy purported targets in potentially endless streams of state killing. Here, crucially, fantasies of military omniscience and omnipotence, which blur seamlessly into wider sci-fi and cyberpunk imaginations of future military technoscience, become indistinguishable from major US military research and development programmes. The fantasies of linking sentient, automated and omnipotent surveillance – which bring God-like levels of 'situational awareness' to US forces attempting to control intrinsically devious global south megacities – to automated machines of killing, pervades the discourses of the urban turn in the RMA.

'We really *do* want an Orwellian future not in Manhattan, but in Kabul,' argue Huber and Mills (2001), two defence consultants who are leading advocates of the automation of counter-insurgency and urban operations as part of the 'war on terror'. To them, the United States' 'longer-term objective must be to infiltrate their homelands electronically, to the point where we can listen to and track anything that moves' (Huber and Mills 2001: 30) (sic). They predict that:

> Terrorist wars will continue, in one form or another, for as long as we live … We are destined to fight a never-ending succession of microscale battles, which will require us to spread military resources across vast expanses of empty land and penetrate deep into the shadows of lives lived at the margins of human existence. *Their* conscripts dwell in those expanses and shadows. Our soldiers don't, and can't for any extended period of time. What we have instead is microscale technology that is both smarter and more expendable than their fanatics, that is more easily concealed and more mobile, that requires no food and sleep, and that can endure even harsher conditions (Huber and Mills 2001: 29).

Huber and Mills go on to envisage a near-future scenario where target cities are so saturated by targeting sensors that US forces are then able to:

> project destructive power precisely, judiciously, and from a safe distance week after week, year after year, for as long as may be necessary … it will end up as their sons against our silicon. Our silicon will win (Huber and Mills 2001: 31–4).

A second telling example comes from the discussion of a model near-future US 'urban operation', described by *Defense Watch* magazine during its discussions of DARPA's CTS programme (2004). In their scenario, swarms of microscale and nanoscale networked sensors pervade the target city, providing continuous streams of target information to arrays of automated weaponry. Together, these systems produce continuous killing and 'target' destruction: a kind of robotized counter-insurgency operation with US commanders and soldiers doing little but overseeing the cyborganized, interlinked and increasingly automated killing systems from a safe distance.

Defense Watch (2004) thus fantasize about 'a battlefield in the near future' that is wired up with the systems that result from the CTS programme and its followers. Here, unbound technophiliac fantasies of omnipotent urban control blur into longstanding dreams of cyborganized and robotized warfare. These often involve dehumanizing racism and the demonization of whole cities through 'terrorist' labelling. 'Several large fans are stationed outside the city limits of an urban target that our [sic] guys need to take' (Defense Watch 2004), they begin:

> upon appropriate signal, what appears like a dust cloud emanates from each fan. The cloud is blown into town where it quickly dissipates. After a few minutes of processing by laptop-size processors, a squadron of small, disposable aircraft ascends over the city. The little drones dive into selected areas determined by the initial analysis of data transmitted by the fan-propelled swarm. Where they disperse their nano-payloads (Defense Watch 2004).

'After this, the processors get even more busy', continues the scenario:

> Within minutes the mobile tactical center have a detailed visual and audio picture of every street and building in the entire city. Every hostile [person] has been identified and located. From this point on, nobody in the city moves without the full and complete knowledge of the mobile tactical center. As blind spots are discovered, they can quickly be covered by additional dispersal of more nano-devices. Unmanned air and ground vehicles can now be vectored directly to selected targets to take them out, one by one. Those enemy combatants clever enough to evade actually being taken out by the unmanned units can then be captured or killed by human elements who are guided directly to their locations, with full and complete knowledge of their individual fortifications and defenses ... When the dust settles on competitive bidding for BAA 03-15 [the code number for the 'Combat Zones That See' programme], and after the first prototypes are delivered several years from now, our guys are in for a mind-boggling treat at the expense of the bad guys (Defense Watch 2004).

Such omnipotence fantasies extend even further to the automated surveillance, through brain scanning, of people's inner mental attitudes to any US invasion so that 'targets' deemed to be resistant can be automatically identified and destroyed:

Robotic systems push deeper into the urban area ... Behind the fighters, military police and intelligence personnel process the inhabitants, electronically reading their attitudes toward the intervention and cataloguing them into a database immediately recoverable by every fire team in the city (even individual weapons might be able to read personal signatures, firing immediately upon cueing ... Smart munitions track enemy systems and profiled individuals ... Satellites monitor the city for any air defense fires, curing immediate responses from near-space orbiting 'guns'. Drones track inhabitants who have been 'read' as potentially hostile and 'tagged' (Defense Watch 2004).

Disturbingly, such fantasies of continuous, automated and robotized urban targeting and killing are far from the realms of sci-fi fantasy. Rather, as with the CTS and HURT programmes, they are fuelling very real multimillion dollar research and weapons development programmes aimed at developing ground and aerial vehicles, which not only navigate and move robotically, but also select and destroy targets without 'humans in the loop' based on algorithmically driven 'decisions'.

Lawlor (2004), for example, discusses the development of 'autonomous mechanized combatant' air and ground vehicles or 'tactical autonomous combatants' for the US Air Force. These are being designed, he notes, to use 'pattern recognition' software for what he calls 'time-critical targeting'. This links sensors very quickly to automated weapons so that fleeting 'targets' both within and outside cities can be continually destroyed. Such doctrine is widely termed 'compressing the kill chain' or 'sensor to shooter warfare' in US military parlance (Hebert 2003). The 'swarming of unmanned systems' project team at US forces JOINT Command Experimentation Directorate, based in Suffolk, Virginia, Lawlor (2004) states, are so advanced in such experimentation that 'autonomous, networked and integrated robots may be the norm rather than the exception by 2025' (Lawlor 2004: 2).

By that date, Lawlor predicts that 'technologies could be developed ... that would allow machines to sense a report of gunfire in an urban environment to within one meter, triangulating the position of the shooter and return fire within a fraction of a second' (Lawlor 2004: 2) This would provide a completely automated weapon system devoid of human involvement. He quotes Gordon Johnson, the 'Unmanned Effects' team leader for the US army's 'Project Alpha', as saying that such a system:

if it can get within one meter, it's killed the person who's firing. So, essentially, what we're saying is that anyone who would shoot at our forces would die. Before he can drop that weapon and run, he's probably already dead. Well now, these cowards in Baghdad would have to pay with blood and guts every time they shoot at one of our folks. The costs of poker went up significantly … The enemy, are they going to give up blood and guts to kill machines? I'm guessing not (Hebert 2003: 3).

Lawlor predicts that such robo-war systems will 'help save lives by taking humans out of harm's way' (Lawlor 2004: 2); here, tellingly, only US forces are considered to fall within the category of 'human'.

In addition, unmanned aerial vehicles armed with 'intelligent munitions' are already being designed that will eventually be programmed to fire on and kill 'targets' detected by US Forces' real-time surveillance grids, in a completely autonomous way. Such munitions will loiter over targets for days at a time, linked into the data links, until 'targets' are detected for destruction. A programme called TUDLS (Total Urban Dominance Layered System) for example, is currently underway to provide what Plenge describes as:

> long hover and loiter propulsion systems, multidiscriminant sensors and seekers, mini- and micro-air vehicles, mini-lethal and non-lethal warheads, autonomous and man-in-the loop control algorithms, and a strong interface with the [urban] battlespace in formation network (Plenge 2004).

Plenge stresses further that the loitering munitions developed through the TUDLS programme will 'be capable of completing the entire kill chain … with minimal human involvement'. They will be able to cooperate to maximize their autonomous destructive power or, where there are 'more stringent rules of engagement', through referring back each time they strike to human-in-the-loop ways on working when they are 'in close proximity to friendly forces' (Plenge 2004). In other words, Plenge envisages 'swarms' of autonomous, robotic weapons systems working completely autonomously through cooperative artificial intelligence and surveillance systems, unless it is deemed necessary to have human beings approve their targeting decisions.

Crucially, such munitions will be equipped with algorithms designed to separate 'targets' from 'non-targets' automatically. The ultimate goals, according to Pinney, an engineer at Raytheon, is a 'kill chain solution' based on '1st look, 1st feed, 1st kill' where each armed unmanned vehicle continuously 'seeks out targets on its own' (Pinney 2003: 16). Tirpak, a US air force specialist, envisages that humans will be required to make the decisions to launch weapons at targets only 'until UCAVs (Unmanned Aerial Combat Vehicles) establish a track record of reliability in finding the right targets and employing weapons properly'. Then the 'machines will be trusted to do even that' (Tirpak 2001: 32).

The munitions that will be tasked with such algorithmic killing weapons are already under development. One, termed LOCAAS ('Low Cost Autonomous Attack Systems'), the United States Air Force has already committed to buy. This system loiters and searches over an area of 80 square miles, scanning the area and comparing signals received with 'stored target templates' using the 'advanced algorithms' of what is known as 'automated target recognition' (ATR) software (Marzolf 2004: 29). When the signature of a known target is detected, the missile homes in to destroy it. The software currently has 'difficulty in discriminating real targets from look-alike targets, especially in cluttered terrain' like cities (Marzolf 2004: 30). Whilst having a human being to approve each weapon's final attack would 'keep the question of accountability solidly answered at all times', Marzolf admits that the USAF has rejected this 'mainly to limit the munition's cost' (2004: 23).

Conclusions

> The ultimate expression of sovereignty resides ... in the power and capacity to dictate who may live and who must die (Mbembe 2003: 11).

This chapter has sought to 'open up' the connections between military technoscience, the military problematization of global south cities, and the doctrines, discourses and fantasies that drive the elaboration of a globe-spanning and hegemonic US military presence in the post-Cold War period. With the bloody morass of the Iraqi insurgency continuing at the time of writing (April 2006), such intersections could hardly be more politically charged, or more pregnant with significance. This chapter has demonstrated very clearly that a large-scale military research and development programme is currently underway in the United States to, quite literally, 'urbanize' the 'revolution in military affairs'. Here the cutting-edge technoscientific efforts and priorities of the world's military hegemon are being shifted from an emphasis on globe-spanning control, networking and vertical targeting, treating planet earth as some unitary, ageographical 'battlespace', to one aimed at bringing maximum control, surveillance and killing power to the detailed micro-geographies of global south cities.

Such dreams of omnipotence, of course, must be treated with caution. The US military, and its associated complex of research and development outfits, has, after all, long held fantasies of superweapons that would deterministically realize their dreams of mastery and omnipotence (Franklin 1988). As now, such technophiliac dreams of mastery have usually evolved closely with the wider discourses of speculative fiction and popular geopolitical domains and entertainment industries (Gannon 2003). The 'technological fanaticism' of both has deep roots within US political, popular and military culture (Sherry 1987). Certainly, future research into the central role of surveillance within the RMA needs to do much more to theorize and address the ways in which popular cultural discourses and fantasies of future war cross-fertilize with military fantasies and real research and development programmes in agencies like DARPA (see Gannon 2003).

We must also remember that the 'US military' is far from being some single, unitary actor. All of the discourses, projects and programmes analyzed in this chapter remain extremely contested. Within the vast institutional complex that together constitutes the 'US military', major political battles are underway – fuelled by the ongoing nightmare in Iraq – over the degree to which technophiliac fantasies of omnipotence, through some urbanized 'RMA' or 'network-centric warfare', are realistic, even in military terms.

Many in the US army, for example, are deeply sceptical that the horrors and 'fog of war' in bloody 'urban operations' like the Iraqi insurgency, can ever really be technologized, mediated, and saturated with sentient surveillance and targeting systems, to anything like the degree that is common in the discursive imaginings driving the programmes discussed above (see for example, Price 2001). The relatively high casualty rates of US forces – forced to come down from 40,000 ft, or withdraw from ceramic armour, to attempt to control and 'pacify' violent insurgencies within sprawling Iraqi cities – are a testament to the dangerous wishful thinking that pervades all military fantasies of 'clean', 'automated' or 'cyborganized' urban 'battlespace' (Graham 2004b). It should also be remembered that, in Iraq, even rudimentary high-tech devices have routinely failed due to technical malfunctions or extreme operating conditions (Hills 2004).

Such caveats about the inevitable gulf between fantasies and reality should not, however, distract from the stark messages that emerge from this chapter. Whilst the urbanized RMA is, of course, being driven by often wild and fantastical discourses, its effects will be very material and profound. Massive technoscientific efforts to saturate global south cities with real-time surveillance, targeting and killing systems are undoubtedly underway as the latest military-industrial research drive focuses on using new algorithmic surveillance capabilities to try to overcome the ways in which the micro-geographies of global south cities interrupt wider fantasies of US military omnipotence.

Whether such systems will ever function as imagined even in military terms is, then, beside the point. For, as the death of an estimated 100,000 Iraqi civilians within the first 21 months of the US–UK invasion testifies (Roberts *et al.* 2004), the very existence of an imperial project of launching the world's military hegemon's high-tech killing systems into global south cities will inevitably lead to mass civilian deaths. This seems especially so as the new algorithmic systems emerge to be the actual agents of continuous, autonomous killing as 'kill chains' are 'compressed', 'sensors' are linked automatically to 'shooters', and the fantasies of 'persistent area dominance' achieve full expression through the favourable context of President Bush's huge increases in defence spending and ideologies of pre-emptive war. To put it mildly, dreams of clinically identifying and surgically killing only 'fighters' within sprawling megacities, through the agency of autonomous computer algorithms, are dangerously deluded. The results of such systems, inevitably, would be large numbers of civilians killed and injured with the added and deeply troubling development of software agency as the ultimate 'intelligence', manufacturing such violence and automatically stipulating who should die and who should live.

The gravity of the developments reported means that a major challenge for both theorists of surveillance, and the wider bodies of critical social and political researchers and activists, is to incorporate the intersections of urbanization, a US-dominated neoliberal Empire (Hardt and Negri 2004), and military technoscience as a critical domain within their work. It is no longer adequate, for example, to solely consider the proliferation of algorithmic techniques, and the shift to ubiquitous surveillance, within the 'civil' domains of cities – as the surveillance literature has overwhelmingly tended to do so far. Nor is it adequate to consider transnational, military surveillance, simulation, and the convergence of what Der Derian (2001) has called the 'military-industrial-entertainment network', in isolation from the military problematization of global south urbanization, the purported effects of 'urbanizing terrain' on digital military systems of surveillance, targeting and killing, and the urban turn in the RMA reported here (see for example, Der Derian 1990). If this chapter makes one thing clear it is this: the intricate and intensifying connections between micro-geographies of control and power on urban streets, and wider geopolitical, military and political economic strategies backed up by military research, must be centrally addressed by all future theorists of urban, social and military surveillance.

An example of such research challenges comes from the deepening intersections between 'algorithmic' and digitized CCTV on city streets and the products of the urbanized RMA. Such cross-overs are especially important given the growing privatization of Western militaries, law enforcement and security industries, and the efforts by a small number of military-security 'prison industrial complex' conglomerates to colonize both 'homeland' and 'war zone battlespaces' equally. As the barriers separating the technoscience of 'civil' law enforcement and military urban operations are progressively dismantled, so the algorithmic surveillance systems embedded into the urbanizing zones of pre-emptive, continuous war will increasingly resemble those in the increasingly securitized cities policed by national security states (and associated private military corporations). Here we confront the latest stage in a long history where disciplinary devices are developed to try and assert control and dominance for colonizing powers within colonized cities being later transmuted back into 'homeland' cities by military and political elites. With the sorts of wide-area, algorithmic urban surveillance system being developed by DARPA and their like so similar to systems envisaged as part of the 'homeland security' drive to securitize cities in the capitalist heartlands of the global north, these cross-overs are already rapidly strengthening further.

As an initial exposé of the close links between the problematization of global south urban areas within US military rhetoric, and the efforts to customize surveillance, targeting and killing systems of the RMA to sustain 'persistent dominance' of such cities, this chapter inevitably raises as many questions as it answers. What implications, for example, does the urban 'turn' in the RMA have for theorizations and analyses of globalization, the geopolitics of neoliberal 'Empire', the nature of the colonial present (Gregory 2004). How might it effect the intensifying nexus between military technologies and entertainment and simulation industries, and the scope for nurturing progressive alternatives to aggressive US hegemony? What are the links between longstanding popular fantasies and imaginations of cyborg war (Gannon 2003) and the emerging automated killing systems discussed in this chapter? What are the implications of such emerging military systems and doctrines for analyses of global south urbanization and the geopolitics of the Middle East? How might systems for continuous, low-level and automated killing alter the nature of warfare, state violence and organized political violence and what are the implications of algorithmic state killing for the laws of war and notions of state criminality and illegality? How might they impact on imagined and real separations between securitized 'homelands' and the 'frontier zones' subjected to pre-emptive and increasingly continuous 'wars on terror' by US strategy? Finally, how can discussions of 'persistent area dominance' best be incorporated into wider debates and activism surrounding the broader challenges thrown down by ubiquitous ICTs, global mobilities, pervasive tracking, sentient environments, the changing links between corporeality, technology and urbanity, and the growing importance of systems of algorithmic surveillance which fuse seamlessly into electronic simulations (Bogard this volume; Graham 1998)?

Addressing such questions entails profound interdisciplinary challenges. It demands that urban social scientists work closely with critical theorists of international relations and state power and violence. It lays down an imperative for multi-scale engagement to track the telescoping dynamics of the military technoscience being unleashed and imagined. It raises questions about the nature of sovereignty, or urban space, of globalization, and of the technoscientific underpinnings to contemporary colonial power (and responses to it). And it necessitates specialists of the social construction of technoscientific and military systems engaging closely with political and urban theorists so as to address the role of imagined geographies, and military surveillant simulations, in constituting and reshaping US Empire in particular, and the political economies and geographies of post-Cold War globalization more generally.

Theorists of surveillance will also need to be mindful that these processes are being further fuelled by proliferating cultures of fear, and the widespread demonization of Arab and global south urbanites and urban places, generated and perpetuated by both 'war on terror' discourses and the Orientalized products of Western entertainment industries (novels, video games, films) (Graham 2004a, b). In these, Islamic and global south cities are often discursively constructed as little more than receiving points for US military technoscience and ordnance, as intrinsically 'terroristic' or 'nest'-like spaces which must be unveiled, controlled and 'pacified' through the colonial technoscience and digitized surveillance and targeting technologies that produced by the urbanized RMA (Graham 2004b).

The final challenge – drawing on theorists as diverse as Foucault (1977), Agamben (1998), Deleuze and Guattari (1987), Gregory (2004) and Said (1978) – is to expose in detail the ways in which urbanized RMA weapons programmes – and the discourses which fuel them – embed stark biopolitical judgements about the varying worth of human subjects, according to their location, beneath the intensifying, transnational gaze of militarized surveillance. Such a theme must be at the very core of any future re-theorizations of the links between corporeal, urban and transnational power in what Derek Gregory has called our 'colonial present' (2004).

Here, attention should fall in particular on the ways in which biopolitical stipulations of the worth – or lack of worth – of human subjects are, quite literally, cast into the software code that operates increasingly automated and multi-scale surveillance, targeting and killing systems. Thus, the new technoscience of the urbanized RMA concentrates on distinguishing 'normal' urban space-times and ecologies in the global north, so that the apparatus of an increasingly militarized security state can be used to discipline those deemed 'abnormal'.

By contrast, those deemed to be 'abnormal' within surveilled and simulated urban space-times and ecologies in global south cities will, as examples of what Agamben (1998) has called 'bare life', be exposed to increasingly autonomous surveillance systems designed to sustain continuous, automated and cyborganized state violence. Here, the very technological architectures of such systems inscribe the cast-out bare life of global south urbanites, whose bodies can pile up unnoticed and without political fallout under the rubric of 'collateral damage', and who can be exposed to automated and cyborganized killing systems without hope of legal or ethical protection.

Crucially, of course, these stark biopolitical realities are endlessly veiled beneath the layers of technological fetishism and dominant political, military, technoscientific and popular-geopolitical discourses. Together, the infinite lexicon of military 'geekspeak' acronyms and euphemisms work to veil even the very humanity of 'target' people and places, whilst glorifying the cyborganized 'warriors' who are piecing together these 'persistent area dominance' systems (Davis 2002). The task, then, is to launch a powerful effort to assert the essential humanity of global south cities, and to so undermine the dehumanizing rhetoric of the urbanized RMA, in which cities become mere physical objects and people mere 'targets' to be attacked through automated weapons systems brought in to animation by the deepest omnipotence fantasies of the United States military.

Note: The author would like to thank the British Academy for the support of a Research Readership, without which this research would not have been possible.

References

Ackerman, R.K. (2002) 'Persistent Surveillance Comes into View', *Signal Magazine*, May. Available at: http://www.afcea.org/signal/articles/anmviewer.asp?a=97 (accessed February 2005).

Agamben, G. (1998) *Homo Sacer: Sovereign Power and Bare Life* (Stanford, CA: Stanford University Press).

Arquilla, J. and Ronfeldt, D. (eds) (2001) *Networks and Netwars* (Santa Monica, CA: RAND).

Bishop, R. and Clancey, G. (2004) 'The City-as-Target, or Perpetuation and Death', in S. Graham (ed.) *Cities, War and Terrorism: Towards an Urban Geopolitics* (Oxford: Blackwell), 74–94.

Blackmore, T. (2005) *War X: Human Extensions in Battlespace* (Toronto: University of Toronto Press).

Cohen, E. (2004) 'Change and Transformation in Military Affairs', *Journal of Strategic Studies*, 27 (3), 395–407.

Davis, M. (2004) 'The Pentagon as Global Slum Lord', *TomDispatch* (19 April 2004). Available at: http://www.tomdispatch.com/ (accessed 10 June 2005).

Davis, M. (2003) 'Shock and Awe', *Socialist Review*. Available at: http://www.socialistreview.org.uk/article.php?articlenumber=8352 (accessed February 2005).

Defense Advanced Research Projects Agency (DARPA) (2003) *Combat Zones That See Program: Proper Information*. Available at: http://www.darpa.mil/baa/baa03-15.htm (accessed February 2005).

Defense Advanced Research Projects Agency (DARPA) (2004) *HURT – Heterogeneous Urban RSTA Team, Briefing to Industry* (Washington: Defense Advanced Research Projects Agency).

Defense Intelligence Reference Document [DIRC] (1997) *The Urban Century: Developing World Urban Trends and Possible Factors Affecting Military Operations* (Quantico, VA: Marine Corps Intelligence Agency).

Defense Watch (2004) 'Combat Zones That "See" Everything'. Available at: http://www.argee.net/DefenseWatch/Combat%20Zones%20that%20'See'%20Everything.html (accessed March 2005).

De Landa, M. (1991) *War in the Age of Intelligent Machines* (New York: Zone).

Deleuze, G. and Guattari, F. (1987) *A Thousand Plateaus* (Minneapolis: University of Minnesota Press).

Der Derian, J. (1990) 'The (S) pace of International Relations: Simulation, Surveillance, and Speed', International *Studies Quarterly*, 34, 295–310.

Der Derian, J. (2001) *Virtuous War: Mapping the Military-Industrial-Media-Entertainment Complex* (Boulder, CO: Westview).

Dickson, K. (2002) *The War on Terror: Cities as the Strategic High Ground* (Mimeo).

Duffield, M. (2002) 'War as a Network Enterprise: The New Security Terrain and its Implications', *Cultural Values*, 6, 153–65.

Foucault (1977) *Discipline and Punish* (New York: Pantheon).

Franklin, H.B. (1988) *War Stars: The Superweapon and the American Imagination* (Oxford: Oxford University Press).

Gannon, C. (2003) *Rumours of War and Infernal Machines: Technomilitary Agenda Setting in American and British Speculative Fiction* (Liverpool: Liverpool University Press).

Graham, S. (1998) 'Spaces of Surveillant-Simulation: New Technologies, Digital Representations, and Material Geographies', *Environment and Planning D: Society and Space*, 16, 483–504.

Graham, S. (2003) 'Lessons in Urbicide', *New Left Review*, 19, January/February, 63–78.

Graham, S. (ed.) (2004a) *Cities, War and Terrorism: Towards an Urban Geopolitics* (Oxford: Blackwell).

Graham, S. (2004b) 'Vertical Geopolitics: Baghdad and After', *Antipode*, 36 (1), 12–19.

Gray, C. (2003) 'Posthuman Soldiers and Postmodern War', *Body and Society*, 9 (4), 215–26.

Gray, C. (1997) *Postmodern War: The New Politics of Conflict* (London: Routledge).

Gregory, D. (2004) *The Colonial Present* (Oxford: Blackwell).

Grubbs, L. (2003) *In Search of a Joint Urban Operational Concept* (Fort Leavenworth, KS: Army Command and General Staff College, School of Advanced Military Studies).

Hardt, M. and Negri, A. (2004) *Multitude: War and Democracy in the Age of Empire* (London: Hamish Hamilton).

Hebert, A. (2003) 'Compressing the Kill Chain', *Air Force Magazine*, March, 34–42.

Hills, A. (2004) *Future Wars in Cities* (London: Frank Cass).

Houlgate, K. (2004) 'Urban Warfare Transforms the Corps', *Naval Institute Proceedings*, November. Available at: http://www.military.com/NewContent/0,13190,NI_1104_Urban-P1,00.html (accessed February 2005).

Huber, P. and Mills, M. (2002) 'How Technology Will Defeat Terrorism', *City Journal*, 12, 24–34.

Lawlor M. (2003) 'Robotic Concepts Take Shape', *Signal Magazine*. Available at: http://www.afcea.org/signal/articles/anmviewer.asp?a=64 (accessed February 2005).

Marzolf, G. (2004) *Time-Critical Targeting: Predictive Versus Reactionary Methods: An Analysis for the Future* (Maxwell Air Base, AL: Air University Press).

Mbembe, A. (2003) 'Necropolitics', *Public Culture*, 15 (1), 11–40.

Perkins, B. (2004) 'Seamless Surveillance', *Technology Review*, February, 71–4.

Peters, R. (1996) 'Our Soldiers, Their Cities', *Parameters*, Spring, 1–7.

Pieterse, J. (2004) 'Neoliberal Empire', *Theory, Culture and Society*, 21 (3), 118–40.

Pinney, C. (2003) 'UAV Weaponization: The Next 100 Years', seminar at International Air and Space Symposium, 14–17 July 2003, Dayton, OH. Available at http://www.raytheon.com/feature/stellent/groups/public/documents/legacy_site/ms01_042879.pdf.

Plenge, B. (2004) 'Area Dominance: Area Dominance with Air-Delivered Loitering Munitions Aids the Warfighter', *AFLR Briefs*. Available at: www.afrlhorizons.com/Briefs/Apr04/MN0308.html.

Price, D. (2001) *Technology in Transformation: Critical Strength or Critical Vulnerability?* (Newport, RI: Naval War College). Available at: http://handle. dtic.mil/100.2/ADA393536.

Roberts, L., Lafta, R., Garfield, R., Khudhairi, J. and Burnham, G. (2004) 'Mortality Before and After the 2003 Invasion of Iraq: Cluster Sample Survey', *The Lancet*, 364 (9448), 1857–64.

Said, E. (1978) *Orientalism* (London: Routledge and Keegan Paul).

Sherry, M. (1987) *The Rise of American Air Power: The Creation of Armageddon* (New Haven, CT: Yale University Press).

Sniffen, M. (2003) 'Pentagon Project Could Keep a Close Eye on Cities', *Philadelphia Inquirer*, Wednesday 2 July 2003, A02.

Stone, J. (2004) 'Politics, Technology and the Revolution in Military Affairs', *Journal of Strategic Studies*, 27 (3), 408–27.

Tirpak, J. (2001) 'Send in the UCAVs', *Air Force Magazine*, August, 31–3.

Toepfer, E., Wood, D. and Graham, S. (2005) 'Surveillance and Violent Conflict', *Surveillance and Society*, 3:2/3. Available at: http://www.surveillance-and-society.org/call.htm#vio.

Virilo, P. (1998) *Open Sky* (London: Verso).

Wark, M. (2002) 'To the Vector the Spoils', in T.Y. Levin, U. Frohne and P. Weibel (eds) *CTRL [Space]: Rhetorics of Surveillance from Bentham to Big Brother* (Cambridge, MA and London: MIT Press), 396–401.

Chapter 13

Electronic government and surveillance-oriented society

Toshimaru Ogura

Introduction: surveillance-oriented society[1]

The purpose of this chapter is to clarify that surveillance technology as an information and communication technology (ICT) has brought about significant transformations in the characteristics of capitalist nation states that are based on the rule of law. Modern society is an information-intensive society, but it also brought about the undermining of modernist preconditions of the state and individuals. With the development of surveillance based on ICT, not only privacy and civil liberty, but also democracy and identity politics, are in serious crisis. There are several questions to be addressed in this complicated process: Why does modern society result in the undermining of its positive values, such as privacy, civil liberty, democracy and freedom? What kind of transformation is taking place in these values? What are some effective alternatives to a surveillance-oriented society based on ICT?

In order to try to answer the above questions, I outline, firstly, the socio-historical background of the present surveillance-oriented society based on ICT. Secondly, I examine the specific intentions of population management in the modern capitalist nation state, which define characteristics of surveillance. Thirdly, I outline a reconsideration of privacy rights. Fourthly, I address problems with electronic government (e-government), and finally, I propose the possibility of an alternative identity politics against a surveillance-oriented society based on ICT.

Before taking up the main theme, I must explain my fundamental viewpoints on surveillance and technology. Issues of surveillance are essentially problems of intention and motive by the watcher. The motive to monitor all behaviour of prisoners without being seen by them brought about the idea of the panopticon. The motive to know the behaviours of unknown customers has brought about innovative technology for marketing. The hidden intention of police on the street watching citizens is to detect the citizens' likelihood of committing crime based on their attitude, fashion, age, race, gender and other appearances. Before the highly developed ICT age, police were not able to identify the criminal potential of individuals by their appearance alone. From the commercial sector to law enforcement, the desire to identify has become widespread. The desire to identify the unknown is the social background for the innovation of surveillance technology. Identification issues are very closely related to privacy and civil liberty issues. It tends to be neglected that the development of surveillance technology embedded in social progress has dangerous characteristics for positive values. Post-September 11, the desire to identify is bound to national security more than ever. But how we misunderstand technology determines the surveillance-oriented society: the unconscious desire to identify the unknown in modern capitalist nation states defines the tendency towards technology solutions.

Socio-historical background of surveillance-oriented society

Generally speaking, society does not transform from one mode to another; rather, social elements in preceding societies persist and reproduce with changing shapes. By 'historical layers', I do not mean historical materialism, such as the base/superstructure models of orthodox Marxism or modernist linear historical progress, but geological strata, where earlier social structures function with alteration in subsequent eras. Cultural elements especially have such a layer structure. Racism and patriarchy are not residual elements of a pre-modern age, they are authentic components that are reproduced in the context of capitalism. This kind of cultural dimension functions as an ideological apparatus to legitimize surveillance and to weaken privacy rights and civil liberties. For example, Japan has a different historical background of privacy than the United States. During the 300-year-long Edo[2] era from the early seventeenth century to the

271

mid-nineteenth century, there were very few urban riots even though the population of Edo was over one million at the dawn of modern age in the early nineteenth century. Because of this history, Japan has a different governance for population management than Western urban places. Many have betrayed the police. During the Edo era, the basic form of mutual surveillance was a short segmented section of houses composed of poor people. The ordinary working poor were monitored by employers and house owners who were responsible for employees and tenants. Public space in Edo was tightly controlled by police–neighbour connections based on the mutual surveillance system embedded in the neighbour relationship. Privacy basically did not exist for ordinary people and urban public space belonged to market interests or political authorities. Thus, the market economy and commercial capital developed but there were very few developments in political freedom. Urban space was regarded as a political and market-oriented space; political opinions in the newspaper were highly censored. This kind of pre-modern urban space is the unconscious parent of a sense of 'public space' in modern Japan. Therefore, seeing public space in this way encourages tolerance of authoritarian state power, commercialism and the self-restriction of people's right to urban space.

Each society has its own specific characteristics for surveillance of the population. However, at the same time, it is necessary to extract the fundamental common characteristics among modern societies in order to make a theoretical framework for surveillance-oriented society. It is my view that the common characteristics of surveillance are the management of population based on capitalism and the nation state.

Modern surveillance-oriented society has five socio-historical layers. The base layer was formed around the eighteenth or nineteenth century in Western countries, especially England as a country of the first Industrial Revolution. Its social structure, in terms of management of the population, was an urban-industrial labour power which was a new phenomenon of population completely different from rural populations. The working class was regarded as a 'dangerous' class. The creation of workplace surveillance technology was to dissolve skilled labour into unskilled labour and to replace workers with machines. From the Industrial Revolution in the nineteenth century to the ICT-oriented society of the late twentieth century, workplace control has been a common interest of capitalism. Surveillance meant that capitalists could keep watch over the behaviour of manual workers in factories. Both the deskilling and segmentation of labour and the replacement of workers with machines were the result of the capitalist motive to control the human body from the outside.

Scientific management strategies by Frederick Winslow Taylor in the late nineteenth century in the United States resulted in surveillance of workers' behaviours. Taylor intended to control the human body by dividing human behaviours into segments constituted by a single action. Fordism took over the ideas of Taylor with the mechanization of human behaviours. Mechanization meant not only the pursuit of economic effectiveness but also the surveillance of working people. This means, as Antonio Gramsci refers in his *Prison Notebooks* (1984: 277–320), capitalists intend to control human behaviour because they cannot control the human mind. This, however, does not mean that capitalists give up the desire to control the human mind because they usually intend to detect what workers are thinking. This hidden desire to invade the latent enemy's inner side is a necessary condition of the technological innovation of surveillance in a capitalist class society.

From the Luddite era to the present time, skilled workers have been struggling against mechanization. This process means the reappropriation of the workers' own body labour that has been deprived by capital. In the nineteenth century, however, outside of the factory, the everyday life of the working class or the unemployed population was kept out of control.

The second socio-historical layer appeared in the late nineteenth century, when management of the population was extended beyond the factory nationwide. Beyond this, one can argue that democracy and colonialism are two sides of the same coin. The universal suffrage movement and labour movement in imperial countries, and more sophisticated management of the population in colonies, occurred simultaneously. In western European countries that were in the age of classical imperialism, surveillance technology was extended to everyday life. Social policy gradually emerged for the integration of unemployment and low-income classes into the nation state. A 'carrot and stick' policy was adopted, where the majority of the working class was integrated into the capitalist order by the legalization of trade unions and the development of social policy for the unemployed. On the other hand, socialists, anarchists and other subversive parts of the working class were excluded. Prejudice based on race and gender was strengthened by the science of crime. Criminology, based on the use of physical features with genetic factors, was invented, which down-played the impact of social circumstances in crimes. In colonial regions, the native population was managed in different ways than in imperial countries. Fingerprint and other classic biometric identifiers were introduced to manage the population.

The two world wars, fascism and the New Deal were the final phase of the second layer. They prepared primitive mass mobilization of the

273

population as a nation in both private and public life. There was an institutionalization of leisure time in fascist Italy along with a war-oriented neighbourhood community association in Japan. There was also the integration of migrant workers into the American way-of-life with the five dollars-a-day policy of the Ford Motor Company.[3] These events led to the mass management of the population.

The third layer appeared in the Cold War era. Surveillance as a tool to manage the population spread from the control of appearance to control of the human mind. While women, ethnic minorities and other social minority groups were requiring their own rights, the dominant strategy used to control identity politics was to integrate these groups into a high consumer society called the 'affluent society', based on the Keynesian policy of income redistribution. Surveillance became an extension into constructing the consumer's life, although identifying each individual as an inherent subject was difficult. Unknown consumers were regarded as mass consumers and unknown voters were the basis of mass democracy. The individual was regarded as an element of an unknown mass to be monitored. Mass media and advertising became two of the major tools of mind manipulation, making people in developed countries look as though they enjoy freedom and democracy.

From Henri Lefebvre (1991) or the Frankfurt school (see Adorno 1991; Benjamin 2003; Marcuse 1964) to the Situationist movement (Debord 1970), resistance against the highly controlled society had problematized the domination of everyday life by the mass-consumption capitalism and bloated bureaucratic state power. In the late 1960s, resistance spread from urban to rural, factory to university, street to family. The management of the population based on mass workers and mass consumers came into crisis.

The fourth socio-historical layer resulted from the crisis of control and surveillance-based mass consumption and mass democracy. The decentralization of mass workers and mass consumers was introduced by computerization as hi-mix, low-volume production systems, based on the availability of computer-processing-based marketing. Mass consumption, which was the social background of what Herbert Marcuse called the 'one-dimensional man', and other critiques of uniformed consumer society, were out of date (Marcuse 1964). Mass anonymous consumers were dissolved into various consumer groups and even individuals. Diversity based on identity politics was taken over by the market economy, commodification of diversity, and the rediscovery of individuals with proper names based on marketing.

Anonymity is the basis of freedom in modern society. However, politicians are eager to know who votes for whom. Also, for capitalists, who buys what is important data for investment. As Karl Marx pointed out, the sale process of commodities is a kind of 'desperate leap' (Marx 1867) for transforming commodities into dollar value because the decision of selling and buying does not belong to capitalists as sellers but to consumers as buyers. For a long time, the behaviour of anonymous buyers was not under the control of capital. Under capitalist control, the marketplace is different from the office or factory. The development of manipulation and profiling technology for consumers was needed. Computerization of marketing and the management of customers caused the capitalist dream to be realized. Progress in information processing caused the advancement of the segmentation of mass consumers into many categories of consumers. Elaborate categorization enabled by computer technology allowed differentiation among individuals. Concrete individuals, as they really are, were reduced to abstract data and categorized in line with commercial requirements. After this data was processed, each individual was reconstructed as a concrete person and was profiled again.

The Cold War brought about the development of computer science in the military. Computers were created for calculating trajectory. In the 1960s, the Defense Advanced Research Projects Agency (DARPA) began to research the possibility of long-distance computer communication networks capable of surviving in a nuclear attack (Edwards 1996). However, the research was dominated not only by military researchers, but also many people who were not strongly interested in national security issues and who were concerned with the new possibilities of computer communication networks for scientific research in general. The Internet also had another origin with grassroots personal computer (PC) network activists (see Randall 1997; Rheingold 1985). The counter-culture of social circumstances in the late 1960s formed an important background to the characteristics of cyberspace. Cyberspace had an arena of hegemony between national security and civil liberty from the very beginning.

The fifth layer is surveillance based on ICT, emerging at the end of Cold War and continuing until the present. Dissemination of the Internet and cell phones brings the reconstruction of previous layers of surveillance. In the 1990s, the Internet was commercialized and institutionalized as a social infrastructure. Its forerunner was 'The Information Super Highway', a term coined by the administration of US President Bill Clinton. The dissemination of ICT for identification and certification spread from welfare to policing and national security activities. So-called electronic government (e-government), which I examine further later in this chapter, is the necessary result of this layer. E-government aims to redefine human identity by introducing

275

networked databases, certification agent systems, identity cards, radio-frequency identification (RFID) and biological identification technology such as biometrics. Another important aim of e-government is to import administration methods of the commercial sector so that the administrative structure of government is regarded as the same as that of a commercial company. This significantly strengthens the surveillance power of government, while democracy based on anonymity becomes weak.

The Internet gives ordinary people equal power to transmit messages to others as the government and mass media. The Internet is a decentralized, anonymous and transnational network without any governance body that is dominated by government; although it does have a private governance body called the Internet Corporation for Assigned Names and Numbers (ICANN). Cell phones also have the ability to allow communication in transit. The government lags behind in terms of trace and surveillance capability in these areas. But on the other hand, the government intends to regain lost ground using ICT. Therefore, the Internet and cell phones are an arena of argument/contention for surveillance.

The transnationality of ICT and the globalization of surveillance, such as data sharing by computer networks, has posed a serious dilemma for the nation state. Under the pressure of neo-liberal globalization, the nation state has been forced to jeopardize its supreme political power limited within its geographical territory because ordinary people as well as transnational corporations realized the capability of global communications. Yet privacy rights and other human rights are basically protected only by national laws. International relations dominated by the hegemony of the Group of Eight (G8) countries and the Organization for Economic Cooperation and Development (OECD) lack democratic governance based on individuals. Therefore, transnational personal data sharing puts privacy rights in crisis. The US and other developed countries intend to extend their political power to other countries. This is not for traditional militarism, but to control the population in the age of globalization. This is also a symptom of a nation state in crisis.

Informatics are a meta-technology that have a great influence on every domain of society. From biology to political science, informatics functions as a convergent science (Thomas 2003). Human beings, or at least their bodies, are reduced to digital data or information. Decoding of the human genome by computer science creates a new myth of human beings, in that human beings are no longer recognized as living organisms, but as information. Just as patented generic modification technology in agriculture is a tool of surveillance for farmers on how they use seeds, ICT becomes a common social technological infrastructure beyond borders between commercial and public sectors. Also, the development of ICT is commonly believed to be a sign of social progress by ordinary people.

Surveillance-oriented society has had extensive and intensive growth historically. Watching the appearance and control of behaviour in the workplace has been extended to public space. Simultaneously, watching internally and analyzing the intention of the human mind in order to control future behaviour has also been developed. The intention of surveillance in modern capitalist society is to control and mobilize each individual as labour power and to integrate various subject identities into a national identity.

Surveillance-oriented society is a dialectic process between the excluded population and the dominant socio-economic political regime. Surveillance is a technique of redefinition and making clear the boundaries between exclusion and inclusion, separation and integration, absence and presence, disregard and consideration. Modern/postmodern surveillance-oriented society is rooted in a deep skepticism of humans. In other words, modern/postmodern society inherently has a kind of machine fetishism at the core of its worldview. It assumes, therefore, that being human lies at the root of uncertainty, that machines are without error, and that following instructions faithfully is an ideal model of humans.

In light of the several theoretical assumptions mentioned above, I have outlined what specific kind of characteristics the present socio-historical layer has and where we are able to see resistance against the present surveillance-oriented society.

Limits of the privacy approach

During the Cold War, the capitalist bloc upgraded freedom and privacy as the specific ideology of capitalism, which was different from the commonly understood ideology of communism. However, few people in developed democratic countries could recognize that freedom and privacy did not belong as essential characteristics of modern capitalism because they were only ideologies used for tackling the socialist bloc. After September 11, the myth of freedom and privacy has been breaking up. The management of the population for national security has become a policy priority. From migrant control to community-based neighbourhood watch groups, national security has been proposed as a precondition of freedom and privacy because, according to government officials, the threat of terrorism has destroyed freedom. Privacy and freedom are nothing related to the essential idea of capitalism; rather, they are the result of power politics between the people's struggle and counter-strategies to the socialist bloc in the Cold War. Democracy and dictatorship, slavery and free workers are poles apart in typical capitalism. Both have very different political and legal structures from each other. However, they intend to achieve a common result: a profit-oriented market economy and nation state through the management of the population by the state. The post-Cold War globalization of capitalism brings about the looseness of legitimacy of the nation state. Capital and population flow beyond national borders more easily than before. The present surveillance-oriented society transcends modernist traditional power relations and accompanies the formation of a new structure of sovereignty, while maintaining the core structure of the capitalist social constitution.

Critiques of surveillance-oriented society have focused on privacy rights. As many critics have pointed out, ICT used for surveillance has undermined the basis of privacy rights (see Lyon 2001; Garfinkel 2001). The main causes lie in the accumulation and sharing of digitized personal data on networks. This kind of function of communication had few supporters in the telephone communication-centred era when communication privacy was problematized.

Originally, privacy rights were defined as the right to leave one alone. The right to privacy prohibits anyone else from entering an occupied or owned space and hearing conversations or watching actions without permission from the occupant or owner. The private property of space is a precondition of privacy rights, which has been guaranteed strongly as a right belonging to the bourgeois as a private property right.

However, with the development of long-distance communications like the telephone, privacy rights based on private property of physical space have become inadequate not only to cover all conversations and communication, but also to face the contradiction within property rights. According to privacy based on private property rights, as the owner of communication equipment, telecommunication companies have the right to access customers' communication. There have been debates that override the customer or telecommunication company. In order to protect a customer's privacy, privacy rights needed a new definition that was not based on private property rights. In the early twentieth century, the main concern was how to protect the secrecy of long-distance communication, as well as face-to-face private conversations.[4] Throughout the twentieth century, the privacy rights of long distance communications were legalized by restricting the ownership rights of telecommunication companies (in some cases, state-owned companies). However, ICT brings about a backlash against users' privacy.

As computer communication became more widespread, the retention and preservation of communication data increasingly became a routine affair. E-mail is held at mail servers until the user downloads and removes it from the server. Super-users of the mail server could read, copy or manipulate data during the time the mail is kept. In order to back up data on the mail server, the computer is able to duplicate the data automatically. Also, networked computers make it easy to transfer the data to other computers without losing their original data. These are very different characteristics than those of data on paper. Computer networks make it possible to record, duplicate and preserve or retain personal data without using a human being that can recognize it by intuition and experience. As a result of these characteristics, once computers are networked, personal data are scattered on the network and become jeopardized and fragile. Under the administrator's rights over the network server computer, private property rights are widely reconstructed in a more complex context over privacy rights. Provisions of due process regarding the access rights of law enforcement to computer data prove that the rights of computer equipment have a preferred position to the privacy rights of users. Law enforcement usually implements the search and seizure of server computers without announcing this to its users. The Cybercrime Convention held by the Council of Europe 2001 intends to legalize the retention of data even without a court warrant.

Conversely, privacy protection technologies such as cryptography and digital data erasers have also been developed. Law enforcement is apt to recognize these privacy protection technologies as facilitating computer crimes and as an obstruction to investigative capability. Certain technology violates privacy because it gives traceability and evidence to be presented before a court. The network administrator is legally obligated to share data with law enforcement that has been retained in the appropriate management and control of the network. The ability to protect privacy is deprived from individuals and is concentrated in the law enforcement and security industry. Also, the security industry increases the possibility of privacy violation by creating stronger surveillance devices for law enforcement and private sectors. There are various reasons for accumulating personal data in computer networks. ICT has versatility and supports various areas such as public service, customer service by private companies, system administration by Internet Service Providers (ISPs) and investigation by law enforcement. Therefore, innovation in one area is easily transferred to other areas; civilian use of surveillance technology has military potential and vice versa. Through this vicious spiral of surveillance, society institutionalizes surveillance based on ICT in both the private and public, political and economic, civilian and military, cyberspace and the real world.

Avoidance technology

Given computer communication, rights for self-control over personal data have been regarded as an effective protection measure against the violation of privacy. However, this has less of an effect than traditional privacy rights, which can no longer be recovered.

Surveillance-oriented society has various networked data storage systems: remote control closed-circuit television (CCTV) network systems, automatic scanning systems for car licence numbers or verification of drivers' faces with those in a database, biometric security check systems for entering or leaving a room, DNA authentication for crime investigation, and so on. These mostly automatically collect and manage personal data without human recognition. The final aim of accumulation of personal data is the construction of profiling.

Surveillance technology gives law enforcement and the ICT industry measures to avoid the application of privacy laws. It is clear that the action of peeking into a bedroom violates privacy rights, but it is more difficult to accuse CCTV cameras in shopping malls that record customers as a violation of privacy rights. In the beginning, CCTV was connected only to a TV monitor in a monitoring room. After many upgrades, CCTV has become networked with other CCTV systems, and now they carry biometric information that is networked with various databases for personal identification. Biometric data are accumulated as digital data, which are easy to check with other databases containing sensitive data, such as criminal records, medical records, tax payments and others. CCTV systems have been evolving as a technology for probing the anonymous appearance of the recorded image to uncover who the person is. The person in charge of setting up the CCTV would plead the case that someone's appearance before the general public is exempt from protection by privacy law, but this is no longer acceptable. If CCTV is equipped with only facial recognition technology, from biometric personal data, the watcher has the ability to consult this data with any biometric database on the network. After this process, if the watcher can match the facial data with any name, ID number or something like this kind of index for personal data, sensitive data may be accessible.

An individual who shows their face before the general public does not necessarily intend to give their name, address, phone number or more sensitive personal data to others. Election candidates who put their name placards on the street want to let constituents recognize their name, but individuals on the street usually implicitly want to be anonymous. However, individuals who are watching for marketing or security reasons intend to identify anonymous people in public space. Surveillance technology has developed to realize the watchers' motivation.

The airport is the epitome of surveillance-oriented society. Airport security uses technology to deny the anonymity of passengers; the identity of travellers is increasingly known as they pass through the airport entrance and security checks, as CCTV is operating in the waiting lounge and at immigration checks. The airport is a highly integrated space for surveillance by government, hand-in-hand with the private sector, beyond national borders. Also, as is the case with US-VISIT and the technological standard platform of biometrics in the identity card (IC)/passports defined by the International Civil Aviation Organization (ICAO), the data are digitized by way of a common platform that can be transferred to law enforcement, intelligence agencies and foreign governments. However, we do not know how our personal data are used in foreign countries. There are no legal restrictions for the accumulation of personal data in passports but it is technologically possible.[5] Though the airport is a limited space, the data exploited from passengers and visitors in the airport are networked beyond this physical space to be connected to a series of security databases inside and outside of the host country. In such a comprehensive surveillance space like an airport, we have no other choice but to sacrifice our privacy rights. This means that surveillance-oriented society has made it difficult to be anonymous.

Before the emergence of computerized society, to know a name differed with knowing a face from the privacy point of view. From personal experience, we can identify very easily who someone is by his or her name and by checking the phone book and other name lists. We could also try to identify who someone is by using his or her photo, voice or other nonverbal information. To explain in words what one's face looks like is more difficult than using just one's name. For human communication and memory, verbalization is an important precondition of information handling. The reason why name has been used for such a long history, as an index of human memory and for the identification of individuals, is its adaptability for information handled by the human brain. Based on the long historical tradition of classification by names, various data that have been extracted by name indices have been accumulated by private corporations, government and individuals. The existence of these name databases gives an indication on how to extract sensitive data. To be anonymous means to hide one's name in order to restrict more sensitive personal data from being extracted from one's name. Therefore anonymity rights are a fundamental and essential condition to privacy rights.

ICT has drastically extended the function that a name plays as an index of identifying who someone is, including every human attribute from biological features to a kind of commemorative photo. Mediated by computer, digitized facial images have the ability to be the index that is used to extract other personal data like name. This is what biometrics are intended for. An unknown face does not mean anonymity, at least not anymore, as it is more difficult to be in public space without exposing one's face. As long as we expose our faces, we cannot maintain privacy even if we reject giving our name, ID card, social security number, resident registration number or something of the kind. Also, we have no other choice but to leave behind some biological trace such as a fingerprint, body temperature, hair and so on. By collecting this information, present surveillance technology is improved by being composed of something one does not want anybody to know about independent of the party concerned. Also, we have no information regarding what kind of technology and programs are being used in criminal record systems, national ID card systems, or other personal database systems used by government. Moreover, once personal data are collected, they are easily transferred beyond borders, spread over the network and integrated into mutual referenced systems in a very short time. This is a decisively different character of the computer-networked database than the database and reference system based on paper; that is restricted by place, human organization and the human ability to sort.

As a precondition, the traditional term of 'privacy rights' means that something one does not want anybody to know about is completely separate from something one does not care to be known. But surveillance in a computer network is not able to separate these from each other. Rather, the creation of avoidance technology in ICT enables the government and private corporations to undermine the detachment between the former and the latter. Therefore, the social consensus of privacy rights as commonsense among ordinary people has been degraded.

The right to control personal data about the self, which is a newer right than privacy rights, only has a limited effect that cannot cover all personal data held on computer networks. This right means that individuals should have the right to control data about them that is held by others; it retreats from privacy rights. As long as the data belong to others, even data protected by the right to control personal data, it is unavoidable to be jeopardized by leaks, manipulation, unjust usage and so on.

Also of importance is the exploitation of identity certification by governments or authorized commercial certification systems. Under an official certification authority system, governments and a few commercial companies monopolize defining who an individual is. Personal identification must be authorized; this is not a fundamental characteristic of ICT. Before establishing certified authority systems by government or commercial corporations, the individuals in close relationships (like Pretty Good Privacy (PGP) (Garfinkel 1994)) were the dominant authority. Hospitality towards others is a fundamental precondition to extend these unofficial confidential human networks. Mutual certification based on equal membership of society and hospitality is compatible with grassroots cyberculture. But by replacing this kind of horizontal certification structure with certified authority, confidential relationships in the community become weakened. The basic motive of certification and identification systems is to deprive an individual's right to decide who one is and is malicious against others.

Electronic government and surveillance-oriented society

Electronic government (e-government) has a fundamental role in surveillance-oriented society. I define e-government as a fundamental governance structure with highly computerized administration and communication networks and digitalized personal databases as a necessary precondition to implement administrative work. E-government inherits functions for management of the population from existing traditional modern bureaucracy and has partly mechanized administrative office work. But another more important characteristic is the qualitative transformation of management of the population and its capability to make decisive social-economic circumstances different from the previous nation state bureaucracies. The ICT industry is its core industry of economic growth. Globalization of the information infrastructure based on the Internet is an indispensable condition for governance of the nation state. E-government has three phases; computerization of the governance structure, computerization of administrative implementation of the public and data sharing among governments (Ogura 2005).

283

Computerization of the government structure: e-government

The main issue of this topic is how bureaucracy suffers from the computerization of administrative work. Bureaucracy has functioned to control the population along with the government's own will, yet it has limited the human capability to handle data and information. In the traditional administration process, residents who had to file any documents with an administrative office used to have to write down their basic personal data such as name, sex, address, age and so on. An officer would confirm, accept and handle the written documents. Numbers of entries were restricted by the human ability of officers to write down and make confirmations in a short time. The output of data and information processing per day defined the upper limit of input per day. This limited capability of human data handling gave a natural limitation of personal data flow from a person to the administration.

However, computers break the barrier of the human limitation of data handling. With computerizing administrative work supported by the ICT industry, the government has the ability to collect personal data more easily and broadly. The surveillance capability of government, therefore, has been remarkably expanded.[6]

Various divisions in government have introduced computer systems since the 1960s. The dissemination of personal computers, downsizing and dispersing of data processing by computer networks, and the emergence of the Internet as a communication infrastructure around the 1990s were turning points in the involvement of ICT characteristics in the governance structure. The government had to deal with the fallout of the rapid development of the information transmission capacity of individuals having become equal to that of mass media and government. Additionally, so-called office automation in private sectors produced strong pressure to transform existing administrative procedures.

E-government has significantly accelerated the centralization of political power. This means the demolition of modern bureaucracy. As Max Weber pointed out in the early twentieth century, modern bureaucracy is a kind of human 'precision instrument' (Weber 1956). The exercise of bureaucracy is defined clearly by the rule of law. This was the most effective organization for handling the huge administrative documents by human power. Legislatures enact laws and courtrooms authorize the legitimacy of laws. Checks and balances are put into place by the three pillars of political power: the bureaucratic administration, the legislative congress and the courtroom that supports the fundamental structure of a law-governing state based on democracy. ICT has the potential to erode this division of power. Rapid sophisticated data processing by computers degrades bureaucracy to an inefficient organization. Democratic decision-making processes based on deliberations in congress and the courtroom are insufficient. The frame of reference in terms of democracy has been the transforming of the human activity base into data and information processing by computers; instead of law, data processing by computer programs becomes a predominant characteristic. Instead of a representative democracy, public political marketing by ICT such as opinion polls, public comments, electronic voting systems and resident participation in public works projects are considered to make government administration run faster and easier than the parliamentary representative system.

New public management (NPM) for political surveillance

The idea of new public management[7] was introduced under Thacherism and Reaganomics in the 1980s and equates to the governance of private corporations. E-government emulates the methods of commercial companies.

NPM is convenient for concealing the political force of surveillance power. Residents are not regarded as subjects of the sovereign in democracy, but as mere customers, like consumers in the marketplace. Research on residents' political needs assimilates to marketing for consumers. Residents are able to choose only given options. Taxpayers are placed in a similar position as shareholders. As democracy based on shareholders is liable to ignore the rights of workers and consumers, the democracy of taxpayers is difficult to reflect in the political process of low-income classes and the socially excluded. Economic efficiency and profitability dominated the motivation of government. NPM does not consider that government monopolizes the political power including physical restraint, which is completely different from corporate power in the market economy. People cannot choose their government as well as commodity choices by consumers in the marketplace. Therefore, political marketing and monitoring residents' behaviours as constituents undoubtedly have negative effects on privacy and civil liberty.

The decline of the rule of law

Until now, it has been uninteresting that e-government has negative influences on the rule of law. As Lessig (1999) points out, in a computerized society the code of computer programs determines social relations more effectively than law. Also as Galloway (2004) insists, decentralized network management systems have to depend on technologically centralized infrastructures such as domain name systems (DNS). The Internet protocols play a more important role in the regulation of communication than laws in terms of communication.

In other words, modern legal systems are facing a major turning point in the regulation of political power; law is directed at the regulation of human behaviour, but it cannot control computers. Code and protocol are able to control the behaviour of computers. E-government uses code and protocol in order to avoid the rule of law. Democratic regulation based on the rule of law has lost regulatory power to e-government's administrative power of implementation.

The rule of law assumes that one must handle technology lawfully. Automobiles usually have the ability to run over the legal speed, but this is lawful because the law assumes individuals will drive a car lawfully. However, many speeding offences are committed. Is it rational to suppose that e-government will use ICT lawfully, when it has unlawful capabilities? Rather, should we consider that it is possible for e-government to use ICT as a technology to avoid privacy rights in order to expand the governmental political power of surveillance? As the rule of law is undermined, legislative bodies, such as parliament, face a decline of their influence on government as an administrative body. For example, most wire-tapping laws have no articles regarding the obligation to disclose the source codes of computer programs of wire-tapping devices. Even if source code is disclosed, most members of parliament would not be able to understand it. Parliament cannot examine whether law enforcement indeed uses wire-tapping devices lawfully. Also, traffic data are sensitive to privacy.

Telecommunication companies use ICT for their own marketing and billing. Computer programs used for the retention of traffic data also allow easy access for law enforcement. Rianon Talbot points out, 'retention and access to this information is not limited to terrorism offences or even activities indirectly linked to national security issues' (Talbot 2002: 155).

E-government will extend its power to foreign territories through computer networks. The global transfer of goods, money, population and information based on the Internet make existing international relations between states obsolete. Instead of inter-state relations, national security policy has been targeting non-state actors such as transnational crimes, terrorism and globalizing resistance against neo-liberalism of the people. Although these non-state actors have no common characteristics, they depend on the common infrastructure of transnational communication, like the Internet. The Internet is also an essential infrastructure for governments and corporations. E-government is protected not by geographical territory, but by the security programs of communication networks.

Each country has its own diplomatic communication network established abroad, in intelligence agencies or military bases. The code name ECHELON, based on a UK–US agreement during the Second World War for monitoring international communication via satellites, is a familiar case that occurred before the Internet age. The present situation is completely different. Government outreach abroad is not confined to national security; rather e-government is under pressure to monitor all of the non-state actors in communication networks. Articles about mutual assistance of law enforcement in the Convention on Cybercrime[8] approve access to any criminal evidence in computers held in networks beyond national borders. National security targeting non-state actors, including individuals, makes a difference in criminal investigations and aims to extend its authority to the realm of domestic policing. Exceptional authority in the realm of national security becomes a general rule. Especially the international 'War on Terror' regime, under the hegemony of the US–UK, promotes e-government in each country as a highly surveillance-oriented one.

Ordinary people use the Internet and cell phones not only as essentials of life, but also as tools expressing their intentions. For e-government, cyberspace is an important vital space to control the population in order to integrate people into national order and national interests. This is very similar to the problems that the modern nation state faced in the nineteenth century, about how to control the urban working-class population, which brought the modernist idea of urban planning. Management of the population has been extending from urban space to cyberspace. But as CCTV on the streets has been increasing more than ever before, e-government extends its outreach from real space to cyberspace. E-government is not the replacement for the existing government structure, but the over-determination of the existing one. This means partly that the state increases its political power, but also that the state is unable to control the population based on the rule of law in both urban and cyber communication space.

Informatic cybernetics as a tool of political exclusion

Representative democracy in the modern state has advantages and disadvantages. It is a serious disadvantage that migrants with foreign nationality cannot have the right to vote and have their civil rights restricted. However, under the freedom of political expression, various interest groups from communists to far right-wing nationalists, sexists to feminists, and ecologists to adherents of economic growth are able to participate in election campaigns. Representative democracy creates the possibility of choice in political regimes. From Allende in Chile to Chavez in Venezuela, or from the construction of the European Union to religious fundamentalist revolution in Iran, there are many options in representative democracy.

E-government creates another route for making consensus with the public by using ICT. ICT allows government to access the constituency online, and monitor their political needs. As public comments online exemplify the case, the government tries to make any interactive discourse with people who want to participate in the policy-making process. This looks more democratic and more effective than the representative decision-making system. However, online democracy only has a narrow basis of permissible scope for discussion because it is based on an 'if/and/or' feedback system of cybernetics. It cannot raise concerns about the fundamental preconditions and essential alternatives or transformation of regime. It ignores the opposition forces outside of partnership strategies that refuse the feedback system itself. Antagonistic constituencies or subjects are excluded beforehand, while participation and partnership with government are welcome as the basis of a dialogue-type of politics based on appearance.

Endless growth of the surveillance system: is there an end?

Political surveillance would be of no use if the system enjoyed stability or equilibrium. As mentioned in the discussion of the historical layers of surveillance-oriented society, the fundamental characteristics of surveillance are to forecast and remove the elements that may constitute barriers to fundamental preconditions of the capitalist regime. The most important thing is how to control the population in an age of ICT. From crime to military conflict, and micro-politics based on individuals to macro-politics based on international relations, there are several different dimensions of friction. As aforementioned, in the 1990s before September 11, developed countries' main enemies transferred from being from the socialist bloc to transnational crimes and anti-globalization movements by non-state actors. Surveillance-oriented society was constructed around these two factors.

Capitalist globalization could not achieve political triumph against the odds but faced new resistance based on diverse and transnational mobilization by intricate subjects among leftists, anarchists, feminists, ecologists, migrants, the unemployed, the excluded and so on. Decentralized networked movements, which are called a 'movement of movements', aim to set up a new notion of freedom and democracy from below. The Internet especially has been a significant influence of the characteristics of people's resistance (see Dyer-Whitheford 1999; van de Donk 2004). From the Zapatistas to the Seattle uprising, various social forums, anti-war movements and autonomous movements have been connected by the Internet.

Capitalist globalization has been mobilizing huge migrant populations from rural to urban in the Third World, to global cities in developed countries. Border control also brings risks to undocumented migrant workers. It allows transnational organized crime to find good business opportunities in such things as human trafficking to fake passports. The latter stimulates stricter border control to introduce more innovative and less privacy-protective surveillance technology. However, usually the targets of surveillance are not only criminal organizations like the Mafia, but also undocumented migrants who are unfairly criminalized.

Crime and political resistance are two sides of the same phenomenon of legitimate crisis. From a viewpoint of the maintenance of security by law enforcement, control of political mass movement on the street has the same meaning as control of street crime. In most democratic countries law enforcement cracks down on political activities as criminal cases. Therefore, transnational organized crimes categorically include not only mafias, but also political terrorism or anti-globalization movements. Surveillance by ICTs is the most versatile system from crime control to political management of the population, as CCTV on the streets as a technology of crime control is easily converted into surveillance of demonstrators on the streets.

Another important issue is the background of economic infrastructure. The ICT industry found their business opportunity in various crime control strategies. The 'secure life' and 'national security' give convenient excuses to commodify various surveillance devices with the latent possibility of privacy violation. As the high technology of surveillance capability, such as biometrics or radio-frequency identification (RFID), becomes popular and embeds in everyday life, these technologies will be acceptable and the sense of privacy changes its nature. The formation of consumer culture favours the use of surveillance in the security of everyday life. This sense of security based on everyday life implicitly has racial and gender prejudice, and is apt to legitimize the exclusion of social minorities. Therefore, ICT easily supports the expansion of the authority of law enforcement and national security oriented legislation.

This kind of tendency has been expanding especially since September 11, 2001.

The old-fashioned modernist view of humankind in ICT

Management of the population by surveillance-oriented society in present postmodern capitalism depends on the theoretical pre-supposition of human terms based on a variation of traditional modernist methodological individualism and biological determinism. This view of human beings is a decisive limitation of the present surveillance society.

From management of the population as an anonymous mass in the early modern age to the management of population as individual certification and identification by ICT in the present time, a common understanding of human beings presupposes that a person with various personal data is able to be reduced to an individual determined by biological attributes. Methodological individualism and biological determinism make individuals able to reconfigure as a unique unit even from various personal data scattered in the network. Under the present ICT surveillance-oriented society, facial data, fingerprints, iris and other biometrics data, as well as name, converge with a unique biological body. This biological body is only substance. It is presupposed that there is no subject outside of the biological body and that the body includes one and only one subject. Personal certification by biometrics or DNA is a typical way of thinking based on this kind of methodological individualism. In the modern tradition of administration processes, one is required to have a unique official name because name is a symbol of personal identity and an index for certification of who one is.

The government or ICT industry are eager to reduce the social identities of individuals into a unique biological identity. But everybody has the latent possibility and desire for having multiple identities in various social contexts. It is not uncommon to have several email addresses, domain names or anonymity for posting on message boards on the Internet. These identities are not able to be reduced into a unique biological identity nor are they interchangeable with each other. The individual has been regarded as indivisible, but the individual is dividable and rather includes multiple individuals as social identities that are inseparable with other identities in the individual and irreducible into biological identities. Additionally, the individuals are inter-subjective and are inseparable in relation to others. In essence, the others are not discarded persons for individuals.

According to the present dominant viewpoint on human beings, network means the summation of individuals as single atoms. In the case of a lost child in a crowd, surveillance-oriented society depends on CCTV or wireless ID tags worn on the body to locate children. This rationality assumes that the crowd does not in any way provide effective support; rather they seem to be fraught with risk and threat. The lost child is deemed to be an isolated individual who is related only to their parents, police or surveillance devices. Surveillance-oriented society weakens mutual assistance based on anonymity and drives people into isolation as individuals. Surveillance-oriented society has the disadvantage of undermining autonomous mutual aids to power from below.

Identity composed by various databases in government institutions or official certification agencies are preferred to my own words regarding who I am or certification by my friends. This means that the government has the authority to create artificial identity from its personal database. The government becomes an official biographer for our lives in favour of its own politics. Also, the fate of our future is like that of a prophet, even preventative restraint will take place.

Conclusion: identity of identities as an alternative to identity politics

The never-ending quest for surveillance brings the fundamental view of postmodernist human beings into question. Especially, personal identity based on an individual is one of the important arenas where we can create space for freedom from the surveillance-oriented society.

Positive values in modern society such as privacy, civil liberty, democracy and freedom presuppose that society would realize a kind of predetermined harmony as Adam Smith's 'invisible hand'. Management of the population with surveillance in modern history proves society has shown various contradictions. Anonymity is a basis of freedom but it is a formidable difficulty for management of the population. With this antinomy, the technology of governance with 'avoidance technology' has been creating management of the population while people have been struggling for freedom. The idea of e-government is a key issue for what the present surveillance society is. We should, therefore, consider more deeply how to consolidate the right to control technology.

I think the transformation of modernist positive values stemming from Western society inevitably bring about the fatalistic surveillance-oriented society. The greatest obstacle to freedom is not unknown others, but the greater governance of population management by the nation state. A sense of freedom based on hospitality to others is one important precondition for a society with less surveillance. Nation states make borders between outsiders and insiders to manage the population. This kind of management of the population has often brought insecurity of the people by risking political instability and military conflict, which are the main causes of the acceleration of surveillance. Therefore, surveillance-oriented society should be tackled with issues of how to separate freedom, privacy and other positive values including even democracy and other political decision-making processes from the modernist governance structure. In other words, without the nation state, or national boundaries, or inter-state organizations, a governance body should be created based on the hospitality of others.

We do not have a panacea for an effective alternative against surveillance-oriented society based on ICT. Surveillance-oriented society usually targets the people who are excluded or marginalized and criminalizes them. Most of those targeted are racial minorities or poor working-class citizens whose bad situation is defined by present neoliberal globalization and the 'War on Terror'. Therefore, we should look at the whole macro picture. Various social movements, transnational and transcultural alliances based on people's diversity are a necessary part of the alternatives.

On the basis of what is mentioned above, I would like to make some conclusionary remarks regarding 'identities'. Traditional privacy rights and other civil rights are important measures against surveillance-oriented society. As I mentioned above, privacy rights have been undermined by avoidance technology in ICT. One of the important negative results of surveillance-oriented society is identity exploitation by government and commercial sectors, deprivation of anonymity and the right to certify who one is, and monopoly of data mining and profiling by government and commercial sectors. In these circumstances, I think identity politics have to be transformed drastically. Identity politics so far have been discussed regarding how to establish the collective identity of social minority groups against cultural, ideological or political integration or affiliation by dominant social groups.

Identity politics that are against surveillance-oriented society need a new characteristic, such as de-convergent politics against convergent politics based on methodological individualism and the biological determinism of ICT. Multiple identities are diffusing on networks by various forms, like personal data to blogs and wikis. In these latter cases, we often corroborate with others to create texts and documents. These are not available to any one person. They do not converge with one person but form decentralized inter-subjectivity. These phenomena also shake the foundation of intellectual property rights that are based on the certification of their original creator. DJ culture, pirate culture in the Third World, or person-to-person (P2P) file exchange in youth culture have had unconscious resistance against certification politics of the surveillance-oriented society. We should consider such popular culture as a symptom of the identity of identities, as elusive as water running through one's fingers in surveillance-oriented society.

Another important thing is how to liberate ourselves from national identity. If we have diversity of identity essentially independent from our biological entity because human beings communicate to others beyond national borders, what kind of positive meaning does national identity have? Non-state actors are becoming more dominant in international relations than ever before and the legitimacy of the nation state is becoming contested terrain. Visas and passports based on nationality are too rigidly regulated compared with the reality of the mobilization of population and communication.

We have not yet seen visible resistance movements based on the above alternative identity politics. Crimes related to identity, such as fake ID, spoofing or masquerading, forged passports, violations of intellectual property and so on, are symptoms of resistance regarding identity politics, even though they are not proper social movements. Identity theft crimes are flipside of the coin of surveillance-oriented society. As long as surveillance-oriented society depends on biological personal identification systems, biological determinism based on methodological individualism becomes a point of concern. Anonymity and unofficial names are regarded as a breeding ground of crimes by the government; anonymity will be criminalized and the use of unofficial names will be regarded as fraud. The right to define who I am and to be anonymous will be deprived even though they are the fundamental bases of civil liberty that make it different from feudal society. If the exploitation of identity expands and deepens, resistance against it to achieve self-determination rights of who 'is' will also follow. In the very near future, we may grab hold of an alternative identity politics based on an identity of identities that is against identity exploitation.

Notes

1 I do not use the term 'surveillance society' because it is confusing terminology. Instead of 'surveillance society' I use 'surveillance-oriented society'. By using this term instead, I intend to make it clear that this is a different dimension than capitalist society, civil society or other types of societies. Surveillance-

oriented society is constituted from several historical layers and is a sub-category of modern/postmodern capitalist society.

2 The old name of Tokyo.
3 The significance of the Ford system is not only its wage and work system, such as mass production based on conveyer-belt manufacturing system, but its education model for migrant workers. See Ogura 1984; Gramsci 1984; Meyer 1981.
4 The most well-known opinion in the early twentieth century in the US for the protection of privacy rights in telephone calls in police investigations was from Justice Louis Brandeis's dissent in 1928. See Diffie and Landau (1998).
5 The international technological standard for passports is authorized by the International Civil Aviation Organization (ICAO), an umbrella organization of the UN. ICAO decided to adopt face-recognition methods as a biometric in the IC passport. Privacy International and other civil liberty groups have criticized this decision. See http://www.privacyinternational.org/issues/terrorism/rpt/icaoletter.pdf.
6 In terms of the present situation of e-government worldwide, see, 'Global E-Government, 2004', by Darrel Wast of Brown University, http://www.insidepolitics.org/egovt04int.html.
7 The neo-liberalist administrative reform since the 1980s spread NPM. The National Performance Review and Government Performance and Result Act in the US are a typical implementation of NPM.
8 The Convention on Cybercrime was drafted by the Council of Europe in 2001. It includes close mutual cooperation among the law enforcement of each country including the compulsory investigation in foreign countries without dual criminology. See website of the Council of Europe, http://conventions.coe.int/Treaty/en/Treaties/Html/185.htm.

References

Adorno, T. (1991) *The Culture Industry: Selected Essays on Mass Culture* (New York: Routledge).

Benjamin, W. (2003) 'The Work of Art in the Age of its Technological Reproducibility', in H. Eiland and M.W. Jennings (eds) *Walter Benjamin: Selected Writings, Volume 4, 1938–1940* (Cambridge, MA: Belknap).

Council of Europe (2001) *Convention on Cybercrime*, Budapest, 23. XI. Available at: http://conventions.coe.int/Treaty/en/Treaties/Html/185.htm.

Debord, G. (1970) *Society of the Spectacle* (Detroit: Black and Red).

Diffie, W. and Landau, S. (1998) *Privacy on the Line: The Politics of Wiretapping and Encryption* (Cambridge, MA: MIT Press).

Dyer-Whitheford, N. (1999) *Cyber Marx: Cycles and Circuits of Struggle in High-Technology Capitalism* (Urbana, IL: University of Illinois Press).

Edwards, P.N. (1996) *The Closed World: Computers and Politics of Discourse in Cold War America* (Cambridge, MA: MIT Press).

Galloway, A.R. (2004) *Protocol: How Control Exists After Decentralization* (Cambridge, MA: MIT Press).

Garfinkel, S. (1994) *PGP: Pretty Good Privacy* (Cambridge, MA: O'Reilly).

Garfinkel, S. (2001) *Database Nation: The Death of Privacy in the 21st Century* (Cambridge, MA: O'Reilly).

Gramsci, A. (1984) 'Americanism and Fordism', in Q. Hoare and G. Nowell Smith (trans.) *Selection from the Prison Notebooks* (New York: International Publishers).

Lefebvre, H. (1991) *Critique of Everyday Life [Japanese edition]* (Gendai: Sichou Sha).

Lessig, L. (1999) *CODE and Other Laws of Cyberspace* (New York: Basic Books).

Lyon, D. (2001) *Surveillance Society* (Philadelphia: Open University Press).

Marcuse, H. (1964) *One-Dimensional Man: Studies in the Ideology of Advanced Industrial Society*, (London: Routledge and Kegan Paul).

Marx, K. (1867) *Capital: The Process of Production of Capital, Volume 1* (Moscow: Progress).

Meyer, S., III. (1981) *The Five Dollar Day: Labor Management and Social Control in the Ford Motor Company, 1908–1921* (Albany: State University of New York Press).

Ogura, T. (1985) *Shihai No Keizaigaku ['Economics of Domination']* (Tokyo: Renga Shobou Shinsha).

Ogura, T. (2005) *Gurogaruka To Kanshikeisatukokka Heno Teikou ['Resistance against Globalization and Surveillance-Police-State']*, Kinohanasha.

Pradip, T. (2003) 'Digital Cohabitations: The Social Consequences of Convergent Technologies, Media Development' [Japanese edition], in *Gendaishisou*, February 2003.

Privacy International (2004) *An Open Letter to the ICAO: A Second Report on 'Towards an International Infrastructure for Surveillance of Movement'*, Tuesday, March 30, Available at: http://www.privacyinternational.org/issues/terrorism/rpt/icaoletter.pdf.

Rheingold, H. (1985) *Tools for Thought: The People and Ideas of the Next Computer Revolution* (New York: Simon and Schuster).

Randall, N. (1997) *The Soul of the Internet* (Stamson, CT: Thomson Learning).

Talbot, R. (2002) 'The Balancing Act: Counter-terrorism and Civil Liberties in British Anti-terrorism Law', in J. Strawson (ed.) *Law after Ground Zero* (London: The Glasshouse Press).

van de Donk, V. (ed.) (2004) *Cyber Protest: New Media, Citizens and Social Movements* (London: Routledge).

Weber, M. (1956) *Wirtschaft Und Geselschaft [Japanese edition]* (Teubingen: J.C.B. Mohr).

West, D. (2003) *Global E-Government: 2004* (Providence, RI: Brown University Press).

Chapter 14

Organization, surveillance and the body: towards a politics of resistance

Kirstie Ball

We now have discrimination down to a science
Vincent, Gattaca (Niccol 1997)

Introduction

In autumn 2004 the UK government was engaged in debate about implementing a national identity card scheme featuring biometric data – fingerprints and iris scans – as the main authenticators of an individual's identity, to be held in a computer chip on the card. Fear of crime and terrorism arguments were employed to support the policy, stating that an increased external security threat required higher levels of internal security. Civil libertarian groups such as Privacy International opposed the scheme on the grounds that placing higher stakes on individual identity would play into the hands of fraudsters who were able to replicate the cards. Moreover, data protection activists were concerned about the integrity of the databases that held this information. Questions concerning whether biometric identifiers were more or less likely to predict or control criminal behaviour, or whether they were likely to instigate new forms of crime, and drive criminal activity even further underground dominated public debate.

These questions reference perennial debates in organization and surveillance studies too. Apart from the civil libertarian arguments that arise, state power and resistance are also foregrounded, with the body taking centre stage, as a subject and object of state practices. Parallel developments in organizational practices that hold the body as a source of 'truth' or 'authenticity' with regards to the employee suggest that a systematic examination of biometric, or biocentric, measures is overdue. With the body now being positioned as an indicator of truth and authenticity about the individual, what potentialities are there for resistance? More generally, how can we theorize the body in the context of biometric surveillance systems? This chapter attempts to address these two questions and its structure is as follows. First, recent developments in organizational biometric surveillance will be reviewed. Then surveillance and organizational theory which interpellates the body will be discussed, as will the recent corporeal turn in sociological theory. Ultimately the chapter draws upon feminist studies of the body to conceptualize how a politics of resistance to biometric surveillance might emerge.

Surveillance in organizations

Surveillance is defined as 'any collection and processing of personal data, whether identifiable or not, for the purposes of influencing or managing those whose data have been garnered' (Lyon 2001: 2). While this is somewhat general, and it may not initially appear to have application in the organizational field, it does establish an important point. Surveillance is the practice of gathering and sorting data with the explicit purpose of influencing and managing the data target. This interpellates many modern organizational processes, and the networks of actors and institutions that are involved: consumer monitoring through loyalty cards, credit scoring and geo-demographic profiling; workforce monitoring through various recruitment practices, email and Internet usage, keystroke monitoring, access control and performance management.

Regan (1998) has provided a useful taxonomy of workplace surveillance practices. She observes that workforce surveillance focuses on three areas: surveillance of performance, behaviour and personal characteristics. Of the former, we can include monitoring of output; monitoring of resource use, using 'Japanized' production techniques of the type described by Sewell and Wilkinson (1992); and the monitoring of communications contents by remote listening, email and Internet monitoring. Behaviours are monitored via the latter two techniques, as they are by CCTV, and access control is discussed at length by McCahill and Norris (1999). Recent developments in access control technologies feature retinal and iris scanning, electronic fingerprinting techniques, hand geometry and voice pattern recognition technologies.[1] Behaviours are also predicted by psychometric, ability testing and hair strand testing on recruitment. These latter technologies give the organization distinct measurements of personal characteristics and lifestyle. North American organizations are particularly adept here. They have even been reported to use lie detector testing as a recruitment practice, as well as aspects of genetic screening, as parodied by Marx (1987). Recent developments are reviewed by Marx (1999), including the rather alarming 'smart toilet' which is popular in Japan. On use, the toilet can measure one's body temperature and weight, and can detect pregnancy, diabetes, etc., via urine. Marx originally joked about the then fictitious device in a 1987 newspaper article.

Current organizational surveillance practices feature the collection of information from the body and contain detailed information about individuals, their habits and lifestyles, which they may not ordinarily reveal in face-to-face interactions such as the recruitment interview. The

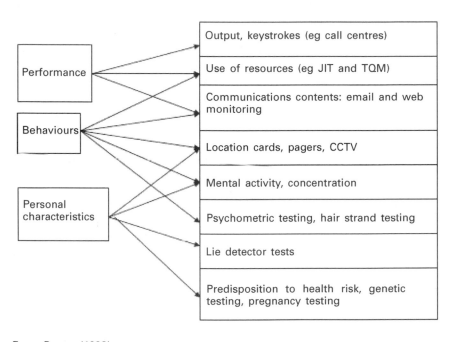

From Regan (1998)

retinal or iris scan, or the electronic fingerprint, provides conclusive evidence as to our identity. The body itself has emerged as a legitimate surveillance target because of the immense level of detail and 'truth' about the person it is thought to provide. Body data enable the organization to divide and classify *par excellence* at the level of the individual.

There are some questions as to what resisting organizational body surveillance would entail. Current organizational thinking on resistance does not shed that much light on this problematic. Body surveillance challenges most, if not all, organizational thinking about resistance, which, to a greater or lesser extent, crystallizes around discursive conceptions of consciousness and social action (Knights 1992; Prasad and Prasad 2001), and, until recently, formalized collective resistance, both of which do not address the difficult issues of embodiment and interiority. Even recent, post-structural work which questions the formation of subjectivities in the workplace, conceptualizes resistance in terms of whether subjectivities, at the level of the individual, coincide with dominant managerial ideas (Knights 1992). Nevertheless, some conceptual advances have been made. Resistance is now understood to be an inevitability and part of the more mundane social fabric of organizational life reflecting its changing nature in the face of hegemonic forms of organizational control (Barker 1993; Sewell 1998), the erosion of long-term employment and the decline of trade unionism in concert with the rise of the tertiary sector (Prasad and Prasad 2001). The central problematic is its observation and analysis in the absence of large-scale formal protest and collective antagonism observed in the mid-twentieth century. The second point is that resistant positions are understood to be discursively achieved by organizational members (Prasad and Prasad 2001). This conceptual move is accomplished by questioning the causal link made by labour process theorists between intentionality, consciousness and resistance (Braverman 1974; Jermier 1988; Clegg 1994), and assertions made as to the calculative, purposive and deliberate nature of worker participation therein. It is argued instead that everyday worker resistance is 'a configuration of emotional responses, patterned behaviour, intellectual assumptions and reasoned decisions – related to specific worker subjectivities' (Prasad and Prasad 2001: 110). Whilst agency has been problematized, and resistance positioned as a local activity, this work does little to challenge a gendered and Cartesian privileging of the mind over the body, or indeed, to consider the embodied basis of resistance and other materialities that are involved. A review of surveillance theory begins to consider these issues, as well as raising further questions about theorizing resistance.

Developments in surveillance theory

Recent theorizing about surveillance practices has turned to the centrality of the body, not least of those at the workplace. While many acknowledge Foucault's nod towards the rehabilitated body of the incarcerated subject in the panopticon, and the political technologies of the body identified in *The History of Sexuality* (Foucault 1976), the theoretical turn is towards Latourian and Deleuzian ideas. These approaches highlight the disparate arrays of people, technologies and organizations which become connected to make 'surveillance assemblages', in contrast to the static, unidirectional panopticon metaphor. Other chapters in this volume emphasize, for example, the body as the panopticon's undoing (Lyon this volume); as a source of spectacle, pleasure or seduction (Haggerty this volume); as questioning the certainty of the data double (Los this volume); and as deterritorialized by simulation practices (Bogard this volume). Indeed Gandy (1998) asserts that it would be a mistake to assume that surveillance in practice is as complete and totalizing as the panoptic ideal type would have us believe. Similarly, Rule (1998: 68), observes that the panopticon alone offers 'little help' in understanding new forms of electronic surveillance, particularly if the question is whether people are subject to more or more severe forms of control. Moreover, Boyne (2000) observes that disciplinary power, with its perfection through technology, and the resultant docile, accepting, self-disciplining population, is the exception rather than the norm. It is, rather, a question of how individuals, organizations, state bodies and the media connect to these technologies which influence whose data are collected, where they go, and what happens as a result.

I began to address this point in an earlier paper entitled 'Elements of Surveillance' (Ball 2002) in which I describe four elements in a surveillance domain. 'Re-presentation' refers to the technological element, acknowledging how surveillance technologies can re-present data that are collected at source, or gathered from another technological medium. 'Meaning' refers to the potential of new surveillance technologies to enable different interpretations of life to be made, as well as interpretations of surveillance itself. At least three common meanings are attributed to surveillance practice: surveillance as knowledge, surveillance as information, and surveillance as protection from threat. 'Manipulation' refers to the inevitability of power relations under surveillance, not least because surveillance practices capture and create different versions of life as lived by surveilled subjects. Power relations are evident by the way in which watching institutions or groups are able to regulate the flow of information and knowledge about the surveilled domain between various parties, and resistant strategies concern breaking or disrupting those flows, and creating spatio-temporal gaps between watcher and watched. Finally, I refer to actors within a surveilled domain as 'intermediaries'– where meaning is inscribed, where technologies re-present information, where power/ resistance operates, and where networks are bound together. Each party, at each level of analysis, assumes a role in a surveillance network, and becomes inscribed as such through embodied compliance, the exchange of money, the inscription of text and the use of artefacts (Michael 1996). I argue that intermediation is an important socio-technical process in the perpetuation of surveillance practices.

Using Deleuze and Guatarri's (1987) concept of the assemblage, Haggerty and Ericson (2000) also describe the convergence and spread of data-gathering systems between different social domains and at multiple levels. Their argument centres on the notion that the target of the generic 'surveillance assemblage' is the human body, which is broken into a series of data flows, to the end of feeding the information categories on which the surveillance process is based (Hier 2003). As such it is not the identity or subjectivity of the individual that is of interest, rather the data it can yield, the categories to which it can contribute, which are reapplied to the body as part of the 'influencing and managing' process to which Lyon (2001) refers. Accordingly Haggerty and Ericson argue that surveillance has a rhizomatic character – that it has many and diverse instances, connected to an underlying, invisible infrastructure, which concerns interconnected technologies in multiple contexts.

Haggerty and Ericson (2000) pose a new challenge concerning how resistance is to be conceptualized. Unlike organizational conceptions of resistance, which are built around the imaginary of some arboreal, centralizing dominant force, Haggerty and Ericson (2000) suggest that more widespread and decentred notions are to be employed. It is no longer sufficient to resist surveillance practices by restricting or controlling one technology; one must also consider the impulse to integrate, simulate and apply disparate information categories across a range of contexts which intersect at those 'surfaces of contact or interfaces between organic and non-organic borders, between life forms and webs of information, or between organs/body parts and entry/projection systems' (Bogard 1996: 33). They characterize the human body as 'flesh made information', drawing on arguments that emphasize hybridity and cyborgism (Haraway 1991), positioning it as a marginality, a state of 'in-between-ness' of technologies and the local (Leigh-Starr 1991). This is a point to which I will return.

However, although they argue that rhizomatic surveillance opens more opportunities for scrutiny of surveillance practices, they privilege the breaking of the body into flows to feed the assemblage over the reconstitution of the body with such flows (Hier 2003), and as such the question of resistance is not sufficiently addressed in their analysis. The main advantage of Haggerty and Ericson's work is that they shatter the notion underlying many of the claims made by proponents of biodata: that the body is a source of truth, enabling a critique of these practices as somehow 'definitive', 'absolute' or 'final' to be established. However, they do not venture far enough: the degree of tension and inbetween-ness which characterizes the hybrid or cyborgian subject (Haraway 1991) is underemphasized. In a manner similar to my previous arguments (Ball 2002), the identification of the body is more akin to Callon's (1991) 'intermediary' – a hybrid entity which 'points back' to the network of which it is part, and defines roles for other actors within it (Michael 1996). A politicization of the constitutive instability of the body is needed to augment a practical and analytical understanding of how resistance to surveillance practices might be conceptualized. In order to address this argument, a brief review of developments concerning a sociology of the body will be reviewed, and its contribution to an understanding of resistance to surveillance will be considered.

The body in sociology and organization theory

Since the early 1990s, sociology, and organizational sociology, like many other social science disciplines, has taken a 'corporeal turn'. This turn was born, in part of the feminist impact in the academy, new patterns of disease such as AIDS, and, of course, new forms of biotechnology which raise ethical issues and challenging political questions about social control. Thus, there was a perceived need to explore sociologically the experience of being embodied, as the subject's sensual interaction with and construction of the world, as well as the body as a social object, as the source or bearer of cultures, practices, signs and symbols. Sociological discussion of the presence of the body revolves around the exploration of its omission in the established sociological canon; its restricted expression within the two-dimensional confines of the practice of writing, the main mode of academic communication; and the exploration and resolution of various tensions that surround the understanding of subjectivity and intersubjectivity beyond Cartesian mind–body dualisms.

It is this final concern that will be explored at length in this section. Briefly, the corporeal turn in sociology emerged from an identification of the body as an 'absent-presence' (Shilling 1993) in the work of Marx, Weber and latterly a number of social constructionists (Butler 1990; Burkitt 1999). More recent writers such as Goffman (1963), Foucault (1980), Bourdieu (1977, 1990) and Elias (1991) have also alluded to the concept of the body in their various analyses of social action and structure. Debate surrounding this reclaiming of the body has been raised by feminist writers who have called for careful reflexivity in the process (Witz 2000). Challenging many of the dualisms through which work on the body has been explored as gendered, Witz (2000) claims that the bodies originally written out of sociology were gendered as embodied males. This is because of a tendency in traditional sociology to over-corporealize women, in other words, to explain women in terms of bodily capacities of sex, sexuality and reproduction, affording them little sociality. Without feminist reflection on an embodied ontology within sociology, the subject is in danger of reclaiming an abject male body, rather than those of males and females. It is with this, and the difficulties with writing about the embodied sensual world in mind, that an embodied politics of resistance to surveillance is considered.

Recent works on the sociology of the body have expended considerable intellectual effort towards exploring the tensions between understanding the phenomenology of the body as lived, and the body as a social object. A history of the development of this dualism is discussed at length by Jackson and Scott (1996). An ontological tension has also arisen from organizational studies of the body, between regulative and informational body ontologies. Each will be discussed in turn.

Body phenomenologies: embodied/object; inscription/incorporation; inner/outer

Numerous theorists have articulated the tension that exists between understanding the body as lived and the body as a social object. All involved (for example, Hayles 1999; Crossley 2001; and feminist writers such as Grosz 1994 and Bell 1999) are careful to work around Cartesian dualisms, which privilege the mind over the body, reflect gendered dualisms, and write the body out of the social. The challenge is to capture the import/proximity of the body in sociological analysis, without lapsing into essentialisms, and to examine how bodies become signified and significant in relation to other bodies, contexts and strategies. Various writers have different strategies for resolving the tension, but all except feminist writers such as Grosz (1994) fall short on addressing resistant alternatives. Crossley opts for a third term, 'body subject'; Hayles argues for simultaneity and Grosz highlights mathematical models. Each of these contributions is considered in turn.

To demonstrate how bodily and mental life are connected (in a manner similar to Burkitt 1999), Crossley draws upon Merleau Ponty, and is informed by Goffman's (1971) *umwelt* (meaning the immediate, sensible environment surrounding social action) to establish that human embodiment is central to the constitution of the social world, since social interactions are sensuous, i.e. of the senses. He makes three main points. First, that perception is not an inner representation of an outer world; second, that the mind is not a separate substance from the body, although the body has a sentient and sensible side; and third, that perception is rooted in behaviour (Crossley 1995). Social interaction depends on the public availability of 'mental states', which necessitates their embodiment. Similarly, the meaning that is derived from this interaction is irreducible to the physical level. Consequently, our consciousness – our perception – is embodied, as to perceive is to be in a two-way sensuous relationship with other things and people. It is intersubjective processes which establish embodiment, described thus:

> we are never in complete possession of ourselves ... our perceptible being is captured in schemas of collective representation ... our anatomical state and embodied visibility are made to signify social meanings and we, accordingly, are positioned in social space ... we only come to have ourselves by first enjoining this intersubjective order and learning to see ourselves from the outside, as 'other' (Crossley 2001: 141).

The body is thus something more than a social object, and yet it is not quite a subject – an identity produced by the social world in and of itself. Crossley proposes that there is a third term to describe this position, between subject and object, as 'body–subject'. The key mediator between the self and the world is the corporeal schema, or what Merleau Ponty terms *le sens pratique* – an incorporated bodily know-how and practical sense. New habits and experiences are merged into the corporeal schema, which shapes its reactions and responses to the social world, and so the body–subject needs to be carnally reflective to fully experience itself. There is potential within Crossley's work for an intersubjective conception of the emergence of resistant corporeal schema to body surveillance.

The work of Hayles (1999) is also reminiscent of these arguments. She maintains the analytical distinction between body-as-lived and body-as-social-object, introducing two simultaneous notions that have consequences at the level of the body–subject: inscription and incorporation practices. Use and interaction with technology incorporate the body as a material entity, but also inscribe it: mark, record and trace its actions in other textual and material media, which abstract from the body, mark and govern it, but do not essentialize it. Put briefly, incorporation practices are defined as 'an action' (such as a mouse click) that is recorded in bodily memory by repeated performances until it becomes 'habitual'. This clearly has great affinities with Crossley's 'corporeal schema'. Learning to type is an incorporating practice – when we say someone knows how to type, it is not to say that they can recite all the positions of the keys on the keyboard, it is to say that they know where to place their hands over the keyboard until the keys seem to be an extension of his or her fingers. Characteristic ways of performing incorporating practices are culturally specific. Particular email shorthands, ways of dressing, walking or gesticulating begin in the body, construct an environment, and flow from the environment to the body through learning. Incorporation practices, which govern the performativity of bodily content, are regulated and corrected by normalizing inscription practices, whether by 'unwritten' norms or formal rules.

Grosz (1994) again maintains the irreducibility of the distinction between the body's neurophysiological and psychological dimensions, characterizing them as inner and outer analytical surfaces of the body. As a feminist scholar, Grosz is concerned with how the human body is able to produce wholenesses, integrations and cohesions, and 'fragmentations, fracturings, dislocations that orient bodies and body parts toward other bodies and body parts' (Grosz 1994: 13), as well as being amenable to politico-historical influences. The need is to identify felt embodiment as central to identity, while simultaneously placing that sense within a critique of dualisms. Grosz, uses the mathematical notion of the Möbius[2] strip, a twisting connection between the body's inner and outer analytical surfaces, to describe the continuous nature of embodied existence. Using empirical research on phantom limbs, body image, torture and scarification, she argues for the continuous conception of inner/outer; inscription/incorporation and embodied/object studies of the body, because it enables a more singular interface with politico-historical and technological dimensions of dominant and alternative accounts of embodied personhood.

Despite the fact that these descriptions are necessarily brief, each has its own set of problems when exploring potentialities for an embodied theory of resistance to surveillance. Crossley's (2001) comments on intersubjectivity are invaluable in respect of the development of resistant positions and strategies, although he does not consider how the importance of the perceptual field and the physical vulnerability of the body become more complex in the time–space distanciated surveillance systems to which the body–subject is now increasingly exposed. Frequently surveillance systems operate silently on the body at a distance (Ball 2002) (for example, electronic work-monitoring systems which regulate productive activity and employee mobility around their workstations), and as such the potential for one revising one's corporeal schema to resist or test these processes is much curtailed. Indeed, the problem with Merleau Ponty's work (and hence that of Crossley) is that the politico-historical is not readily found in the corporeal schema or in the body–subject, and hence make it very difficult to politicize, even at the most micro level. When claims are made that one's body is not completely one's own, forming the corporeal schema in a relativistic way alludes to the presence of ideological forces or influences that inscribe the body with meanings which value-code (Spivak 1990) it in ways that are not welcome, appropriate or solicited (Bell 1999). Gatens (1996) suggests that a politics of remembering might be useful here by analyzing what we have been constituted to be, to ask what we might become. Within the context of biometrics, all manner of political positions may arise.

And though Hayles (1999) concentrates on the incorporation–inscription tension, she chooses to maintain the dualism, arguing that the two processes occur simultaneously. Actual acts of resistance to surveillance occur at the interface of body surfaces and technologies (Bogard 1996). The notion of simultaneity of inscription on and incorporation of the body underplays the negotiation of body boundaries which occurs between technological systems and the body–subject, and the boundaries which necessarily move when biocentric surveillance techniques are used. Hayles' (1999) work does not enable the body-subject to gain control over the movement of these boundaries, nor does it highlight the tensions which occur at that boundary, and hence may not serve to adequately conceptualize resistance.

There is, however, hope in Grosz's work, particularly in her use of the Möbius strip to describe the body as a monism of substance which hovers at the pivot point of binaries, at the threshold of a singularity which interfaces with machineries, technologies, histories and cultures. The body is presented as a constitutive uncertainty, but which has continuous inner/outer dimensions. Grosz is also keen to establish the historicity of the body in terms of its ability to enable potentialities for resistance and political behaviour. This is a point to which I will return.

Body ontologies: containment/informatization

Studies of the organizational body have highlighted a further dimension to this tension. As well as the organization being a complex of forces acting on the body to ensure its performance, gathering information on that performance, studies of embodied organizational life concentrate on how organization tries to ensure containment of the body's more fluid properties. A discussion of the work of Longhurst (2001), McDowell (1997), van der Ploeg (2002) and Gibson (2001) highlights the debate.

Reminiscent of Turner (1984, 1991), Longhurst (2001) asserts that business organizations exhibit a regulative body ontology which concern the integrity of its boundaries, fluidity, ability and impairment. Her main thesis addresses the tension inherent in norms of corporate comportment: between strong, upright, clean-cut business attire, and the less firm, fluid sides of the human body, signifying the creation of a norm about the impenetrability of bodily boundaries at work. She argues that, in the workplace, it is considered inappropriate for matter to make its way in to or out of the body: 'farting, burping, urinating, spitting, dribbling, sneezing, coughing, having a runny nose, crying and sweating' (Longhurst 2001: 99) are all unacceptable. Drinking or eating at one's desk, or smoking, are also examples. The business suit has a normalizing effect on the more fluid or squashy sides of the body to render it more acceptable and normal: Longhurst relates cases of larger-bodied people who feel that the structured suit firms up their curves, creating an image of the controlled, firm body. Sometimes bodies can seep, or even burst through this barrier: anything that is not appropriately concealed arouses desire and disgust. Irigaray (1985) notes the gendering of these ideas, constructing body fluidity as feminine: in organizational body ontologies, the fluid is subordinated to the firm. This is supported by McDowell (1997) who examines the precarious choices to be made by the female office worker. She argues that women must be careful to choose something that isn't too bright, too revealing or too masculine. Women who 'play down their feminine side' are considered 'butch'; women who do not conceal their curves according to the 'norm' run the risk of arousing desire in their male colleagues. According to these writers, modern organization produces the old, Taylorist Cartesian body ontology of regulation.

This reference to Taylorism is not accidental. Whilst early forms of recruitment, assessment, training and performance management

307

perpetuated a traditional view of body boundaries, the assemblage of biometric and biocentric technologies of assessment outlined earlier makes no such distinction. Van der Ploeg (2002) explores the specific problem of the informatization of the human body. She argues that biodata are a different category of information – rather than being about persons it is of the body, giving rise to a new ontology of the body as information. As such, the human genome project, and excursions into DNA analysis, gas chromatography, hand geometry, etc., enable a reading of the body by its codification in information. During the act of extracting information from the body, stringent rules apply as to how the body and the integrity of its boundaries are treated, in the test or experimental scenario. However, if an informatized body ontology is emerging, the point at which the body itself ends, and the body as information starts, will begin to shift. For example, the use of an iris scanner to ensure access to a building is perhaps a much more severe breach of bodily integrity than a search of the lower body openings for drugs, because the former has the potential to reveal much more information about the identity of the person than the latter. Moreover, there are ways of collecting DNA samples which do not even involve touching the body – after all, we involuntarily leave our DNA all over the place. In her analysis of lie detector testing Gibson (2001) characterizes the polygraph machine as a translator of the body, inscribing it as holding an ultimate truth, hence becoming a specific site of truth investments. She argues that the repeated subjection of the body to pain-free truth tests (the comparison is made to torture), such as polygraphy, DNA testing, hair strand testing and retinal scanning, renders the body a 'fragmented site of cross referenced zones or assemblages of meaning' (Gibson 2001: 63). In a manner similar to van der Ploeg, she notes that techniques such as the polygraph do away with notions of bodily integrity and interiority, by virtue of their informatization of the body, arguing:

> This borderless body technology may indeed be preferable to a torturous play between inside and outside, where the border is the site for a battle of wills over what is revealed or imagined as concealed. Yet this graphic writing of the living, breathing and speaking subject is a form of capture or incarceration within seemingly limitless decipherability (Gibson 2001: 73).

Paradoxically, organization simultaneously shores up and breaks down bodily boundaries in the name of control, regulation and predictability. Cultural regulation and informatization of the body are mutually supportive in the public domain of embodiment; that which cannot be measured, that which may disrupt is hidden from view by the cultural, but is hunted down by the informational. The public availability of our organizational embodiment is regulated, corporeal schema are exacting, and the mediating, body, at the heart of surveillance networks, becomes a contested domain. How, then, to resist?

Organization, surveillance and the body: towards a politics of resistance

When building conceptions of resistance to body surveillance, I shall be taking three analytical turns. Drawing, *inter alia*, on Haraway (1991), Grosz (1994) and Crossley (2001), I will explore the politicization of boundaries, coding and fixity as ways in which the incidence of body-surveillance rhizomes can be politicized and resisted. Akin to Vincent in the film *Gattaca* who manipulated and managed his embodiment to fool the industrial complex that extracted body information at every turn, and had determined his life-chances, resistance to body surveillance begins at second-guessing interfaces but (of course) does not end there. The key is to understand the nature, multiplicity and simultaneity of contact points between bodies and surveillance technologies. These points of contact need no longer be on the surface of the body – rather they are heterogeneously located and distributed throughout the rhizomic networks which constitute the surveillance assemblage.

The first move is to acknowledge the significance of Grosz's (1994) conception of the inner/outer body as the Möbius strip. Using Spinozan ideas, Grosz argues that the constant twisting and non-linear oscillations of inner and outer body layers, reconstitutes the body in a sustained sequence of states, each of which is materially different from its predecessor. The oscillation of inner and outer introduces and absorbs new substances into the inner/outer monism as it relates to other entities in its vicinity. As with McNay (1999), embodiment is discussed as a mind/body univocity, as a set of unstable potentialities. The questioning of the extent to which the body can be pinpointed as a source of truth, as it is constantly reconstituted and inherently unstable, is the starting point for challenging biotechnologies that specifically locate the body as a site of ultimate truth or authenticity about the person. It also follows that, because of continuous reconstitution, the positioning of the body as 'natural', beyond the social, technological, political and intersubjective becomes problematic, and refocuses our attention on body interfaces and connections which merely begin at its physical boundaries.

309

There are two lines of argument which can be pursued at this point. The first concerns what happens at contact points, or interfaces, and the second concerns the fixity of the body monism in relation to other entities. Viewers of *Gattaca* will recall the many close-up shots of Vincent placing latex fingerprint copies over the end of his finger, with small sachets of blood hidden underneath to fool access systems, hence disrupting the boundary over which information flows, by which a judgement is made. Even in 1941, William Scott Stewart examined how to resist polygraph tests, referring to the ways in which the person can manipulate the information flow from the body to the machine:

> In beating the lie detector, conceal no emotions; intensify them as much as possible, even on those preliminary innocent questions calculated to obtain your normal reaction. When you're asked a harmless question, think about something unpleasant. Deviations in the chart are not great in any case, and if you cause the needle to act up on innocent questions the operator will be baffled, whether he admits it or not ... if you bite the inside of your mouth or tongue on a question of no importance, unbeknown to the operator, he will begin to wonder what's the matter with his machine. You can make sudden muscular movements inside the skin, or twitch your leg in such a manner that the operator will see no outward sign of movement. Try moving your big toe inside your shoe, for instance. It's easy. Or, to confuse the test from the start, you might tense your muscles when the rubber is wrapped around your arm. If you appear to relax in spite of this tenseness, the operator will set his gauge to a false medium (Stewart 1941).

Using Haraway's (1991) comments on cyborgism and hybridity, it is possible to discuss the question of interface and boundary more broadly, as well as supporting analytical moves away from the body as nature and truth. The de-naturalization of the body raises the mythical figure of the cyborg, a product of electronic systems with biotic componentry – systems which interface with bodies and code information about the body into a single language of computer coding. It is constructed at the boundary of information systems and flesh, is necessarily momentary, and dispersed, as information passes through. The cyborg identity is thus constructed as a resistant multiplicity, a partial identity, and contradictory standpoint. Control strategies, therefore, address not the existence of a cyborg identity *per se* but the rates of flow of information and code between the body and the system, and the writing of code which inscribes and recrafts the cyborg body. Politicizing resistance to body surveillance entails disrupting flows of information and code, problematizing the enduring nature of what is transmitted, recodifying, rewriting and resignifying categorizations of flesh-made-information at local rhizomes. Haraway's cyborg is an appropriate figure of resistance to interlinked surveillance systems which no longer eschew an arboreal dominance. The question of boundary negotiation and control between individual people, intersubjectivities and systems is framed as a potential site for sociological inquiry into empowerment under surveillance. Such field investigation may want to adopt a monist conception of the embodied person in order to examine all aspects of resistance to body surveillance.

The second line of argument concerns fixity. Although we have established that the body is not a stable or fixed entity, biometric surveillance systems indeed do attempt to fix bodies as authenticators of identity in space and time. Research into surveillance in action has also demonstrated that the opening of spatio-temporal gaps between watcher and watched enable resistance to occur (Ball 2002). The human body interface with the majority of surveillance systems is necessarily time- and space-bound, giving a momentary and partial account of the individual. Biometrically fed surveillance systems produce predictive and preventative simulations, or momentary snap-shots of life wherein the informatized body exists in statis. As such, the question of the fixity of bodies is not only troubled from a Spinozan viewpoint, Deleuzian notions of becoming can also be employed to explain resistance.

In making this argument, I draw on Grosz (1994), who uses Deleuzian notions in constructing a feminist account of the body. Grosz argues that the connection of the body with other systems constitutes a congealing, fixing or solidifying of identity. Becoming is the trajectory or flight through which the body forms these connections with other entities. Achieving or seeking connectivity is not based on liberal humanist notions of choice; it involves a substantial remaking of the subject, resignifying them in different social and historical locations. Grosz is particularly interested in Deleuze and Guatarri's (1987) fascination with Lewis Caroll's character 'Alice', because, as an embodied girl she is found 'in between', slipping in and out of worlds, orders and groups. Grosz's argument positions Alice as 'becoming-woman': the most resistant state which disrupts the binaries privileging the patriarchal and capitalist structures, marking the female body as 'other' and which, incidentally, creates widespread surveillance practices. 'Becoming-woman' destabilizes histories that have already been inscribed, categories which are taken for granted and transparent, and is a state that is available to all. Indeed, the multiplicity of becomings, and the shattering of binaries emphasized by Grosz (1994) highlights fixity as transient and momentary entrapment within the surveillance assemblage as minor in terms of the full potentiality and resistant capacity of the body. It also enables a disruption of surveillance categories generated by fixed bodies, and a reflection on whose body is connected, how it has been constituted in the past, and what it is likely to be constituted as in future (Gatens 1996). Hence the volatility of the body and the importance of multiple microstruggles at the level of the subject is a vital point to make when surveillance is so rhizomatic in character. The most important conclusion to be drawn from this work is that resistance to the surveillance assemblage is never final, finished or complete.

This discussion is not unproblematic, however. Reliance on radical feminist and post-structuralist concepts as the basis for a politics of resistance to body surveillance, while emphasizing specific problems associated with it, do little to engender a discussion of an ethics of the self (McNay 1999). Even as Haraway recommends strategies for resistance and action, a question remains over how a challenge to categories might actually be mediated at the level of the embodied self. The general question of agency has also not been resolved, particularly that which concerns the work of McNay (1999) and Bell (1999), who use Pierre Bourdieu and Judith Butler's ideas to discuss the possibility of building reflexive, feminist, creative and proactive agencies. Whilst this problematic cannot be resolved here, it is suitably acknowledged as an ongoing debate within feminist writings on the body, and will need to be addressed in future. The core issue for any embodied sociology of surveillance must remain as being primarily concerned with whose body information is appropriated, how it is encoded, how encoded information is reapplied, how effectively this fixes, and how it is resisted.

Conclusion

From this chapter it can be concluded that resistance to body surveillance can be politicized using feminist work on body monisms, univocity, and historicity and post-structural work which articulates alternatives to the fixities engendered by body surveillance. Current developments in biometric surveillance, which position the body as a source of authenticity and truth, are intensely troubled by this conclusion. Resistant strategies occur at the boundary of the body and surveillance, and at an intersubjective level. They include disrupting flows of information from the body to the information system, disrupting the time it takes to encode the body, coding the body in an alternative way, troubling or moving the interface/boundary between the body and the surveillance system. The political bases of these strategies delight in boundary ambiguities and becoming, recognizing the dominant patriarchal and capitalist tendencies behind these technologies, and resisting that through textual strategies which question the impulse to surveil.

These conclusions were reached by first, examining body-surveillance practices in organizations, and recent arguments concerning organizational resistance as being inadequate in terms of engendering any embodied notion of resistance. Developments in the sociology of the body were examined, with phenomenological and ontological tensions being highlighted which reflect theoretical developments in sociology and practical developments in surveillance practice. Arguments were made that applied particularly to the problematic of body surveillance, and are described above.

In making these arguments, I am aware that it might appear that first, I have overlooked organizational specificities to concentrate on a wider surveillance assemblage, and second, that I view all body surveillance as bad, and that it must be resisted in all instances. My response to both would be to return to the central pillar of this chapter, which is Haggerty and Ericson's identification of modern surveillance practice as rhizomatic and body-centred. In respect of the former point, though organizational surveillance is significant, it is one of a set of surveillance rhizomes which are now appearing, particularly in the wake of September 11, and are reflective of an underlying connectivity between the private sector, government, and military complexes. All of these complexes attempt to interface with the human body as the feed-point for their respective information systems (Wood, Konvitz and Ball 2003). Any argument which applies at an organizational rhizome would also need to apply at other rhizomes too. My response to the latter would be that it is not. The centrality of Deleuze and Guatarri's work to their discussion enables an assertion of the point that surveillance practice is primarily productive: it synthesizes and conjoins – indeed it must, before a critique can be offered. In organizational rhizomes, the collection of body data enables the organization to exist, to function and to be staffed. The rationale and justification for an extensive study of embodied resistance stems from the need to challenge any local totalities that would arise should it be left undisrupted, unquestioned and untroubled.

Taking a corporeal turn in surveillance theory certainly reflects the observations of Howson and Inglis (2001) – given the increasing use of biodata in everyday life, a sociology of such practices which highlighted ethical concerns about control, autonomy and privacy (to name but a few) is certainly timely. Surveillance involves the mobilization of information categories that order by hidden criteria, they determine which groups are more likely to be surveillance targets, and the nature of the gaze they are likely to attract. Surveillance, through its categorizing tendencies, is thus bestowed with a genetic, gender, racial and cultural politics; an economic politics at the macro and meso level, and a 'big P' politics if we are to consider the role of national and local government in promoting and sustaining street surveillance as part of public policy. Organizational surveillance practices do not escape this agenda. The person, in making their embodiment publicly available for inspection, intermediates between surveillance technologies, organizational actors, categories, standards, targets, cultures, subcultures and the organization itself. The surveilled organizational body is thus an entity which achieves co-incidence of performance objectives and person specifications, with the immeasurable and invisible elements of lived, embodied experience. An examination of organizational worlds has supported and enhanced a move towards a politics of resistance to body surveillance.

Notes

1   For a range of available products, see www.cybersigns.com; www.retinaltech. com; www.ergosis.com.tr (Accessed 5 November 2002).
2   A Möbius strip is a continuous closed surface with only one side; formed from a rectangular strip by rotating one end 180 degrees and joining it with the other end.

References

Ball, K.S. (2002) 'Elements of Surveillance: A New Framework and Future Research Direction', *Information, Communication and Society,* 5 (4), 573–90.
Barker, J. (1993) 'Tightening the Iron Cage: Concertive Control in Self-Managing Work Teams', *Administrative Science Quarterly,* 38, 408–37.
Bell, V. (1999) *Feminist Imagination* (London: Sage).
Bogard, W. (1996) *The Simulation of Surveillance: Hypercontrol in Telematic Societies* (Cambridge: Cambridge University Press).
Bourdieu, P. (1977) *Outline of a Theory of Practice* (translated by R. Nice) (Cambridge and New York: Cambridge University Press).
Bourdieu, P. (1990) *The Logic of Practice* (translated by R. Nice) (Cambridge: Polity).
Boyne, R. (2000) 'Post Panopticism' *Economy and Society,* 29 (2), 285.
Braverman, H. (1974) *Labour and Monopoly Capital: The Degradation of Work in the Twentieth Century* (New York: Monthly Review Press).

Burkitt, I. (1999) *Bodies of Thought: Embodiment, Identity and Modernity* (London: Sage).

Butler, J. (1990) *Gender Trouble: Feminism and the Subversion of Identity* (New York: Routledge).

Callon, M. (1991) 'Techno-Economic Networks and Irreversibility', in J. Law (ed.) *A Sociology of Monsters* (London: Routledge), 132–64.

Clegg, S. (1994) 'Power Relations and the Constitution of the Resistant Subject', in J.M. Jermier, D. Knights and W.R. Nord (eds) *Resistance and Power in Organizations* (London: Routledge), 274–325.

Crossley, N. (1995) 'Merleau Ponty, The Illusive Body and Carnal Sociology', *Body and Society*, 1 (1), 43–63.

Crossley, N. (2001) *The Social Body: Habit, Identity and Desire* (London: Sage).

Deleuze, G. and Guatarri, F. (1987) A *Thousand Plateaus: Capitalism and Schizophrenia* (Minneapolis: University of Minnesota Press).

Elias, N. (1991) *The Symbol Theory* (London: Sage).

Foucault, M. (1976) *The History of Sexuality*, volume 1 (Harmondsworth: Penguin).

Foucault, M. (1977) *Discipline and Punish: The Birth of the Prison* (Harmondsworth: Penguin).

Foucault, M. (1980) 'Body/Power' in C. Gordon (ed.) *Michel Foucault: Power/ Knowledge* (Brighton: Harvester), 55–62.

Gandy, O. (1998) 'Coming to Terms with the Panoptic Sort', in D. Lyon and E. Zureik (eds) *Computers, Surveillance and Privacy* (Minneapolis: Minnesota University Press), 132–155.

Gatens, M. (1996) *Imaginary Bodies: Ethics, Power and Corporeality* (London: Routledge).

Gibson, M. (2001) 'The Truth Machine: Polygraphs, Popular Culture and the Confessing Body', *Social Semiotics*, 11 (1), 61–73.

Goffman, E. (1963) *Behaviour in Public Places: Notes on the Social Organization of Gatherings* (New York: Free Press).

Goffman, E. (1971) *Relations in Public* (Harmondsworth: Penguin).

Grosz, E. (1994) *Volatile Bodies: Towards a Corporeal Feminism* (Bloomington, IN: Indiana University Press).

Haggerty, K.D. and Ericson, R.V. (2000) 'The Surveillant Assemblage', *British Journal of Sociology*, 51 (4), 605–22.

Haraway, D. (1991) *Simians, Cyborgs and Women: The Reinvention of Nature* (London: Free Association Books).

Hayles, N.K. (1999) *How We Became Posthuman: Virtual Bodies in Cybernetics, Literature and Informatics* (Chicago: University of Chicago Press).

Hier, S. (2003) 'Probing the Surveillance Assemblage: On the Dialectics of Surveillance Practices as Process of Social Control', *Surveillance and Society*, 1 (3), 399–411. Available at: http://www.surveillance-and-society.org/ articles1(3)/probing.pdf.

Howson, A. and Inglis, D. (2001) 'The Body in Sociology: Tensions Inside and Outside Sociological Thought', *The Sociological Review,* 49 (3), 297–317.

Irigaray, L. (1985) *Speculum of the Other Woman* (translated by C. Gillian) (Ithaca, NY: Cornell University Press).

Jackson, S. and Scott, S. (1996) *Feminism and Sexuality: A Reader* (Edinburgh: Edinburgh University Press).

Jermier, J. (1988) 'Sabotage at Work: The Rational View', *Research in the Sociology of Organizations* 6, Greenwich, CT: JAI Press, 101–34.

Knights, D. (1992) 'Subjectivity, Power and the Labour Process', in D. Knights and H. Willmott (eds) *Labour Process Theory* (Basingstoke: Macmillan), 297–335.

Leigh-Star, S. (1991) 'Power, Technologies and the Phenomenology of Conventions: On Being Allergic to Onions', in J. Law (ed.) *A Sociology of Monsters: Essays on Power, Technology and Domination* (London: Routledge), 26–56.

Longhurst, R. (2001) *Bodies: Exploring Fluid Boundaries* (London: Routledge).

Lyon, D. (2001) *Surveillance Society: Monitoring Everyday Life* (Milton Keyes: Open University Press).

Marx, G.T. (1987) 'Raising Your Hand Just Won't Do', *Los Angeles Times*, 1 April.

Marx, G.T. (1990) 'The Case of the Omniscient Organization', *Harvard Business Review*, March–April, 4–12.

Marx, G.T. (1999) 'Measuring Everything that Moves: The New Surveillance at Work', in I. Simpson and R. Simpson (eds) *The Workplace and Deviance*, JAI series on Research in the Sociology of Work (Greenwich, CT: JAI Press). http://web.mit.edu/gtmarx/www/ida6.html (accessed 26th August 2004).

McCahill, M. and Norris, C. (1999) 'Watching the Workers: Crime, CCTV and the Workplace', in P. Davis, P. Francis and V. Jupp (eds) *Invisible Crimes: Their Victims and their Regulation* (London: Macmillan), 208–31.

McDowell, L. (1997) *Capital Culture: Gender at Work* (Oxford: Blackwell).

McNay, L. (1999) 'Gender, Habitus and the Field: Pierre Bourdieu and the Limits of Reflexivity Theory', *Culture and Society*, 16 (1), 95–117.

Michael, M. (1996) *Constructing Identities* (London: Sage).

Niccol, A. (1997) *Gattaca*. Columbia Pictures.

Prasad, A. and Prasad, P. (2001) '(Un)Willing to Resist? The Discursive Production of Local Workplace Opposition', *Studies in Cultures, Organizations and Societies* 7, 105–25.

Regan, P. (1998) 'Genetic Testing and Workplace Surveillance: Implications for Privacy', in D. Lyon and E. Zureik (eds) *Computers, Surveillance and Privacy*. (Minneapolis: University of Minnesota Press), 21–46.

Rule, J. (1998) 'High-Tech Workplace Surveillance: What's Really New?', in D. Lyon and E. Zureik (eds) *Computers, Surveillance and Privacy* (Minneapolis: Minnesota University Press), 66–78.

Sewell, G. (1998) 'The Discipline of Teams: The Control of Team-Based Industrial Work Through Electronic and Peer Surveillance', *Administrative Science Quarterly*, 43 (2), 397–428.

Sewell, G. and Wilkinson, B. (1992) 'Someone to Watch Over Me: Surveillance and Discipline and the JIT Labour Process', *Sociology*, 26 (2), 271.

Shilling, C. (1993) The *Body and Social Theory* (London: Sage).

Spinoza, B. (1986) *The Ethics and On the Correction of the Understanding* (translated by A. Boyle) (London: Dent).

Spivak, G. (1990) *The Post-Colonial Critic* (London: Routledge).

Stewart, W.S. (1941) 'How to Beat the Lie Detector', *Esquire*, November 1941, at http://antipolygraph.org/articles/article-034.shtml (accessed 26 August 2004).

Turner, B.S. (1984) *The Body and Society: Explorations in Social Theory* (Oxford: Basil Blackwell).

Turner, B.S. (1991) 'Recent Developments in the Theory of the Body', in M. Featherstone, M. Hepworth and B.S. Turner (eds) *The Body: Social Process and Cultural Theory* (London: Sage), 1–35.

van der Ploeg, I. (2002) 'Biometrics and the Body as Information: Normative Issues of the Socio-Technical Coding of the Body', in D. Lyon (ed.) *Surveillance as Social Sorting* (London: Routledge), 57–73.

Witz, A. (2000) 'Whose Body Matters: Sociology and the Corporeal Turn in Sociology and Feminism', *Body and Society*, 6 (2), 1–24.

Wood, D., Konvitz, E. and Ball, K. (2003) 'The Constant State of Emergency', in K. Ball and F. Webster (eds) *The Intensification of Surveillance: Crime, Terrorism and Warfare in the Information Era* (London: Pluto Press), 137–150.

Chapter 15

Quixotics unite! Engaging the pragmatists on rational discrimination

Oscar H. Gandy, Jr.

Introduction

Although there are moments within the ebb and flow of talk about the human genome that focus on the amount of genetic material we share in common with all living things, especially among those defined as human (Tishkoff and Kidd 2004), the real interest and attention these days is focused on those fractions of genetic material that set us apart, that distinguish between us, and when we get right down to it, that allow us to discriminate between those who have the 'right stuff', and those who do not (Jones and Smith 2005).

The pursuit of difference is part and parcel of the drive to understand and manage uncertainty and risk through differentiation, classification and identification. Bowker and Star (1999) have argued quite convincingly that 'to classify is human'; it is what we have come to do. However, our tendency toward limiting our attention to those who classify and the techniques they develop and use often leads us to ignore the consequences that befall the objects of classification. We do so at our collective peril.

While they recognize that classifications are 'powerful technologies' that tend to become 'naturalized', Bowker and Starr (1999: 319) offer little hope for the persons who are the objects of classification to do more than recognize how they are a part of this 'thicket of classification' that not only describes, but defines the 'possibilities for action' that make sense in this environment (Bowker and Star 1999: 326). Classification becomes one of the structural features of contemporary society that shape life chances (Dahrendorf 1979) beyond those which we traditionally assume to flow from our locations within the social structure. Risk classification is rapidly emerging as one of the most important forms of constraint on autonomous social choice in modern society (Baker 2003).

I have been moved toward this view in part by some of the arguments laid out by Frederick Schauer (2003) against the use of race and gender as components in predictive models and decision systems. While all decisions involving choices made by powerful actors usually result in an unequal distribution of harms, Schauer reminds us that these negative consequences tend to be especially problematic when they are cued by race and gender because these markers of difference are readily available, and tend to be overused.

In addition, because of the ways in which past decisions are linked to future options, hardships tend to cluster, and contribute to what is increasingly being discussed as *cumulative disadvantage* (Blank, Dabady and Citro 2004: 233–8). Critics also suggest (Andrews 2001; Carlson and Stimeling 2002) that using some information, such as that provided by genetic tests, may also provide a 'pretext for further discrimination' Dolgin (2000: 787). Unlike Dolgin, however, I do not suggest that the most important concerns are those associated with pretext or subterfuge; the problem that confronts us is the routine and apparently legitimate use of classifications that may include, but are not limited to, race as a basis for excluding, denying or in some other way restricting the life chances (Dahrendorf 1979) of substantial numbers of persons.

For those who choose to resist the limitations on action that systems of classification impose on its objects, it becomes important to discover the best way out of a bag that seems to draw tighter against resistance. I have come to believe even more strongly in the wake of September 11 that crying out against the invasion of privacy or the weight of social stigma will not suffice to mobilize the public will. An alternative construction of collective concerns will have to be found. I believe that the rallying cry of a social movement that will be capable of challenging this march toward the valorization of invidious distinction will have to be 'It's discrimination stupid!' (Gandy 1995).

Classification

Bowker and Star define classification as a 'spatio-temporal segmentation of the world' (1999: 10). This is obviously quite broad. My concern, of course, is with something a bit more specific – the classification of persons into categories often associated with risk, or hazard, or potential loss. Such classifications increasingly expand the organization of difference to include predictions about paths to the future. Through such classifications, persons with a disease, like tuberculosis, can be assigned a trajectory reflecting the usual 'course' of the disease, and the prognosis for the sort of life such a person might enjoy (Bowker and Star 1999: 170–1). The application of surveillance and classification as an aid to the management of cardiac patients is illustrated well in the chapter by Dubbeld (this volume).

Although we continually expand the classes and categories of persons as we learn more and more about what sets us apart, some distinctions tend to remain. Classification by race is one of those distinctions that seem to resist attempts to replace them.

Progressive social theorists attempted to define away the foundations of racism by transforming race into a social construct rather than a meaningful distinction with some basis in science (Littlefield, Lieberman and Reynolds 1982). Not surprisingly they find themselves once again embroiled in a high-stakes debate, only this time over the use of geographic origins as a substitute marker of difference (Gannett 2001, 2004).

Where the challenge of racial identification is only the assignment of persons to one of three populations (East Asian, African and European), the current rate of success is quite high, exceeding 95 per cent with 150 genetic markers. The problem, of course, becomes one of deciding just how much precision is actually required for a given decision. For those in need of greater certainty, we are told that one need only add more polymorphisms to the clustering model and then even 'members of "admixed" American populations, such as Hispanics, African-Americans and European-Americans can be accurately identified' by origin (Jorde and Wooding 2004: S31).

Racial identification by statistical programme obviously represents a distinct departure from the ways in which people have traditionally identified themselves as members of racial and ethnic groups (Cornell and Hartmann 1998; Dolgin 2000; Gandy 2000). The possibility that the identification of groups by 'highly reliable estimates' of geographic origin, as well as by 'reliable predictors' of behaviour will become the norm is the source of mounting concern about discrimination (Andrews 1999; Rothstein 1999a).

Evaluating social technology

I would like to suggest that we think about classification as a social technology. Like any other technology, its use ought to be justified on the basis of its effectiveness. We ask: does it do what it is supposed to do? This criterion for assessment may reasonably be extended to include a determination of its reliability: how often, or how well, does it work? In some cases, the evaluation of some technology or technique is likely to be comparative; we want to know how well it works in comparison with available alternatives.

It is here that assessments about social technology become more troublesome as more and more aspects of a comparison may be seen as relevant. We might ask how easy it is to use, in comparison with available alternatives. And of course, we will want to know about its relative cost. It may or may not matter to us as individuals whether the 'true' costs of alternatives have been modified by taxes, subsidies or monopolization. Of course, our consideration of costs should not be limited to the costs of acquisition. The total costs of alternatives should include the costs of operation; the variable costs of resources acquired and used up in the production of decisions about how to act. These costs are part and parcel of our assessment of efficiency as it relates to the productive use of scarce and valuable resources.

Of course, we have more recently been invited to identify the competitive market as the social technology best able to manage such choices (Aune 2001). In the absence of such an idealized market, it becomes important to examine the assumptions of the received theory and then to consider the extent to which they are not met. Among the most critical departures from the ideal is the dependence of decision-makers on incomplete and perhaps strategically biased information (Kleindorfer, Kunreuther and Shoemaker 1993: 350–1).

The assessment of technologies along the lines just described becomes more complicated as a function of the extent to which its use serves more than one goal or purpose. It is generally recognized by decision theorists that it is difficult to maximize several objectives at the same time, especially when the outcomes may be incompatible. The difficulties that we associate with maximizing incompatible outcomes are amplified when our evaluations of the process rely on historically distinct, if not orthogonal criteria, such as efficiency and equality (Kleindorfer, Kunreuther and Shoemaker 1993: 354–8).

What is far less often considered are the unintended and therefore unanticipated consequences of the use of technological systems (Tenner 1996). These 'externalities' are often quite substantial. Among the most important external costs are those that are generated on those occasions when the 'device' does not work as well as it might; when it makes a mistake, or affects systems, activities and relationships well beyond the expected boundaries of concern.

Of course, it is important to consider that all devices always operate with some degree of error; perfection is never really obtained. However, the costs of those errors are rarely considered, and the distribution of those costs is beyond consideration by any but the most severely distracted (or quixotic, if you will allow). In addition, decisions about efficiency and effectiveness are not quite the same as those we might make if considerations of justice, fairness or other social values (Roemer 1996) must also be included in our decisions about the use of technology. But it is precisely this set of considerations that should come into play as we evaluate the use of racial profiles and other discriminatory techniques to make decisions about the quality of the lives some of us may get to lead.

Discrimination

Obviously, by choosing to use the term 'discrimination', rather than talking about choice, or selection, I am engaging in an act of strategic communication, which may make my motives suspect. As a term, discrimination bears the weight of its history. Discrimination is felt as a pejorative; it implies an injustice, an unwarranted harm.

Discrimination involves differential treatment of objects, including persons, on the basis of their membership in disfavoured groups. While discriminatory choices can be made in favour of members of some group, our concerns usually focus on those who are discriminated against, or suffer as a result of choices made. While Bowker and Star (1999) say without hesitation that classification is what we do, they are strangely silent on discrimination, which seem logically to follow, if not to lead as the motivating force guiding classificatory efforts these days. Sufficient evidence for this claim can be found in the chapter by Bigo (this volume). Our challenge is to determine the basis upon which discriminatory acts, enabled by the development of classificatory techniques, ought to be subject to 'strict scrutiny' as a matter of law, and perhaps to active restraint as a matter of politically vetted common sense.

Rational discrimination

In discussing the economics of information, Roger Noll (1993) makes a distinction between decisions made by a private firm on the basis of racial prejudice, referred to among some economists as a 'taste for discrimination' (Sunstein 1997: 153), and similar decisions thought to be less troublesome when based on a statistical generalization. Noll provides the example of a bank that charges higher interest rates to borrowers from one community than another on the basis of a 2 per cent difference in default rates. This is a decision that is thought by financial experts to make good business sense because, as he suggests:

> the identity of a person, because it is correlated with a useful attribute, even if the correlation is extremely weak, is nonetheless a valuable signal to the decision maker. To ignore the signal (and not to discriminate) is then costly, inducing decision makers to discriminate while honestly proclaiming themselves not to be prejudiced (Noll 1993: 41).

Noll notes, however, that while the 'ethical distinction' between the two kinds of decisions may be 'nonexistent', the economic consequences are not.

On the other hand, Sunstein (1997) suggests that people would act on the basis of 'irrational prejudice' if they acted on a belief that members of a group have characteristics that they in fact do not; for example, a belief that many or most of the members of the group have those characteristics, when only a relatively small number actually do, or even using 'fairly-accurate group based generalizations when more accurate classifying devices are relatively inexpensive and available' (Sunstein 1997: 155). Sunstein suggests that other more common uses of stereotypes are 'not only pervasive; they are entirely legitimate in most settings ... People may use stereotypes not because they are very accurate but because they are less costly to use than any more individualized inquiry' (Sunstein 1997: 155).

But Sunstein invites reflection on the fact that our laws still seek to restrict racial and other forms of discrimination even though they may be 'rational'. Even though our laws allow other forms of rational discrimination, including that which is based on widely varying probability estimates, legislators in many areas seek to limit discrimination on the basis of race and other bearers of information. We need to understand why this line is drawn in the shifting sands of social policy, especially with regard to decisions made by government agencies.

Rational discrimination, informed by statistical inference within the criminal justice system, is best represented by claims made by or through references to the perspectives of an idealized 'Intelligent Bayesian' (Armour 1997: 35–60). The Intelligent Bayesian uses available racial statistics, without regard to, or understanding of, the factors that generate the data being brought to bear on the decision (Best 2001; Gandy 2001). The fact of disproportionate arrest and imprisonment of African American males is offered as proof of criminality, and a justification for pre-emptive strikes in self-defence against whatever risks might be assumed. The Intelligent Bayesian has become a lightening calculator of risk as it relates to race, and his willingness to use deadly force in moments of stress has been demonstrated in the courts, and in the laboratory as well (Kang 2005: 1525–8). As we see in the examples provided by Bigo (this volume), Los (this volume) and Walby *et al.* (this volume), the impact of risk modelling as an aspect of institutional rationality is a substantial multiple of the impact of individual Bayesians.

For example, the Commonwealth of Virginia reportedly 'encourages its judges to sentence nonviolent offenders the way insurance agents write policies, based on a short list of factors with a proven relationship to future risk' (Bazelon 2005). Using a risk assessment scale developed by the state's sentencing commission, judges determine whether a defendant goes to prison, or is given an alternative that might include probation or house arrest. As a result, the state has been able to reverse the rate of growth in its prison population, without suffering what would be seen as an unacceptable increase in recidivism. Indeed, for those whose scores exceeded an upper limit, sentencing guidelines were adjusted to triple the years served by the average offender (Bazelon 2005). The fact that this particular risk assessment model makes use of age and gender as predictors raises questions about the limits of permissible discrimination on the basis of immutable characteristics. The fact that the Commonwealth of Virginia has hesitated to include race in its model should not be assumed to reflect its limited utility as a predictor, or even the fact that race is so closely associated with poverty and related dimensions of cumulative disadvantage (Blank, Dabady and Citro 2004). What we observe is the fact that the use of race as an aid to law enforcement has become politically charged in light of rising concerns about racial and ethnic profiling (Harris 2003).

Racial profiling

Racial profiling has emerged as an especially harmful form of discriminatory classification, despite the fact that it has achieved a rather spectacular level of notoriety. Because of its basis in actual or imagined data regarding the base rates or probability of some set of target behaviours, racial profiling can be understood as a form of statistical discrimination (Blank, Dabady and Citro 2004). We understand that profiling is a form of rational discrimination in which one or more characteristics of an individual or their behaviour are used as a basis for selection, and subsequent investigation 'to determine whether they have committed or intend to commit a criminal act … or other act of interest' (Blank, Dabady and Citro 2004: 186).

Racial profiling refers to those cases in which a person's apparent race or ethnic group membership is used as a basis for selection (along, or in combination with, other characteristics). The use of race as a factor in a predictive model means that 'race is perceived by police officials doing the profiling as a negative trait that marks the bearer of that trait as a person more likely to cause a criminal problem than similarly situated people without the trait' (Kennedy 2001: 3). Racial profiling is generally used to refer to a set of routine practices used by police in the 'prosecution, identification, and prevention of crimes' (Risse and Zeckhauser 2004: 138). Although, as we will discuss, it is a label that also applies in a great many other domains (Squires 2003), including the delivery of health care (Lillquist and Sullivan 2004).

I want to suggest that racial profiling in all these domains is problematic. Schauer (2003) helps us to understand why. Schauer explores the moral, ethical and technical criteria that might be used in deciding when the use of race or other sensitive characteristics can be justified, or balanced against what might be called the common good (Etzioni 1999: 2–4). A number of critical considerations are identified: (1) whether the characteristic is 'statistically sound' – that is, it bears some non-random association with the behaviour of interest; and (2) whether the association is strong or weak, reflecting the extent to which the activity or behaviour is characteristic of most, many, or merely a few members of the population. Schauer notes that many characteristics of persons may be statistically linked with a racial group without their being a 'universal' tendency among members of that population group (Schauer 2003: 96). As a result, the issues raised by the use of 'non-spurious' but 'non-universal' characteristics of racial and ethnic groups are moral, ethical and intensely political.

Like gathering proof of racial discrimination more generally, gathering evidence for the existence and impact of racial profiling is difficult. Since the practice is either illegal, or unpopular, it is unlikely that law enforcement personnel will admit to using race as a predictor of criminality. It does not mean, however, that racial profiling will soon be eliminated. Indeed, some observers suggest that 'racial profiling is likely to continue as a lawful form of police practice for the foreseeable future, so long as it is implemented with sufficient politeness and subtlety to avoid a clear confrontation with the racial logic that it embodies' (Kennedy 2001: 7). It falls to the critic to make a statistical case – to identify a disparity in relative risk ratios among similar age cohorts across racial or ethnic groups. Unfortunately, even a compelling body of statistical evidence of discrimination may not lead a court to declare that an unconstitutional harm exists (*McCleskey* v *Kemp* 1987). The US Supreme Court has suggested that rather than inferring risk from a historical pattern, defendants claiming bias should have to provide evidence of purposeful racial discrimination in their own individual case (Kennedy 2001: 13).

Racial profiling in the delivery of health care

The bases for concerns about the use of racial profiling in the administration of justice are readily identified, and they are also relatively clear in the case of redlining and discrimination in the housing market (Squires 2003), but they are far from obvious when they are examined in the context of a health care system being assigned responsibility for continuing and substantial health disparities along racial lines (Lilliquist and Sullivan 2004; Shields *et al.* 2005). Yet, the public is reluctant to interpret these disparities as being the products of racial discrimination (Gandy and Li 2005; Williams 2001: 392–5). Assigning responsibility becomes especially problematic in the context of disparities in health that are attributable to genetic predispositions because of the historic associations between genetics and racist assumptions regarding biological inferiority (Cho and Sankar 2004; Duster 1990; Lillquist and Sullivan 2004; Rotimi 2004; Stevens 2003).

Lillquist and Sullivan (2004) identify a number of examples of what they call racial profiling in the medical arena. They suggest that statutory limitations on the use of racial classification in the offering of contracts should raise critical questions about the development and testing of drugs designed to be used solely, or primarily, by African Americans. Although the history of the transformation of a failed drug into a marketing success is marked by claims of statistical misrepresentation (Kahn 2003), the fact that this particular discrimination is framed as actually providing an advantage to African Americans has helped to fend off harsher critiques. If the goals of the equal protection clause of the Fourteenth Amendment are taken seriously, however, selecting individuals for clinical trials and even for preventive screening on the basis of race should raise concerns and invite government scrutiny because there are other valid criteria for selection that do not make use of this historically troubled classification (Lilliquist and Sullivan 2004: 403).

A similar point is made by Stevens, who suggests that:

> in light of the vast similarities among most people, and the very common and similar causes of most diseases afflicting us, and given known interventions for addressing these that are not currently being pursued, it is not at all 'clear' that it is 'important' to know more about individual-level variations in order to significantly improve the country's health (Stevens 2003: 1059).

Because the threats to health associated with exposure to environmental toxins can be attributed far more directly to racism and other forms of discrimination than to differences in genetics, it makes little sense to focus on one while ignoring the other (Popescu and Gandy 2004). Fortunately, there is a growing awareness that genetic research may actually exacerbate health disparities in the United States, and some suggest that such disparities may serve as 'one critical measure against which the enormous public investment in genetics research ought to be judged' (Shields et al. 2005: 98).

The genetic threat horizon

In the world of health insurance, a little knowledge is a dangerous thing. A surprisingly high proportion of all those who apply for individual health insurance are denied coverage by some carrier (Greely 1992). This denial is usually based on the information that the applicant provides, or is accessed by the insurer from a common database. The numbers of applicants who might be denied insurance, or be offered policies with specific exclusions on the basis of information about genetic predispositions to some medical risk, is expected to grow.

It is important to keep in mind that information about behaviour or lifestyle is not information about a person's health status, but about the probability that they will become ill, or incapacitated because of their risk-related behaviours (Murray 1997). Thus, there may indeed be a basis for distinguishing between exclusionary or limiting decisions based upon a medical condition and those based on a higher than average risk of developing some medical condition at some point in the future.

Unfortunately, concerns about genetic discrimination extend far beyond the boundaries of the health care system. Rothstein (1999b) identifies a number of policy concerns that extend concerns about privacy and discrimination to the workplace and other settings, in which people uninformed about the factors that link the presence of genetic markers and a host of behavioural expressions may nevertheless make decisions that limit the opportunities people may take advantage of. Widespread knowledge of the possible uses of genetic information for identification, classification and evaluation contributes to the growing demand that such testing is performed, and that all sorts of people are informed about the results of those tests (Carlson and Stimeling 2002: 211).

Efforts to limit the use of this information once gathered appear destined to fall further and further behind the new discriminatory applications that appear each day. Rothstein (1999b) doubts that traditional anti-discrimination legislation will be up to the task. As he sees it:

> since the mid-1960s there have been laws enacted prohibiting discrimination based on race, colour, religion, sex, national origin, and age. Nobody would seriously contend that discrimination on the basis of these factors has been eliminated, and discrimination on the basis of these criteria do not have the actual or perceived economic incentives that discrimination on the basis of future health status do (Rothstein 1999b: 475).

The new eugenics

The medical community is understandably concerned about the rapid growth in direct-to-consumer marketing of genetic testing. Already having lost the battle to control the marketing of prescription drugs to consumers, physicians are preparing for the next onslaught of requests for referrals or administration of a widening array of diagnostic and predictive tests designed to identify and evaluate the genetic status of patients, and patients to be (Gollust, Chandros-Hull and Wilfond 2002).

Genetic testing has quickly become a prominent feature of the new surveillance (Marx 2002; Nelkin and Andrews 2003; Silva 2005). Genetic information provides a basis upon which segments of the population can be marked as deficient – a damaged race (Rosen 2003).

Because of its association with the eugenics movement and the abuse of sterilization taken to an extreme under Nazi rule (Kevles 1992: 10–11), the emergence of a market for prenatal and pre-implantation genetic diagnosis raises concerns about the moral and ethical basis upon which decisions about reproduction will increasingly come to be made (Alexander 2002). The fact that the ability to identify markers of genetic risk far exceeds the ability to intervene to correct or modify these risks has led to the emergence of a new form of preventative medicine. One avoids facing the problems of 'genetically compromised' persons by preventing them from being born in the first place (Silva 2005: 102). It seems likely that concerns about liability, as well as social responsibility, will serve to increase the pressure on individuals to pursue the imperfect knowledge of the future that rests within their genomic arrays.

The availability of genetic tests will increase the pressure on individuals to have their genetic status determined. This will be only a part of the new genetic responsibility. It will also include a responsibility to share, or make this information available to others who will claim, or will be thought to have a right, and perhaps a responsibility to know. This responsibility seems most likely to arise in the context of reproductive decisions, where the transmission of this genetic material to a new person raises questions about one's responsibility for the assignment of risk.

It is not always the case that knowledge of one's future is a good thing. Rawl's 'veil of ignorance' assumes that individuals will make just social decisions if they are unaware of the 'genetic traits' and other 'morally arbitrary' resources or constraints that will be theirs in the future (Roemer 1996: 175). Will it be only the rich (or those who have good reason to expect that they will be rich) who can or should allow less than perfect children to be born? Will public policies be established that will shape the social distribution of such decision-making in the future? These are some of the questions that Schauer's (2003) analysis begins to explore.

Cumulative disadvantage

Schauer reminds us that the standards for evaluating the 'difference' or the predictive utility of some model or criterion will vary with a host of factors, including the social, economic and political costs of being wrong. But, as Schauer and others (Etzioni 1999) also remind us, the costs of being wrong have to be weighed against the costs of not acting until we are certain.

The critical concern that Schauer (2003) identifies as it applies to the use of race, gender, age and ethnicity is the fact of their visibility, or their availability. It is this accessibility that makes it likely that these identifiers will be used more often than their contribution to the reduction of uncertainty would suggest (Gandy 2001). Thus, Schauer concludes that 'the strongest argument against including race is not that race is irrelevant, although it may sometimes be, but that race, even if relevant, is so likely to be overused that it is necessary to prohibit its use – to mandate its underuse – just to ensure that things come out even in the end' (Schauer 2003: 196).

To 'come out even' is what an accountant expects to find when income, expenses and reserves are added up. Social accounts are not so easily kept. Part of the challenge we face, at least theoretically, if not practically, is including all the relevant costs on both sides of the balance. How likely are we to include the costs to society that flow from further stigmatization of African Americans and other people of colour (Major and O'Brien 2005) by stopping them along the side of the road, or pulling them out of the line at airports in order to subject them to more intensive assessment?

Part of the problem within the economics of regard that Loury (2002) has begun to develop is the fact that the people we value less to begin with are assured of being seen as less valuable in the future because of the ways in which they are treated today. It is for this reason that the expressive harms that flow from the reproduction and use of negative stereotypes complicate the rational calculus of choice.

By granting that statistical discrimination may be rational, Loury and others who would question the wisdom of this rational path suggest that an 'iron gate' will almost certainly appear to block further progress. Loury (2002) offers the case of the taxi driver who refuses to pick up African American male passengers out of a fear of being robbed. Ironically, this seemingly rational action is likely to increase this particular risk by ensuring that most of the right-meaning black men who can do otherwise will abandon the hopelessness of waving at passing cars. This means, of course, that unless the driver's doors are securely locked, the next passenger to open the door and claim a seat may claim his wallet as well. As Loury puts it, 'the drivers' own behaviours have created the facts upon which their pessimistic expectations are grounded' (2002: 31). These 'feedback effects' or 'self-fulfilling prophesies' abound within the literature on the reinforcement of stereotypes (Schneider 2004: 215–24). Unfortunately, they are just beginning to be explored in the context of the administration of justice (Armour 1997).

Cumulative disadvantage is the result of repeated and unique discriminations that pile misery upon hardship for many who have been classified by race (Blank, Dabady and Citro 2004: 223–46). Risse and Zeckhauser (2004) argue that racial profiling is troublesome not because it is profiling, but because it aggravates hardships occasioned by racism.

We may understand the consequences for individuals that flow from racial profiling in the household mortgage and property insurance markets, but we tend to forget about the ways in which these harms are likely to accumulate and spread within communities that become effectively, if not actually, redlined (Squires 2003: 403). In this way, the aggregation of racial statistics makes it possible for people to be victims of racial discrimination even though they are not themselves members of a devalued race (Popescu and Gandy 2004). The weight of cumulative racial disadvantage anchors the markers of differential value that geodemographic profiles release into the market (Elmer 2004: 82–9; Monmonier 2002: 140–53). It is often enough to merely live among African Americans to be assessed a share of the 'Black Tax' (Armour 1997: 13–18).

How likely are we to use an appropriate valuation scheme to combine the harms to dignity, the harms to the economy, and the harms to the public sphere that are produced each time we use race as a marker of spoiled identity? Do we even consider the costs to ourselves or to society more generally, in terms of the opportunities forgone when stigmatization reinforces a set of aversive responses that have become automatic (Kang 2005)?

Moving quixotically beyond race

While we have seen some evidence to suggest that there are indeed some brave souls who are willing to demand restrictions on the use of race, and perhaps even gender, as inputs in discriminatory models, despite their predictive value, the general sense is that this is an uphill battle. It seems even less likely that there is a social movement to be formed around the theme of cumulative disadvantage. Yet, that is what it means to be quixotic. That's what it means to pursue an impossible dream.

Racism and the burdens of racism clearly exist, and racial profiling only compounds the harm. The same is true of sexism, and the burdens of gender discrimination argue against the use of gender within decision models common to a whole host of insurance markets and other structures of opportunity. Quixotics will have to work to identify other particularly salient 'isms' that might be identified as a basis for mobilizing resistance against the use of group membership as a basis for decisions about the allocation of resources and opportunity.

Risse and Zeckhauser (2004) suggest that some of the 'harm' produced by racial profiling is to be found in its expressive character. Powerful actors within society who act with the consent of the majority express disrespect and disregard for African Americans by treating them disproportionately as suspects. They identify other forms of profiling that are not seen as morally suspect because they do not seem to affect a core basis for individual identity formation. Our identities are not likely to be tied up with our status as a 'vacation traveller' even though that objective status may subject us all to increased surveillance during holiday seasons.

The challenge for quixotics is to identify the bonds, linkages or ligatures, including the rising authority of insurance-dependent decisions based on actuarial assumptions that help to shape the 'life chances that identifiable groups of persons encounter' (Dahrendorf 1979: 31). This is particularly important despite the fact that as 'insurance has become an accepted mode of governance, it has become increasingly difficult to raise questions in the political realm, for instance about who should drive and how drivers should behave' (Heimer 2003: 301). At the same time, Heimer also suggests that new forms of social solidarity may be an unintended consequence of the rise of such power among insurers.

We are reminded that Weber was ultimately a critic of rationalization, and the evils that it brings. He also felt that opposition to these bad effects was likely to develop as the basis for social movements, even though these movements would ultimately fail. Giddens suggests that Habermas actually extended Weber's thoughts along these same lines. But Giddens concluded that Habermas was being quixotic because there was nothing in his analyses that might lead to a different conclusion regarding the path and consequences of rationalization (Giddens 1987: 251–2).

It is not clear that a social movement based on the development of risk profiles generated by insurers, as (Los this volume), describes, or on the basis of the more acute risks that terrorism represents (Bigo this volume) will ever develop into an effective counterforce to profiling and rational discrimination.

Of course, it does seem quixotic to select the actuarial assumption as a windmill against which to tilt. Gigerenzer and his colleagues make it pretty clear that 'numbers rule the world', in that 'probability theory has become the arbiter of practical rationality, not merely its mathematical codification' (Gigerenzer *et al.* 1989: 255). It is not that the predictions that guide the choices of those with the power to choose are false, or off the mark. Rather it is that those who choose to discriminate on the basis of those predictions also choose to ignore alternative futures that might also be predicted with greater confidence if our attention had been directed toward those ends.

It is the responsibility of the quixotics among us to help them see the light.

Quixotics unite!

References

Alexander, B. (2002) 'The Remastered Race', *Wired*, 10 (5). Available at: http://www.wired.com/wired/archives/10.05/eugenics.html.

Andrews, L.B. (1999) 'Predicting and Punishing Antisocial Acts: How the Criminal Justice System Might use Behavioral Genetics', in R.A. Carson and M.A. Rothstein (eds) *Behavioral Genetics: The Clash of Culture and Biology* (Baltimore, MD: Johns Hopkins University Press), 116–55.

Andrews, L.B. (2001) *Future Perfect: Confronting Decisions About Genetics* (New York: Columbia University Press).

Armour, J.D. (1997) *Negrophobia and Reasonable Racism: The Hidden Costs of Being Black in America* (New York: New York University Press).

Aune, J.A. (2001) *Selling the Free Market: The Rhetoric of Economic Correctness* (New York: Guilford Press).

Baker, T. (2003) 'Containing the Promise of Insurance: Adverse Selection and Risk Classification', in R.V. Ericson and A. Doyle (eds) *Risk and Morality* (Toronto: University of Toronto Press), 258–83.

Bazelon, E. (2005) 'Sentencing by the Numbers', *New York Times*, Sunday 2 January 2005. Available at: http://www.nytimes.com/2005/01/02/magazine/02IDEA.html

Best, J. (2001) *Damned Lies and Statistics: Untangling Numbers from the Media, Politicians, and Activists* (Berkeley, CA: University of California Press).

Blank, R.M., Dabady, M. and Citro, C.F. (eds) (2004) *Measuring Racial Discrimination* (Washington: National Academies Press).

Bowker, G.C. and Star, S.L. (1999) *Sorting Things Out: Classification and its Consequences* (Cambridge, MA: MIT Press).

Carlson, R.J. and Stimeling, G. (2002) *The Terrible Gift: The Brave New World of Genetic Medicine* (New York: Perseus Books).

Cho, M.K. and Sankar, P. (2004) 'Forensic Genetics and Ethical, Legal and Social Implications Beyond the Clinic', *Nature Genetics Supplement*, 36 (1), S8–S12.

Cornell, S. and Hartmann, D. (1998) *Ethnicity and Race: Making Identities in a Changing World* (Thousand Oaks, CA: Pine Forge Press).

Dahrendorf, R. (1979) *Life Chances* (Chicago: University of Chicago Press).

Dolgin, J.L. (2000) 'Personhood, Discrimination, and the New Genetics', *Brooklyn Law Review*, 66, 755–822.

Duster, T. (1990) *Back Door to Eugenics* (New York: Routledge).

Elmer, G. (2004) *Profiling Machines: Mapping the Personal Information Economy* (Cambridge, MA: MIT Press).

Etzioni, A. (1999) *The Limits of Privacy* (New York: Basic Books).

French, M. (2005) 'Abstract Machines and Making up Identities', poster presentation at Theorizing Surveillance: The Panopticon and Beyond, 12–14 May 2005, Queen's University, Kingston, ON.

Gandy, O.H. (1995) 'It's Discrimination Stupid!', in J. Brook and I.A. Boal (eds) *Resisting the Virtual Life: The Culture and Politics of Information* (San Francisco: City Light Books), 35–48.

Gandy, O.H. (2000) 'Exploring Identity and Identification in Cyberspace', *Notre Dame Journal of Law, Ethics & Public Policy*, 14 (2), 1085–111.

Gandy, O.H. (2001) 'Journalists and Academics and the Delivery of Race Statistics: Being a Statistician Means Never Having to Say You're Certain', *Race and Society*, 4, 149–60.

Gandy, O.H. and Li, Z. (2005) 'Framing Comparative Risk: A Preliminary Analysis', *The Howard Journal of Communications*, 16 (2), 71–86.

Gannett, L. (2001) 'Racism and Human Genome Diversity Research: The Ethical Limits of "Population Thinking"', *Philosophy of Science*, 68 (3), S479.

Gannett, L. (2004) 'The Biological Reification of Race', *British Journal for the Philosophy of Science*, 55, 323–45.

Giddens, A. (1987) *Social Theory and Modern Sociology* (Stanford, CA: Stanford University Press).

Gigerenzer, G., Swijtink, Z., Porter, T., Datson, L., Beatty, J. and Krüger, L. (1989) *The Empire of Chance: How Probability Changed Science and Everyday Life* (New York: Cambridge University Press).

Gollust, S.E., Chandros-Hull, S. and Wilfond, B.S. (2002) 'Limitations of Direct-to-Consumer Advertising for Clinical Genetic Testing', *Journal of the American Medical Association*, 288 (14), 1762–7.

Greely, H.T. (1992) 'Health Insurance, Employment Discrimination, and the Genetics Revolution', in D.J. Kevles and L. Hood (eds) *The Code of Codes: Scientific and Social Issues in the Human Genome Project* (Cambridge, MA: Harvard University Press), 264–80.

Harris, D.A. (2003) *Profiles in Injustice: Why Racial Profiling Cannot Work* (New York: New Press).

Heimer, C.A. (2003) 'Insurers as Moral Actors', in R.V. Ericson and A. Doyle (eds) *Risk and Morality* (Toronto: University of Toronto Press), 284–316.

Jones, N.L. and Smith, A.M. (2005) 'Genetic Information: Legal Issues Relating to Discrimination and Privacy', *CRS Report for Congress* (RL3006) (Washington: Congressional Research Service, Library of Congress).

Jorde, K.B. and Wooding, S.P. (2004) 'Genetic Variation, Classification and "Race"', *Nature Genetics Supplement*, 36 (11), S28–S33.

Kahn, J. (2003) 'Getting the Numbers Right: Statistical Mischief and Racial Profiling in Heart Failure Research', *Perspectives in Biology and Medicine*, 46 (4), 473–83.

Kang, J. (2005) 'Trojan Horses of Race', *Harvard Law Review*, 118 (5), 1489–593.

Kennedy, R. (2001) 'Racial Trends in the Administration of Criminal Justice', in N. Smelser, W.J. Wilson and F. Mitchell (eds) *America Becoming: Racial Trends and Their Consequences*, vol. 2 (Washington: National Academies Press), 1–20.

Kevles, D.J. (1992) 'Out of Eugenics: The Historical Politics of the Human Genome', in D.J. Kevles and L. Hood (eds) *The Code of Codes: Scientific and Social Issues in the Human Genome Project* (Cambridge, MA: Harvard University Press), 3–36.

Kleindorfer, P.R., Kunreuther, H.C. and Shoemaker, P.J.H. (1993) *Decision Sciences: An Integrative Perspective* (New York: Cambridge University Press).

Lillquist, R.E. and Sullivan, C.A. (2004) 'The Law and Genetics of Racial Profiling in Medicine', *Harvard Civil Rights-Civil Liberties Law Review*, 39 (2), 391–483.

Littlefield, A., Lieberman, L. and Reynolds, L.T. (1982) 'Redefining Race: The Potential Demise of a Concept in Physical Anthropology', *Current Anthropology*, 23 (6), 641–55.

Loury, G.C. (2002) *The Anatomy of Racial Inequality* (Cambridge, MA: Harvard University Press).

Major, B. and O'Brien, L. (2005) 'The Social Psychology of Stigma', *American Review of Psychology*, 56, 393–421.

Marx, G.T. (2002) 'What's New About the "New Surveillance"'? Classifying for Change and Continuity', *Surveillance and Society* 1 (1), 9–29. Available at: http://www.surveillance-and-society.org/articles1/whatsnew.pdf.

McClesky v *Kemp* (1987) LexisNexis Academic, Supreme Court of the United States, 84–6811.

Monmonier, M. (2002) *Spying with Maps: Surveillance Technologies and the Future of Privacy* (Chicago: University of Chicago Press).

Murray, T.H. (1997) 'Genetic Exceptionalism and "Future Diaries": Is Genetic Information Different from Other Medical Information?', in M.A. Rothstein (ed.) *Genetic Secrets: Protecting Privacy and Confidentiality in the Genetic Era* (New Haven, CT: Yale University Press), 60–73.

Nelkin, D. and Andrews, L. (2003) 'Surveillance Creep in the Genetic Age', in D. Lyon (ed.) *Surveillance as Social Sorting: Privacy, Risk and Digital Discrimination* (New York and London: Routledge), 94–110.

Noll, R.G. (1993) 'The Economics of Information: A User's Guide', *Annual Review of the Institute for Information Studies, 1993–1994* (Queenstown, MD: Institute for Information Studies), 25–52.

Popescu, M. and Gandy, O.H. (2004) 'Whose Environmental Justice? Social Identity and Institutional Rationality', *Journal of Environmental Law and Litigation*, 19 (1), 141–92.

Risse, M. and Zeckhauser, R. (2004) 'Racial Profiling', *Philosophy and Public Affairs*, 32 (2), 131–70.

Roemer, J.E. (1996) *Theories of Distributive Justice* (Cambridge, MA: Harvard University Press).

Rosen, C. (2003) 'Eugenics: Sacred and Profane', *The New Atlantis*, 2 (Summer), 79–89.

Rothstein, M.A. (1999a) 'Behavioral Genetic Determinism: Its Effects on Culture and Law', in R.A. Carson and M.A. Rothstein (eds) *Behavioral Genetics: The Clash of Culture and Biology* (Baltimore, MD: Johns Hopkins University Press), 89–115.

Rothstein, M.A. (1999b) 'Genetic Secrets: A Policy Framework', in M.A. Rothstein (ed.) *Genetic Secrets: Protecting Privacy and Confidentiality in the Genetic Era* (New Haven, CT: Yale University Press), 451–95.

Rotimi, C.N. (2004) 'Are Medical and Nonmedical Uses of Large-Scale Genomic Markers Conflating Genetics and "Race"?' *Nature Genetics Supplement*, 36 (11), S43–S47.

Schauer, F.M. (2003) *Profiles, Probabilities, and Stereotypes* (Cambridge, MA: Harvard University Press).

Schneider, D.J. (2004) *The Psychology of Stereotyping* (New York: Guilford).

Shields, A.E., Fortun, M., Hammonds, E.M., King, P.A., Lerman, C., Rapp, R. and Sullivan, P.F. (2005) 'The Use of Race Variables in Genetic Studies of Complex Traits and the Goal of Reducing Health Disparities', *American Psychologist*, 60 (1), 77–103.

Silva, V.T. (2005) 'In the Beginning was the Gene: The Hegemony of Genetic Thinking in Contemporary Culture', *Communication Theory*, 15 (1), 100–23.

Squires, G.D. (2003) 'Racial Profiling, Insurance Style: Insurance Redlining and the Uneven Development of Metropolitan Areas', *Journal of Urban Affairs*, 25 (4), 391–410.

Stevens, J. (2003) 'Racial Meanings and Scientific Methods: Changing policies for NIH-Sponsored Publications Reporting Human Variation', *Journal of Health Politics, Policy and Law*, 28 (6), 1033–87.

Sunstein, C.R. (1997) 'Why Markets Don't Stop Discrimination', in Sunstein, C.R. *Free Markets and Social Justice* (New York: Oxford University Press), 151–66.

Tenner, E. (1996) *Why Things Bite Back: Technology and the Revenge of Unanticipated Consequences* (New York: Knopf).

Tishkoff, S.A. and Kidd, K.K. (2004) 'Implications of Biogeography of Human Populations for "Race" and Medicine', *Nature Genetics Supplement*, 36 (11), S21–S27.

Williams, D.R. (2001) 'Racial Variation in Adult Health Status: Patterns, Paradoxes, and Prospects', in N.J. Smelser, W.J. Wilson and F. Mitchell (eds) *America Becoming: Racial Trends and Their Consequences*, vol. 2 (Washington: National Academies Press), 371–410.

Index

access control technologies 298
accountability 223
administrative surveillance, alcohol
    125–7, 128–9, 130, 132–3
administrative work, computerization
    284–5
advertising 274
affective labour 119n
affluent society 274
Afghanistan war 62
Agamben Giorgio 4, 9, 11,12, 50, 142,
    265, 266
agency 175, 312
agents of surveillance 32–4
airport security 56–7, 281
Al Qaeda 50–1
algorithmic killing 260, 261, 263
algorithmic surveillance systems
    16–17, 254–5, 264
ambulatory ECG recorders 187, 188,
    189, 192, 194, 200–1n
American Civil Liberties Union
    (ACLU) 34, 60
Andrejevic, Mark 6–7
anomalies, in research 24

anonymity 291, 293
anthrax scare 141
ARPANET 151
Arendt, Hannah 11
Armstrong, Gary 170, 187
Ashcroft, John 147
audiences, panoptic 8
automated target recognition (ATR)
    261
autonomous mechanized combatant
    vehicles 259
avoidance technology 280–3, 291, 292
awareness of surveillance 34–5, 77, 81

Ball, Kirstie ix, 17, 42, 296–317
ban-opticon
    concept of 12, 46–7
    declarations of emergency 47–8
"bare life" 6, 9, 11
Baudrillard, Jean 10, 65, 99, 112, 119,
    130–1
Bauman, Zygmunt 11, 27, 232
Beck, Ulrich 10, 112
behaviours, monitoring 298
"being seen" 174–5

337